12⁵⁵

5ᵃ

Michael Stutman
914-329-
3888

ART AS AN INVESTMENT

ART

AS AN INVESTMENT

By RICHARD H. RUSH

BONANZA BOOKS · NEW YORK

Dedication

To Julie

Library of Congress Catalog Card Number: 61-11358

Printed in the United States of America

This edition published by Bonanza Books,
a division of Crown Publishers, Inc.,
by arrangement with Prentice-Hall, Inc.
a b c d e f g h

Acknowledgments

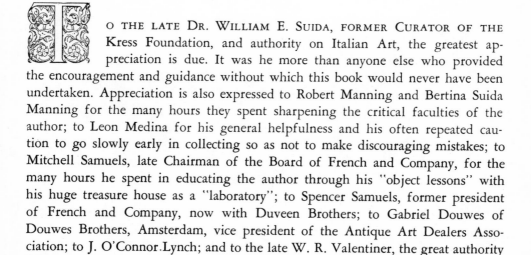

O THE LATE DR. WILLIAM E. SUIDA, FORMER CURATOR OF THE Kress Foundation, and authority on Italian Art, the greatest appreciation is due. It was he more than anyone else who provided the encouragement and guidance without which this book would never have been undertaken. Appreciation is also expressed to Robert Manning and Bertina Suida Manning for the many hours they spent sharpening the critical faculties of the author; to Leon Medina for his general helpfulness and his often repeated caution to go slowly early in collecting so as not to make discouraging mistakes; to Mitchell Samuels, late Chairman of the Board of French and Company, for the many hours he spent in educating the author through his "object lessons" with his huge treasure house as a "laboratory"; to Spencer Samuels, former president of French and Company, now with Duveen Brothers; to Gabriel Douwes of Douwes Brothers, Amsterdam, vice president of the Antique Art Dealers Association; to J. O'Connor Lynch; and to the late W. R. Valentiner, the great authority on Rembrandt.

Many thanks are expressed to Leslie Hyam, President, and Mary Vandegrift, vice president of the Parke-Bernet Galleries for their helpful information and advice as well as their kindness in making available photographs from their files; to the Arnold Witt Library of the Courtauld Institute of the University of London, and to Peter Murray of that organization in particular for opening their picture files to the author; to the Netherlands Royal Art Archives and especially to Dr. S. J. Gudlaugssen for his invaluable assistance in attribution; and to Professor Dr. Ulrich Middeldorf, director of the Kunsthistorisches Institut in Florence for his continuous flow of help in attributions.

The National Gallery of Art in Washington supplied invaluable help, not only in making available their entire files, including auction catalogues from all over the world, but the staff of the library produced books and documents required for a period extending to well over a year.

The greatest appreciation is expressed to Helen Clark, the author's aunt, for her invaluable assistance in the preparation of the manuscript.

To the American dealers, museums, and business corporations who so kindly cooperated in the author's surveys, appreciation is expressed.

Appreciation is also expressed to Christie's and Sotheby's in London for their helpfulness and to the museums, artists and collectors who so graciously permitted the reproduction of their paintings in this book. To the Frick Art Reference Library staff and to the staff of the Art Division of the Public Library, Washington, D. C. acknowledgment for many kindnesses is also due.

Finally, thanks go to the author's wife for accompanying him on visits to nearly 1000 dealers throughout the United States and Europe, and for reviewing with him the sales catalogues of the major world auctions covering the past 35 years in order to obtain price trends on authentic paintings. Her professional background as an artist provided the critical element required in selecting exemplary works of art to reproduce and discuss in this book as well as to record pricewise.

Preface

T O ENTITLE A BOOK *Art as an Investment* MAY SEEM TO BE A SAC-
rilege. The general public has long considered art to belong to
an élite group of intellectuals who seemed to be the only ones who
could really understand the greatness of the Old Masters, or decipher the otherwise unintelligible abstractions that some extreme modern and contemporary artists
produce. While fine works of art are certainly "above money," art, at the same
time, is intimately connected with and is an attribute of money. Recently a modern
painting sold for $145,000 and a Rubens for $770,000. Obviously such art was
valued in monetary terms and could only be purchased by persons or museums
with sufficient means.

On the other hand, those specializing in art in one way or another often considered the money part of art as something unmentionable, and a person who
"invested" in art, as contrasted with someone who purchased art for the sheer
love of art alone, as beneath the notice of the art intelligentsia.

It is doubtful, however, whether collectors have ever been unmindful of the
investment value of art. We cannot, of course, be certain of what went through
the mind of Andrew Mellon when he purchased Raphael's "Alba Madonna" for
$1,166,000 and Raphael's "St. George and the Dragon," a little painting the size
of a sheet of typing paper, for $747,000, and some other paintings which brought
his total purchase in this particular lot to almost $7,000,000. Maybe he said, "They
are beautiful. Here is a check for $7,000,000." But I doubt it. Mr. Mellon's
background, and the backgrounds of the great collectors, Kress, Widener, Frick,

Lehman, Phillips, and Dale, are much too eminently along business and financial lines for them to ignore the market value of what they purchased. When anyone puts out $10,000 for a painting—let alone a million—whoever he is and however wealthy he may be, it is very, very probable that he weighs the cost with extreme care against what he is getting. Were this not so, there would not be a market price for each major artist and each major School of art. And there is most certainly a market price.

It is no sin to think of what a painting may be worth in terms of market price. In fact, only a very foolish man would buy a painting without thoroughly understanding the market and price for the artist and for his School of art, whether French Modern, Impressionist, or Sienese Primitive. A part of this knowledge concerns the future market and the future market price. It is doubtful whether many collectors would want to buy a $10,000 painting if they knew that the painting would be worth half of what they paid for it next year.

For a person who has earned his money by his own efforts, it is hard to part with $10,000 for anything: a cruiser, a house in the mountains, or a Rolls Royce. For some of us it is even harder to part with $10,000 for a painting. It can't carry us on the water and thus afford weekend relaxation, or provide entertainment for a possible client. It isn't a mountain hideaway and a retreat to go to if times get hard, or to retire to some day. And a painting will not carry us around the city or on business or personal trips as a fine motor car can.

The chief benefit of a painting is intangible. It is the pleasure, pride, and admiration felt when looking at it. Ten thousand dollars is a good deal of money for such an intangible benefit, particularly when in a rising stock market ten per cent might be realized on the money annually.

"The investment value of art" provides not only a real reason for investing in art, but at the same time a splendid excuse for a person to buy what he loves. If this book does not provide an answer that is entirely favorable to art from the point of view of a safe, high-appreciation investment subject only to the capital gains tax, at least it may provide some excuse for the art lover to indulge himself with a little more freedom.

A small collection of paintings inherited from my father and my uncle, the latter having lived for many years in Germany and in Constantinople, started my wife and myself on the tremendously adventurous road of collecting. I remember well the first picture we bought. It was a real discovery. We came upon it quite accidentally, and surprisingly enough we found it torn and dirty in the "Flea Market" in Arlington, Virginia. My wife is an artist and has had eleven one-man shows here and abroad, but the verification of this painting was something new for us. We laboriously started on our research and verification work. The painting turned out to be a fairly well-known one that had been in several collections.

From here our collecting finally settled down to two main Schools of art: early Sixteenth Century Italian and Seventeenth Century Dutch. We gravitated to these Schools because we liked these the best; and to know what we should collect we made ourselves proficient in these Schools and the major artists in each. This started us collecting in earnest and we have kept up the pace to the present. We collect by means of the "Case Method" as developed by the Harvard Business School. This is the way it works:

We see a painting for sale, either in a dealer's shop or in an auction. Let us say it is supposed to be a Fragonard. Before we buy it we first have to like it, and second to make sure it is done by Fragonard. Labels too often mean little. Before we buy the painting we get out every book we can find on Fragonard, look at all the photos of Fragonard paintings in the books and in photo collections in art libraries, note exactly how he painted and what his usual scenes were, look at every available painting by Fragonard in museums nearby.

Sometimes we find that while paintings are not what they are labeled, they still can be assigned to an artist of equal merit, or even greater merit and worth. We considered a painting which had long been known as being a Magnasco. It turned out to be a Castiglione, and a good one. Castiglione is as eminent an artist as Magnasco.

One of our favorite pastimes is touring art museums. In nine weeks we visited 64 museums and about 700 dealers in Europe. I estimate that we looked at 10,000 paintings. Out of this lot of 10,000 paintings we bought exactly four. Then it occurred to us that while we had not discovered the "long lost Leonardo da Vinci" (every collector hopes he will find one on the next trip), we had "discovered" the Art Market. We had seen everything from Verrocchio to Gilbert Stuart, from Fra Angelico to van Gogh. That trip was the immediate origin of this book, and the things we have learned in our program of constant collecting provide the general background.

Since the opening of the new building of New York's Museum of Modern Art in 1939, a gala event at which President Roosevelt gave a radio address from the White House in Washington, Modern and Contemporary art has been a great concern of ours academically. We use the word academically because, while we have collected a few Impressionists, we have not yet collected the latest Schools of art. But because the later Schools are so much in the public eye at the present time, have experienced such a huge rise in price, and because of the increasing sales of Contemporary Art throughout the country, if not throughout the world, a disproportionate amount of attention has been given to the Modern and Contemporary Schools in this book.

We have been fortunate in having had available expert help and guidance which will never, unfortunately, be available to anyone again: the advice of the late Dr. William E. Suida, former Curator of the Kress Foundation. Through the right proportion of criticism and encouragement, he changed the direction of our lives. While Dr. Suida was an authority on Renaissance Italian art, and particularly on the art of Leonardo da Vinci, Dr. W. R. Valentiner helped us on Dutch art of the seventeenth century, especially the art of Rembrandt.

We spent considerable time in the files and with the staff of the Courtauld Institute of the University of London and the Netherlands Royal Art Archives, but we arrived in Florence, Italy, too late to talk to Bernard Berenson who, together with his sponsor, Lord Duveen, did so much to bring Old Masters to America in the era of the financial giants.

It takes the same qualities to make an art expert as it does to make an expert in any other field, or to develop talent, for that matter: innate ability, excellent and long training, and continuous practice. The field of art is a peculiar one in that learning is a constant process. The art expert can keep on learning at a rapid rate until he is in his eighties or nineties.

For this reason the three great art experts who all passed on within twelve months' time are difficult if not impossible to replace: Berenson, Suida, and Valentiner.

To identify a painting and tell who painted it is a talent which can only be developed by a person who first of all has an eye for painting style, method and detail, and who, secondly, studies the technique of artists ceaselessly. Fortunately for me, my wife has that native ability and has developed it. It is not unusual for her to stand for as long as 30 minutes in front of an important painting studying every detail. Most people become tired after the first three minutes. That tiredness is probably what makes the difference between the expert and the layman. Only when this intense study is continued for months and years is expert identification developed.

We came into art at the tail end of the era of the great American collectors. Fortunately we were taken back into the atmosphere of this era by Mitchell Samuels, the late Chairman of the Board of French and Company, probably the world's largest antique dealer. Just to walk casually through French and Company's old 57th street building in New York required four hours. The paintings, tapestries, sculpture and antiques housed in this building plus two warehouses might possibly be worth $30,000,000, but more important, they are irreplaceable. Mr. Samuels spent many hours with us telling us interesting anecdotes, the most interesting of which I have recorded in the chapter on "Discoveries," and trying to give us a faint glimmering of what art had meant to him. He gave us this insight by using the contents of his treasure house as examples. He told us he could identify, blindfolded, every object that had any form in his entire collection.

One New York art dealer must have spent a material part of his time for years helping us to learn to buy intelligently, letting us buy an item from his stock at just a little over his cost, consistently refusing to allow us to buy expensive things until we learned more. He told us again and again, "What America needs is more collectors of beautiful antiquities, more young people who will learn of their beauty and will buy them. But until you know, don't buy; and early in the game, don't pay too much. America needs real collectors, and I don't want you to get discouraged in your collecting career by sinking large sums in mistakes."

Out of our study, collecting and the writing up of it in this book, a few lessons emerge with absolute clarity:

1. A person starting to collect art must not assume after reading a few books that he understands art and can walk into any shop and put down a sum of money for a picture and expect either to get a good one or to get his money's-worth. In the first place, he must deal with reputable dealers who will sell him authenticated paintings. Unfortunately, to the novice, works by imitators and copyists appear to be as good as works by the Master.

2. Art must be of primary interest to the collector, and he should concentrate on one School, such as Impressionism or French Moderns, learn it thoroughly, and know the technique of the various artists extremely well. Only in that way will he himself know what he is buying and its value, and whether a picture offered him is typical of the artist. In the last analysis fine quality, good condition, and a quality typical of the artist are the attributes that give a painting value.

3. The purchase of one painting may satisfy a person to some extent, but if he considers investment value, one painting purchased at a very high price is too risky. He must think in terms of a collection of paintings—a dozen or more. By creating a collection over a period of time, he spreads his investment; and the ownership of a collection more or less forces him to pay good attention to what he is doing in his art purchasing program.

4. Finally, the purchase of art is, unfortunately, not the road to quick profits, at least for the inexpert collector.

The purpose of this book is to develop, caution, and guide American collectors of art, to stimulate them to recognize and preserve the world's treasures and to lead the uninitiated into one of the most thrilling and rewarding activities of all time.

Contents

I

The Painting Boom

N MAY 14, 1952, AN EVENT TOOK PLACE IN PARIS WHICH CALLED the attention of a major part of the Western world to the value of art. A painting of apples and biscuits by the Post-Impressionist Cézanne was sold from the Gabriel Cognacq Collection to Mme. Jean Walter for 33 million francs, the equivalent of $113,141.

Not only did the people at the auction gasp. The art world gasped. This was the first time an Impressionist or Post-Impressionist painting had been auctioned for such a price.

Four years later in the Charpentier Galleries in Paris another Cézanne, "Still Life with Apples," sold for $116,000. It was clear that the earlier price of a similar Post-Impressionist painting was not a freak.

On June 14, 1957, the painting "Still Life Apples" by the Post-Impressionist, Paul Gauguin, sold in Paris for $255,000 from the estate of Mrs. M. T. Biddle.

The stage was well set for the sale at the Parke-Bernet Galleries in New York of the Georges Lurcy Collection on November 7 in the same year, 1957.

The salesrooms were jam-packed long before the sale began. Several rooms were set aside for the bidding, each with its sub-auctioneer and each with a closed circuit television set which pictured the particular painting up for auction. The television camera switched back and forth during the auction between the painting up for sale and the chief auctioneer, Mr. Louis J. Marion.

Many of those who came to buy or to look on were in evening clothes, and the whole affair had the atmosphere of an opening night. The Henry Fords II were there, the Chester Dales, the Billy Roses, Mrs. Eleanor Roosevelt, and the director of the Metropolitan Museum of Art, Mr. James J. Rorimer, to name only a few.

Then the bidding started. After the first few minutes the whole atmosphere became electrified. It was obvious that history was being made. New high prices were not simply being established, but a boom in art works throughout the world was being signaled.

Each time the occupant of a particular room made a high bid, the other members of the same room cheered. When the painting was finally knocked down by the auctioneer, most of those at the sale applauded, especially those in the room where the high bidder sat. One handsome lady gradually bid up to $170,000 for a Gauguin. When someone topped her bid, many of those in the seats around her encouraged her vociferously to bid higher. She graciously shook her head and smiled. The painting went for $180,000 to one of the Greek shipping kings. In the same sale a Renoir sold for $200,000.

Prices rose to heights that at the time became more and more difficult to grasp the higher they rose. One had a feeling, "This is it! This is the high point. Nothing can ever go higher in the Impressionist category. This is the time people finally have taken leave of their senses *en masse.*"

Yet on May 13, 1959, at the same Parke-Bernet Galleries in New York, one painting from the collection of Mrs. Byron Foy (daughter of Walter P. Chrysler) by Renoir entitled "Daughters of Durand-Ruel" (the great Parisian art dealer) sold for $255,000.

The all-time high point in Impressionists was yet to come, however. In the middle of October, 1959, seven paintings from the collection of the former German industrialist, Jakob Goldschmidt, were offered for sale. More remarkable about the sale than the extremely high average price per painting was the fact that one painting, Cézanne's "Boy in a Red Vest," (see frontispiece) went for $616,000 to Paul Mellon of the Pittsburgh banking family. This figure was over twice as much as an Impressionist or Post-Impressionist painting had ever brought at auction. But the rest of the prices were noteworthy as well:

Manet	............$182,000	van Gogh	........$369,600
Manet	 249,200	Cézanne	 252,000
Manet	 316,400	Renoir	 201,000

The price of every major Impressionist and Post-Impressionist had risen enormously in this decade of the 1950's. What the sellers paid for these paintings is quite another matter, and this will be taken up later.

Let us look at the total amount received *per sale*.

The grand total for the 1952 Cognacq sale was 302 million francs ($860,000).

Headlines were also made at the sale at Christie's in London in November, 1954, when the Rees Jeffries Collection brought in a total of £44,320.

We can use this sale as a benchmark to trace the course of prices up to that time. The paintings that sold for a total of £44,320 ($124,100) cost the seller when he bought them £3,332. The sale price at auction was over 13 times the purchase price in pounds sterling. Here are some of the selling prices and costs:

	Selling Price	Cost	When Purchased
Matisse	$19,700	$1,700	1928
Bonnard	11,760	750	1928
Braque	3,400	210	1935

In June of the next year (1955), in two afternoon sessions, 99 million francs were turned over for paintings at the Paris Galerie Charpentier ($282,900). Four days later this total was surpassed in the same gallery with a total receipt of 177 million francs ($500,000).

On July 15 of the same year (1955), Christie's in London racked up the biggest total day's sale since the war—£154,174 ($431,700).

This was by no means the end of the art price rise. The never-to-be-forgotten theatrical of the sale of the Georges Lurcy Collection at the Parke-Bernet Galleries in New York in 1957 brought in $1,708,550—the greatest total for Parke-Bernet or any other auction house in the world up to that time. The only comparable sale in history was the month long sale of the Duke of Hamilton in 1882 which brought in £397,562.

The Goldschmidt Collection of only seven paintings brought in $2,186,800 in just 22 minutes of auctioning in London—a new world record total in October, 1958.

The next month in New York the 29 paintings of the hotel-man Arnold Kirkeby brought $1,548,500—the second highest amount taken in by any U. S. art auction, the Lurcy total being a little higher.

On May 6, 1959, Sotheby's of London brought in $1,102,676—the second highest sale in the history of English collections.

One week later in New York the 17 paintings of Mrs. Byron Foy returned $1,166,400.

Finally, on June 24, 1959, at Sotheby's in London, 89 Old Master paintings

brought in $2,074,184. In this sale a new high was established for the auction
sale of any one painting. The "Adoration of the Magi," a large altarpiece by the
Seventeenth Century Flemish artist, Peter Paul Rubens, reached an all-time high
of $770,000.

On April 27, 1960, art sales went nation-wide. For the first time in the history
of art auctions an inter-city closed circuit television system was established. While
the paintings were displayed and auctioned at the Parke-Bernet Galleries in New
York City, prospective buyers in Chicago, New York and Dallas could assemble
in those cities and not only view on a large television screen the paintings up for
sale, but could bid on them as well.

There were 1800 people in New York at the Parke-Bernet Galleries, some in
the main auction room and some in the adjacent rooms, each room having its own
television screen. In Dallas 700 gathered at the Preston Royal Theatre to view
and bid, and free scotch and bourbon were served before the bidding began.

Three hundred people gathered at the Arts Club of Chicago.

PETER PAUL RUBENS. *Adoration of the Magi*

About 400 gathered in the Los Angeles County Museum to bid, including actresses Arlene Dahl, Greer Garson and Nanette Fabray.

Not only was the auction unique in that it provided a transcontinental television hookup, but it was unique in that all 51 paintings and sculptures were donated by their respective owners for the benefit of the 30th Anniversary Fund of the Museum of Modern Art in New York.

The total receipts of the auction were $871,750, including "Les Pommes" by Cézanne, donated by Ambassador to Belgium and Mrs. William A. M. Burden, which brought $200,000, and Braque's "Composition: The Violin," donated by Governor Nelson Rockefeller, which brought the huge price for a French Modern of $145,000.

While the New York buyers bought most of the paintings, over $100,000 worth was bought by Dallas, Chicago and Los Angeles buyers.

The events of the past several years seem to indicate that the art auction, aside from providing a place where buyers and sellers can come together in competition and through their buying reflect the level of the art market, is becoming an event rivalling the Metropolitan Opera in New York as an élite social event.

What is happening to total sales of art objects, and paintings in particular?

The art year begins in the fall and generally ends the following June. Sales are tallied for this period.

The 1956 to 1957 season for the largest American art auction house, Parke-Bernet Galleries in New York, was a record season. An all-time high was reached in sales of $7,028,295. The nearest figure was for the 1945-1946 season when sales were $6,684,045.

Over 2000 paintings were sold for a total of $1,123,568.

The next season, 1957-1958, established another new high when the total for all art objects sold by Parke-Bernet was $7,244,547. Nearly 2000 paintings were sold for a total of $2,604,190. The average price per painting more than doubled.

It should be pointed out that most of this season was in the period of business recession. Yet sales of art objects in general, and paintings in particular, rose.

The season 1958-1959 established a new Parke-Bernet high—$10,208,879, an increase of nearly $3,000,000, over 40 per cent above the sales of the previous season.

The total received for the 1550 paintings sold was $4,379,367, compared with $1,123,568, for the approximately 2000 paintings sold two years earlier.

In 1960 total sales were comparable with 1959—$9,240,000. In this season 1950 paintings were sold for a total of $3,078,000.

There are two great art auction houses in London—Sotheby's and Christie's. For the 1955-1956 auction year Sotheby's sales were £2,250,000 ($6,300,000). The following year sales topped £3,000,000 ($8,400,000) and for the 1958-1959 season sales were £5,756,742 ($16,119,000). In 1960 sales were $19,254,000.

In 1959, Christie's took in £2,783,490 ($7,793,000). In 1960 sales were $10,360,000.

For the year 1959, the imports of art works into England exceeded the exports by almost £4,000,000 ($11,200,000). Five million pounds sterling of art objects were imported into England for sale at auction but were delivered out of the country to foreign buyers ($14,000,000 worth).

By any standard the late 1950's inaugurated a boom in art sales and in the prices of works of art.

What lies ahead? Can the art market continue to climb, and does the rise mean that all works of art are rising in this manner? The answer is yes and no. Some Schools are rising in importance and others are not. In order to understand some of the factors influencing the market we shall study the major Schools, sample the prices within these various Schools and, in a final analysis, put the price history of these Schools together in order to form an art market price index.

II

The Schools of Art

HE PARKE-BERNET GALLERIES, THE LARGEST AUCTION HOUSE FOR art in America, in the fall, 1956 to summer, 1957 season sold $1,123,568 worth of paintings. In the 1957-1958 season they sold $2,604,190 worth and in the 1959 season painting sales reached $4,379,367.

Out of the total Parke-Bernet sales of art and furnishings in the 1957 season, paintings amounted to 16 per cent, the rest being furniture, statuary, jewels, and other objects. In the next season paintings had jumped to 36 per cent of total sales and in the 1959 season to 43 per cent. Paintings in the 1958 season were 232 per cent of those in the previous season, and in the 1959 season were 390 per cent of the 1957 season.

Out of Sotheby's sales in London for the 1959 season of $16,119,000 and Christie's sales for the same season of $7,794,000, and in the other score of auction houses throughout Europe, paintings amount to perhaps half (or a little under half) of the total.

Out of this total volume of paintings sold each year by these auction houses, the Impressionists and Post-Impressionists form only a very small percentage. When we speak of the art market for paintings, we are not by any means confining ourselves to the Impressionist and Post-Impressionist Schools—Renoir, Degas, Monet, Manet, Cézanne, etc. Nor are we considering these to be the major Schools of art. They have recently received the greatest publicity because they are "the

Schools to have," and because they rose in value from the turn of the century when paintings in these two Schools often sold for well under $1000 to the high point for one painting of over half a million dollars.

What about the other Schools of art—their price range, their importance in the world art market, their beauty and general desirability and the outlook for their price level in the future? Possibly the best way to analyze the art market is to break down art into its Schools, briefly outlining each School and moving from there to a detailed study of each major School of art and the price history of the paintings belonging to that School.

While it would be entirely possible to write a volume or more on what art is, it is sufficient simply to define what is meant in this particular book by "art." Then we know, at least, what we are talking about.

The words "art" and "paintings" are used interchangeably here, and while art in the broad sense certainly includes sculpture, pottery, and many other items, we shall confine ourselves to paintings when we use the word "art."

A painting or an art object in the limited sense here used is a representation of nature, thoughts or feelings depicted by means of colors, usually oil or tempera, on canvas or wood panel, metal or other similar surface, by a person or persons who have devoted a certain amount of time and energy to securing an education and training in this occupation, with the result that enough people like to see it hanging on their walls to give it a commercial value.

A School of art is a prevailing method of painting, and this prevailing method is usually connected with a particular country or section of a country of the world during a particular period of years.

The early fifteenth century art of what is now Belgium can readily be identified by anyone familiar with art as Flemish Primitive. It is readily distinguishable from, let us say, the Italian art of the same period, which is known as Italian Primitive. Yet the paintings within each School, such as the Flemish Primitive School, are enough alike to be distinguished as a group or School from other Schools.

Many Schools of art arose from a revolt against the type of painting in vogue at a particular time. Impressionism is an example. Yet most of the Impressionist paintings can readily be identified as Impressionists and distinguished from other Schools of art. Again, one familiar with art can point to a Monet, for example, and say (although he has not read the signature or label and has never seen the painting), "That is an Impressionist."

In the same way the Cubist revolt led to a School which is fairly easily identifiable—Braque, Picasso, Léger, etc.

Even the most violent revolt, one characterized at times by blasphemy, as, for instance, the Dada School, results in works which look more or less alike.

The ironical part of these revolts against the extant methods of painting is that while the revolt represents an extreme dissatisfaction with the art that is, and places a tremendous emphasis on individuality, the art of all of the "individuals" has recognizable similarities. Because of this inevitable alikeness, it is possible to classify almost all art into Schools.

Certain artists might object to this categorizing of art into Schools by saying, "Yes, but I was the first to use this technique. I was unique." Such a statement could be correct. In the case of many, if not most, Schools those artists who make up the School follow the lead of the founders and vary their basic techniques.

It is next to impossible to categorize *all* painting, and there is no point in it, as far as our purpose goes.

The Schools of art selected are those which form the major part of the art market for paintings in the Western world, with particular emphasis on the interests of the American investor. These Schools are classified according to buyer interest today beginning with the most popular School—the Impressionists.

TWELVE SCHOOLS OF ART

I. *French Impressionist and Post-Impressionist*

There is little doubt that the art which is in the greatest vogue today and in the greatest demand is Impressionism. The result is that prices of paintings of this School have risen to astronomical heights, particularly considering the fact that it is a late School, not an Old Master School that has had centuries in which to secure acceptance—or rejection, and that because it is a late School, time has not removed the paintings from the market into museums or into oblivion through neglect, fire, pillage, and the other hazards of time and history. Renoir, one of the most popular of the Impressionists, painted close to 6000 pictures, and the majority of these are in existence today. By way of contrast, there are under forty known Vermeers in existence.

The Impressionists were beginning their painting careers in the late 1860's —Monet, Manet, Renoir, Degas, and the rest—and the Post-Impressionists—van Gogh, Gauguin, Cézanne, Seurat, and Signac—were becoming important two decades later.

These Schools of art caught on and captured public approval after the turn of the century, but particularly after World War II. Although some of the greatest

RENOIR. *La Serre.* Collection Henry Ford II

CLAUDE MONET. *Venice, Palazzo da Mula.*
National Gallery, Washington, D.C.
(Dale Collection, Loan)

UTRILLO. *Marizy—Saint-Genevieve.*
National Gallery, Washington, D.C.
(Dale Collection, Loan)

collectors accumulated paintings of the Impressionist and Post-Impressionist Schools even before World War I, the huge supply of these canvases which was available kept prices low, and it required a period of time which ran into the middle of the century for the paintings to realize prices in line with other great Schools on the art market.

An Impressionist painting might be described as a painting characterized by vibrant color and light effects achieved by an ingenious placement of colors which under close examination do not seem to produce a coherent or pleasing effect but suddenly blend in the eye as one moves away from the canvas.

These "impressions" are bright, airy and cheerful, with subjects tending toward outdoor scenes of Paris and rural France. While the Impressionists may not have had the rigorous training of the earlier Schools of art, they produced inherently beautiful and pleasing works which almost everyone would enjoy having on the walls of his home.

II. *French Modern*

Shortly after the turn of the century a new but related School arose and although it embraced several subdivisions and various "isms," it can generally be described as French Modern. The French Moderns continued the use of bright color and imprecise drawing and chose subjects somewhat similar to those of their predecessors, but whereas the Impressionists emphasized the representation of light and strove to create a painting which, by the use of bright, contrasting, contiguous colors, blended in the eye as in nature, a characteristic of these Moderns is that they did not attempt to achieve novel, surface light effects and cohesion of the painting as a representation of nature. For the first time in art history the representation of nature was played down and artists depended for their acceptance on pleasing rhythms, forms, and colors regardless of how accurate the representation of nature was.

The Impressionists and Post-Impressionists would have been embarrassed if the viewer did not recognize what was represented. Not so with the Moderns. If the viewer asked whether the object was supposed to be a house, the artist of the French Modern School might well have replied, "Yes, but forget about the house. Notice the bright color, the form, the contrast of colors between the object and its surroundings, and see if you can obtain pleasure from these things, regardless of whether the representation of a house is accurate or not."

The leaders of this Modern School are Matisse, Picasso, Braque, and Léger.

III. *Contemporary*

Contemporary art is the art of the day and is produced either by living artists or by artists only recently deceased. There is a great lag before the auction market accepts paintings by Contemporaries in any volume, so that the classification "Contemporary" is somewhat ambiguous when it refers to a large group of artists (and it does) a good number of whom were born prior to 1890 and many of whom are now dead.

Despite the fact that Contemporary art seems to be going off in all directions at once and the volume of canvases turned out is the phenomenon of all time (probably 50,000 Contemporary paintings are sold yearly in New York City alone), this general classification of art—it is hardly to be considered a School as it bridges many countries, many "isms" and many Schools—can be broken down for our purposes into two categories:

1. Naturalistic   2. Abstract

Among our more recognized young American Contemporaries in the first group is Andrew Wyeth. He continues in the tradition of the strictly American artists, Thomas Eakins and Winslow Homer, who painted America in the spirit of America. Wyeth's paintings seldom appear on the auction market. His watercolors retail in the medium four figures.

ANDREW WYETH. *Groundhog Day.*
Philadelphia Museum of Art

A leader of the second group is Jackson Pollock, the "drip" artist. While Pollock is known as an Abstract Expressionist, Salvador Dali has produced a number of Abstract Surrealistic paintings, and is certainly the leader of the Surrealistic School.

The major portion of the work of Nicholas de Staël falls midway between abstract painting and naturalistic painting. His objects are usually recognizable as pears, pitchers, glasses, bottles, etc., but they are painted without much concern for perspective, shading or naturalistic shape and coloring.

Bernard Buffet's work is halfway between de Staël and the more naturalistic Contemporaries. His paintings—more in detail than those of de Staël, but considerably less in detail than the objects really appear—are characterized by a strong, straight, dark outline. His large volume of paintings are selling in the middle four figures at the present time.

IV. *Old Master Italian*

Old Master Italian art is the art of museums. It is found in almost every general art museum in the world. To indicate the significance of this world collection of Italian paintings, if they were suddenly removed from all museums many of the museums, if not most, would lose their importance.

TITIAN. *Venus with a Mirror.*
National Gallery, Washington, D.C.
(Mellon Collection)

PAOLO VERONESE. *The Finding of Moses.*
National Gallery, Washington, D.C.
(Mellon Collection)

CANALETTO. *The Square of St. Mark's.*
National Gallery, Washington, D.C.
(Gift, Mrs. Barbara Hutton)

PITTONI. *Rest on the Flight into Egypt.*
National Gallery, London

14

The production of paintings by Italian artists over the centuries has been prodigious. In Italian art we can trace the development of the craft from the most
primitive, no-perspective painting of the thirteenth century, through the exquisite
works of the Renaissance to the glorious and mature art of the Great Venetians,
Titian, Tintoretto and Veronese. If the Italians did not pioneer all of the great
developments in art up to the nineteenth century, at least Italian art paralleled the
forward strides in art throughout the world.

We shall start our review of Italian painting with the eighteenth century and
work back to the Primitives.

A. *Eighteenth Century*.   In this century there were two main groups of painters. The first is the Canal painters, Guardi, Bellotto and Canaletto who, as the
name implies, specialized in the painting of Venetian canals. Canal painting has
for several years been in ever greater demand, particularly in Europe. The great
Venetian Canal painter, Canaletto, found many buyers in England at the time he
painted, and the artist's paintings come onto the market frequently from the descendants of these original buyers.

Aside from the Canal painters, eighteenth century art and that of the prior
Baroque period are characterized by a well developed technique based on the Great
Venetians, the use of flamboyant color, a capturing of movement and a refinement
and polish not as evident in the prior century. The fluid brushwork of Tiepolo
epitomizes this technique as does the bright color so skillfully employed by Ricci
and Pittoni.

B. *Baroque* (*Late Sixteenth and Seventeenth Century*).   The master of the
use of light, Caravaggio, typifies this period in Italian art. His influence extended
all the way to Rembrandt. The canvases of this period are often dramatic compositions with well developed lighting effects which accent form and convey a feeling
of depth and space.

C. *Middle Sixteenth Century*.   The great masters of the middle sixteenth century are the Venetian painters, Veronese, Titian, and Tintoretto. One has only to
visit the churches of Venice and the Doge's Palace to learn what a welter of artists
there were in Venice at this time, all painting in the grand, flowing, silvery style
of the three leaders. There are relatively few paintings offered for sale either at
auction or privately which can absolutely be attributed to one of the three leaders
but there are a good number of works by their contemporaries available.

The word that best describes this period in Italian art is monumentality expressed in large canvases depicting colorful pageants, legends, and Biblical scenes.

CASTIGLIONE. *Allegory.*
National Gallery, Washington, D.C.
(Kress Collection, Loan)

D. *Middle Fifteenth to Early Sixteenth Century.*   This is the era of Leonardo, Michelangelo and Raphael, the era of literal perfection in the development of Western art and an era in which sheer beauty was at a premium. The subjects of the works of this and earlier eras were mainly religious.

The total number of authentic, accepted paintings by Michelangelo can be counted on the fingers, and we can dispense with him as part of the art market. His fresco painting in the Sistine Chapel might well be considered the most valuable work of art in the world, but we can be fairly certain that it will never be sold.

There is speculation from time to time that the Liechtenstein family will sell their portrait of "Genevra di Benci" now recognized as by Leonardo, and the portrait if sold today would easily command seven figures. In fact, a million dollar offer was refused.

There may be a few Raphaels available, but to our knowledge no absolutely authentic and unquestioned one has been on the market (at least not at auction) for some time.

Besides these fabled names there is a secondary group of slightly lesser artists. In this category is Perugino, the teacher of Raphael.

Fine lesser painters who are in a still lower price range of this School are Pinturicchio, Fiorenzo di Lorenzo, and Antoniazzo Romano.

E. *Early Fifteenth Century.*   The early fifteenth century in Italy is brought beautifully to mind by the artist-monk, Fra Angelico. This kind, devout man's

RAPHAEL. *St. George and the Dragon.*
National Gallery, Washington, D.C.
(Mellon Collection)

FRA ANGELICO and FRA FILIPPO LIPPI.
Adoration of the Magi.
National Gallery, Washington, D.C.
(Kress Collection)

personality and purity of life come through in his paintings, which seem to radiate an uplifting, angelic quality, particularly when they are seen in abundance, as in the Monastery of San Marco in Florence, where he lived and worked.

One characteristic of this period in Italian art, and the middle fifteenth and early sixteenth century, is that the subjects depicted are almost exclusively religious. The Popes were the great patrons along with the ruling families of each of the states into which Italy was then divided. The primary concern of the artist was considered to be the veneration of the Deity. Later, in the time of Titian, Veronese, and Tintoretto, in addition to the religious paintings and paintings of important personages, there were pictures depicting historical scenes and many more portraits.

In the fifteenth century sureness of drawing and fineness of painting were particularly emphasized. *Chiaroscuro* was developed under the deft brush of Leonardo. In the following century the Venetians applied the paint in bolder strokes and emphasis was shifted to over-all grandeur of composition and color—foretold perhaps by the magnificent composition by Michelangelo on the ceiling of the Sistine Chapel.

F. *Primitives.* The early fifteenth century shades off into Primitives. These are what the name implies. The drawing and modeling of form are primitive as

SASSETTA. *Meeting of St. Anthony and St. Paul.*
National Gallery, Washington, D.C.
(Kress Collection)

TER BORCH. *The Suitor's Visit.*
National Gallery, Washington, D.C.
(Mellon Collection)

compared to the more perfect rendering of form by later Schools. These sensitive early attempts to portray the subjects do not appear lifelike. Most particularly there is a lack of third dimension. These works, usually religious in theme, are more interesting because of their place in art history than because of their intrinsic beauty, although many of these jewel-like panels, usually painted in tempera on a gold background, are refreshing to look at—pure in form and religious concept.

Two greats of this period, which are highly treasured by those museums and collectors fortunate enough to own them, are Duccio (1255-1319) and Cimabue (1240-1302), but these highly valued masters seldom appear on the market today. There has been a return of interest in this School partly because of its simplicity and similarity to Modern art.

V. *Seventeenth Century Dutch and Flemish*

There are known to be in existence about 200,000 paintings by approximately 2,000 artists of seventeenth century Holland. This is an extremely large and popular School with an active market throughout the Western world. This is the School of such Masters as Rembrandt, Vermeer, Hals, Ter Borch, Jacob and Salomon Ruisdael, Hobbema, and van Goyen.

VAN DYCK. *Marchesa Balbi.*
National Gallery, Washington, D.C.
(Mellon Collection)

JOHN CONSTABLE. *View of Salisbury Cathedral.*
National Gallery, Washington, D.C.
(Mellon Collection)

The gamut of Seventeenth Century Dutch art is great—from the precise, perfectly painted portraits by Ter Borch and the subdued but dramatic Ruisdael landscapes to the masterful psychological studies by Rembrandt.

The Seventeenth Century Flemish School of art is as big in volume of paintings as the Seventeenth Century Dutch. The two Schools are very similar in style, one explanation being that the countries are small in area and adjacent to one another. Three artists in the Flemish School stand out as the leaders—Rubens, van Dyck and Teniers. There is a drop in renown to artists in the rest of the group. R. H. Wilenski in his two volume work on Flemish painting, with particular emphasis on the seventeenth century, has done much to bring this School before the public.

VI. *Eighteenth Century British Art*

The great industrialists of the United States, the pioneers who developed the railroad systems, the steel mills, and who enabled great aggregations of capital to be brought together to advance industrial America through their investment banking houses, were also the great collectors of this country—Morgan, Bache, Frick, Mellon. Their successors, the Fords, the Lehmans, the Paul Mellons, and the Rockefellers continue in this tradition.

ROMNEY. *Portrait of Henry Thornton, Esq.*
Private Collection

At the end of the nineteenth century, and in the first decade of the twentieth century, Eighteenth Century British art was collected probably more avidly than any other art by these prime collectors. There is some evidence that the hard working industrialists, many of whom rose from obscurity to a position of national pre-eminence in relatively few years, wanted to grasp culture in a hurry, even though it had to be bought in the form of paintings—paintings that gave the home and the owners an elegance and an air of nobility, as only the British portraitists could.

This School includes the great portraitists: Gainsborough, Reynolds, Romney, Lawrence, Hoppner, and the Scotsman Raeburn, as well as the landscapists: Constable, Crome, and Wilson. The price history of this School, although at times unfortunate, is among the most interesting—as we shall see later.

VII. *Old Master French*

A. *Nineteenth Century.* The nineteenth century in France brought forth several Schools and groups, the most popular today being the Impressionists. Another notable group was the Barbizon School which included Daubigny, Rousseau, Diaz, Troyon, Millet, and Corot. This was a naturalistic School, fairly true to nature but

RAEBURN. *John Tait and His Grandson.*
National Gallery, Washington, D.C.
(Mellon Collection)

DAUBIGNY. *The Farm*. National Gallery, Washington, D.C. (Dale Collection)

TOULOUSE-LAUTREC.
Quadrille at the Moulin Rouge.
National Gallery, Washington, D.C.
(Dale Collection)

not typified by the brilliant coloring so favored by the later Impressionists who were, nevertheless, greatly influenced by the Barbizons. Renoir is said to have painted with Daubigny on the latter's houseboat, and Corot's influence on Renoir can be detected in Renoir's early landscapes and figure studies.

Although the landscapes of the Barbizon School are not as spectacular as the Impressionist landscapes, they are very pleasing and wear well with the viewer, adding greatly to the charm and livability of a home.

Also included in the nineteenth century group of important painters in France are such diverse artists as:

Toulouse-Lautrec	Courbet
Daumier	Ingres
Gericault	David
Fantin-Latour	Delacroix

B. *Eighteenth Century French.* The eighteenth century in France was the decorative century (also known as the Rococo Age) and considerable thought was given to what would look attractive on the walls of fine homes and palaces. The subjects have been criticized as being trivial, but the polished technique, the beautifully blended flesh tones, and the pleasing colors cannot help but be admired. This was the age of the court painters, Boucher and Fragonard, and the painter of everyday life, Chardin. Some of the more frivolous subjects (in light of the troubled times just prior to the Revolution) incline one to shake his head and say, "I see why there was a French Revolution."

Other important painters of this period were Watteau, Greuze, and Hubert Robert.

C. *Seventeenth Century French.* The seventeenth century was the era of Lorrain, Poussin, Georges de la Tour, Le Nain, Vouet, Largillière, Le Sueur, Philippe de Champaigne, and the Boullognes.

In many ways the School combines the best qualities of the Dutch and Italian Schools of this century. The rendering of form and shading are excellent, sometimes superb, and not unlike the painstaking work of the Dutch, yet the colors are usually bright and show the Italian influence. This influence is also seen in the strong lighting and figure composition.

"The Splendid Century," an exhibition of French art from 1600-1715, at the National Gallery of Art, Washington, The Toledo Museum of Art and the Metropolitan Museum of Art, 1960 and 1961, was the first major exhibition we have had of this era—and shows a revival of interest in this period of art.

BOUCHER. *Madame Bergeret.*
National Gallery, Washington, D.C.
(Kress Collection)

GEORGES DE LA TOUR. *The Fortuneteller.*
The Metropolitan Museum of Art, New York
(Rogers Fund, 1960)

VIII. *Expressionists*

Expressionism is a Central European art movement which arose in the early part of this century. The painting is to a considerable extent a caricature of whatever is represented. Through a distortion of the form an effect of strong emotion is achieved. The paintings do not have a restful aspect. The Expressionists convey something to the viewer other than the object painted. It is an attempt to impart a feeling. The paintings are essentially strong and command attention and in the late 1950's gained a strong foothold in the art market.

The big names in Expressionism are Oskar Kokoschka, Kirchner, Nolde, Kandinsky, Schmidt-Rottluff, Marc, Klee, Soutine, Munch, and "the painter of clowns"—Rouault. When we review the amazing price history of this School in the chapter on Modern Art, we shall also study further what this School hoped to accomplish, how it started, and how it conflicted with Hitler's Nazis.

The eight Schools of painting we have just highlighted represented the majority of the interest in the art market in the late fifties and early sixties. They occupy this position because of the rising nature of the market for these Schools and because of the percentage of total sales represented by these Schools.

MAX BECKMANN. *Descent from the Cross.*
Museum of Modern Art, New York

VELÁSQUEZ. *Coronation of the Virgin*. The Prado

IX. *Spanish*

The relatively few Spanish Masters that are popular are very highly priced. Probably the most sought after is Velásquez. His paintings are scarce, and a top-notch painting by him rarely appears on the market. Certainly Velásquez was one of the most remarkably adept painters of all time. Bernard Berenson, the distinguished authority on Italian painting, implies throughout his writings that Velásquez is certainly the equal of the greatest Italian artists.

Paintings by El Greco are much sought after at the present time, and the prestige of owning an El Greco is great indeed.

X. *Flemish Primitives*

The great Flemish Primitives are among the most highly prized paintings in the world. They are characterized by infinite detail, freshness of form and jewel-like color as well as a stylization which makes them distinguishable immediately. Their rendering of textures has not been surpassed.

The astonishing thing about this School is that it accomplished what it did so early in art history. The School is essentially a School of the early 1400's; yet the exquisite perfection of the works of the leaders of this group has hardly been exceeded in the five hundred years which have passed since the artists completed these paintings.

The first great painters of the School were Hubert and Jan van Eyck, who are credited with the invention of "oil painting." Masterfully using the new medium of oil these Flemish craftsmen painted large altarpieces composed of as many as a dozen complete, individual pictures—portraits, landscapes and interior scenes—all blending into a perfect, harmonious whole.

HOLBEIN. *Edward VI.*
The Metropolitan Museum of Art, New York
(Bache Collection, 1949)

XI. *Sixteenth Century German*

The significant Sixteenth Century German artists are Albrecht Dürer and Hans Holbein the Younger. When these names are mentioned one thinks only in terms of superlatives to describe their work. Between these greats and the other German painters of the same century there is a difference in quality and price, but this does not mean that the lesser artists are not important. As we shall see, many have great merit and the prices of this School are not low.

XII. *American*

Because this book is primarily for the American Collector historical American has been featured. The adjective "historical" is used to distinguish this group from Contemporary American. The group includes Gilbert Stuart, Charles Willson Peale, Thomas Sully, Winslow Homer, James McNeill Whistler, John Singer Sargent, Albert Pinkham Ryder, and a good number of other important Americans. A collector beginning today can select a number of fine examples from the American Schools—which should increase in value over the years and which are still comparatively reasonable in price.

These twelve Schools comprise the major portion of what we will be considering in this book, and they comprise a substantial percentage of the art market

GILBERT STUART. *The Skater.*
National Gallery, Washington, D.C.
(Mellon Collection)

in the Western world today. Oriental art and Near and Middle Eastern art as well as Egyptian, Greek and Roman art are sold in the Western world but this is a very distinct segment of the art industry and should be considered as separate from the Schools of art noted here.

An objection to confining ourselves to the twelve Schools is that the tremendous group of nineteenth and early twentieth century paintings is not emphasized. Every country has a large trade in the paintings by its artists in this period. In most cases the price per painting is relatively low, and the market is more of a national market than a world-wide or Western market. The painters are diverse as to School, but are frequently traditional in style, rather than members of an "innovation" School. If they were innovators like, for example, the Central European Expressionists, they might have secured world-wide attention, as this group has done, and they would consequently have become a part of the world market.

A number of Schools have been omitted because too few paintings from the School appear on the market to make the School of much market significance; however, it is advisable that the collector make himself familiar with these Schools as they can be very important from an artistic point of view (and for investment) as for instance: Sixteenth Century Flemish, Sixteenth Century Dutch, and the French Primitives.

Where examples are given in the following chapters, each painting is considered to be a typical example of the work of the artist as judged from an examination of a photograph. The works chosen for the charts are not poor works, nor are they necessarily masterpieces. A work with a good background of authenticity is often selected, and it represents what is considered to be the fair market price for a painting of good quality by the particular artist at the time of sale. The dimensions are usually given, and the paintings selected are generally the optimum sized paintings which can be hung on the wall of an apartment or modern home of reasonable space.

A very small painting or sketch is frequently less valuable, as is an extremely large one—except for the oversize important painting of museum quality which would appeal to museum buyers.

Our period for the study of price trends is 1925 to the present; and now that we have a general idea of what we shall be covering, let us begin our study of these Schools in more detail.

III

The Impressionists

N OCTOBER 15, 1958, AT THE JAKOB GOLDSCHMIDT SALE OF SEVEN
paintings, a Cézanne, a Post-Impressionist, sold for the record auction price of any painting of this School of art—$616,000. The buyer
was Paul Mellon of the famous Pittsburgh banking family. Admittedly, Mr. Mellon is a multimillionaire and can afford such a price. Yet he would not have had
to pay this price had not someone else forced him to pay it by bidding against
him. In other words, someone else was willing to pay nearly that much. But the
rest of the prices were remarkable as well, ranging from $182,000 to $369,000.
Later we will look into these paintings in detail, studying prices as compared with
costs to Mr. Goldschmidt.

At the end of the decade of the 1950's, the Impressionists were the thing to
have, a symbol of wealth. Throughout the decade of the 1950's a good Impressionist was a prime investment, and the price level of this School rose steadily
and steeply.

The style of painting known as Impressionism arose in the late 1860's. The
name was derived from a canvas by Monet exhibited in 1874 entitled "Sunrise:
an Impression."

In this School of painting precision drawing and careful modeling of form,
which up to that time had been stressed by almost every School of art, declined
in importance. Figures and objects became vague and sketchy. Outlines became

31

RENOIR. *Bather Arranging Her Hair.*
National Gallery, Washington, D.C.
(Dale Collection, Loan)

indistinct. The "impression" on the viewer was more important than the fineness
of drawing. Because of the concern of the Impressionists with the effect of light
falling on a subject, the majority of their canvases are landscapes. These were
painted out in the open air directly from nature, whereas the great Seventeenth
Century Dutch artists of landscape, Ruisdael, Hobbema, and van Goyen, painted
landscapes in their studios from memory. By this "open air" painting the Impressionists believed that they could duplicate the colors of nature. They brightened
up their canvases through the use of pure primary colors—bright reds, blues
and yellows, and the inclusion of complementary colors in the shadows. They
would paint the same subject at different times during the day, carefully recording
the light effect.

When an Impressionist painting is examined in detail it becomes apparent
that the paint is applied in small strokes of different colors. Green grass will not
be green, but will contain blue and yellow strokes. The effect is unnatural if one
is a foot away from the canvas, but when one stands farther away the individual
brush strokes seem to blend, giving a pleasing and vibrant effect.

CLAUDE MONET. *Banks of the Seine, Vetheuil.*
National Gallery, Washington, D.C. (Dale Collection)

MANET. *Landscape.* Private Collection

EDGAR DEGAS. *Four Dancers.*
National Gallery, Washington, D.C.
(Dale Collection, Loan)

VINCENT VAN GOGH. *The Olive Orchard.*
National Gallery, Washington, D.C.
(Dale Collection, Loan)

PAUL GAUGUIN. *Fatata Te Miti.*
National Gallery, Washington, D.C.
(Dale Collection, Loan)

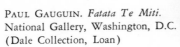

The Impressionists emphasized happy scenes, partly in response to an effort to escape from the dreary, poverty-ridden lives that most of them led. They were further borne down by the severity of the criticism which they received from the adherents to the orthodox Schools.

The leaders of this Impressionist School were Monet, Renoir, Pissarro, Sisley, Bazille, Morisot, Manet, and Degas.

In the 1880's a modification of the Impressionist School took place, and the exponents of this School are known as Post-Impressionists. The leaders are Cézanne, van Gogh, Gauguin, Seurat, and Signac. While Seurat and Signac experimented with Pointillism, the use of "scientifically" placed small dots and squares of different colors which were supposed to blend in the eye from a distance to give a new effect, Cézanne, van Gogh, and Gauguin went off in a different direction in experimentation. Van Gogh appears to have painted all of his pictures in a great hurry with short, choppy strokes. Gauguin gradually developed into a painter of flattened, two-dimensional surfaces, instead of three dimensional, and produced his most sought-after works in Tahiti where he painted the primitive, native life in warm, tropical, close-harmony colors. Cézanne attempted to combine the characteristics of the new style with the monumentality of the Old Masters.

We have traced the price history of the Impressionists (and each other School that we have reviewed) from the year 1925 up to the present. We could have traced some of the Schools and artists to a year much earlier than 1925, but we have chosen this year as a starting point for several reasons.

In the first place, 35 years is a reasonable period of time to hold an investment. It does us little good to know that at the time Vermeer died, and later on

CÉZANNE. *Landscape in Provence.*
National Gallery, Washington, D.C.
(Dale Collection)

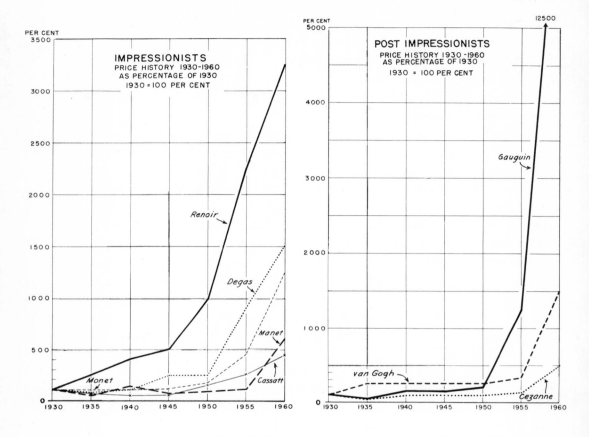

in the same century, his paintings could have been bought for $200 each or less. An investment extending over a time span of 275 years has little meaning. Thirty-five years has meaning. A man 30 years old in 1925 would be 65 in 1960. This span is a reasonable limit to investment during one's lifetime.

In the years 1920 and 1921 we had the post-World War I depression. By 1925 the country was well out of it and definitely on the road to the peak year 1929. The business cycle was in the upswing phase.

The period 1925 through the '50's includes the great depression years of 1930 to 1934, with the trough in 1932 and 1933, so that we can study painting prices in depression.

The period also includes the war years 1940-1945, so that the effect of this cataclysm on art prices can be determined.

Finally, the post-war period and the boom of the 1950's can be studied in its relation to art prices.

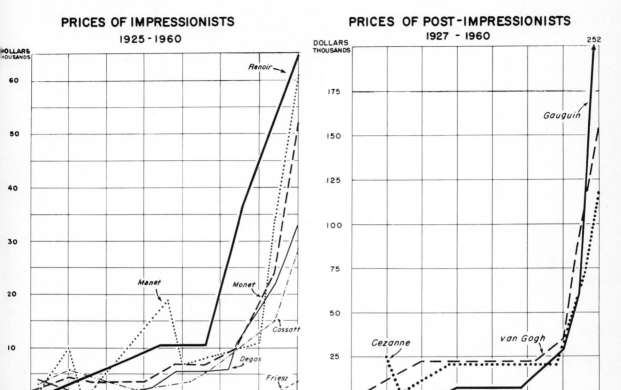

PRICES OF IMPRESSIONISTS
1925 - 1960

PRICES OF POST-IMPRESSIONISTS
1927 - 1960

We have mainly confined our study to three great auctions in two of the major art centers of the world: the Parke-Bernet Galleries in New York and Christie's and Sotheby's in London. While many of the auctions in Paris were studied as well as some in other art centers, over 95 per cent of the auctions in Parke-Bernet, Sotheby's, and Christie's were studied.

In determining a price trend *what* we are tracing must be carefully defined in advance. When a person says, "I have a Renoir," the sentence has relatively little meaning. It might mean that the owner has a Renoir drawing worth $2000, or a small, late, sketchy painting worth $4000, or it might be Duncan Phillips referring to his painting "The Canoeists at Lunch" which was worth at the beginning of the 1960's at least $1,000,000.

The following standards were used in charting the prices of particular artists:

1. No painting which seemed of doubtful authenticity was selected for the recording of price. Usually only those paintings which had reproductions in pho-

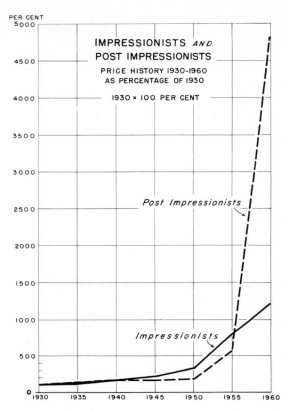

tograph form in the auction catalogues were considered.

2. The paintings chosen were typical works of the artist so that one with a good degree of knowledge, such as a dealer, would recognize the painting as being a Renoir or a Gauguin or whoever else it was supposed to be by.

3. The painting selected had to be of excellent quality. This qualification means that poor Renoirs were not put in, and among the 6000 paintings he produced, some were of much lower quality than others. The same qualification holds true of the works of any artist. Some are good and some are bad, and there are all degrees of quality from the hand of one artist. The paintings selected were not all necessarily of museum quality. While some of them undoubtedly went into museums, masterpieces were deliberately avoided since they command such high prices as to be atypical, are not representative of the average prices for the artist's good paintings, and are not generally available to buyers because of their extremely limited supply. Such a museum quality painting is Gainsborough's "Mr. and Mrs. Robert Andrews" which sold in early 1960 for £130,000 or $364,000.

In the same way the highest priced auction paintings of the Lurcy sale, the Kirkeby sale, the Goldschmidt sale and a few other élite sales were discounted price-wise because of their top quality and because of the unusual aggregation of moneyed buyers at the sales.

4. The size of the painting selected was medium. The smaller paintings, as for instance, 10 by 12 inches and smaller, were usually not recorded here, as these go generally cheaper than larger paintings. The very large paintings were also rejected for price recording. Large paintings by certain Masters bring premium prices. On the other hand, large paintings by certain other artists are known as "outsize paintings" and bring low prices. Some very large Italian and French paintings are in this "outsize" category. However, a large Rubens Biblical or mythological scene brings a premium price. Such paintings are very often sold to museums which have the necessary wall space. Private demand comes generally from apartment or modern home dwellers who want paintings of perhaps 20 by 30 inches or thereabouts—a convenient size to hang on the wall without having the painting dominate the room.

Size is most important in value, especially in the work of certain artists. A good large Renoir can bring $100,000 or more, with measurements of perhaps 25 by 35 inches. The same quality in 8 by 10 might bring $12,000.

It should be stressed that all price charts are based strictly on auction prices, and they reflect the actual figures received for the paintings, not some theoretical price. There are these difficulties in using auction prices, however:

A. The retail price is frequently higher than auction prices for the same quality painting.

B. The more important galleries frequently have quality paintings not found in auctions. While the Goldschmidt Collection was of superb quality, not all auction items are of this quality so that auction prices might be somewhat below dealer prices because of this difference.

C. In determining a price trend we can rarely compare exactly alike items. In 1925 ten Renoirs might have sold for prices ranging from $10,000 to $12,000. The sizes might all be close to 25 by 30 inches. In 1960 ten Renoirs might sell for from $50,000 to $60,000, and the sizes might be in the same range as the paintings sold in 1925. The conclusion would seem to be that Renoir rose to about five times the 1925 level in this period, but the paintings are not the same. The value of one painting, even at the same minute, is rarely exactly the same as the value of another painting. We are then, always to a large degree, comparing unlike things. Two paintings of the same size and of the same quality by the same artist are never as comparable as two shares of stock of the same company. In order to modify this difference somewhat, we approximate paintings of the same quality and size. In some years only small paintings by the artist might be used for price comparison because no larger paintings were sold. We thus have to estimate from these smaller paintings what a larger one would have sold for, and this approximation offers room for error.

D. Where we use British price quotations, and sometimes French and other quotations, we have converted the price to dollars to make prices comparable with American auction figures. There is an error in conversion where currencies were devalued. When the pound went from $3.68 in 1949 to $2.80 in 1950, it obviously took fewer American dollars to buy the same number of pounds sterling, and the price of paintings in England dropped in dollars immediately. We must make an adjustment here or the chart on prices would be in error.

E. The auction price may reflect the existence and operation of a buying "ring" of dealers who artificially depress the price of a painting which would otherwise go at a very much higher figure if this collusion did not exist. We have no way of knowing in which auctions and for which paintings "rings" artificially depressed the price.

F. Buy backs by the owners can artificially establish high prices. There is an advantage in reselling when a person (usually a dealer) can point to the high price he paid for the painting. In one small auction house, at least, a dealer frequently offered excellent paintings in order to help the auction house lure in buyers. These paintings, however, would never be permitted by the seller to go at the very low price an auction buyer might expect. If officially recorded these prices are unrealistic.

G. Sometimes paintings have non-commercial values. These are often sentimental and connected with estate sales on the demise of the owner. A member of the family or a friend might be willing to pay an unrealistically high price to keep the picture out of the hands of the public.

H. The restriction of the paintings selected for the recording of price to typical, authentic works of the artist of house or apartment size, and of excellent, but not necessarily top museum, quality, and to pictures which have been reproduced in the sales catalogue so that they can be studied, drastically cuts down the number of paintings on which prices were recorded. The sample of prices is thus sometimes limited. In this case, where sample prices are few, recorded prices of paintings which have not been actually studied from photographs are consulted in establishing the price line. It must be stressed that where photographs have not been seen, much care has been exercised. As an example of misattributed works, several paintings now in our collection had in the past gone through major auctions and were carefully recorded by the price guides, but the artist had been misstated, and thus in these cases the quotations are without meaning.

I. There is a difficulty in using the three markets of the United States, England, and France. Each market has a certain bias, either for or against a particular artist. Some of the French Moderns who are new to the American market have long been selling in France and at good prices. The same holds true of the Impressionists in the early part of the present century.

As the world becomes smaller from the point of view of transportation the market differences have a tendency to cancel out, but it is only a tendency. Canaletto canal scenes have not been selling in the United States at auction for the huge prices they bring in London, for instance. Medium grade Seventeenth Century Dutch paintings bring far more in Amsterdam than they do in New York.

There follows a price history of the Impressionists by a sampling of key artists:

Renoir was the most prolific of all of the Impressionist painters. In all he painted 6000 pictures. In New York at the American Art Gallery, an auction house, in 1926 the "Portrait of Madame Samary at the Piano," measuring 23 by 17½ inches, sold for $400. Nine years later at the Newman sale in New York "Jeune Fille à sa Toilette," 16½ by 13, brought $2900, and "La Jeune Mere" brought $4100.

In 1925 at the Hotel Drouot in Paris, however, possibly the largest Renoir sale in history was held. No fewer than 160 Renoirs were sold. The event was the sale of the Maurice Gangnat Collection. There was hardly a mediocre Renoir in the entire sale. For $2000 or less a good Renoir could be purchased, and the sale certainly did not lack moneyed and knowledgeable buyers. These included the Aga Khan, the great French actor Sacha Guitry, Knoedler and Company, and Alphonse Kann, and all purchased paintings. The painting featured on the cover of the collection catalogue, "Injured Nude," 28½ by 36½, brought 505,000 francs, approximately $25,000.

In the same sale were five good Cézannes and three Vuillards. The Cézanne prices were $2300, $5000, $6550 and $26,400. The high price for the Vuillards was $2540.

The entire total of 168 paintings brought $543,000.

By 1942 the price of good Renoirs had reached $10,000. In the Parke-Bernet Galleries in New York in that year "Les Oliviers à Cagnes," a smaller painting,

12½ by 21½, from Durand-Ruel, a top grade dealer, brought $2100 as did "Prunes," 10½ by 18, from Knoedler.

From that point the price of Renoirs rose steadily, until by the end of the decade of the '50's a top quality Renoir cost in excess of $50,000. Toward the end of the decade a Renoir landscape was sold from the Lurcy Collection to Henry Ford II for the high price of the sale: $200,000; and at the Goldschmidt sale even this price was slightly exceeded. With the year 1925 equal to 100 per cent, the 1960 price of a good Renoir had risen to 12,000 per cent of that 1925 base!

In the base year, at the beginning of our study period, Monet, the second great Impressionist, could be purchased for $2000. In January, 1926, the American Art Galleries in New York sold "Spring in Vetheuil," 23 by 31, and "Falaises à Dieppe," 21 by 29, each for $2000. Both paintings came from Durand-Ruel.

Fifteen years later, in 1940, the price of Monet had risen little if at all. In 1944 the Parke-Bernet Galleries in New York sold ten illustrated Monets of good quality. The lowest priced one was $2400 and the highest priced was $8000.

From this figure the price rose slightly in 1952, and then rose sharply, so that in 1960 the price of a good Monet was $50,000. The price rise, with 1925 equal to 100 per cent, was 2600 per cent. The price rise was not quite as abrupt as in the case of Renoir, but it must be remembered that the base period offered slightly lower priced Renoirs than Monets.

The third Impressionist, Edouard Manet, offers a more up and down price history than Renoir or Monet. In 1926 a "Portrait of a Man," 13 by 10, was sold in New York for $310, and in 1929 Sotheby's in London sold "Two Roses in a Vase," 14 by 9, for £300, nearly $1500.

The great exception to these low prices came in 1930 in the sale of the celebrated Havemeyer Collection in New York. Here an excellent "Portrait de Marguerite de Conflans," 22 by 18½, was sold for $10,500. From this point there was a drop during the depression, and in 1932 "The Old Carpenter" was sold in New York for $600.

There was a pull-up from the depression to 1943. In that year "White Lilacs in a Vase" sold for $18,000, an excellent, recorded painting 22 by 18. The Parke-Bernet Galleries sold this picture as well as "Le Petit Lange," 46 by 28, in the following year, a painting of similar high quality and recorded, which brought $18,500.

During the war and immediately thereafter there appears to be a slump in the prices of Manet to 1945 when "Jeune Femme aux Cheveux," 24 by 19¾, a recorded painting, sold for $4750 in New York.

MANET. *Gare St. Lazare*. National Gallery, Washington, D.C. (Gift, Horace Havemeyer)

From this point there was a moderate rise in price to 1955, when the level was about $11,000. Then there was a steep rise to the end of the decade when the price of a good Manet reached over $60,000.

In the famous Goldschmidt sale in late 1958 three Manets sold for $182,000, $249,000 and $316,000 respectively.

The rise in price from 1925 was 6100 per cent.

In the year 1926 Edgar Degas brought $4000, more than the average Renoir, Monet or Manet.

By 1934, during the depression, the excellent "Femme Assise" from Durand-Ruel, 27½ by 19½, was sold for $1125 in New York. This painting was in the Degas sale of 1918.

From this low point the price climbed slowly upward to the year 1951 when "Three Jockeys," a pastel 19½ by 25½, sold in New York for $6000.

The price curve then turned sharply upward until it reached $30,000. It is characteristic of the price of Degas that it started out higher than Renoir, Monet or Manet and rose to a lower peak at the end of the decade of the '60's. In the Kirkeby sale in November, 1958, "Deux Danseuses," a typical picture of ballet dancers, 55 by 31½, sold for $66,000.

MARY CASSATT. *The Boating Party*. National Gallery, Washington, D.C. (Dale Collection)

America produced the excellent Impressionist Mary Cassatt, a daughter of Alexander Cassatt, former President of the Pennsylvania Railroad.

In the twenties Mary Cassatt was classed among the great American artists, including Whistler and Sargent, but as time went on she became more and more identified with the Impressionists to which group she actually belonged and with whom she painted.

From a price level of about $3000 in 1926 she rose to a level of about $7500 in 1930. Her paintings were usually portraits of mother and child or of children. They are of beautiful, gentle quality, combining the best Impressionist characteristics with the American School characteristics.

Prices of Cassatts slumped until 1939 and followed very much the American painting pattern rather than the French Impressionist pattern. In that year a good Cassatt could be purchased for around $2000. From there prices of her paintings rose steadily until 1948. Then they took an upward surge from this average level of $5000 to $25,000 in 1960. In April, 1959, "Alexander Cassatt and Son," 39½ by 32, sold at the Parke-Bernet Galleries in New York for $39,000. The painting was unquestioned, recorded, excellent and of prominent persons, who, incidentally, were members of the artist's own family. Her 1960 prices were 700 per cent of her 1925 prices.

In January, 1961, the same gallery sold a pastel, "Mother and Child," 29½ x 24½, for $30,000.

Othon Friesz illustrates the price history and general popularity of a minor Impressionist. Until 1943 his paintings were hardly ever illustrated in auction catalogues, and in that year $300 would purchase a fair Friesz. By 1956 "The Bathers," 10½ by 13¾, brought $750, and in the following year "Still Life," 29 by 31, brought only $650.

From then on his prices rose sharply, and in November, 1959, "Cassis sur Mar" brought $3500, an increase from 100 per cent in 1943 to 1100 per cent in 1959. While Friesz is most certainly not one of the leading, high priced Impressionists, his prices have risen in the decade of the '50's fairly sharply.

At this point we leave the strict Impressionists and go on to the Post-Impressionists, and first to Vincent van Gogh, the Dutchman who attempted to make use of colors the way Vermeer did. While van Gogh certainly lacked formal training, discipline and emotional balance, his paintings have a distinctive characteristic of highly colored short-stroke brush work that has made him the rage in the '50's along with Gauguin and Cézanne in the Post-Impressionist School.

FRIESZ. *Cassis sur Mar*. Parke-Bernet Galleries, Inc.

In 1927 Christie's in London sold "Vase of Flowers," 15¼ by 12¼, of poppies, daisies and cornflowers for £1260, about $6000.

By 1935 at the Newman sale in New York "Printemps près d'Arles," 25½ by 32, sold for $15,000. This is a typical, recorded work by van Gogh of his most wanted period.

A peculiarity of the paintings of van Gogh is that his works of the so-called Nuenen Period, which are characterized by dark colors, principally dark greens, grays and blacks, are worth very little as compared with his sunburst and bright color paintings. These latter are the paintings that people think of when the name van Gogh is mentioned.

From 1935 to 1951 there is little rise in the auction prices of van Gogh. To 1955 there was a rise in price to about $35,000. The "Bouquet of Flowers," an excellent van Gogh, 21¾ by 18, recorded, was sold by the Parke-Bernet Galleries for $37,000 in 1955.

From here the price of van Gogh's paintings went skyward to over $150,000 by the turn of the decade into the '60's. Sotheby's in November, 1959, sold the excellent painting "Pont sur la Seine à Asniers" for £45,000 ($126,000).

The price rise of van Gogh based on 1927 as 100 per cent was 3100 per cent in 1960.

Paul Gauguin, born in 1848, painted and shared the house in Arles for a short time with van Gogh. Gauguin's most wanted Tahitian period is characterized by the use of bright, tropical, tapestry-like colors, especially reds. As late as 1930 the paintings of Gauguin were not highly in demand. "River Landscape in Brittany" was sold in New York in that year for $2000, although this is not a Tahitian period Gauguin. In 1937, however, "Tahiti" from George Bernheim in Paris was sold for $1700. The painting measured 28 by 17½. There was a slight drop in prices into the depression and a slight rise to 1949.

On June 30, 1939, an unusual sale took place in Lucerne, Switzerland, at the Gallerie Fischer. It was a sale of paintings from German galleries—125 museum pieces, some of top quality, and the artists included Braque, Chagall, Derain, Gauguin, van Gogh, Klee, Kirchner, Kokoschka, Matisse, Modigliani, Nolde, Picasso, and Vlaminck, among others. It was a German government-ordered sale. What the real motives behind the sale of these museum paintings were can be conjectured. Perhaps the German government wanted all the foreign credit it could get since it was preparing to wage all-out war on Europe, and the paintings were in many cases considered to be decadent art by the Nazi party.

Whatever the motives were, the excellent example of Gauguin, "Aus Tahiti,"

36½ by 29, sold for just under $12,000. Gauguin generally did not reach this level of auction price until 1955.

In the same German government sale a van Gogh self-portrait brought the highest price: $39,455.

After 1955 the price of Gauguin rose enormously and extremely rapidly to a quarter of a million level by the end of the decade.

The painting "Te Tai Na Ve I Te Rata" of the same period and the same size as the government sale Gauguin brought £130,000 ($364,000) in London, November 25, 1959.

The 1960 price is 12,600 per cent of the 1930 price.

Of all the Post-Impressionists, the artist who probably has the finest reputation and has exerted the greatest influence on Modern Art because of his concern with geometrical structure is Paul Cézanne. His quality was reflected in price earlier than any of the Impressionists or Post-Impressionists.

In 1930 "L'Enlèvement" sold from the Havemeyer Collection in New York, a painting measuring 35½ by 46, for $24,000, a not inconsiderable price for a member of this group in the year 1930.

From here Cézanne prices declined to the year 1932 when the "Portrait of a Botanist" brought £130 (about $650).

Prices then rose out of the depression to 1939 when a level of about $20,000 was achieved and maintained until 1954. From here prices rose precipitately to 1960 when a level of well over $100,000 was achieved.

The famous "Boy in a Red Vest" sold in October, 1958, from the Jakob Goldschmidt Collection, for £220,000 ($616,000) was a high point for Impressionists and Post-Impressionists at auction.

In November, 1959, the similar, excellent "Peasant in a Blue Blouse" brought £145,000 ($406,000).

Nevertheless, in the same month the "Portrait of Victor Chocquet" brought only £24,000 and the "Portrait of Madame Cézanne" brought £40,000, both fine paintings, the latter bringing $27,000 in 1939, an auction record.

Cézanne has risen from 100 per cent in 1930 to 460 per cent at the end of the '50's, but his base price is high, and often good paintings by Cézanne can be purchased for less than his tremendous peak prices.

We can equalize the growth rates and at the same time make the various artists in the group more comparable in their price rise by using 1930 as a base. Some of the artists were not enough in public vogue in 1925, at least from the point of view of being featured in auctions, so that their prices were not well recorded this early. By the year 1930 we have all of the Impressionists and Post-Impressionists featured from time to time, although by 1930 they were certainly not the School of art in favor with the buying public. By this year a certain rise had taken place from 1925, so that subsequent rises based on the year 1930 would not be so steep as if the year 1925 were used as the base year.

If we base all artists on 1930 as 100 per cent, we have by the year 1960 Renoir at 3250 per cent, Monet at 1250 per cent, Manet 600 per cent, Degas 1500 per cent, and Cassatt 440 per cent. These are the Impressionists.

In the Post-Impressionist group we have van Gogh rising from 100 per cent in 1930 to 1500 per cent in 1960, Gauguin to 12,500 per cent, and Cézanne to 500 per cent. Here again it must be repeated that Cézanne was earlier recognized and consequently priced more highly than the others in the early years; and while in the year 1960 a small painting of fruits sold in the Museum of Modern Art benefit sale for $200,000, good, typical Cézannes could be purchased for a little over $100,000.

Taken as a whole the Impressionist group rose from 100 per cent in 1930 to 107 per cent in 1935, to 154 per cent in 1940, 205 per cent in 1945, 333 per cent in 1950, 794 per cent in 1955, and 1208 per cent in 1960. This is a realistic growth rate and eliminates the extreme rates of percentage growth which result from using a very low price in early years when few paintings of the particular artist were sold, the artists and the School were not in vogue, and the sales of a few outstanding paintings tended to send the price index skyrocketing.

The Post-Impressionists, van Gogh, Gauguin and Cézanne rose from a combined base percentage in 1930 of 100 per cent to 115 per cent in 1935, to 160 per cent in 1940. In 1945 the per cent remained about at the same figure and rose to 177 per cent in 1950, to 566 per cent in 1955, and to 4833 per cent in 1960.

The price increases of the Impressionists and Post-Impressionists were roughly parallel from 1930 until after the war; then the Post-Impressionists greatly exceeded the Impressionists in price rise, although both groups and all the artists in these groups rose greatly in price.

IV

Modern Art

ODERN ART WAS BORN OUT OF THE SCHOOLS OF IMPRESSIONISM
and Post-Impressionism. Impressionism is characterized by an attempt to represent nature primarily by painting directly from nature.
It is also characterized by an attempt to create colors as bright and vibrant as those
seen in nature in contrast to earlier landscape paintings which were somewhat
darker than the scene actually appeared. Akin to this attempt to represent nature
as it really is was an emphasis on light effects, especially sunlight, and experimentation with various methods of color application to show how sunlight actually looks.

The drawing is inexact as compared with the older Schools of art, but from
a distance the weakness in drawing is not so important, and the effect of the
whole painting is pleasing. Finally, there is an emphasis on scenes from life,
especially carefree, happy scenes. The Impressionists started to paint in about
1860.

By 1880 the Post-Impressionists came along and tried to improve on or
modify Impressionism in various ways. The Pointillists, Seurat and Signac,
experimented with dots and small squares of various colors which, from a distance, blended and gave new effects. Van Gogh ran riot in his use of bright and
sharply contrasting colors, while Gauguin, particularly in his popular Tahiti
period, emphasized color, design and flat surfaces.

Modern art began in approximately 1905 with the Autumn Salon Exhibition

MODERNS
PERCENTAGE OF PRICE INCREASE, 1945 - 1960

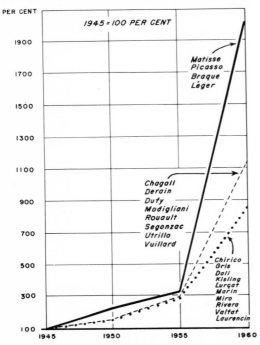

FOUR BIG MODERNS
PRICES IN DOLLARS, 1927-1960

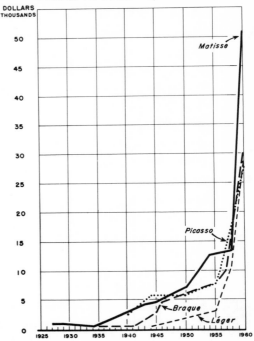

of the Fauves, or Wild Beasts. Just as Impressionism was a revolt against traditional art and its rules and standards, Modern art was in a sense a revolt against Impressionism, although at the same time it was based on Impressionism and carried Impressionism a certain number of steps further.

Henri Matisse may be called the "grand old man" of Modern art. He was trained strictly in the traditional methods of the late nineteenth century and studied under the great painter of charming children and beautiful nudes, Bouguereau. A part of Matisse's early work consisted in copying the works in the Louvre and selling them to the French government for distribution to the French provincial museums. He apparently had some difficulty or unwillingness as regards copying exactly, and the job of selling some of his copies to the government was not an easy one.

From here Matisse absorbed Impressionism, Post-Impressionism, and even Oriental art and finally developed his unique style which is so much in demand at the present time.

His objective was to present form and color for their own sake. Prior to the

Modern School the subjects represented by the artist's brush were the important thing—a field, a house, a person. Now the nature of the forms and the colors and combination of colors, *even though not true to nature,* became the important things. There was a deliberate attempt to *de-emphasize* how things looked so as to emphasize the forms and color.

When one looks at a typical Matisse he usually first notices the fact that it looks flat. There is no depth to the painting. The colors are brighter than in nature. The painting lacks natural shading and perspective and there is no gradation of the colors from bright to dark as they appear in reality. The objects do not always sit solidly on the table or on the floor, but appear to be haphazardly placed. Some of them, without concern for the law of gravity, show little or no support.

This new concept of art was not, however, the result of poor training on the part of Matisse or a lack of self-discipline and industry. It was a deliberate attempt to create a new concept of what art might be. When his paintings in the New York show of 1913 were ridiculed, Matisse wrote, "Tell the American people that I am a devoted husband and father; that I have three fine children, and a fine garden—like any man—that I am not a hoodlum." He could hardly have expressed his sincerity in a more effective way.

HENRI MATISSE. *Woman with Exotic Plant.*
National Gallery, Washington, D.C.
(Dale Collection)

Matisse emphasized color as did van Gogh and Gauguin and flat surfaces as did Gauguin. Whereas these two were still representing nature as they saw it, Matisse was trying to emphasize color and form for their own sake because he thought a picture containing only colors and forms would please the eye and be an end in itself. The representation of nature was of secondary importance. This objective of Matisse is important to keep in mind as we review later Schools of art.

The second great Modern is Pablo Picasso, the Spaniard. Most artists develop a particular style of painting and more or less stick to that style. They progress through their painting lives from being students of someone, and to some extent imitating that teacher, to the development of their own characteristic style which changes gradually over the years, but which has the same general characteristics. For example, the vast majority of Modigliani's paintings look alike in style and resemble no one else's work. The same is true of Renoir and Monet.

Picasso, on the other hand, experimented all through his life with new techniques and new styles, and in each field did about as well as, if not better than, those already established and painting in those Schools. As a result, he is probably the most influential artist of the twentieth century.

In his Blue Period, begun in 1901, he painted pensive looking people, including harlequins, in dull blue colors, emphasizing flat surfaces such as Gauguin produced. To a certain extent Picasso was influenced by his countryman El Greco, with his elongated figures.

In 1905 he started to paint in rose colors, thereby beginning his so-called Rose Period. Later on he drew on African and other primitive art for his subject matter and method of presentation.

At this point let us go back to the Post-Impressionists. The leader of this group, which included van Gogh, Gauguin, and the Pointillists Seurat and Signac, was Paul Cézanne. At the end of the decade of the '50's no other artist in any recent School—Impressionists, Post-Impressionists, Moderns, or Contemporaries —received such acclaim or brought higher prices. A small Cézanne of fruits on a table sold in the $200,000 class at auction in 1960.

Cézanne not only strove to be a good artist; he tried to be a monumental one. He was probably more influenced by the Spanish Master, El Greco, than by any other artist. Cézanne was competent and conservative, and he strove in his paintings to produce something that was worthy of display in the greatest galleries, realizing fully that the standards of these galleries were the greatest art of the past, that this art was good, and that to be on a par with these artists he had to be outstanding also. Cézanne stated his goal in art by simply saying, "I wish to make of Impressionism something solid and durable, like the art of the Old Masters."

Cézanne developed a very effective technique for giving his paintings the look of solidity and permanence. He turned some lines that in real life appear as curves into the *suggestion of angles* and achieved his solidity of form by the suggestion of *cubes* throughout his pictures, even in his portraits.

The Fauves awakened to new vistas opened by Cézanne's breaking down of form into geometric shapes. They revolted against the cold intellectualism of prior art and sought a short cut between what is seen and its representation on canvas.

Science was developing rapidly at the time, and the Fauves picked up an idea from the mineralogists that the *crystal* was the original form of all things. The theory went on to state that all secondary forms arise from the *edges* and *angles* of these primitive forms.

PABLO PICASSO. *Mother and Child*.
Parke-Bernet Galleries, Inc.
Photograph by Taylor & Dull

This revolt and its concomitant return to the simplicity of the far past, plus the use of straight lines and angles of Cézanne, the traditional painter who himself broke away from the Impressionists, resulted in Cubism. The whole art of Cubism is based on two principles: (1) that strength is beauty, and (2) a straight line is stronger than a curved line.

Whether these theories are correct is open to serious question. The strides of science in every period have a way of being popularized for the general public in an outline form, often however, fallacious. One example is the popular interpretation of the Darwinian theory of the late nineteenth century which presumes that man is descended from monkey. Darwin, however, never said this, stating only that both man and monkey are descended from a common ancestor.

In the same way the Cubistic artists, and before them the Fauves, may have misinterpreted what was said about the crystal and straight lines.

This crystallization of the objects painted in pictures is the essence of Cubism. This is simple Cubism, but Cubism did not stop here. The next step was to break up the cubes which together represented the sitter or the scene and shuffle them around. The point in doing this was to show not just the one aspect of the objects painted, but several aspects seen from different standpoints—in different parts of the canvas and from the front, back, sides, top and bottom, in more or less arbitrary presentation or grouping. A glass, for instance, is broken up and the various pieces, presented as cubistic forms, are found all over the canvas; and one must use ingenuity in many cases to put the pieces together in his own mind so that he comes to the conclusion, "Oh, I see now; that's supposed to be a glass on a table. The viewer must reassemble all of the pieces." The paintings in some cases presented a kind of puzzle to determine just what they were, a challenge to the viewer and a demonstration of the ingenuity of the painter. Whether the Cubists succeeded or not, and how fine and acceptable the painting, are things entirely up to the viewer, *not the painter,* and this simple test of the success of a painting is too often lost sight of.

Finally, in order to understand the subject matter of Cubism we must go back to Paul Gauguin. His representative painting is of native life in Tahiti—primitive in every aspect. This is a part of his revolt against civilization and what he considered to be its incorrect developments and complications.

The Cubists were not content to go back to the crystal for *form.* They went back to simple, primitive African art for subject matter. In this way they felt their entire painting was fundamental painting, devoid of the incorrectness of the prior Schools of art which had developed, together with civilization, along the wrong lines.

BRAQUE. *Still Life: Le Jour*. National Gallery, Washington, D.C. (Dale Collection, Loan)

Picasso was probably the primary exponent of Cubism. He was undoubtedly influenced by Cézanne's adherence to geometric principles in drawing. This influence, and other influences, led to his Cubistic Period which began in 1909. In this period he produced a great volume of paintings which frequently appear on the market.

By 1920 he entered a Classical Period during which he painted heavy, ungainly figures. By the middle twenties he entered a Surrealist Period in which he painted tortured forms that were supposed to inspire fear and various other emotions, and by 1939 he produced paintings which qualified him as a member of the Expressionist School.

The third great Modern is Georges Braque, the Cubist. He was influenced by the Fauves and in 1908 by Cézanne. Here again it must be emphasized that Cubism embodies breaking simple objects down into geometric forms because the artist feels they have a pleasing compositional effect, and there is little esoteric or hidden meaning about such painting.

Fernand Léger is the fourth of the important Moderns. He also is a Cubist, but he often employed machine designs instead of simple geometric forms and cubes. He was influenced by both Braque and Picasso, but particularly by the war

machines which were developed during World War I in which he was a com-
batant.

These four: Matisse, Picasso, Braque and Léger constitute the "greats" of
Modern Art. They dominate the broad, general category known as "Modern
Art" and they represent the highest monetary values.

Modern Art is the art of the early twentieth century. Most of its exponents
are either dead or elderly. Although the name of the general category is "Modern," this term has ceased to mean what it apparently did, namely "up-to-date."
The up-to-date art of today, that art produced by living artists, is known as
Contemporary Art, and it will be discussed separately later.

Modern Art is not a School of art. It is an aggregation of Schools, movements
and fads which developed in the twentieth century. It will be appreciated that
one artist may belong to several Schools during different periods of his painting
life. Picasso belonged to many Schools. Rouault belonged to the Fauves, but also
to the **Central European Expressionist School.**

LÉGER. *Woman with Mirror.*
National Gallery, Washington, D.C.
(Dale Collection)

To see the price movement in Modern Art one looks first to the "Big Four."

In 1927 a Matisse could be bought for $1000. In 1934 "Woman Reclining in a Chair" sold at American Art Galleries in New York for $500—just half the pre-depression price. In October, 1940, the Parke-Bernet Galleries in New York sold the peculiar painting "Nature Morte," 71½ by 87, a large painting, for $10,400. It was unusual in that it was based on the famous Seventeenth Century Dutch artist Jan Davidsz de Heem's "Still Life" painting in the Louvre entitled "The Dessert," dated 1640. Matisse in his version of the painting changes the classical Dutch painting to typify his own approach to art; he flattens the whole painting by eliminating the third dimension, brightens the colors until they dominate, and sharpens the outline of every object so that the composition does not look like the traditional version of a still life. (See page 277)

In 1943 a Matisse could be bought for $2500 at auction. By 1954 "Blue Interior," a good, recorded Matisse, brought $12,000 and "Nu au Fauteuil" brought $13,750.

From this point the price of Matisse's paintings rose very rapidly until in the Kirkeby sale in New York in November, 1958, the recorded, illustrated painting "Fleurs et Ceramique" brought $65,000. In March of the following year "Two Girls at Nice," 25½ by 19½, sold in New York at Parke-Bernet for $52,500. A good Matisse could only rarely be purchased at the end of the decade of the '50's for under $50,000.

The price history of Picasso is extremely hard to trace because of his many periods. Some of the periods are very much wanted, and others not so much. This difference in demand is reflected in price. For that reason price comparisons for Picasso are not so reliable as in the case of many other artists.

In 1940 Picasso begins to have enough importance in London and New York auction galleries to merit reproductions of his paintings in the catalogues. There is always a lag in the recognition by auction houses of the works of living artists. In the year 1940 a typical Picasso of good size could be purchased for $2500. By 1944 a good-sized Picasso, recorded, would bring about $5000, and in 1955 $10,000. By the end of the decade of the '50's, a good Picasso would bring around $30,000. This represents a growth to 1100 per cent from 100 per cent in 1940. In January, 1961, the Parke-Bernet Galleries sold the colorful, well-recorded "Fernande," 24 x 16¾ for $75,000. In October, 1960, four Picassos sold for $134,000, $84,000, and $72,000. Picasso had risen to about twice the figure of the 1959-1960 season. Matisse, on the other hand, rose from 100 per cent in 1927 to 6100 per cent at the end of the '50's.

The figures and percentages are, however, somewhat deceptive. In the Kirkeby sale in New York in November, 1958, "Mother and Child" by Picasso, 39½ by 29, brought $152,000, the highest auction price for any work by a living artist. This is not a unique price for Picasso. "La Belle Hollandaise" sold in London at roughly the same time for a comparable price.

In 1934 a Georges Braque "Vase of Anemones," 17½ by 21½, brought $475 in New York. The price of Braque was about the same in 1942. It then rose steadily to about $10,000 in 1957, and from there skyrocketed to approximately $30,000 in 1960, to 6000 per cent of the 1935 figure.

Here again the price of a particular painting can be high. "Femme à la Mandolin" sold in London in July, 1959 for $100,000, and "Composition: the Violin," 31⅞ by 21¼, when sold in New York in April, 1960 for the benefit of the Museum of Modern Art, brought $145,000.

In October, 1960, in the next season, one Braque sold in London for $56,000 and another for $117,000. Prices had risen materially as compared with the past season.

As late as 1944 a Fernand Léger painting could be purchased for $500. In 1944 "Abstraction with Figures," 28¾ inches by 36 inches, brought only $300, and another abstraction, "Still Life," sold in the same year for $700.

By 1955 a few thousand dollars could buy a Léger. By 1958 some of Léger's paintings brought five times this figure, and in March, 1960, his "Still Life with Pipe" brought $20,000, a landscape sold for $25,000 and "Le Fumeur" brought $82,500.

At the beginning of the '60's a good Léger could be purchased at auction for close to $30,000, a price about 6000 per cent of Leger's price in 1944, just 16 years earlier.

If we use the year 1945 as a base for all of the four major artists of Modern Art, we get an idea of the magnitude of the price rise in this general category of painting since the war. This late year is used not simply to emphasize the meteoric rise in prices, but to include all of the artists in one index, since they were not major factors in the international art market prior to the war.

Léger, the least eminent of the four, shows the greatest rise: from 100 per cent in 1945 to 4667 per cent in 1960. Matisse shows a rise in the same period to 1700, Braque to 1200, and Picasso to 467. It will be recalled that Picassos brought well over $100,000 at the end of the period. It is fairly clear from the chart that the greatest rise occurred in the five-year period from 1955 to the end of the decade, when the index rose from 306 to 2009.

In this same five-year span the Impressionists rose from 794 to 1208, and the Post-Impressionists from 566 to 4833. The late rise of the Post-Impressionists and the Moderns were closely parallel, with the Post-Impressionists rising the greatest amount.

If we use the year 1945 as the base year in the case of all three groups of painters, whereas the Moderns rose from 100 per cent to 2009 per cent, the Impressionists rose to 589 per cent and the Post-Impressionists to 3021 per cent. The Impressionists were recognized earlier and their prices rose earlier than did those of the Post-Impressionists and, obviously, the Moderns who came on the scene much later. The Impressionists thus had less distance to rise by the year 1945.

We move now from the leaders of the movement known as Modern Art to the next group within the general category, and for a sample of this larger group which we are considering we include the following:

Marc Chagall	Georges Rouault
André Derain	André Dunoyer de Segonzac
Raoul Dufy	Maurice Utrillo
Amedeo Modigliani	Edouard Vuillard

DERAIN. *Harlequin.*
National Gallery, Washington, D.C.
(Dale Collection)

Marc Chagall is characterized by a fantastic, almost Surrealistic, style of painting in which the figures often float through space. There is no emphasis on perspective; the paintings have a flat quality and the drawing is primitive rather than
precise. There is little attention to the features of the faces and little shading. He
uses rich colors, darkly outlined, and often paints fantasies. In 1940 and 1941 his
paintings might have been purchased for as low as $500. As late as 1955 they had
risen to a level at which a fair sample of his art could be purchased for $2500.
From then on his prices rose rapidly, and they are now over $25,000. In the George
Lurcy sale in November, 1957 "Le Violiniste sous les Roses" brought $12,500 and
"L'Esprit de Roses" sold for $12,000. In April, 1961, two Chagalls brought
$43,000 and $37,000.

André Derain was one of the Fauves identified with Matisse. He painted
in the Fauve style in his early years. Later on he absorbed certain Cubist qualities
and finally went back to painting in much the manner of the traditional French
style. Some of his pleasant and colorful still life paintings seem to be a compromise
between the flat surfaces and unnatural, sharp colors of the Fauves and the true-to-
life colors and perspective of the traditional Schools.

In 1927 in New York two of his paintings sold for $180 and $320, but a large
piece, 4 feet 11 inches by 6 feet 1 inch, brought $1650. There was not much of a
drop in prices during the depression, if any, and in 1943 we find little change in
his 1927 level of prices, except that a large painting, "Au Bal de Suresnes," 71 by
56½, brought $5700. This was formerly in the collection of the dealer Vollard in
Paris.

By the year 1944 Derain's prices had lifted a little to a general level of about
$1500 where they remained through 1951. By 1956 they had risen to the $2000
level, and then a sharp rise took place until the end of the decade when they
reached an average of about $10,000. In the Lurcy sale in 1957 "Arbre dans le
Chemin Creux" brought $22,000.

The price history and price level of Derain are very similar to those of Chagall.
When they first appeared to attract enough attention in the art auctions in America
to merit being reproduced in the sale catalogues, their prices were $500 or there-
abouts. Now they are both well above $10,000. Both experienced their sharp and
large rise in price after 1955. They both rose to about 2000 per cent of their
base period prices which represent 100 per cent.

Raoul Dufy has much the same price history. When he began to attract the
attention of the auctions in 1938 a Dufy could be bought for $500. By 1953 his
prices had risen to $4000, and by the end of the decade they were over $12,000.
The rise represented a figure of 2500 with the base period 100.

DUFY. *Paris*. Parke-Bernet Galleries, Inc.

Dufy was another member of the Fauve group but quickly developed a style of his own which differed markedly from that of the other members of the group. Dufy was technically an excellent painter. His paintings very often emphasize light colors, expanses of sky and space and finely drawn buildings, boats and small figures—these scenes being painted from a distance to include a wide horizon. His Paris scenes are extremely pleasing, gay and decorative. At the Lurcy sale his large canvas "Paris," 76 by 61, brought $26,000.

One important quality of Amedeo Modigliani is that his works are almost instantly recognizable. Practically his entire production of paintings consisted of elongated nudes and portraits, not at all lifelike, but greatly influenced by African art. There is little attempt to represent the third dimension. Very often the faces are without shading, although sometimes there is an exception. The paintings with their bright colored flesh and sensitive, dark outlines have a certain strength, and some of them have a wistful beauty. Probably one reason for their popularity is that when a Modigliani hangs on the wall it advertises itself, and many of the viewers can recognize it.

In 1934 the "Portrait of the Artist" sold in New York for $1200. In 1946 the "Portrait of a Woman," 30¼ by 21¾, brought $3300, and this was a typical price at the time. By 1954 "Raimondo" from the artist's Cubistic Period brought $15,250. His prices then shot up to over $30,000 at the end of the decade. On July 6, 1960, Sotheby's in London sold "Portrait of a Young Girl," 18¼ by 15³⁄₁₆, for £24,000 ($67,000). The portrait was certainly one of his better productions, with strong color and slight shading in the face and a typical elongation of the neck and head and distortion of the chest and shoulders.

Modigliani rose in price from his base of 100 per cent in 1934 to 3100 per cent in 1960, most of the rise taking place in the decade of the '50's.

In October and November, 1960, Sotheby's sold three Modiglianis for £21,000, £22,000 and £38,000 ($58,000, $61,000 and $106,000). The market price of Modigliani about doubled in one year.

Georges Rouault was both a Fauve and, later, a leading Expressionist. We will take the Expressionist School up later in this chapter because it is an important School with a history distinct from that of the French Moderns.

Rouault is the painter of clowns. Early in his painting life, after he had turned from Fauvism to Expressionism, his technique was very sketchy, his surfaces flat and his drawing imprecise. As he developed his style, a certain sad quality appeared in his little groups. The selection of clowns as one of his frequent subjects allowed him to portray effectually this emotion of sadness. Rouault's early training in the making of stained glass is also an apparent influence in his style.

ROUAULT. *Les Trois Juges.*

SEGONZAC. *Paysage.* Parke-Bernet Galleries, Inc.

His dark outlines are reminiscent of leaded stained glass windows. As in the case of Modigliani, Rouault is instantly recognizable to even the less experienced eye, and this quality alone adds to his importance and to his value. There is no need to explain to the art-loving viewer that what one has hanging on the wall is a Rouault. It speaks for itself.

Here again, as in the case of some other French Moderns, a painting by this Master could be purchased for $500 in 1934. The "Head of a Clown," 11 by 8¾, sold for $400 in November, 1934 at the American Art Galleries in New York. By 1939 Rouault's prices were rising, but a plateau existed from 1944 to about 1954, and in this decade $2500 could purchase a Rouault at auction. From there his prices rose rapidly, and by the end of the 1950's they were in the $40,000 range. In the famous Kirkeby sale of 1958 in New York "Crepuscule," 40½ by 28½, a well recorded, illustrated, exhibited Rouault brought $62,000. Rouault's prices rose from the starting 100 per cent in 1934 to 8100 per cent in 1960.

André de Segonzac was, like so many of the Modern French School, identified with the early Fauve movement, and in some ways his paintings resemble those of Derain. They combine the classic quality of the French tradition with the brighter colors and tendency toward lack of detail and flatness of the Moderns.

As late as 1937 Segonzacs could be purchased for under $500. In 1943 "L'Eglise à la Marne," 31¾ by 39½, brought $7250, and the "Gulf at St. Tropez," 25¾ by 31¾, brought $4000.

63

From this point, which represents a steep rise in price and an atypical one, his prices were generally on the $1000 level until 1954. They rose gradually to 1957 when $6000 was paid for "Paysage" in the Parke-Bernet Galleries in New York. Then a tremendous rise began in his prices. In the 1958 Kirkeby sale "Still Life with Apples" achieved a price of $30,000.

From his 100 per cent base in 1937 Segonzac rose to 6350 per cent at the end of the decade of the '50's.

Maurice Utrillo's beautiful little landscapes have long been treasured and conseqeuntly brought fairly substantial prices. He painted charming little scenes around Paris, especially in the Montmartre Section. His drawing is good, his colors are light; there are few experiments which turned out poorly from the point of view of the viewer, and the paintings make excellent and pleasant additions to the decor of any home.

In 1928 "La Rue Bayer, Paris" sold at Christie's in London for £525 (about $2500). There was a drop in price in the depression. In 1937 "Corte, Corsica," 23½ by 32, brought in New York only $450. By 1948 the $2500 level had been achieved again, and by 1953 his prices had risen to over $3000. From here a sharp rise took place until, at the end of the decade, a level of about $18,000 had been reached. In the 1958 Kirkeby sale "Le Lapin Agile à Montmartre" reached a level of $28,000.

In January, 1961, the Parke-Bernet Galleries sold the Utrillo "Rue de Crimee," 28¾ x 39½, for $52,000. Utrillo's price level had risen greatly in one year.

Utrillo painted a great many of his typical Paris street scenes and these often appear on the auction market. Were it not for the great availability of Utrillo's paintings, it is quite possible that his prices would have risen to an even higher point. At the end of 1959 the comparative level was 700 per cent with 1928 representing 100 per cent.

Our final painter in this group of French Moderns is Edouard Vuillard. Vuillard in some ways resembles Derain and Segonzac, but the drawing is much more imprecise, and sometimes the human figures are hardly recognizable as such. The colors are, however, pleasing, and Vuillards have a fine, decorative value.

In 1940 a Vuillard still life brought $1500 in the Parke-Bernet Galleries in New York. Prices rose slowly to a level of about $2500 in 1945 and remained at that level until 1956. Thereupon a rapid rise took place to the end of the decade when an average price of $20,000 was achieved. In the 1957 Lurcy sale "Aux Tuileries," 14½ by 13½, not a large painting, brought $70,000.

This group of eight painters all belonged to the French Modern group, even

though some are identified with other Schools. All of them were born within 19
years of one another, the oldest, Vuillard, being born in 1868, and the youngest,
Chagall, in 1887.

Their great rise in popularity (and this popularity was reflected in price) took
place in the decade of the '50's, and particularly after 1955.

The price pattern since the war is very similar for all of these eight artists,
and with the year 1945 equal to 100 per cent, the rises are roughly comparable,
with the exception of Vuillard who had a higher base period price in 1945 than
the others.

When we compare the combined prices of all of these eight artists with the
Big Four Moderns—Matisse, Picasso, Braque, and Léger—we find a close parallel.
The rise through 1955 is almost identical. From then on the leaders of the Modern
Movement rose more rapidly to a level at the end of the decade of 2009 per cent,
as compared with 1141 per cent, for the eight other artists. This is a general rule
in art value: the leaders of a School or movement usually are the most preferred
and bring the highest prices. They rise the surest and to the highest figures. The
others tend to lag in time and in height of rise.

As of the end of the decade these artists hardly reached the level at auction of
$50,000, and the leaders of the Modern Art Movement sometimes achieved three
times this figure.

VUILLARD. *Repast in a Garden*.
National Gallery, Washington, D.C.
(Dale Collection)

At the same time it should be noted that before the boom in art began after the war, the leaders had a much readier acceptance than the lesser members of the group and brought consistently much higher prices. The boom and the enormous rise of the leaders tended to pull the lesser members along with them, but after a time lag.

A third group of modern artists will now be reviewed:

Giorgio de Chirico   Marie Laurencin
Salvador Dali   John Marin
Juan Gris   Joan Miro
Moise Kisling   Diego Rivera
Jean Lurcat   Louis Valtat

This is also a group sampling and by no means includes all of the Moderns in this price range.

Although these artists can all be classified as Moderns, they vary in Schools and in nationalities, although most of them depend very heavily in their artistic backgrounds and connections on the French Modern group. While Laurencin, Lurcat and Valtat are French, Chirico is Italian, Dali, Gris, and Miro are Spanish, Kisling is Polish, Marin is American, and Rivera is Mexican.

Salvador Dali is the great exponent of the Surrealist School of Art. In this School a painting is supposed to be the result of the operation of the subconscious

DALI. *The Sacrament of the Last Supper.* National Gallery, Washington, D.C. (Dale Collection)

GIORGIO DE CHIRICO.
Conversation among the Ruins.
National Gallery, Washington, D.C.
(Dale Collection)

mind and its expression in concrete form. Dali's canvases, with eerie colors and precisely drawn objects which sometimes have and sometimes do not have a connection with reality, give a feeling of almost endless space. His picture of the melting watches typifies one phase of his painting.

Dali is an excellent draftsman, and there is nothing careless or imprecise about his productions. His "Last Supper" in the National Gallery in Washington, although it has a mystic quality about it, is characterized by excellent draftsmanship, particularly in his fabrics, and is from a compositional aspect well balanced. It draws a larger crowd than perhaps any other painting in the gallery regardless of School or artist. His "Crucifixion" in the Metropolitan in New York is a similarly well painted picture.

When his smaller, less monumental paintings have appeared at auction they could often be bought for a few thousand dollars.

Giorgio de Chirico's painting emphasizes the supernatural. His empty spaces give one the feeling of aloneness, and his objects often have symbolic meaning.

He is very fond of using human figures beside very large horses. In the creation of a dreamlike atmosphere he reminds one of Dali. In 1940 a Chirico could be purchased for $150, but by 1944 his prices had risen to the level of about $500, where they remained until 1954. Now they are at the $2000 level at auction.

Juan Gris was a Spanish-born member of the Paris Cubist group and obviously absorbed much of the Cubist work of Picasso and Braque. He made innovations, and he tended to be precise in his execution of pictures, whereas some of the other Cubists made preciseness secondary to other points they were apparently trying to get across.

In 1944 and 1945 a group of Juan Gris paintings went in New York at auction at the general level of $1000. In 1946 three of his paintings sold for $2600, $3600 and $2000. From then on a rise took place and by 1955 "The Black Guitar" brought $6750 at the Parke-Bernet Galleries in New York. At the end of 1959 "Nature Morte a la Guitare" sold for $14,000. This was not the average price in 1960, although in December of that year Sotheby's sold a large "Harlequin," 50½ x 34½, for $44,000.

Moise Kisling, although Polish, is identified with the School of Paris and came

LAURENCIN. *In the Park.*
National Gallery, Washington, D.C.
(Dale Collection, Loan)

under the influence of Picasso and Braque, although as he matured he developed a more classical and precise style of painting. In 1939 a Kisling could be bought for $100 at auction. The illustrated and recorded Kisling "Lady van Leer," 39½ by 29, an excellent picture, brought $110. It took until 1950 for him to reach the $500 level, and not until 1956 did his prices start to rise rapidly. They reached a level of over $2500 by the year 1960.

Marie Laurencin is identified with the French Modern movement. Her paintings have a flat quality, delicate coloring and little or no modeling. The features of the face are very simply drawn with large, dark eyes accented. To a great extent she concentrates on the painting of women and children, very often repeating the theme of mother and child. The paintings are quite charming and decorative.

In 1932 her "Young Girl," a watercolor 13 by 9¼, sold for $140. By 1943 two of her paintings sold for $1200 and $1600 respectively at the Parke-Bernet Galleries. There was a slight drop in her auction prices in 1945 and 1946 and a rise to $2500 in 1954. Thereafter her paintings show a rise until the end of the decade when they reached a level of $5000.

A Jean Lurcat painting, in 1944 and 1945, could be purchased at auction for $300 more or less. His paintings have a formless quality in many cases, without perspective, but rather decorative. Only after 1955 did the prices of Lurcat rise, and they doubled in the five-year period. At retail they are bringing much higher figures, however.

LURCAT. *The Big Cloud.* National Gallery, Washington, D.C. (Dale Collection)

John Marin, the American watercolorist, is essentially a cross between Cubism and Expressionism. His origins of style are, however, French and his paintings, most of them watercolors, have a distinctly French quality about them. Some of his painting life was spent abroad, and he is thus included in the modern group as well as in the American School.

In 1944 two of his watercolor landscapes sold at the Parke-Bernet Galleries for $525 and $550. His prices rose gradually to 1955 when they reached a level of $1500. By 1960 this figure had been doubled.

Joan Miro, a Spaniard, early came under the influence of the Fauves and re-tained their color throughout most of his painting life. He is, however, classified as an Abstract Surrealist. Most of his paintings do not as much as suggest a third dimension. The subject matter sometimes consists of floating, flat discs suggestive of single cell animals or plants as seen under the microscope—irregular forms of one color or several colored sections in the same flat linear form. Besides these floating forms there are connecting lines in the painting, and the background is usually dark and plain.

A typical Miro abstraction sold at auction in New York in 1946 for $550. It was a large painting, 51 by 38, entitled "Abstraction." His prices did not stay long at this level, however, and another painting bearing the same title "Abstrac-tion," 19 by 25, sold in April, 1959, for $7500.

JOHN MARIN. *Tunk Mountains, Autumn, Maine.* Phillips Collection, Washington, D.C.

Diego Rivera was one of the leading Mexican artists, and during most of his life was a representative Mexican painter. He lived in Paris from 1917 to 1921, during which time he produced cubistic paintings. The paintings of this period are completely different from the great epic canvases and murals that he painted depicting the history of Mexico. The Cubist paintings are those in greatest demand now, and are clearly in the price category of paintings of Picasso and Braque.

In May, 1937, his "Fruit" from his Paris period brought $425 in New York. As late as 1945 his "Caballero," 76½ by 51, a Cubist painting, brought $300 in New York. By 1955 his paintings had generally reached the level of $1400. From this point they rose rapidly. At the Diego Rivera sale in New York in October, 1959, "Le Jeune Homme au Stylograph" from his Cubist period was sold for $17,000. On the other hand, his Mexican painting "Vision of the Conquistadores," 35 by 32, was purchased for $300, the low price of the sale. His general level of prices is now $7500 or a little less, even for his abstract paintings. It must be emphasized in the case of Rivera that his Cubist period paintings are distinct enough from his Mexican paintings to represent the work of two separate artists in subject matter, style, and price.

Louis Valtat is our final example, and a typical French Modern. Until 1949 his paintings attracted very little attention in London or American auctions, and $150 was a fair price. By 1952 this price level had been doubled. Then a rapid price rise set in to arrive at the end of the decade at a level of $5000.

These ten artists represent a cross section of the third group of Moderns. They are of generally diverse nationalities and Schools, but they all fall under the heading of Modern. Perhaps some of them might object and class themselves as Contemporary artists or Expressionists, but it is hoped that no enormous injustice has been done in this classification of them. It is not meant to imply that these artists are not as fine as the previously discussed groups of Moderns, but up to this date their prices have not been as high. The situation can change very rapidly, and history has shown how some artists are recognized late as well as how some fall into disfavor during certain periods in art history.

All of these artists were born before 1900 with the exception of Dali who was born in 1904.

When an index is made out of the 10 artists in this third and lower priced group of Moderns, the pattern of price rise from 1945 to 1955 is almost identical to that of the two groups previously studied. With 1945 as the base year represented by 100 per cent in all three groups, the Big Four (Matisse, Picasso, Braque and Léger) rose to 218 per cent in 1950. The next group of eight artists rose to 147 per cent and the third group of 10 artists to 137 per cent.

By 1955 the Big Four reached 306 per cent, the next eight artists 299 per cent and the last ten artists 288 per cent. In both years, 1950 and 1955, the less popular and lower priced the artist, the less the rise. At the end of the decade the Big Four had risen to 2009 per cent, the next eight artists to 1141 per cent and the lower ten to 850 per cent. Here again the pattern is repeated. It will be noted, however, that in all cases the greatest percentage of rise took place between the year 1955 and the end of the decade.

Mention should be made of the fact that there is a conservative bias in the case of the highest prices received by the Big Four. The top prices are not used in many instances as it has been thought that they might be exceptions and should only *influence* the trend line, but not be a part of it or represent the peaks. This adjustment has not been made in the case of the other artists. Still, the more important the artist, as a general rule, the higher the price rise in this period studied. On any basis and regardless of any generalizations and trend lines based on too few items in the averages, the period since the war has been characterized by an enormous growth in the price of Moderns, a growth which has turned into a boom since the year 1955.

THE EXPRESSIONISTS

Up until the time of the Impressionists, painting was a very formal procedure. Over the centuries, and particularly in the fifteenth and sixteenth centuries, art was an extremely important element in the Church and in the various city-states and countries of the world, especially the city-kingdoms of Italy. The cities and countries used art to glorify God and the Nation. It was an instrument of public policy, and the outstanding painters were greatly sought after, highly paid and honored. Competition among painters became extremely keen under these conditions of demand, and to qualify it was necessary for an artist not only to have intense training extending over a long period of time, but years of practice in improving his technique.

Over the years and centuries the best elements of painting and those techniques which led to the best results as far as the finished product—the painting—was concerned, were carefully culled out of the experience of painters, preserved either in written form or otherwise, and passed down from generation to generation of artists.

Formalism proved to be the most effective way to accomplish the results. To the novice such accumulation of knowledge and such formalism is cause for impatience, particularly if much time and training are required in order to absorb them. Discipline and patience are required of the student and these qualities are not always compatible with an "artistic temperament."

This formalism is similar to the present-day formalism of accounting. Accounting is done by rigid rules. There are, of course, alternative methods of doing things in accounting, but these are all fairly well catalogued. Long treatises, for instance, have been written on how to account for surplus arising from revaluation of property and how to depreciate such accompanying revaluation of assets.

No major company in the United States, and few minor companies, prepare their own financial statements. A member of a "guild" does this, highly trained and educated Certified Public Accountants, and at the beginning of each financial statement the Certified Public Accounting firm states that "This statement is prepared in accordance with established accounting procedures."

In the same way the formalism of painting prior to the Impressionists is like the formalism of law, and there is no greater formalism than legal formalism. To take just one aspect of law's formalism, consider such phrases as *in absentia, donatio causa mortis, de novo, prima facie, amicus curiae, post hoc, de facto, ex parte,* and *nolle prosequi.* This formalism has grown up around law over the centuries.

The revolt of the Impressionists was to an extent a revolt against the formalism of art. The Impressionists sought to short-cut the distance between what is seen and its representation on canvas by painting directly from the subject and allowing the primary colors to blend in the eye rather than on the canvas, which resulted in a picture more visually exciting than that produced when using the formalistic painting rules of the past.

Van Gogh, following the Impressionists, used stronger and more strident color contrasts applied with heavy brush strokes, and, to a degree, his paintings exhibit the intense sensibility of a tormented personality. But it must be remembered that he still painted what he saw in the way he saw it. His canvases presented recognizable subjects.

Paul Gauguin, too, painted scenes the way he saw them. He said the reason he painted things flat was because he saw things flat. He too was beset by conflicts and by an intense desire to revolt against civilization. When he was a minor employee of a stockbrokerage firm, married, and presumably on the way up in the business world, Gauguin deserted his family, gave up his job and finally settled in Pont-Aven, Brittany, in search of people who had not, in his eyes, been "ruined by civilization." Later on he moved from Pont-Aven, which finally attracted too many tourists to suit him, and settled in Le Pouldu.

A few years later his lack of success and poverty induced him to move still farther away from civilization to Tahiti, where he produced the colorful, primitive paintings now sought after. They are definitely lacking in third dimension, and the rendering of the human figure, particularly hands and feet, are primitive and lacking in roundness. But despite these characteristics, some of which are probably deliberate and some unavoidable, Gauguin tried to paint the objects that he saw as *he saw them*. He created contrast and pattern by painting heavy outlines around the various figures and objects in the picture and by so doing he accomplished what he felt was beauty through a flat, brightly colored surface of contrasting colors and shapes.

The Central European Expressionists represent another concept of painting which grew naturally from the unrealistic works of van Gogh, Gauguin, Picasso, Matisse, and the Fauves. The Expressionists were no longer concerned with portraying what they saw, but used the natural objects *as media in themselves* (not as the end result) in an attempt to give a deeper meaning or emotion to the viewer.

It was still another step on the ladder away from (1) the "formalism" prior to Impressionism, (2) the concern for living light in Impressionism, (3) the departure from naturalism of the Post-Impressionists with their new emphasis on the effect of sharply defined forms in sharply contrasting colors, and (4) even the French Moderns who also painted without concern for realism—getting their effects almost solely through the use of simplification of form and color.

EDVARD MUNCH. *The Cry.*
National Gallery, Oslo

One of the most significant and illustrative paintings of this School is "The Cry" by the Norwegian Expressionist, Edvard Munch, who lived from 1863 to 1944. The body of the central character does not look like a human body by any stretch of the imagination. The mouth is oval vertically, not horizontally. The road is represented by parallel streaks converging in a way to create the impression of great distance. Unless one looks at this painting as though it is a cartoon and passes it off lightly, he gets an intense feeling of aloneness, a feeling of horror and of pressures being put on the man which are driving him to the brink of insanity. The hands clasped over the ears and around the head add to this feeling of being overwhelmed.

Through deliberate distortions of forms, human features, colors and placement of figures in space, the attempt is made by the Expressionists to create intense feelings or ideas on the part of the viewer: fear, hatred, decadence and disintegration of the human personality, the power of God, etc.

In order to get this final result of feeling or grand idea, they focused attention on it by simplifying the painting itself, by throwing out many of the refinements of form, color and spatial relations so painstakingly developed by painters in the past. They felt too many details would obscure the meaning they wanted to project to the viewer. The flatness and emphasis on shapes and colors that van Gogh and Gauguin used to represent the objects they saw, the Expressionists used to express the idea or feeling, and these were the objects or end results of their paintings.

KIRCHNER. *The Street.* The Museum of Modern Art, New York

One of the branches of Expressionism grew out of the art of van Gogh—the Bruecke group, represented by Kirchner, Nolde, and Schmidt-Rottluff.

The second branch grew out of Gauguin and is represented by Kandinsky, Klee, Jawlensky, and Marc. This is the so-called Blue Rider group.

The third group is called the New Objectivity (Neue Sachlichkeit) group: Beckmann, Grosz, and Dix.

Besides these three distinct groups there are independent Expressionists such as Kokoschka and Klimt.

The Expressionist group was a Central European group, principally Germans and Austrians, but included are the Norwegian Munch and the Frenchmen Rouault and Soutine. Rouault has been included elsewhere and should be classified as a French Modern, but he is also definitely an Expressionist. The American painter John Marin can also be classified as an Expressionist.

Three years ago Dr. W. R. Valentiner, the great Dutch authority on art, stated to us, "Buy Expressionists. That's the School." To say that we were surprised would have been a gross understatement. For the Rembrandt expert to recommend a School so different from the Seventeenth Century Dutch as Expressionism startled us. At about the same time we met a young man who had sold his seat on the Stock Exchange to start a dealership in Expressionists.

From an investment point of view both of these men were right. In the 12-year period from 1947 to 1959 Munch rose from about the $1500 level to $14,000 and $9000 respectively in the April, 1959 sale at the Parke-Bernet Galleries in New York.

In 1952 a work by the Blue Rider painter, Franz Marc, could be purchased for $1000. A chalk drawing sold for 220 marks and a pencil and watercolor picture sold for 400 marks in Germany in 1952. In 1958 three of his paintings sold in Germany for 28,000 marks, 36,000 marks and 18,000 marks. To convert to dollars, these figures can roughly be divided by four. In March, 1960 the Parke-Bernet Galleries sold an interesting and colorful Blue Rider painting, 20 by 25, for $10,000.

In the 1958 and 1959 season in Germany Nolde's prices were 50,000 marks, 45,000, 40,000, 38,000 and 30,000, to take a sample. In New York, however, in March, 1958, "Old Man and Woman," a true Expressionist painting, brought only $3100, and "Venetian Scene" in 1959 brought $1500.

Kokoschka has had a similar rise in prices, and in the 1958-1959 season two of his paintings sold in England for the equivalent of $8400 and $5040.

In 1944 "White Center" by Kandinsky brought $850, a large painting, 47 by

54. By 1955-1956 one of his works sold in Germany for nearly $15,000.

From the 1949 season to the end of the decade, in a span of approximately 10 years, Kirchner has risen about six times in price. He is close to the $6000 auction level now.

Between the 1955-1956 season and the 1958-1959 season Egon Schiele has risen in price about five times.

All of the major Expressionists were born before 1890. Nolde was born in 1867, shortly after the close of the American Civil War, to give a bench mark. Marin, the American, was born in 1870, Klee in 1879, and Munch in 1863.

These birth dates indicate the lag in public acceptance of new Schools of art. This is a rising School of art, if not *the* rising School, at the present time. Yet their painting goes back to the time of World War I. Nolde, Rohlfs and Marin all went through an Impressionist period before arriving at Expressionism, and probably the two major artists of any period or School to influence the Expressionists were the Post-Impressionists van Gogh and Gauguin.

The group has a very interesting, although unhappy, history. Kokoschka was invalided out of the army after World War I with a mental disturbance. After a series of misfortunes Kirchner committed suicide. Munch had a nervous breakdown and practically retired from the world.

In the year 1937 Hitler confiscated certain paintings which he considered to be degenerate art. Over 600 of Kirchner's paintings were seized at this time. At the same time 609 of Schmidt-Rottluff's pictures were condemned. In the same year Nolde's pictures were confiscated. In 1941 both Nolde and Schmidt-Rottluff were forbidden by the Nazis to paint any more pictures, and a Gestapo policeman was placed outside the door of Schmidt-Rottluff to make sure he obeyed this order.

The ironical part about this policy of Hitler was that while Hitler himself painted pictures, and several have appeared on the auction market recently, he painted no better than the Expressionists.

In the attempt of the Expressionists to dematerialize the objects painted and to distort them in order to create a mood or feeling on the part of the viewer (and this objective was sometimes achieved well), the quality of drawing, composition and perspective deteriorated, either on purpose or inadvertently, while the artists were concentrating on creating the feelings on the part of the viewer. A Klee looks like a grown-up's copy of the painting of a child; and while Munch's "The Cry" speaks for itself and creates the desired mood, too many of the Expressionist pictures create the feeling on the part of the viewer of, "That doesn't look so good. Maybe he is trying to get across a mood or message, but I wonder what it is." This is the great failure of many of the artists and Schools after Impressionism, and worthy objectives are too often left unrealized by the failure of the artist's technique to "put it over."

The whole Expressionist School is an unhappy one with few exceptions. It represents negatives in all its human aspects: fear, aloneness, failure, strife. Very often it is successful in looking inside the man or in getting across from a landscape or a genre scene a specific feeling or mood; but almost invariably the result is negative. Within someone or something the Expressionists might have found beauty, friendliness, human compassion, unselfish devotion to an ideal, or a devotion to religious principles. But the Expressionists did not emphasize beauty. Like attracts like, and the unhappy painters probably gravitated to this School of art.

A criticism made of many of the paintings by the Expressionists is that they are often unpleasant. It is desirable for a painting to do something of a positive nature for the viewer. Perhaps a feeling of awe at the way in which the artist achieved his goal of creating a given mood or feeling will suit the viewer, but too many viewers may say, "I don't understand it. I don't like it!" If so, the artist has missed the goal of painting something that others will want to look at.

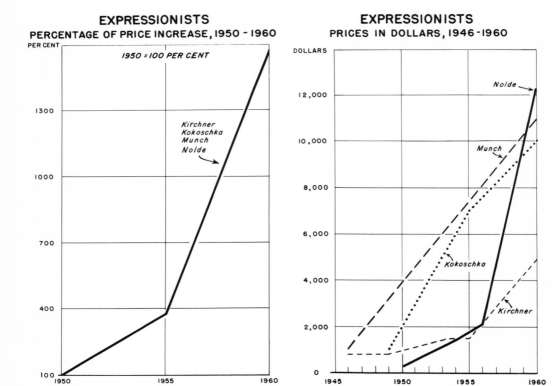

EXPRESSIONISTS
PERCENTAGE OF PRICE INCREASE, 1950 - 1960

EXPRESSIONISTS
PRICES IN DOLLARS, 1946 - 1960

On the more positive side in regard to the Expressionists, the Weinmueller auction in Munich, Germany, on June 22, 1960, sold two landscapes by Oskar Kokoschka—the first entitled "Grinzing Landscape with a View of Vienna," and "View of Prague." These landscapes are impressionistic. The use of color is excellent, the subject is pleasing, and such landscapes could not mar the decor of any home. Also we have noted that several good, impressionistic Kokoschkas are exhibited in the Phillips Collection in Washington.

From the point of view of market behavior the Expressionists present a pattern of price rise that is unique. Until 1950 the Expressionists were rarely high priced, and $1000 was considered a good price. With 1950 as the base year of 100 per cent, the combined index of Kirchner, Kokoschka, Munch, and Nolde rose to 390 per cent in 1955 and to 1586 per cent in 1960. This price rise has not been equaled by any other School of art.

V

Contemporary Art

N New York City there are somewhere between 400 and 450 art dealers. This number includes dealers in Old Master paintings, dealers in specialized types of art, such as Far East and Near East Art, and dealers in Contemporary Art. It is very roughly estimated that in New York approximately 1000 paintings are sold per week at both the retail and wholesale levels. The wholesale level includes those organizations which usually sell only to dealers—dealers either in New York or in other parts of the country.

Probably the majority of the art dealers specialize in Contemporary Art. By Contemporary is meant the most recent Schools of Art represented by either living artists or by those only recently deceased. There is some overlapping of Contemporary Art and other Schools of Art, and because it seemed expedient, we have included some living artists in Schools other than Contemporary as, for instance, Picasso, who is considered to be one of the Great Moderns. Modern Art as distinguished from Contemporary Art, is that School of Art developed by Matisse, Picasso, Braque, and Léger. Contemporary Art is present-day art, and embraces the many Schools which are active today. It is not so much a national or regional School of Art, as the various "isms" have a strong international following.

Never in the history of the United States has there been such a demand for paintings. In 1960 the stock market went into a slump, but not the painting market.

It continued to boom merrily on. Shop after shop along Madison Avenue and other main thoroughfares are devoted to paintings, and even young artists in their twenties sometimes have their entire output contracted for.

At first glance the contemporary paintings appear to be very diverse and not subject to any classification. When one tries to study the Schools of painting and runs afoul of such descriptions as Abstract Surrealists, Nabis, and Dadaists, he is inclined to give up and refer the whole thing to experts.

This is the great weakness of Contemporary Art. It appears to be so technical, so intellectual, and so abstruse that only those with a very advanced education and deep emotional and intellectual understanding of art can even look at a painting.

Nothing could be further from the truth. Relatively few contemporary canvases would be painted for the art market were it not for the buyer and what he likes and will pay for. The artists and the art dealers can extol a particular School of Art or a painting all they want, but if the buying public is unimpressed, the School and the painting go by the wayside, perhaps to wait generations, or forever, in order to secure that recognition which is spelled out in the buyer's check.

The painting is produced for the viewer and not for the artist alone. If it were not something to be seen by others it would not be offered for sale to others by the artist. And if it is to be sold it must contain something that someone wants to see enough to part with his hard earned money. The buyer wants it because he instinctively likes it, or because he admires it as a work of art. To illustrate the point, outside the author's office in the hall is a little painting done in the latter part of the nineteenth century. It is of a single track railroad running through a small town. The name of the artist is not well known. The painting is of little monetary value. It is simply pleasant to look at.

Upstairs there is a painting in a different category, an important Magnasco that has been in several prominent collections, including that of the Director of the Brera Gallery in Milan and the personal collection of Benno Geiger, the author of the authoritative book on Magnasco. The picture is of the dying Saint Francis with an angel hovering nearby. It is a superbly done painting of monumental quality achieved by the use of subdued colors, put on strongly, and fading into blackness. One could hardly enjoy looking at this subject all the time, but it is an excellent and admirable work of art.

Still another category might be added which explains the art buyer's motive: the social prestige paintings. There is good evidence that a person will buy a painting because it is "the painting to buy." If a prominent person or family owns a Picasso, that is a stimulus for others to buy a Picasso simply to put themselves in the Picasso-owning group. In a recent article in the New York *Times* a statement is made to the effect that in Hollywood it is quite chic to own a Rolls Royce and a Matisse.

The artist must earn his living too, just like the accountant or the construction worker, and he earns this living because someone likes his paintings. In the same way the art dealer depends on customers for his existence. There is, however, a certain hesitation on the part of potential buyers of art to walk into a dealer's shop and ask to see paintings. Early in their collecting days many buyers feel that they do not understand paintings well enough, and that to walk into the sacrosanct precincts of Knoedler, or other prominent galleries, would only show them up as ignoramuses.

This is far from the truth. The more potential customers walk in, the better for the dealer. There is nothing whatever the matter with a potential buyer's walking into an art dealer's showroom and following a line of inquiry like this:

"I would like to see some paintings, please."

"What kind of paintings?"

"I don't know. What do you have?"

"What artists do you prefer?"

"I don't really know them too well, but I would like something by a fairly prominent artist."

"Well, here is a watercolor sketch by Marin."

"No, I want something that looks more finished."

"Maybe you would like something earlier in the American School. How about this oil painting by Winslow Homer?"

"Yes, that's more what I had in mind. How much is that?"

"This picture is $35,000."

"No, I don't want to spend $35,000. What have you got along that line that is cheaper, say for $5000."

"How about this Dupré?"

"That looks good. How much is it?"

"This is $4500."

On the other hand, the following inquiry would be just as usual:

"I would like to see some paintings, please."

"What artists do you prefer?"

"I don't know, but I have been reading a lot about paintings in the papers and magazines lately, and I thought I'd see what was being offered for sale."

"What School do you prefer?"

"School? Why, I don't know. What have you got?"

"In the American School we have John Steuart Curry here."

"No. That's not at all what I have in mind. You see paintings like that all the time. I want something modern. I have a new house with modern furniture, and I want something that's going to fit in."

"How about this John Marin watercolor?"

"Now that's more what I'm thinking about. How much is it?"

"Twenty-eight hundred dollars."

It is not to be implied that the novice collector must buy a painting on his first visit to a gallery. The dealers are glad to show paintings to prospective collectors, and in order to determine the Schools and artists which are most pleasing to his taste, a person must begin by *looking* and developing his eye and connoisseurship. This "looking" should include visits to dealers, museums and not least important, the library.

The Contemporary painters of America are perhaps more numerous and better patronized than any other Contemporary painters of the world. In the early days of America painting was very much of a side line, as the rugged pioneers did not take it seriously enough for a vigorous, characteristic American School of Art to develop, with the result that some of our finest painters, Gilbert Stuart, John Singleton Copley, Benjamin West, and later, Whistler, Sargent, and Mary Cassatt became essentially European painters.

Since the latter half of the 1950's, for the first time in American history, a large percentage of the American public is ready for art. This public is not only ready for it, but it is eager for it and has the money to buy.

At the same time there is a distinctly American art for the first time in our history. It is art in an American style about American subjects. In our older Schools it is represented by the Western painters, the painters of Indians—Remington, Russell and King; the painters of monumental Western landscapes—Bierstadt and Thomas Moran; by the "Eight"—Prendergast, Shinn, Glackens, Davies, Luks, Sloan, Lawson, and Henri; and by the painter of the American farm life and sea scenes—Winslow Homer.

The chapter on American art includes Grandma Moses and Thomas Hart Benton. These painters are in a way transitional to the Contemporary American Scene painters, and are actually a part of this group.

The Depression of the 1930's created as well as brought to a head many problems and maladjustments in our American economic system and in our American society generally. "New Deal" was more than a political cliché. It was a focal point for a reform movement that resulted in such controls as the Securities and Exchange Commission, which for the first time provided thoroughgoing regulation of the issuance of securities and of the exchanges on which they were traded; the Wages and Hours Act and the Social Security Act which set minimum wages and maximum hours and provided for payments to the aged and the unemployed; and the Agricultural Adjustment Acts and subsequent attempts to control farm surpluses.

Fresco Panel by GEORGE BIDDLE.
Department of Justice, Washington, D.C.

WILLIAM C. PALMER. *Controlled Medicine.*
Queens General Hospital,
Long Island, New York

The philosophy that led to these social and economic innovations was depicted by the artists of the time, those who painted in the Depression and prior to the Depression. They can best be described as Social Message painters.

George Biddle's "Tenement" pictures hard work, resignation and squalor. At the bottom of the picture he has even painted the message he wants to get across: "If we would guide by the light of reason we must let our minds be bold."

William C. Palmer's "Controlled Medicine" apparently shows all of the persons who would be aided by socialized medicine but who at the time could not afford such aid.

William Gropper's "The Senate" pictures a fat windbag orating while another Senator props his feet on a chair and another reads a paper.

Aaron Bohrod's "Landscape Near Chicago" shows a miserable little tin-covered house, the shingles falling off, with an old touring car in front of it and junk piled around in the yard. The feeling is of abject poverty.

WILLIAM GROPPER. *The Senate.*
The Museum of Modern Art,
New York

AARON BOHROD. *Landscape Near Chicago.*

As time went on and the Depression became more and more a thing of the past, the social message became progressively less important; but the scene remained a typically American scene of one period in our history. Such scenes have a nostalgic value. They are American and only American, just as the Seventeenth Century Dutch paintings are typical only of that country and of that period in the Dutch national life. To look at a Seventeenth Century Dutch landscape or interior scene makes us feel a part of that life. Our American scene painters give us this same feeling, and at the same time they demonstrate a fine technique, in some ways reminiscent of the Dutch painting. In this group of American scene painters are the following:

Andrew Wyeth	Edward Hopper
Eugene Speicher	Georgia O'Keeffe
Leon Kroll	Charles Sheeler
Robert Brackman	Charles Burchfield
Gladys Rockmore Davis	Reginald Marsh
John McCrady	Charles Demuth
Aaron Bohrod	George Biddle

EUGENE SPEICHER. *Sara Rivers*. Corcoran Gallery, Washington, D.C.

FOUR CONTEMPORARY ARTISTS
PRICE HISTORY IN PERCENTAGE
1947 - 1960

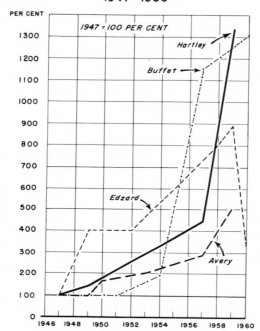

The American Scene painters are discussed again in the chapter on American Art, except that the above group are more the painters of today and those discussed later on are more closely identified with the America of three decades ago.

A watercolor by Andrew Wyeth could be purchased at retail in 1960 for about $4500. A recent painting by Wyeth, now in the collection of the Philadelphia Museum of Art, is reportedly valued at $30,000. A work by Aaron Bohrod could be purchased in 1959 for under $5000 as could a painting by Charles Sheeler or one by Charles Demuth. Fine paintings by Georgia O'Keeffe retailed in the middle-to-high four figures in 1960. Leon Kroll prices range from $3500 to $15,000.

Charles Sheeler specialized in the painting of industrial America with its factories, his pictures done in precise style. Robert Brackman's painting entitled "Arrangement, Life and Still Life" depicts two girls by a table with fruit on it and is reminiscent of both the beauty of the Baroque Italian School and the touch of the Modern French School. Speicher paints in much the same vein. Kroll combines excellently painted nudes with landscapes.

This American Scene School is a School genuinely American and distinct in style from other Schools, either in America or abroad, although there are perhaps analogies in the subject matter with the painters of other countries.

Another important American School is the Modern French-American School. These painters, while American, paint in the style of the Modern French School which began about the turn of the present century. The method of painting is less realistic than that of the American Scene painters. The colors and the patterns are emphasized. The naturalistic element is either ignored or deliberately played down. Some of the leaders of this group are:

Louis Eilshemius	Yasuo Kuniyoshi
Maurice Sterne	(of Japanese background)
Max Weber	

One day, shortly before World War I, the artist Eilshemius turned up at a dealer's establishment and announced that he had painted 10,000 pictures and was interested in disposing of some of them. The art world had not even heard of Eilshemius, much less had they known his works. In the sale of works of art for the benefit of the Museum of Modern Art in April, 1960, Eilshemius's "Beauty by the Waterfall" brought $2750.

In 1943 a Sterne could be bought for $250. Now he is well into four figures. Paintings by Max Weber sell in a wide four figure range.

A Kuniyoshi is becoming a rarity since his death. In the fall of 1960 a good sized painting of his was priced at $6500. A charming small one was a very good buy at $2000.

From here we get into the controversial Schools. It will be remembered that the Impressionists opened the door to abstractionism by blurring the outlines of the objects painted and using broken brush strokes of primary colors which blend in the eye of the viewer rather than on the palette or canvas.

Their "blending in the eye" was taken a step further by the dots and squares of the Pointillists.

While the entire Impressionistic School tried to paint nature as actually seen, two artists modified this objective: van Gogh and Gauguin, and they are generally called Post-Impressionists for want of a better descriptive title. Both of these painters de-emphasized the objects actually seen and emphasized bright colors and bold strokes (van Gogh) and warm hues with contrasting patterns of color (Gauguin). But both of them maintained that they painted what they saw in the way they saw it.

Matisse, the leader of the Modern School, moved further from Realism. He thought only colors and patterns were needed to make a good picture. He flattened the styles of van Gogh and Gauguin still more, until there was little or no perspective. What remained were line and color to provide the picture.

The Central European Expressionists had still a different major objective: they desired to transmit to the viewer not an illustration but an idea or an emotion. To create this effect they eliminated as many of the details of painting as they could, while still retaining enough to indicate what the painting was all about. Through distortion and emphasis they tried to achieve their result.

Now a new idea came along. If this major idea or emotion could be secured by distortion and emphasis of the things seen, why not try to secure the same effect by pictures that did not depict natural objects, but which would project their messages through abstract design, color, and novel brush work? Thus was born what is known as Abstract Expressionism, the "Expressionism" referring to the expression of an idea or emotion and the "Abstract" meaning a departure from the natural.

Willem de Kooning is one of the leading Contemporary Abstract Expressionists. In the United States today and in the immediate past there is a great group of Expressionist painters, both naturalistic and abstract, including:

Kenneth Callahan	George Grosz
Philip Evergood	Marsden Hartley
Stuart Davis	Robert Motherwell
Adolph Gottlieb	Ben Shahn

KUNIYOSHI. *Fish Kite.*

In the year 1960 some of the prevailing retail prices for these artists were: Callahan, $900 to $1500; Evergood, $825 to $2700; Shahn, $5000 to $7000; Davis, $500 to $5000; Motherwell, $1000, and Hartley, $1500 to $5000. Considered one of the important naturalistic Expressionists is a Frenchman, Bernard Buffet, whose works bring upwards of $2500.

This particular School of Art and the one which will be discussed next have been the center of the most bitter controversy for years.

A completely Abstract painting was reproduced some time ago on the cover of one of the art magazines with the following description: "A sort of neo-Dada —pyrotechnic or lyric, earnest but sly, unaggressive ideologically but covered with esthetic spikes."

After puzzling over this imaginatively worded description the author took it to one of the prominent art experts for his comment. He too was puzzled and then suggested it might be best if an explanation was secured directly from the editor of the magazine in which the description appeared, and the matter was dropped there.

The trouble with the description is that it does not seem to fit the picture. Descriptions such as these frighten the ordinary soul away and make him feel that it is useless to try to understand modern art because he has sunk too deep into the uncultured depths.

Along the same line is a description of the work of a very prominent Contemporary artist. This description appeared in a magazine article:

"He was the first successfully to liberate painting from the dominant conventions of the School-of-Paris cuisine. When the interior evolution of his style led him to work with the canvas lying on the floor and, later, to toss and splash pigment on the picture—to throw the picture on the floor and attack it in a violent dance—to use the intellectual, critical faculties of the artist in such a way as to permit and sustain the moment of creativity and violence—and when he emerged from the wrestling with the angel bringing with him paintings that kept intact the action of the fighting—at that point in time a new approach was opened to painters and a new appearance was made possible for pictures."

It is possible that the artist himself, had he been alive to read this description of his work, might have asked, "Who, me?"

One of the local Washington painters went so far as to infer that the Louvre was filled with "junk" and that all art led up to Modern Art; therefore she was of the Modern School.

Now let us look at the other side of Contemporary Art, what those who don't like it have said and done. There is no more prominent Expressionist than Oskar Kokoschka; yet when his show opened in 1911 in Vienna, the Austrian Crown Prince stated that Kokoschka deserved to have "every bone in his body broken."

Hitler went so far as to confiscate the works of the Expressionist Kirschner, as well as those of Nolde and Schmidt-Rottluff.

One wonders what all of the fuss is about. On the one hand if the artists are trying to put one over on the art-buying public, this is nothing new. People are always trying to pull a fast deal on someone: at cards, in oil and gold deals and in investments. Why should art be any different? High binders can operate here just as well as in any other part of the economy. There seems no need to confiscate anyone's paintings no matter how bad they are or how dishonest and reprehensible the motives of the artist. Why isn't it enough to look at the painting and simply say, "I don't like it; I think it's poor art," and go on to something else? In that way the artists and the paintings would die a natural death. The louder the defamation, the more attention is attracted to the art and the artist and the more defending champions arise.

Probably *most* of the artists are sincere and think they are producing something of artistic merit. The great difficulty is that many of the recent Schools of Art do not employ the techniques of art that were so painstakingly developed over the centuries by top artists: skill in drawing which was developed before 1400, roundness of the forms and a sense of third dimension and solidarity developed as early as Giotto, a feeling of action and movement and finally a feeling that the painting exists in space.

The Impressionists with their blurring of line developed a pleasing innovation in painting, but they left the door open to those who could not paint a clear form, try as they might.

When van Gogh and Gauguin flattened surfaces and de-emphasized drawing, they left the door open to those who could not draw and who could not portray the third dimension properly. When Matisse deliberately did away with perspective and perhaps achieved a good result, he provided a way for those painters who knew nothing of perspective.

The Expressionists threw out the "excess baggage" of detail in painting: the outlines, the roundness of forms, the feeling of completeness in the picture in order to convey the "great idea" or the "all-powerful emotion." By this time it was not necessary to be able to paint with a developed technique to come up with an acceptable picture. It became increasingly difficult to know who could paint or who deliberately chose the Abstract Expressionist technique, because he didn't know

KENNETH CALLAHAN. *Revolving World, 1944.*
The Metropolitan Museum of Art, New York
(Gift, Francis Henry Taylor)

how to paint. There was no longer an emphasis on the objective standards of (1) drawing, (2) perspective and third dimension, (3) composition within the edges of the canvas, and (4) space composition. These were skills that took centuries to develop and which any one artist achieved only through years of patient study. There are, unfortunately, few standards by which to judge the excellence or lack of excellence of these new Schools, and if a person says, "That is a fine Abstract Expressionist painting," the immediate counter question is, "Why? How do you know? What are your bases of judgment?"

Our next School of Art is also controversial—Surrealism. As a worthy objective in painting few can have any quarrel with Surrealism. The ideas of the basic psychologists are fairly well accepted now: that we are motivated to a great extent by what is below the surface of our minds—the unconscious mind. The Comptroller of one of our largest corporations a few weeks ago complained that too many of his top executives remember clearly the Depression years and are so fearful of a return to those times that they will not act boldly. A great deal of that motivation is not just common sense based on a historical perspective. It is deep-seated fear, and it is only too clear what being out of a job with an exhausted bank account means. That is the unconscious mind and its power.

It is not at all unusual for a person to have a peculiar type dream, let us say of an old wreck of a house through which he is trying to find his way. If the dreamer were able to paint what he sees in his dream the result would often be a Surrealist painting. Infinite distances which cannot be covered at all, deformed objects such as bent watches and faceless figures are all a part of the unconscious mind and can appear at times in the dreams of normal people. The pictorialization of these things is Surrealist art.

The message is the difficult thing to portray sufficiently well to convey it to the viewer in this Surrealistic painting, even though the viewer may have read the explanation of dream symbolism as expounded by Sigmund Freud. When one departs from the natural phenomena which are contrasted in eerie ways by Dali and goes to pure form and line with no figures, bent watches or perspective, the task of getting something across to the viewer becomes almost hopeless, and the work must be judged solely on the basis of whether the peculiar forms and colors please the viewer or whether they seem to be executed with great skill—or both.

The leading Surrealists are:

Arp	Callahan (also an Expressionist)
Dali	Baziotes
Tanguy	Berman
Masson	Blume

In May, 1960, Sotheby's in London sold the Dali "Old Age, Adolescence and Chivalry" for £4500 ($12,500). Baziotes can be purchased for about $2,000, Callahan for from $900 to $1,500 and Berman in the low four figure range.

We come now to perhaps the two leading Contemporary artists from the point of view of price: the American Jackson Pollock and the Frenchman Nicholas de Staël. Jackson Pollock was the leader of the "Drip School" which achieves its results through dripping paint from a can onto a canvas.

JACKSON POLLACK. *Autumn Rhythm.*
The Metropolitan Museum of Art, New York
(Hearn Fund, 1957)

In 1944 a Pollock could be purchased for about $100. By 1953 his price had risen to about $2000, but by 1960 an important Pollock might bring $50,000, and in December, 1960, one brought over $100,000.

De Staël can best be described as an artist who specialized in Simple Painting. He represents a definite return to simplicity in the same way Gauguin returned to simplicity in his painting of Tahitian life, as the Cubists returned to simplicity (suggested by the quartz crystal) or the French Moderns, including the Cubists, returned to the Primitive African art for their subject matter and form. De Staël did not employ perspective. His forms are not rounded—he used no shading. He either created *collages* (in which various flat colored pieces of paper are pasted or painted on a flat background) or he painted uncomplicated still lifes in which each object had its own simple, unshaded, ungraduated bright color.

In 1944 a de Staël could be purchased for about $100, and in 1953 his works were bringing $2,000, but the price of a good de Staël in 1960 might well be $30,000. In July, 1960, his "Bottle, Pear and Jug," 25 by 31¼ inches, in five colors, one for each of the three objects, one for what they rested upon and one for the background, sold at auction for £9,200 ($25,760). In December, a bottle picture, 25 x 31½, brought $36,000 in London.

The outstanding characteristic of both of these high priced artists is that their style is original. Both employ bright colors. They also represent a movement in the chain of art progression toward the simple—much simpler than the Abstract Expressionists or the Abstract Surrealists, although Pollock is generally classed as an Abstract Expressionist.

We can include with the "Drip" Artists the "Pattern" Artists, of which there are many. Among these are two quite interesting new experimental artists: Foldes and Anuszkiewicz. The first develops clever, bright colored designs that obviously have been carefully worked out, and the latter experiments with small squares of color complements which are almost blinding. The effect is a novel optical experience.

Before we leave the American Contemporary artists we should examine two more who, although they recently passed on, are important members of the American School: Walt Kuhn, the American painter of clowns, and John Marin, also considered an "Expressionist." Each shows a style and technique uniquely his own and because of this individuality the prices of works by these two painters should remain high. This is found to be the general rule with the leader or few leaders of any School of art, or a great innovator who starts a new style.

Kuhn painted large portraits of clowns, usually with whitened faces; but unlike

NICHOLAS DE STAËL. *Composition.*
Parke-Bernet Galleries, Inc.

NICHOLAS DE STAËL. *Parc de Sceaux.*
Phillips Collection, Washington, D.C.

the clowns of Picasso or Rouault, Kuhn's clowns are commanding personalities with strong physiques. A slightly eerie effect and a certain unreality or incorporeality is given to the figures through the whitening of the face. Kuhn's prices are well into five figures and $35,000 is not an unusual asking price for one of his more important works. A New York gallery is handling the sale of paintings left in his estate.

John Marin, best known for his watercolors, was a pioneer Modernist whose paintings were abstract even in his 1903 series. In 1931 he returned to painting in oil after using watercolor almost exclusively for many years. One of his oil paintings, a colorful view of the Maine Coast where he spent many summers, was offered in New York for $6,000. His watercolors (and he is considered by many to be America's greatest watercolorist) are delightful and an excellent investment. A watercolor could be purchased in 1960 for $2,800, as mentioned earlier.

Next let us examine very briefly the French Contemporaries. The most noted as far as number of sales on a world-wide basis is concerned is Bernard Buffet, a young artist classified as an Expressionist, but who has practically started a new

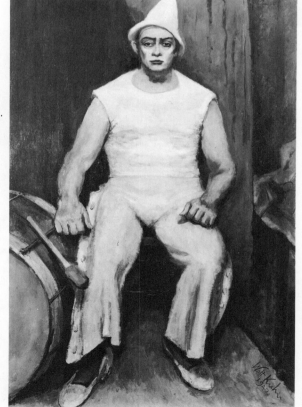

WALT KUHN. *Clown with Drum.*
Maynard Walker
(Photograph by Adolph Studley)

School of his own. His linear technique seems to be taken up by a good number of contemporaries. In 1944 a Buffet could be purchased for $50. By 1950 his prices were nearing $1000, and by the end of the decade he was at the $3000 level—and at times higher. Toward the end of the decade he realized his greatest gain in popularity and price.

Pricewise Pierre Soulages exceeds Buffet. In July, 1960, Sotheby's in London sold a Soulages for £3,000 ($8,400). Soulages too is an Expressionist whose paintings are characterized by thick criss-cross lines, usually black on a neutral ground.

Mathieu is a third contemporary Frenchman of the Abstract School, and Francis Picabia is a fourth. Picabia is an Abstract painter although he went through phases of Impressionism, Cubism and other Schools of art. In May, 1960, Sotheby's sold three Picabias for £280, £350, and £120, all less than $1,000, and Parke-Bernet Galleries recently sold one for $300.

The majority of French contemporary paintings sold on world markets are of the Abstract variety and the realistic Schools have fallen into second place. De Staël's new style of Simplicity, however, is gaining wide acceptance from the buying public.

In the Italian School a realist, Pietro Annigoni, has stepped to the fore. A few years ago a brilliantly painted portrait of Queen Elizabeth II was reproduced in newspapers and magazines. It was by Annigoni, and at about the same time he

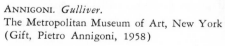

ANNIGONI. *Gulliver.*
The Metropolitan Museum of Art, New York
(Gift, Pietro Annigoni, 1958)

painted a portrait of Princess Margaret Rose which also received a great deal of publicity. Up until this time little had been heard of Annigoni. A review of auction catalogues showed that only a few of his works had been sold in London within the past two years, and at extremely low prices.

Since that time Annigoni has been given a one-man show in New York and has exhibited his fascinating "Witch" in London. There is little doubt that he is a masterful painter. His portraits are skillfully executed and a great amount of work obviously goes into every picture. In reply to the author's inquiry when visiting their offices in New York, Portraits, Inc. advised that Annigoni will consider painting commissioned portraits, but he must meet the sitter first (as he will paint only those whom he chooses to paint) and that if he decides to do the portrait, about four months will be required for sittings in Florence. The price of the portrait runs well into four figures.

Another Italian painter of note is Giorgio Morandi, the painter of bottles. In order to perfect his style, which early in this century was based on that of Cézanne, he decided to narrow his subject matter to bottles and a few other limited objects, including vases, flowers and some landscapes. His formal simplicity possibly influenced de Staël. There is certainly a similar concept of composition in the works of the two artists. Morandi, however, uses subdued colors and executes some detail of construction, although there still remains a distinct impression of two-dimensional representation. Many Italians feel that Morandi is their finest contemporary artist. His prices are in the middle four figure range at the present time and are rising.

Perhaps the most publicized and best accepted contemporary Italian painter is Giorgio di Chirico. He is mentioned as one of the "time proven" Italian artists. His works have been selling in the middle four figure price range.

Renato Guttuso can best be classified as an Expressionist. He emphasizes flat surfaces, sharply contrasting bright colors and angles in his natural subjects rather than curves. Through this angulation he achieves strength without destroying the identification of the natural objects painted.

In May, 1960, a Carlo Carra entitled "I Cavalieri 'dell Apocalisse," 14½ by 37 inches, sold for £2,100 ($5,880). Carra has long been in the forefront of Italian painting, first as a Futurist, and later as a kind of follower of Chirico—with his sharply angled objects. Later he returned to the Renaissance artists for his style, in particular to the very early Giotto and to the Umbrian, Piero della Francesca. Some of his works show the influence of the latter.

The Futurist painter, Giacomo Balla, is perhaps best known for his "Leash in

Motion" also called "Dog in Motion," "Dog on Leash," and "Running Dog." The work, painted in 1912 and in the collection of A. Conger Goodyear of New York, was an interesting and effective experiment in representing a dog hurrying along the street with his master. The dog's legs are painted in various positions of running, and the leash also is shown in innumerable positions so that the effect is clearly of motion. While Balla experimented with abstract forms, his paintings are carefully executed, and the use of natural objects, such as birds—stylized and placed in a thoughtfully created pattern ("Swifts: Paths of Movement")—gives his work a pleasing, finished appearance.

Carra's pupils, Boccioni and Severini, while being Abstract painters, retain a semblance of the objects painted, and they too have the finished, well-patterned look that an abstract painting can have if done carefully.

SEVERINI. *Trois Danseurs.*
Parke-Bernet Galleries, Inc.

Italy boasts a number of excellent painters in the Impressionist and French Modern style; among them are the following:

Tosi   de Pisis
Casorati   Rosai
Campigli

In the purely Expressionist School there are Sironi and Pirandello, while Santomaso and Guidi are Abstract Modern painters, Afro is a Cubist in the manner of Picasso, Mafai combines French Modern style with Expressionism, and Borra combines Modern painting with a return to the Old Masters—some of his works vaguely showing the influence of Caravaggio.

South of the Border of the United States is a School of art which is thoroughly native and of good quality: the Mexican School. Practically all of the students at Dartmouth College were "brought up" on Mexican art—the famous Orozco murals painted on the library walls. The notoriety of these murals came more from the subject matter, however, than from any technique exhibited therein. This is a violently anti-existing-regime series, painted in bold firm lines and strong color, depicting Orozco's version of religion and capitalism. For a while it seemed expedient to cover them from student view but today they are again on display in the library. Orozco did, however, paint colorful, unpolitical pictures of native life in Mexico which are pleasing in style and subject.

Diego Rivera has been mentioned as a member of the Cubist School, but his later works, using peasant life as a favorite subject, are very appealing and typically Mexican. At the same time he would paint strong and monumental murals—

RIVERA. *Potate Vendors.*
Collection Mr. and Mrs. Peter Ellis

JUAN O'GORMAN. *Portrait of Suzana Pradat.*
Courtesy of the Artist

somewhat in the manner of Orozco, representing our highly mechanized society. His paintings of Mexican peasant life bring in the low four figures, and his Cubist period works sometimes sell in the low five figures.

Juan O'Gorman has probably had more effect on the architecture of Mexico that any architect anywhere has had on his native architecture in recent years. His decorative theme has been primitive Indian art, and perhaps his most noted work is the impressive decoration in natural, colored, native stones covering the outside of the library at the University of Mexico. While O'Gorman in his easel paintings shows the influence of the Modern School, he has also experimented with tempera, using the methods of the Old Masters. Juan O'Gorman is a sensitive and unpretentious artist—a sharp contrast to his prodigious output and constant work. The O'Gormans' home, which we visited in 1956, is a fascinating "organic" house—constructed as an integral part of nature around a stone cave and decorated on the outside with his unique and colorful stone mosaics.

David Siqueiros is the fourth Mexican artist of note, primarily a muralist on a grand scale. At times Siqueiros resembles the Expressionists.

101

JUAN O'GORMAN. *On Way to Oaxaca.* Courtesy of the Artist

Rufino Tamayo is less of a muralist than the other "Greats" of Mexico. Many of his works are easel paintings which show the definite influence of the French Modern School, with a distinct Mexican adaptation and subject matter.

Contemporary British artists run the gamut of style and Schools. Walter Sickert was distinctly an Impressionist, perhaps the leading British Impressionist and a man of considerable ability in this School. For a time his works were more or less in eclipse, but with the revival of Impressionism, his prices are beginning to rise, and more of his paintings are appearing on the market, generally in the low four figure range.

We might consider Augustus John as a typical British painter. His works exhibit a solid, well developed technique, but with a distinctly Modern touch, and his portraits are particularly noteworthy. His sitters have included such prominent individuals as George Bernard Shaw and James Joyce.

Sir Matthew Smith is distinctly Fauve—in the manner of Matisse. Probably of all the British painters he uses color the most freely, and to the best advantage. His style is French Modern.

Ivon Hitchens shows the influence of Matisse, but paints more abstractly. Ben Nicholson is one of the most precise painters among the Abstractionists. His work is executed carefully and delicately although it often bears no relation to natural objects. He was very much influenced by Braque and Picasso. His paintings bring anywhere from $1,500 to $5,000.

Although Paul Nash went through several periods of development and identified himself with many Schools of art, including Cubism, his present style is Surrealistic.

Graham Sutherland has shown a development in his artistic career strikingly similar to Paul Nash, and he ended up about in the same place—Surrealism.

Francis Bacon has one of the most unique styles and objectives of any British painter. Through the study of the horrors of war, of accidents and other similar incidents, Bacon developed his art. He uses shockingly bright color, and with a blurring of forms and weird shapes out of a nightmare world he attempts to instill in the viewer a feeling of terror and horror. He succeeds uncomfortably well. One of his comments is interesting. He says, "Painting today is pure intuition and luck and taking advantage of what happens when you splash the stuff down."

Percy Wyndham Lewis is the father of Vorticism. "By Vorticism," Lewis says, "we mean (a) *activity* as opposed to the tasteful Passivity of Picasso; (b) *significance* as opposed to the dull or anecdotal character to which the Naturalist is condemned; (c) *essential movement* and *activity* (such as the energy of the mind) as opposed to the imitative cinematography, the fuss and hysterics of the futurists."

W. R. Sickert.
An Expensive Half-Sovereign.
Leicester Galleries, London

Here was a School of art opposed to what we consider today to be the most modern and accepted School—Cubism. Yet Vorticism died in 1915 and was not revived. The paintings of Lewis look like whirling machines. One can imagine an automobile crankshaft turning at high speed. Since Vorticism, Lewis has executed a number of competent, strong portraits, which show excellent draftsmanship.

Other leading names of the Contemporary British School are William Holman Hunt, Victor Passmore, Stanley Spencer, Philip Wilson Steer, and Alan Reynolds.

In price Paul Nash brought to the low four figures, Sutherland up to $1,000, Nicholson near $5,000, Spencer to $3,000, Passmore under $1,000, John in the low four figures and Sickert to $2,500. Alan Reynolds brought about $500 and Sir Matthew Smith up to $3,000.

One of the outstanding members of the Contemporary German School is the German-American Lionel Feininger, an artist who combines delicately shaded, subdued colors in a painting which shows the influence of both the Cubist and Expressionist Schools. While the Expressionists sometime give the impression of having splashed the paint on the canvas in a big hurry, Feininger, through the careful use of geometric forms, comes up with a pleasing picture.

The remaining leaders of German Contemporary art can be classified, almost without exception, as Abstract. A few use figures, but in an Expressionistic or Surrealistic way. Part of the explanation for the predominance of this type painting is the First World War which produced many of the present German art leaders. The word "produced" is used advisedly, as the art of the Contemporaries in many cases went back to the horrors of World War I and to the disillusionment which resulted from the defeat of Germany and the privations which follow in the wake of war.

The leading German Contemporary artists are:

Hans Hartung	Otto Dix
Ernst Wilhelm Nay	Oskar Schlemmer
Max Ernst	Willi Baumeister
George Grosz	Fritz Winter
Kurt Schwitters	Theodore Werner

An Ernst can be purchased for $5,000, while Feininger and Hartung each bring $10,000 or more, and Baumeister brings in the neighborhood of $1,500.

Very similar to the Germans and their emphasis on Expressionism, Surrealism and other forms of Abstract art are the Belgians. Perhaps the leader of this group

FEININGER. *Side Wheeler*. Detroit Institute of Arts

is Constant Permeke whose strong, heavy strokes and dark, muddy colors emphasize large, awkward figures which dominate his canvases. Permeke is probably the highest priced Belgian Expressionist and his auction prices run into five figures.

It is difficult to summarize Contemporary art. The Schools of Abstract Expressionism and Surrealism form a large part of this ever growing, constantly changing group. Schools and "isms" shoot forward in popularity and then sink back until they find their level—like a sea shell projected onto the beach by a wave, only to be gathered up by the force of the next wave and returned to the ocean floor.

As the wave of public taste carries an artist on its crest, so does it pull him down in the undertow of changing fashion and standards. The curse of being "out of date" is not undone until the years have mellowed memory and once again bring back the art of inherent quality to "greatness." Fifty years is time enough for testing public taste. In one hundred years the style is often "out of date" and not until two or three hundred years have passed is the art of quality a treasure once again.

Paintings are primarily for the viewer. The buyer is the ultimate critic, not the artist or the School of artists or the art dealer. This is a most simple fact that is too often forgotten.

Contemporary art is the art of today, and reflects our present-day culture. From the vast array of works offered by many Schools of art throughout the world each viewer and each buyer will make his choice as to what is good and what is not. Two quotations may help us to get the right slant in making our selections. The first is the opening sentence of Bernard Berenson in his *Italian Painters of the Renaissance:*

"Many see pictures without knowing what to look at. They are asked to admire works of pretended art and they do not know enough to say, like the child in Andersen's tale, 'Look, the Emperor has nothing on.' "

The second quotation is from the most popular of all Impressionists, Pierre-Auguste Renoir:

"A thing of beauty needs no commentary. Theories don't make a good picture. Most of the time they only serve to mask an artist's shortcomings. Theories are only worked out afterwards anyhow. Painting is not a matter of dreaming up or being inspired. It's a handicraft first of all and a good craftsman is wanted to do it well.

"Don't ask me whether painting ought to be objective or subjective. All I can say is I don't give a damn one way or another. Our craft is not an easy one by any means, and I can understand the doubts and anxiety it gives rise to. But, after all, a little simplicity, a little sincerity."

VI

British and French Art

URING THE NINETEENTH CENTURY IN ENGLAND A FAIRLY LARGE group of artists painted in a peculiarly British manner and can roughly be grouped into a nineteenth century British category. They are actually in many respects too diverse to be placed in a "School," although they, of course, all belong generally to the British School.

The artists selected for study here were born between the 1780's and the 1830's. They have been selected because their price history is somewhat different from the price history of the Impressionists, the Post-Impressionists, the Moderns, and the Contemporaries. They have also been chosen because they form a general grouping, although not strictly a School, because they have a long record of auction prices which can be traced, and because there is little question as to the authenticity of the paintings. This question often arises when one attempts to trace prices back beyond the time in which paintings were illustrated in the price catalogues.

The first of these artists is the famous Sir Lawrence Alma-Tadema (1836-1912), a Dutchman who painted in England and is identified with British art. His characteristic paintings employ Greek or Roman themes and represent a high degree of painting skill.

In May, 1925, his "Love in Idleness," 33½ by 65, sold for £1050 (about $5000) at Christie's in London. In 1933 his "Roman Bath," 23 by 11½, a well-known and exhibited painting, sold in New York for $375. Prices revived some-

ALMA-TADEMA. *The Sculpture Gallery.*
Parke-Bernet Galleries, Inc.

what and in 1945 his "Spring," 70 by 31½, went for $3600 at the Parke-Bernet Galleries in New York. From there they slid off until in 1958 a good example of his work brought around $700 in London.

David Cox (1783-1859) was an eminent landscapist in both oil and water-color, and one who painted with vigor. In 1925, $1250 would buy a good David Cox. In 1932, $40 or $50 would purchase a Cox. His prices then recovered until in 1945 two of his paintings brought £420 each, one brought £525 and one £357. At about $4 to the pound, his prices were in the $2000 range. From this point there is an almost steady drop in auction prices for his works until the year 1960 when $300 was a high price, with many good examples of his pictures going in this neighborhood.

Myles Birket Foster specialized in painting the rustic cottage scenes of Surrey, England. He painted hamlets, countrysides, winding lanes and similar country views. From 1925 to 1930 there was a rise in his prices, although this rise may be more apparent than real, since only three auction paintings are used in the price chart for the 1925-1926 season. In 1930 his "Venice," a watercolor 23½ by 35½, brought £892 (over $4000). From then on there was a general lag in his prices, partly, of course, due to the devaluation of the pound sterling at the end of the decade of the '40's, but there is little indication that his prices have done anything but weaken in the last 30 years.

John Pettie was a painter of historical and genre pictures. Although he used rich colors and painted dramatically and vigorously, his titles give a clue to his characteristics of painting: "Little Lessons," "False Dice," "The Rivals," "What d'ye Lack, Madame?" His paintings in a way look like advertisements in which a construction worker is saying, "Do I want a Fizz-Cola? I've been waiting all day for one!"

From a general price level of $2500 in 1926 his prices went down about 90 per cent to 1931. There was no apparent recovery, but rather a decline, to under $100 in the '40's. Since that time his works have practically disappeared from the auction market.

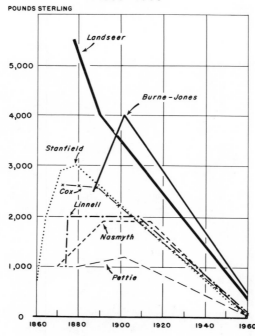

NINETEENTH CENTURY BRITISH ARTISTS
PRICE HISTORY IN POUNDS STERLING
1860 - 1960

Although we are concerned only with charting prices for the 35 year period from 1925 to the present, in the case of this general category of painters it is interesting to chart the price history from earlier times down to the end of the '50's.

Accurate price histories back into the 1800's were secured for seven painters. The seven include Cox and Pettie who are mentioned above and the following:

Sir Edward Burne-Jones (1833-1898) was one of the most eminent painters that England ever produced. The subject matter for his paintings came from the Bible, medieval ballads and legends, classical myths, the poems of Chaucer and Spenser, allegory and imagination. His form and color were good and his attention to detail most painstaking.

He received the Knighthood of the Legion of Honor. In 1882 he and one other English artist, Lord Leighton, were invited by the French government to represent England at the International Exhibition of Contemporary Art. In 1897 he received the First Class Medal at Antwerp, and in 1897 the Queen bestowed upon him a Baronetcy.

Sir Edwin Landseer (1802-1873) was a distinguished artist, a Royal Academician, who specialized in animal pictures. He was offered the immense honor of the Presidency of the Royal Academy and at one time the National Gallery in London owned fourteen of his paintings.

BURNE-JONES. *The Garden of Pan*. Parke-Bernet Galleries, Inc.

John Linnell was an eminent portrait and landscape painter who specialized in scenes of suburban London. He lived from 1792 to 1882.

Patrick Nasmyth (1787-1831) was once known as the "English Hobbema." Possibly there is no landscapist any better recognized at the present time for quality paintings than Hobbema, so that this epithet was an honor indeed. Nasmyth painted pleasing landscapes of England, and at one time seven were in the National Gallery in London.

William Clarkson Stanfield (1793-1867) of the Royal Academy was one of the pre-eminent British marine painters of his time. He painted churning waves, and turned out a number of coastal scenes painted in Holland. A certain coldness and affectation characterized his work, setting it aside from the work of the other British marine painters.

The price history of these seven artists has been traced back into the 1800's. All of them brought over £1000 as an average price at one time in the price history of each, and this represents about $5000. Landseer, prior to 1880, averaged over £5000 ($25,000). The story about Sir Lawrence Alma-Tadema is well-known in which he was offered roughly $66,000 for one of his paintings but held out for $82,500.

In the case of every one of these seven painters, the average auction price at the end of the decade of the 1950's was $500 or less. A good Alma-Tadema in 1958 brought $700.

With several of these artists the price appears to go down percentage-wise to zero. While it is not actually zero, it is such a small fraction of the prices received for their work in the nineteenth century as to approximate zero.

The price history was, as a general rule, first recorded when the prices of the works of the particular artist in his growing acceptance by the art buying public had reached £1000 or $5000. Even with this high starting point, in the case of Linnell, Stanfield, and Burne-Jones the price rise over a short period of time in the 1800's was very rapid.

Despite the extremely active art market of the 1950's, this group of artists showed little or no tendency to rise in price. The price level for each one is so low as to make the works of this group speculative at the present time as an investment. If a collector prefers this School to others, an exemplary collection can be made on a limited budget and there is no reason to believe that the value will not increase somewhat over the years.

Fortunately this group does not characterize all British art. The next group we consider includes J. M. W. Turner, George Romney, John Hoppner and Sir

ROMNEY. *Mrs. Davenport.*
National Gallery, Washington, D.C.
(Mellon Collection)

Thomas Gainsborough. Turner is one of the leading British landscapists of any era, and has been highly admired throughout the art world. His skill of representation rivaled that of the great Seventeenth Century Dutchmen, and his later concern for painting sunlight or haze, fog, or the awesome quality of fire provided a steppingstone to Impressionism. Unfortunately the pigments which Turner used faded in many cases, and the canvases which have been exposed to strong light now have a dull, yellow color where such color was not originally intended.

In July of 1927, Turner's "Venice: the Dogana and Salute," 24 by 36, brought £30,450 (about $150,000), and in that year a fair estimation of his American price at auction would be $50,000. In 1930 "Venice," 39 by 49, with a good background, brought $85,000 in New York. This painting did not have the eminence of the painting sold earlier, but it was excellent.

From this point Turner's prices decreased. In 1932 "Fitz Allen Chapel" brought $4000 in New York. From this low point there was a gradual rise in prices to a level of around $45,000 at the end of the '50's. In the New York

Public Library sale in 1956 "Staffa, Fingle's Cave" brought $47,000, and "Scene on the French Coast" sold for $56,000. These were great and typical works of Turner. Near the end of 1960, "Port Ruysdael," a good, large canvas, but uncleaned, brought $31,000 at the Parke-Bernet Galleries.

George Romney is one of the three or four leading Eighteenth Century British painters. In his price history he has reached some of the highest auction levels. On June 13, 1913, Romney's "Anne, Lady de la Pole" brought the equivalent of $206,850. In July, 1919, in the great Hamilton Palace sale, following the death of the Duke of Hamilton, Romney's picture of the "Misses Beckford when Children" brought a record auction price: £54,600 ($273,000).

In the year 1926 the "Portrait of Mrs. Davenport," an outstanding portrait, was sold for £60,900 in London, or the equivalent of $296,000. In this year, however, a good Romney could be purchased for about $75,000 at auction.

From this point there is a sharp drop into the depression. Prices declined to a general level of $25,000 by 1932. This general level was maintained until 1944, or for 12 years, when there occurred a decline to 1956 when $12,000 would be an average price of a good Romney. In 1959 the "Double Portrait of Edward Bootle and his Brother" sold for £8000 ($22,400). This same painting sold in July, 1925 for £8925, a comparable price. This price similarity indicates some of

TURNER. *Port Ruysdael*. Parke-Bernet Galleries, Inc.

the difficulties in price comparisons. The £8925 translates at $4.83 per pound sterling into $43,100, almost double the £8000 figure at $2.80 per pound sterling which the picture brought in 1959.

John Hoppner is the second Eighteenth Century British portraitist to be studied here. His level of prices was approximately $30,000 in 1925. "Lady Elizabeth Bligh as a Child" brought £10,710 in that year (about $50,000). In the year 1930 "Miss Charlotte Papendiek when a Child" sold for £14,700 (about $75,000). In 1934 "Master William Russell as a Child" brought £3400 (about $14,000). In the year 1935 one Hoppner went for £12,075 and one for £5040.

From this point there is a definite price decline, and in 1941 "Miss Frances Beresford" sold for $39,000 and the "Hon. Charlotte Chetwynd" brought $16,000. This represents the 1925 level. By 1944 the $10,000 price level was reached and by 1953 "Lady Catherine Harris" was sold for $3100. It was an excellent Hoppner portrait, 49½ by 40. By 1957 a price strengthening began to be noticeable, with the smaller portrait, 30 by 25, of "Emilia Charlotte" bringing $4000.

JOHN HOPPNER. *The Frankland Sisters.*
National Gallery, Washington, D.C.
(Mellon Collection)

RAEBURN. *Miss Eleanor Urquhart*.
National Gallery, Washington, D.C.
(Mellon Collection)

Romney and Hoppner represent the great School of British portraitists, and the distinguished period of British portraiture was the eighteenth century. Along with Romney and Hoppner go Sir Thomas Gainsborough, Sir Joshua Reynolds, Sir Thomas Lawrence and the Scotsman, Sir Henry Raeburn. Just why these portraitists became so popular and so high priced is explained by several facts. In the first place, their painting technique was excellent. The works they produced created an impression of charm and monumentality.

Prior to the great depression a large part of the demand for these portraits came from the United States. Royalty and nobility have always, consciously or unconsciously, impressed Americans. The purchase of such a portrait results in the acquisition by the purchaser of at least a small part of the elegance contained in such a painting. The exquisitely feminine women portrayed by the British portraitists convey a tranquil atmosphere far above worldly things and just "one step below the gods."

There is a theory about the timing of the appearance of British portraits on the art market which is an interesting side light. A man does not generally put the portrait of his mother up for sale at auction. He is not inclined to sell the portrait of his grandmother either. His great-grandmother, however, is a different matter

GAINSBOROUGH. *Georgiana, Duchess of Devonshire.*
National Gallery, Washington, D.C.
(Mellon Collection)

as in all probability he never knew her personally and therefore has not the same emotional attachment to her.

England's number one Eighteenth Century portraitist in point of recognition and of price is Sir Thomas Gainsborough. In the year 1925 his price level was about $25,000. "Mrs. William Monck," 29 by 24, sold for £5040 in 1925. A larger portrait would have sold for more, particularly one with more than one figure in it. This general level was maintained until 1930 when there was some decline to 1935. In that year the "Charleton Children," 57 by 46, a good size, sold for £3465 (over $14,000). This level was maintained until 1948 when prices declined some until 1951.

In November, 1959, the "Countess of Chesterfield," 86 by 61, sold for £34,000 ($95,000), and this is felt to be the fair level of a good painting by Gainsborough at the present time.

In March, 1960, "Mr. and Mrs. Robert Andrews in the Park at Auberies," 27½ by 47, a very famous Gainsborough, brought £130,000 ($364,000). At the end of the decade of the 1950's there was a portrait of a woman on the market in New York for $125,000, and a double portrait of two children for $300,000.

116

The price increase since 1951 has been substantial. It still does not equal the price in the high six figures paid by Collis Huntington for "The Blue Boy" three decades earlier.

The pattern of all three portraitists—Romney, Hoppner and Gainsborough— is the same: decline after 1930, a low point in the '50's and an increase since that time, but not a substantial one in all cases, at least at the end of the decade. The leader, Gainsborough, shows the greatest increase, or recovery, in price.

In addition to the painter's reputation there are a bewildering number of technicalities on which the value of British portraits depend. The condition of the painting and its excellence are, of course, primary. Portraits of women often bring more than those of men, and probably children bring the most. More than one figure results in a higher price. A large portrait usually brings more than a small one, and the standard size of about 25 by 30 does not bring the highest price. What the man is wearing has a bearing on the price, and a colorful uniform, for example, usually brings more than a plum-colored or black jacket.

A peculiarity of Sir Thomas Gainsborough is that his paintings are classified into two categories from the point of view of the art market: portraits and land-scapes. He earned his reputation as a portraitist, but his real love was the painting of landscapes. He considered himself, strangely enough, to be primarily a land-scapist, not a portraitist. His landscapes have a sketchy quality, in many ways an unfinished and carelessly done quality. This is partly their charm, however, and

GAINSBOROUGH. *Landscape with a Bridge.*
National Gallery, Washington, D.C.
(Mellon Collection)

in this respect they are somewhat akin to Impressionist paintings with their de-emphasis of line and precision. At a time when the Impressionists are in vogue, it can be expected that Gainsborough's landscapes would be in favor in the market. They are.

In the year 1930 "On the Orwell," a landscape 25 by 42, brought £1155 (about $5000), while his portraits were bringing at least five times this figure. There is a very slight drop in values into the depression, and then an almost steady rise. A plateau in prices was reached in 1937 which lasted well into the war years, after which a steady rise took place to the end of the decade of the '50's. In 1953 the "Cottage Door," 39 by 49, brought £27,300 and "Crossing the Ford," also 39 by 49, brought an identical price. Each painting was sold for $76,000. The general price level of a good Gainsborough landscape is over $100,000. Landscape prices outstripped portrait prices after the war, and only at the turn into the decade of the '60's have his portraits been catching up in price.

The entire British School has been characterized by a drop in popularity which started early in the twentieth century and which was accentuated after the decade of the '20's. Prices declined in the '30's and did not readily recover with prosperity. After the war, Turner landscapes and Gainsborough landscapes grew in popularity, but only in the active art market of the '50's have the great portraitists, Gainsborough, Romney, Raeburn, Lawrence, Hoppner and Reynolds shown definite signs of recovering their former pre-eminence.

The creation of an index of British portraitists presents very real problems and embodies inaccuracies. In the first place, Gainsborough has a pattern which is unique. His popularity, particularly in important paintings of women and children, is increasing rapidly, and his prices are high. At the end of the decade of the '50's he was still rising in price and achieved high prices by any standards. The other portrait artists of the eighteenth century tended to lag, however. Yet there were signs that although there was a lag, the direction of price movement was the same as Gainsborough, although their rise was not of the same magnitude. One of the major dealers offered for sale at the close of the decade a Romney portrait, about 25 by 30, of a pretty woman, a well-known figure in her time, an extremely beautiful as well as decorative painting. The price was $75,000, but the average auction prices for Romney were considerably lower.

Another objection to the use of an index is that it does not include the minor portraitists such as Beechey and Opie. These portraitists are relatively low in price, and an attempt to add into the combined index their indexes would give them too great weight.

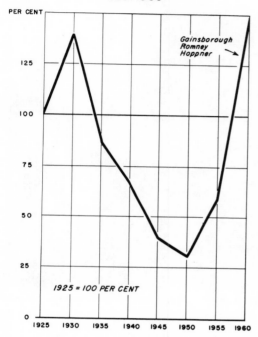

BRITISH PORTRAIT ARTISTS
PRICE HISTORY IN PERCENTAGE
1925-1960

PER CENT

Gainsborough
Romney
Hoppner

125

100

75

50

25

1925 = 100 PER CENT

0

1925 1930 1935 1940 1945 1950 1955 1960

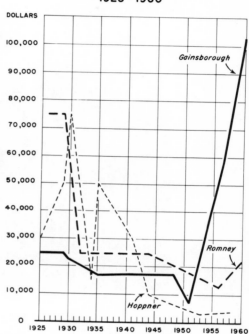

BRITISH PORTRAIT ARTISTS
PRICE HISTORY IN DOLLARS
1925 - 1960

DOLLARS

100,000

Gainsborough

90,000

80,000

70,000

60,000

50,000

40,000

30,000

Romney

20,000

10,000

Hoppner

0

1925 1930 1935 1940 1945 1950 1955 1960

The pattern of the price curve is nevertheless not far off, and only the degree of magnitude and turning point upward are open to serious question. From a base of 100 per cent in 1925 the index went upward to 141 per cent just before the depression. This rise may be exaggerated and due to the influence of the sale of important Hoppners at the end of the decade of the '20's. From the year 1930 there is a definite drop which continues down more or less steadily to the post-war period. In 1950 a low was reached of 31 per cent of the 1925 price level. From that point there is a steady rise to the end of the decade when 150 per cent of the 1925 price level is reached, and this rise is accounted for, at least in its magnitude, primarily by Gainsborough. The pattern of prices in the 1950's parallels the art market in the Schools of art previously reviewed, with the exception of the Nineteenth Century British landscape and marine painters noted.

FRENCH ART

French art is included in this chapter with British art, not because there is any special kinship between the two, but because of certain parallels in the art market.

POUSSIN. *The Baptism of Christ*. National Gallery, Washington, D.C. (Kress Collection)

To make comparisons, French art has been classified into Schools and periods.

The French School of art which immediately preceded the Impressionists was the Barbizon School, an early and middle Nineteenth Century School which derived its name from the town of Barbizon on the edge of the Forest of Fontainebleau where most of the artists in this group painted. The most important member of the group was Corot. Other significant members were Daubigny, Diaz, Troyon, Theodore Rousseau, Millet, Dupré, Francois, Jacque, and Harpignies.

The School's interest was centered around landscape painting. Landscapes *per se* had never been a specialty of France until this time. The artists of the earlier Schools painted landscapes in their studios from sketches and memory according to well established principles. The Barbizon School represented a revolt against these "traditional methods" of painting. When one reads the objectives of the School it is evident that these objectives do not differ in very many respects from those of the Impressionists who later revolted against the earlier Schools, including the Barbizons. Actually the Barbizons followed by Courbet and Manet formed a natural transition to the Impressionists. Whereas the Barbizons were influenced by the great British landscapists, notably Constable, and the traditional Dutch

Seventeenth Century landscapists, such as Cuyp and Ruisdael, plus the landscape elements of the great French painters Claude Lorrain and Nicholas Poussin, Charles Daubigny, one of the leading members of the Barbizon School, exerted an influence on Claude Monet who was one of the leaders of the Impressionists. Daubigny, incidentally, in his search for natural qualities of painting, constructed a houseboat and painted what he saw from the boat, particularly sunrises and sunsets.

Despite the emphasis of the Barbizon School on realism as against traditional methods of painting from memory, and despite their working out-of-doors, their successors, the Impressionists, outdid them in the portrayal of the vividness of the out-of-doors and sunlight.

Corot did, however, have some of the elements of Impressionism in one period of his painting. His art is not by any means uniform, and the paintings of one period do not resemble those of another. In his early years he painted Italian landscapes, and these employ warm colors, especially a sand color close to yellow ochre. Buildings, ruins, and other structures were featured in these carefully and precisely painted landscapes. In the 1840's and '50's he developed the cool, green, more loosely painted, misty landscapes that are so representative of the artist and

COROT. *Agostina.*
National Gallery, Washington, D.C.
(Dale Collection)

which have been so long in demand. The dominant color of these landscapes, which he seems to have repeated over and over again, is a bluish green. The trees and shrubbery have an indistinct appearance, not that they were painted originally that way, but the artist brushed over his colors while the paint was still wet to cast a kind of film over the picture through which it is viewed. In these landscapes are sometimes found little figures, frequently dancing figures, and almost always a spot of bright red is to be found as an accent.

In his portraits of ladies, usually costumed as gypsies or peasants, and often in landscape backgrounds, he achieves excellence and admirable strength. These portraits are in great demand at the present time and bring by far the highest prices of any of Corot's paintings.

In 1926 "Les Baigneuses," a painting of bathers in a landscape, from the Billings Collection, brought $50,500. Probably the average price of a Corot woodland scene at that time was about $25,000.

In the '30's there was a precipitous decline in prices, and $2500 could have purchased a Corot at the bottom of the depression.

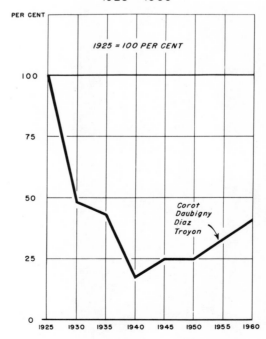

BARBIZON SCHOOL
PRICE HISTORY IN PERCENTAGE
1925 - 1960

From the low point of 1933 there was a gradual increase in prices, an almost level line of growth, up through 1958, when the level of nearly $15,000 was reached. At the end of the decade a good Corot of ample size was worth around $20,000. Sotheby's in London sold "Flesselles," 13 by 15, a rather small painting, in November, 1959, for £6800, and in May, 1960, "La Solitude," 38¼ by 51, for £6500, both paintings being just under the $20,000 level. In 1956 Sotheby's sold "Venus au Bain," 46 by 45½, for £27,000 ($75,000). This is the price received for a good, fairly large figure painting by this Master. The price was typical of the time, but was higher at the end of the decade. The index is not based on this infrequently sold figure group of paintings, but rather on the blue-green, filmy landscape paintings.

Charles François Daubigny painted picture after picture of the River Oise, most of them apparently being done from his houseboat studio. He painted frequently on mahogany panels, often 15 by 25, wider than high, and in many of his paintings he included a family of ducks swimming in a line across the water. The landscapes are well done with sure brush work, the colors good although subdued, and his paintings have the quality of offering pleasing and restful wall decorations.

From a level of $10,000 in 1925, the price of Daubigny plummeted to $1000 and $1200 in the depression. About 90 per cent of the price in the '20's was lost. The painting "La Saulaie," 14¾ by 26¼, that sold in January, 1926 for $12,500, brought exactly $2100 when resold in November, 1934.

By 1935 prices had risen to approximately the $2500 to $3000 level, but by 1939 they had slumped to $1200 where they remained until 1952, when apparently the general activity in the art market caught up Daubigny, and his prices started upward, but rather gradually. The $3000 level had been achieved at auction by the end of the decade, as compared with $10,000 in the '20's, although individual, brightly colored paintings reminiscent of the Impressionists sometimes reached five figures at retail.

The history of Diaz is much the same. Diaz is characterized by natural green foliage, especially the use of thickets and twisting trees covered with leaves. He used larger figures than Corot did in his landscapes but tended to blur the outlines, giving a mystical effect.

From a level of $2500 in 1926, his plentiful pictures dropped in price to $500 in 1934, and except for a rise during the war years, remained at the $500 level until 1956 when they rose to around $800 by the end of the decade.

Constant Troyon, the final representative of the Barbizon School, brought

$15,000 in the '20's. He specialized in rural scenes with cattle, and to a great extent he based his art, including the use of cattle, on the Seventeenth Century Dutch landscapist Albert Cuyp. Troyon's "Milking Time at la Celle" sold in April, 1926 for $17,750 at American Art Galleries in New York.

By the year 1935, $2500 was a fair auction price for Troyon's paintings. They remained at this level until 1943, and since that time have shown no improvement, and perhaps even a decline.

These prices are a far cry from the £13,650 ($66,200) received for Corot's "Bird's-nesters" at Christie's in London in 1910, or the $42,800 received in 1912 for his "Souvenir of Italy," or the $29,650 and $28,124 received for two Troyons in 1914, or the $22,000 received for a Daubigny in 1910 at Christie's.

If we compare these four members of the Barbizon School, from the very popular and high priced Corot to Daubigny, Diaz and Troyon who are in the low price class, we see a similarity in their popularity and price behavior. If we combine the four into an index and use 1925 as 100 per cent, the index drops to 48 per cent in 1930, to a bottom of 17 per cent in 1940, and a gradual rise to 41 per cent by the end of the 1950's. Corot is primarily, although not solely, responsible for the upturn, especially that prior to the 1950's. If we weighted the index by the level of Corot's prices, the curve would rise more rapidly.

In the early years of the twentieth century the Barbizon School was the "School to have." One of the great estates of New York City, the Billings estate, in the Washington Heights-Fort Tryon Park Section, included among its collection of. paintings Corot, Diaz, Dupré, Troyon, Rousseau, and Daubigny. This was one of the truly great New York mansions. I well remember how just the sight of it impressed me when I was a boy of twelve.

The home of Cornelius Vanderbilt was likewise filled with Barbizon paintings. These were sold April 18, 1945.

The George A. Hearn Collection catalogue of 1908 includes three Corots, two Daubignys, two Duprés, two Harpignies, and two Troyons.

What the Impressionists and Post-Impressionists are to collectors today the Barbizons were in the early years of the century. The Barbizons were *the* paintings to be owned by those who could afford them, and those who could afford them were only the very rich. These paintings were a symbol of wealth, at the same time being very pleasant additions to the home. But times and taste changed, and the Barbizons went out. Now, however, there is something of a comeback, especially in the case of Corot.

Gustave Courbet painted in this same period but was not a member of the

Barbizon group. He too threw aside the Romantic background and the historical paintings and insisted that history was in the present, that the present should be emphasized in painting, not the past. His paintings have a strength which, combined with a peculiar and characteristic shade of green which might almost be called "Courbet green," makes them easily recognizable. His most characteristic works are landscapes embodying the green tone. From a level of $2000 in the '20's, Courbet dropped to close to $500 in the depression, rose very gradually to the $1000 level in 1943 and remained at that level until 1954. From there his prices shot up to just under the $10,000 mark at auction by the decade's end. At retail his best works now bring much more than this.

Another Nineteenth Century French painter has been included because of his popularity at the time of the heydey of the Barbizons—the early years of the century—Bouguereau. He painted generally large pictures of historical or mythological subjects, but specialized in nudes painted with extreme precision and near-photographic realism modified by a Victorian sweetness. Bouguereau was a great craftsman. From a level of $5000 in 1926 his prices dropped to $1000 in the year 1933, rose to just under $3000 in 1936, dropped to under $1000 in 1938 and rose again in the war years and shortly thereafter to the $2500 level in 1950. From

COURBET. *Young Woman Reading*. National Gallery, Washington, D.C. (Dale Collection)

there he dropped back toward $1000 and shows little sign of increasing in price at the present time.

Bouguereau went out of style. Perhaps his inherent weakness was that although he was a skillful painter and craftsman, he was not an innovator. He did not develop a new style that was a break with the past, and it becomes clear that paintings to gain their place in society are generally new types which represent innovations in technique. Bouguereau is criticized for his sentimentality. One of his paintings was entitled, for instance, "Far from Home." It represents two homesick little girls far from home. While they may have been very homesick, and their feelings were certainly presented effectively in the painting, sentimentalism went out of vogue and is now considered *passé* Victorianism.

The Barbizon group of painters and Bouguereau have been presented at this point so that they may be compared in price characteristics with the other French Schools: the Impressionists, the Post-Impressionists, the Moderns, and the Contemporaries. Their price history, in the years studied, has been far different from that of the later Schools.

BOUGEREAU. *Far From Home.*
Savoy Art and Auction Galleries,
New York

The Barbizon group has also been considered along with the British Schools, both the Eighteenth Century portrait artists who went down in price and then recovered, and the Nineteenth Century painters who went down in price and did not recover.

From this group painting in the nineteenth century, let us turn to the painters of the eighteenth century in France. This was the century of Boucher and Fragonard, the painters of doll-like, exquisite women, and of landscapes with beautiful and varied colors. The decorative value of these two artists has been and still is immense. They portrayed the rich, extravagant, frivolous side of life, the life at Court. Among their favorite subjects were various outdoor and parlor games at a time when an emphasis on such trivialities characterized the French Court prior to the Revolution.

In 1926 Boucher's "Vertumnus and Pomona," 45 by 52½, a good sized painting, sold at Christie's for £2100 (around $10,000). In 1932 "Venus Consolant l'Amour," 43 by 33½, brought $31,000 in New York. The effects of the depression are not clear on this artist. From this point there is a downward trend of prices in the London and New York auctions to 1950 when the Parke-Bernet Galleries sold "Pastorale," a fine, oval painting, 30½ by 24, for $13,000.

From here there was a price rise steep and steady to 1957 when two ovals, 25 by 21, from the Rovensky collection brought $34,500 each. They were not large paintings. In July, 1958, a landscape brought £15,000 ($42,000). The present price of a good Boucher can well be over $50,000.

The seventeenth century was the classic century of French painting. This was the century of Poussin, Lorrain, le Sueur, the Le Nain Brothers, la Hire, Le Brun, de la Tour, Vouet, and Philippe de Champaigne. Largillière was a popular portrait painter as was Rigaud, the latter a favorite at court.

For the leaders of this period, Poussin and Lorrain, prices are hard to trace because so few of their important, authentic pictures appear on the American and English auction markets. In June, 1953, Sotheby's sold Lorrain's "A Landscape Near Rome," 28½ by 37¼, for £13,000 ($36,400).

In July, 1956, Poussin's "The Nativity," 38½ by 29¼, was sold for £29,000 ($81,000).

There has been some tendency for Poussin to drop gradually from 1925 to the early 1950's and then rise sharply, while Lorrain's prices have tended to weaken in the period.

In the year 1960 a sale took place which may well result in a drastic increase all through the Seventeenth Century French School. A Georges de la Tour of strictly museum quality was sold privately to the Metropolitan Museum of Art for a price which was reported to be somewhere in the neighborhood of $750,000. The painting was a superb example of this century and School, but it does not represent the average price of works which usually come onto the market. The painting, although French in character, combines some of the best elements of Seventeenth Century Dutch and Seventeenth Century Italian art. It features the precision of the Dutch painting and the lighting, color and composition of Italian painting, particularly of Caravaggio.

In sheer technique of painting few Schools equal Seventeenth Century French. Yet, with the exception of the leaders and a handful of other members of this School, it is not very well recognized throughout the world. A few years ago Simon Vouet was practically nonexistent in American art galleries or in private collections. The entire family of Boullogne (Louis Sr., Louis Jr., Bon Boullogne, the brother of Louis Jr., and Bon's two sisters), all excellent artists, artists who painted directly for the King of France, are unknown in most museums and collections outside of France. Yet the quality of their paintings, the use of shading and of light, the flesh tones, the composition and the landscape background put the paintings of these artists in the masterpiece category.

Important paintings of museum quality by leaders of this School should bring in the neighborhood of $100,000 to $150,000 in the 1960's.

VII

Dutch, Flemish, Spanish and German Art

HE GREAT ERA OF DUTCH PAINTING WAS THE SEVENTEENTH CEN-
tury. This was the time of Rembrandt, Hals, Vermeer, and Ter Borch
and of the landscapists Jakob and Salomon Ruisdael, Hobbema, and
van Goyen. This century produced 2000 Dutch artists who turned out about
200,000 paintings. (In contrast there were a handful of important Impressionists, fewer Post-Impressionists, and only slightly more in the French Modern
School.) The Seventeenth Century Dutch School is one of the two leading Schools
of art in the world from the point of view of representation in the museums of
the world, the other great representative School being Italian. Seventeenth Century Dutch art is of extreme importance from the point of view of supplying the
demands of the international art market, and this School has held its high position
down through the centuries since the 1600's.

The British monarch, Charles I, accumulated what at the time was by far the
finest collection of paintings in England and one of the finest in the world. But
in England it was an innovation. Paintings had not been collected to any great
extent prior to this time.

When Charles I was beheaded in 1649, Oliver Cromwell who, as Protector
of the Realm, replaced the king and abolished the kingship, dispersed Charles'
collection. Such demand as there was for paintings was satiated by throwing onto
the market this large collection.

For upwards of 100 years there was little buying or selling of paintings in England, and what paintings were bought were primarily of this Seventeenth Century Dutch and Flemish School. It is difficult to conceive of such a situation since London in the twentieth century is the world's greatest art market.

Market-wise, we shall consider the Seventeenth Century Dutch Landscapists as a group. They, like the Impressionists and the Barbizons, developed a characteristic method of painting, so that there are obvious similarities in the style of the Ruisdaels, Hobbema and van Goyen, as well as in the style of every other Dutch landscapist. As a general rule it can be said that these landscape artists did not paint directly from nature. They looked at the subject they desired to paint, made a sketch or mental note of what it looked like, and returned to their studios to paint.

The entire School, portraitists and landscapists, uses subdued colors, and this tendency is probably a concomitant of the mores of the time. The ability to draw and to produce near photographic likenesses reached an extremely high degree with this School.

HOBBEMA. *Farm in the Sunlight.*
National Gallery, Washington, D.C.
(Mellon Collection)

The guild system, embodying standards of artistic training and standards for the production of paints, was no doubt responsible for the technical excellence of the School. Behind the guild system and the extensive training required of young artists was the high position of art in the entire life of the country. With the successful termination of the Dutch-Spanish War and with the rise of the new class of businessmen, primarily traders, an excess of money was produced which could be used to buy luxuries. Works of art were important purchases and each town boasted its own local guild of artists with president and other officers. This guild performed a great many services, not the least being to develop formulas for the preparation of colors which would not only give the desired effect, but which would not fade or otherwise deteriorate with time. After 1795, with the onset of the Industrial Revolution and the rise of the textile industry with its requirements for dyes, these new industrial dyes were used as the basis of the artists' colors. They were suitable for garments and other textiles, but unfortunately were not always permanent enough to be used for paintings. This is evident in works by Turner in which the colors have dulled over the years, and in several paintings by Renoir where certain colors have faded (as in the case of the charming and important Renoir in the Frick Collection) and in Blakelock's paintings where much of the pigment has darkened.

Although subdued, the colors of the Seventeenth Century Dutch landscapes were not so far from natural as to merit the violent criticism that the Impressionists heaped on them. It is true that the Dutch paintings did not as a rule contain the bright colors that are pleasing simply because of brightness. The emphasis was rather on beautiful brushwork, harmony of color, third dimension, and form.

The important Seventeenth Century Dutch landscapists frequently did not paint the figures in their landscapes. Landscape painters specialized in landscapes, and figure painters specialized in the painting of figures. The great Jakob Ruisdael commissioned such painters as Nicholas Berchem, Adrian van Ostade, and Phillips Wouvermans to paint figures in his pictures. It is reported that Ruisdael never actually saw the pine woods and waterfalls that he often painted, but that the artist Everdingen, who traveled in Sweden, sketched and painted what he saw and showed Ruisdael the pictures so that Ruisdael could create the mountainous country in his own paintings. There are many Ruisdaels which depict rocky pine woods, hillsides and waterfalls.

Jan van Goyen specialized in coastal and river scenes with boats and figures in the boats, usually with a town in the background. In 1928 van Goyen's "A Squally Day at the Mouth of a River," 46½ by 60, a large painting, particularly

JAKOB RUISDAEL. *Quay at Amsterdam.* The Frick Collection, New York

as Seventeenth Century Dutch landscapes go, sold for £1176 ($5700). The next year "A Market Day in a Village," 42 by 59, also a large painting, sold for £2047 ($10,000), and "A View of Nymegen," one of his favorite scenes, 26½ by 55½, brought £3465 ($16,840).

From this point there is a slight rise in his prices to 1930 and a drop in 1934 to a level of about $3000. By 1949 prices had returned to the level of the 1920's. Then they rose in 1959 when a river landscape in November of that year, 25¾ by 37⅝, brought £6000 ($16,800). In the same season an important work brought £24,000 ($67,000), and one brought £9500 ($26,600). A general level of $30,000 for his good sized paintings had been reached by the end of the decade.

Salomon Ruisdael, a student of van Goyen, is another of the great Dutch landscapists. He was the uncle of Jakob Ruisdael who has sometimes been called the world's greatest landscapist. Salomon's most typical scenes are river scenes with figures in a boat fishing, as well as coastal scenes. Whereas van Goyen is identifiable by his characteristic, fluid brush work and short, linear strokes, Salomon Ruisdael has a similar but even more stylized brush stroke, particularly in painting trees and shrubbery. His predominant colors are a misty green and burnt sienna, warm in tone.

In 1927 his general level of prices was about $15,000 (£2940 for a large painting of a "Ferry Boat," 38½ by 56½). There is a slight rise in prices to 1929

SEVENTEENTH CENTURY DUTCH ARTISTS
PRICE HISTORY IN PERCENTAGE
1925-1960

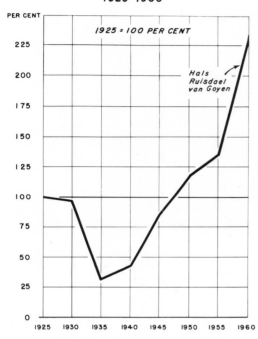

SEVENTEENTH CENTURY DUTCH ARTISTS
PRICE HISTORY IN DOLLARS
1927-1960

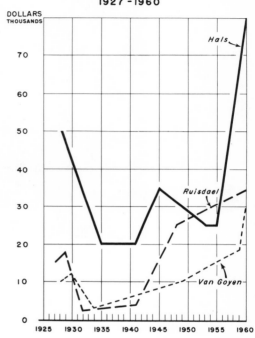

VAN GOYEN. *View of Rhenen.*
Corcoran Gallery, Washington, D.C.
(Clark Collection)

SALOMON RUISDAEL. *River View with Fishermen Hauling in Net.*
Walter's Art Gallery, Baltimore

and then a drop. In 1932 one painting of good quality sold for £630 and another for $800. From there on prices recovered, and in 1941 a good and fairly large "River Landscape," 34 by 46, sold for $4300. The price rise from this point, and especially after the war, was rapid, and by 1948 the $25,000 level was reached. The general rise continued past this point, but gradually, and not sharply, up to the late 1950's.

Nicholas Berchem has a strange history. He is one of the finest of the Dutch landscapists. He specialized in pastoral scenes, featuring hilly, Italian landscapes with sheep, cows, dogs, shepherds and shepherdesses. His brushstroke is smooth and sure and he used a typical vivid blue, which could be called "Berchem Blue," for his skies.

In the year 1925 a Berchem could be purchased at auction for the extremely low sum of $75, or about £15. The price level may have risen a little in terms of dollars or pounds sterling to the end of the '20's, but a Berchem could certainly have been purchased for under $500. In 1932 prices dropped down to about half this low level, pulled out of the slump to a level a little over the peak at the end of the '30's, dropped off again in the war, and then rose gradually to a level of about $2500 at the end of the 1950's. Although this price is over 3000 per cent of the 1925 price, it has little significance because the whole price range involves such low figures, and it is clear that in this period Berchem was not in vogue and was a speculative investment.

Let us go back to the beginning of the period studied again, and then go back beyond this period.

In the 1926-1927 season, Berchems sold for 37, 25, 23, 11, 23, 19, 31, 157, 29 and 15 pounds sterling, lower, but not too much lower, than the van Goyens sold in the same period.

Not one of the major paintings mentioned as having been sold in the 1929-1930 peak London season by a major auction was a Berchem. He was too unimportant.

In the 1931-1932 season "Italian River Scene," 28½ by 38½ inches, an excellent size, was sold at Christie's for £31. At Sotheby's, "Coast of Italy with a Hawking Party" was sold for £32.

The depression low was a true low, but as late as 1950 Berchem prices were not quoted.

In the present high market for art, $5000 would buy the quality Berchem which belongs in a museum, while a van Goyen of similar quality sells for $75,000.

BERCHEM. *Landscape*. National Gallery, London

Berchem versus van Goyen is a prime illustration of the change in public taste even within a particular School.

In the 1876-1889 period five Berchems brought 1207, 514, 735, 472, and 241 pounds. The high price was about $6000. At the same time no van Goyen was even quoted. In the 1780-1791 period Berchem prices were 120, 320, 200, 315, and 31 pounds, a much lower level.

Let us go back to a slightly earlier period in the Brussels market. Here not the absolute prices in the local currency, but the relative prices, are what should be noted in the period 1773-1803. Berchem prices in the currency of the time were 3266, 700, 505, and 610.

Now let us look at Rembrandt's prices in the same market at the same time— 1290, 774, 202 and 186—under Berchem!

And Titian's prices—400, 250, 168 and 106—still lower.

Both Rembrandt and Titian are now in the hundreds of thousands of dollars class.

The leading Dutch landscapists are Jakob and Salomon Ruisdael, Meindert Hobbema and Jan van Goyen, and to this group we may possibly add Albert Cuÿp who specialized in cattle scenes but also painted coastal and other landscapes.

Hobbema is comparable in quality to the other landscapists, and perhaps over the years his prices have been somewhat above even those of Jakob Ruisdael. Whereas Jakob painted scenes from a distance showing a wide, low horizon with from two-thirds to three-fourths of his canvas devoted to sky, with the landscape often flat and featuring rutted roads and a few carefully placed little figures walking or riding over them to give the effect of serene space and monumentality, Hobbema was more concerned with close-up views of woods and houses and with less sky in relation to the whole picture. We can consider the price movements of Ruisdael and Hobbema to be comparable. When we trace Hobbema back to 1878, beyond the start of our study period which began in 1925, we are in effect also tracing Ruisdael's price pattern, and to some extent patterns of the other leading Seventeenth Century Dutch landscapists. Hobbema is not difficult to trace as his sales are well recorded. These are some of the auction prices for his better works:

1878	$10,716	1901	$48,000
1892	9,696	1902	46,950
1899	46,437	1913	76,545
1900	31,640	1922	28,800

It becomes immediately apparent from this table and from a study of the prices of the other Dutch landscapists during this period that these artists were in great demand and commanded high prices; but even in the boom of the late 1920's their day had passed. In the early years of the twentieth century they were in greatest demand.

Yet when we go back earlier we find that there was a decline in price from 1878 to 1892. One particular picture was sold in 1878 and again in 1892. In 1878 it sold for $10,716 and the second time for $9696. In 1875 a Jakob Ruisdael brought $10,648 and the same picture in 1892 brought $7144. In the year 1919 two Ruisdaels brought $60,000 and $47,480.

This level of prices has hardly been reached even now with a far higher general level of prices than prevailed at that time. There is thus a repetition of price level and a cycle of prices which reflects the change in public taste.

The "greats" in the Seventeenth Century Dutch School are Rembrandt, Hals, Vermeer, and Ter Borch. While there have been possibly only 36 genuine and thoroughly accepted Vermeers on the market, Vermeer is now so much in demand as to make his prices entirely out of range for most pocketbooks. Rembrandt is difficult at times to trace because of a certain amount of confusion between his own paintings and some paintings by members of his School who imitated his style. Hals is easier to trace as he is hard to confuse with artists who imitated him.

HALS. *Portrait of a Man.*
National Gallery, Washington, D.C.
(Mellon Collection)

He developed a sure, strong brush stroke and sketchy style, using bright skin color tones and often chose laughing, jovial subjects.

In 1928 his "Dutch Lady," 32½ by 26, brought $55,000 at the Anderson Galleries in New York. In 1935 "Two Singing Boys," 23¼ by 19½, a painting which was typical of his best and most wanted period, and a painting thoroughly accepted as a Hals and recorded in most major books on Hals, sold in New York for $20,000. It was clear that the price of Hals had declined fairly substantially. This price level was maintained until 1941 when there was an increase. The excellent portrait of "Joseph Coymans," 33 by 27, sold in 1945 for $34,250. This was typical and thoroughly recorded. It represented the price level of his good paintings. In 1953 a "Portrait of a Gentleman," 34½ by 26¾, excellent and recorded, sold for $24,500. In 1954 a similar painting sold for $23,000.

Since that year prices are hard to trace. One large Hals was on the market in 1958 for $50,000, and a very small portrait was on the market for $80,000. Eighty thousand dollars at the present time should buy a good, typical Hals. Museum quality paintings, such as the one in the St. Louis Museum, should bring $150,000, and this is reported to be the purchase price of that comparatively recent St. Louis acquisition.

It is interesting to go back in the case of Hals to a period prior to 1925. In the year 1919 a Hals brought £26,775 ($127,449) and in 1923 one brought 19,000 guineas ($86,830).

Let us go back still further. Up to the year 1880 the paintings of the Seventeenth Century Dutch School that were in demand were the genre and landscape paintings, paintings done in a tight, not a sketchy, style. Frans Hals with his free, sketchy style was *not in demand at all*. In 1855 "Admiral de Ruyter with Page," from the Bernal Collection, 18 by 16, brought exactly £14 (considerably less than $100), and a "Lady in a Black Dress Holding a Jewel at Her Bosom," brought £2/15 shillings. In 1872 a full length portrait from the Pourtales Collection brought £151 ($730), the highest auction price for Hals in England to that date. Only in 1885 did his prices reach the four figure level.

In the great Stowe sale of 1848 "A Gentleman with Grey Hair Dressed in Black" brought seven guineas, and "A Lady in a White Cap and Black Dress" brought 10½ guineas. Both were in the $50 class or below.

In the Sir Cecil Miles sales held May 13, 1891, these same paintings brought £3150 and £2100 ($15,310 and $10,200 respectively).

In the *Record of Christie's* the chronicler, H. C. Marillier, states in regard to these two pictures, page 247, "Today (1926) either of them would be worth £50,000 in the open market, or an American would probably pay £150,000."

Fifty thousand pounds in 1926 would have been worth $242,500, and £150,000 about $727,500.

The average price of a Hals was not at this high level at the beginning of the decade of the 1960's, even though his rise in price even from the late year 1955 has been immense. One portrait, however, in late 1960, brought $509,000.

To summarize the Seventeenth Century Dutch School, van Goyen and Salomon Ruisdael can be combined into an index. They are similar painters and have similar market characteristics. Nicholas Berchem was at a very low level in the 1920's from which he declined even further. While his rise has been tremendous percentagewise since this low point, his prices are still low compared with other significant painters of the Dutch School. He has therefore not been combined into the index. While the Hals pattern is much like that of Ruisdael and van Goyen, his is a special case. He is a portrait artist and as such is not strictly comparable with the landscapists.

From a level of 100 per cent in the late '20's, van Goyen, Ruisdael, and Hals all dropped down to 40 per cent of this level or less in the depression and from that low point rose more or less steadily to about 300 per cent of the level of the '20's in the late '50's. The growth since the start of the period, in the year 1925, is certainly not remarkable and cannot be compared with that of the more recent Schools of art, but it is substantial, nevertheless, especially when compared with the depression low.

Rembrandt offers many difficulties in charting a price history. In the first place, there are few absolutely authentic, first class paintings by him that come onto the auction market. "Titus in an Arm Chair," 32 by 27, from the Stillman Collection sold in February, 1927, for $270,000. It was a fair size, and was bought by Sir Joseph Duveen. In March of the next year "Portrait of a Young Man with a Cleft Chin," 29½ by 24½, sold for £46,200, about the same price. This was a good painting from the famous Holford Collection. In the same sale "Portrait of a Man Holding the Torah," 39 by 34, sold for £50,400 ($245,000). A "Portrait of a Lady," 49 by 39½, sold for £31,500. All three paintings were well recorded and accepted.

In 1930, when prices had begun to sag, the "Portrait of an Old Man," 34 by 28, brought £19,950 ($97,000), but it must be remembered that the Holford paintings, because of their eminent collector, brought premium prices just for this reason, and the fact that three were offered for sale at the same time helped accumulate more interest and more buyers. Also, other fine paintings from his collection were sold at the same sale, drawing in even more painting buyers.

In 1932 the "Woman Plucking a Fowl" from the Kleinberger Collection was

sold for $26,000. This painting had more certificates of authentication by promi-
nent experts than almost any painting ever offered on the auction market. It may
not look as typically Rembrandt as other pictures, but its authentications were not
lacking. The painting now hangs in the National Gallery in Washington.

In 1945 a "Pilgrim at Prayer," once exhibited at the World's Fair, 37 by 31½,
and well accepted by experts, brought $75,000. This painting has recently been
on loan to the Metropolitan.

In 1950, the fine "Portrait of the Artist" was sold at Sotheby's, a painting
28½ by 23½, for £21,000, which was equal to only $59,000 as the result of the
devaluation of the pound sterling. The price was roughly comparable to that of
the "Pilgrim at Prayer" sold in 1945.

We now come to March, 1960. In that month the "Portrait of a Man," 27½
by 21½, brought £40,000 ($112,000), and in April, 1960, "Juno" reached a
high bid price of 50,000 guineas ($150,000), although the painting was finally
withdrawn. The pattern of Rembrandt is almost identical with that of the other
major Dutch artists, except that Rembrandt's price has not come back as the other
prices have. This failure to return may be due in part to the fact that in the case of
this particular artist it is hard to get comparable paintings for price tabulation
purposes. The "Horse and Rider" now in the National Gallery in London and
bought at the turn of the decade into the 1960's is not a comparable painting. It
is a masterpiece and in a different category. It is reported that the purchase price
was around $1,500,000, and wonder was expressed as to why an offer from abroad
which might have been considerably higher was not taken. A fine Rembrandt,
however, not one of his greatest masterpieces, but of unquestioned background,
typical, and of his late and most desired period, would at the end of the 1950's
bring perhaps the same price as it did at the beginning of the study period—1925.

There is another type Rembrandt that is in a different class and has its own
price peculiarities. This is the small Rembrandt, roughly the size of a sheet of
paper. Throughout the period in question Rembrandts of this size could be purchased for from $10,000 to $15,000 at auction. A painting, well accepted and well
recorded, of this size was offered in 1960 in New York for $50,000. This size
painting, too, has risen in price.

For centuries museums have been seeking Rembrandts, and the name Rembrandt is almost synonymous with "Old Master." For some years perhaps two
new Rembrandts, hitherto undiscovered, appeared each year. These usually do
not bring the prices of the well established ones and are not so highly in demand.
The fact that a number of the associates and pupils of Rembrandt are so close
to him in style and technique makes absolute proof of the authorship harder in

his case than in the case of most other masters. Even with exhibitions in museums, attributions and other authentications, a Rembrandt may often still be considered by some to be a doubtful painting.

This confusion sometimes works both ways. In the sale of paintings from the van Aalst Collection at Christie's in April, 1960, a "Portrait of Rembrandt" by Carel Fabritius, 14¾ by 12 inches, brought £14,000 ($39,000). There is a possibility, judging from the high price, that there were buyers present who thought the painting that was represented as being by Fabritius was actually a Rembrandt. In the Delft, Holland, sale of 1959, a painting was offered as being by Govaert Flinck, an associate of Rembrandt. It was as close to being by Rembrandt as any not actually labeled Rembrandt.

In the eighteenth century the style of painting in Holland changed in some details. Much of it became less fresh in quality and gravitated or was refined to enamel-like finishes, more painstaking technique, and unfortunately less originality.

However, in the eighteenth century the great Dutch flower painters came to the fore, artists who painted with such perfect precision and such carefully chosen colors that it was difficult to tell the objects painted from the real things. These skillful artists would paint a drop of water, a fly, or butterfly on the flowers so perfectly that one still finds himself looking close to be sure it isn't real. Rachel Ruysch, Jan van Huysum, and Jan Davidsz de Heem are representative of the best of this School.

141

In the nineteenth century the art of Holland still was based on that of the great Seventeenth Century Dutch painters, but it had developed into a kind of general nineteenth century traditional style of painting that was more like the same period painting of Germany, England and elsewhere than peculiar to itself. This was the period of Jongkind, Maris, and Israels. Jongkind was first a Barbizon painter and then was closely allied with the Impressionists, and can best be identified with the latter group, rather than with the Nineteenth Century Dutch group.

Israels is a better example. He specialized in homely interior scenes featuring a few pensive, forlorn figures sitting around a table or a fire, and bearing such titles as "At the Spinet," "The Peasant's Home," "Rabbi Reading," and "Motherly Care."

Israels belonged to that great group of artists who were popular in the early part of the twentieth century, and he took his place along with Diaz, Daubigny, and Troyon. From a price level of $2500 in 1929, he dropped to about $500 in 1932 and 1933. There was a price recovery up through the war and then came a gradual price sag until now he is at the $1000 level. He never recovered even his 1929 level of prices, and he, like the other artists so popular in the early twentieth century, particularly the Barbizons, went out of public favor. He in great measure represents the present position of the Nineteenth Century Dutch School, and from the view of number of artists and works produced this is a very large school.

ISRAELS. *Motherly Care.*
Parke-Bernet Galleries, Inc.

It is interesting to note that Jongkind parallels Israels down from the late '20's and into the depression years. In 1948 one of his paintings brought $1750, roughly the price of an Israels at the time. There was then a decline to the '50's, as in the case of Israels. Then the change takes place. Jongkind was identified with the Impressionists and with their price rise, so that in November, 1959, "View of Grenoble," 12½ by 21½, brought £7200 ($20,160) in Sotheby's.

FLEMISH PAINTING

Flanders, or what is now Belgium, is next door to Holland, and there is a close relationship between the two countries, both in past political ties and in nationality. The streets of Brussels are designated in both French and Dutch, and the country is bilingual.

Similarly many of the paintings done in the seventeenth century in both countries are of the same general style and composition. There were probably as many Seventeenth Century Flemish painters as there were Dutch painters of the same century. The quality of their painting is roughly comparable to that of Holland. Whereas Dutch painters of the seventeenth century have been carefully studied and their paintings that were known recorded, the Flemish artists of the same century have not been so fortunate. At least three major catalogues of Dutch works exist (Hofstede de Groot, Smith, and Walter Bernt). Only recently has the excellent Flemish art of the seventeenth century been systematically studied and recorded by R. H. Wilenski.

Partly because of this neglect there are very few Seventeenth Century Flemish painters of first rank in the world market: Peter Paul Rubens, Anthony van Dyck, David Teniers, and Jakob Jordaens.

Rubens would be included in a group of the dozen greatest painters of all time, and would stand high on the list. Rubens could and did paint practically anything, from portraits to Biblical and mythological scenes, great altarpieces and landscapes. His dexterity allowed him to paint in sizes from a sheet of paper to heights as great as the ceiling of the Louvre. During our visits to some sixty European museums we could not help but be impressed with the paintings that Rubens produced: their size, complexity, variety of subject matter and sheer number. It seems inconceivable that one man could turn out the work that Rubens did, or even supervise a shop turning out paintings of such quality and style. Like the works of many great masters, the works of Rubens have been classified as those produced by his own hand and those produced by his workshop, or with the assistance of his workshop. When we consider only those works which are attributed

SEVENTEENTH CENTURY FLEMISH ARTISTS
PRICE HISTORY IN DOLLARS
1927-1960

to his hand alone, it is still hard to imagine the immense work schedule of this painter.

On June 24, 1959, "The Adoration of the Magi" by Peter Paul Rubens, a painting 11 feet by over 8 feet, so large that it could not conveniently get into Christie's auction rooms, from the collection of the Duke of Westminster, brought the highest price ever received for a painting at auction: £275,000 ($770,000). It brought this price despite the fact that along with the photograph of the painting in the sales catalogue were diverse opinions in regard to the painting by several experts. Included in these opinions was one to the effect that the painting was not entirely by the hand of Rubens, that it was not in the best condition, and that the pose of the Virgin was awkward. Billionaire J. Paul Getty is reported to have bid up to $500,000 for the painting.

On July 4, 1924, the Duke of Westminster sold 63 paintings from Grosvenor House at Christie's. Featured at the sale were three gigantic paintings by Rubens, but they failed to find buyers. It could have been that they were considered to be too big and awkward to be of any use. Whether these paintings were from Rubens' own hand or from his workshop is not known, except that a large sum was paid for them when they were purchased in 1818 from Mr. Edmund Bourke, the Danish envoy. When the French army entered Madrid in 1808 they took two others back to the Louvre. These, plus the above three, were part of a set.

On July 8, 1927, at the start of our review period, Rubens' painting of "The Departure of Lot and His Daughters from Sodom," 85½ by 96, with life size figures, a painting almost as large as the one sold in 1959, brought £2205 ($10,716). This painting had been presented by the City of Antwerp to John, Duke of Marlborough. (In 1886 the painting sold for £1942/10s.)

On June 8, 1928, the "Portrait of Anton Triest, Archbishop of Ghent," 47 by 41½, sold for £9660 ($47,000). In 1931, "The Mystic Marriage of St. Catherine," 35 by 50, brought $2100 in New York. In London the prices were considerably higher, but they fell nevertheless.

From this point there is a slow but steady rise to 1957 when a level of about $50,000 was reached, five times the level of the 1920's.

In the year 1958 the "Meeting of Abraham and Melchizedek," 26 by 32½, brought £33,000 (nearly $100,000). This painting is now in the National Gallery in Washington. In the following year, "Head of a Bearded Man," 27 by 21, certainly not large, brought £35,000. At the end of the decade good quality Rubens paintings were in the range of over $100,000. This level is 1100 per cent of the 1927 level, and the sharpest rise took place in the 1950's.

RUBENS. *Rape of the Sabine Women.* National Gallery, Washington, D.C. (Widener Collection)

Sir Anthony van Dyck was the pupil and assistant of Peter Paul Rubens, and in the early period of his career he painted in much the same manner as Rubens, so that at times his works are almost indistinguishable from those of the Master.

For a time van Dyck painted in Italy and there absorbed the Italian style of painting, particularly that of Titian. He then became Court Painter to Charles I, King of England, and in that country painted several hundred portraits, and incidentally, in the process became rich. While he painted in Flanders under Rubens his style was strictly the Flemish style of Rubens, with voluptuous nudes, action scenes and warm colors. When he went to England he painted elegant portraits in a distinctly formal style, using blacks and relatively subdued colors. He painted with great restraint and laid down the general style principles followed by the great Eighteenth Century Portrait artists.

In 1928 the "Portrait of the Abbe Scaglia" from the famous Holford Collection, 79 by 48½, brought £31,500 ($153,000) and this price was comparable to the Rembrandts sold at the same time. In the year 1938 five portraits of the English period of van Dyck sold in the Viscount Feilding sale. The highest price

VAN DYCK. *William II of Nassau and Orange.*
National Gallery, Washington, D.C.
(Mellon Collection)

for these portraits was £2100 ($8475). The decline in van Dyck's prices had been precipitate. They remained at this level for 12 years. A gradual rise then took place, and in 1958 "Portrait of a Man," 26¼ by 21½, brought £7000 ($19,600) at Sotheby's. This is not a well recorded van Dyck. The subject's identity is unknown and there are several replicas or variations of this painting in existence, one being in the author's collection. The $30,000 level for good paintings of van Dyck had been reached by the end of the decade. What a large Flemish period altarpiece, similar to that of Rubens which brought the record auction price, would bring is not known, except that it would be several times the price of the unknown man. Van Dyck has probably not recovered his price level of the 1920's, but his prices have been heading in that direction. In this respect his prices somewhat parallel those of the British portraitists, and he was certainly close to these both in period and in style, although earlier and of Flemish background.

At the time David Teniers lived he was the most popular of all Flemish painters, and for years his prices were extremely high in relation to those of other great masters of all countries. He painted outdoor and indoor scenes featuring finely rendered figures performing various tasks, very often dancing, and other merrymaking.

In April, 1768, at the Louis-Jean Gaignat sale, Gaignat being Secretary to the King of France, a Teniers brought the highest price of the 55 paintings offered for sale. The price of this painting exceeded that of paintings by Murillo, van Dyck, Rembrandt, Ter Borch, and Claude Lorrain.

By the 1920's Teniers was at the $10,000 level. From here a drastic decline in price set in, and by 1938 a Teniers could be bought for less than $1,000. Prices recovered through the war, and in 1944 "The Prodigal Son," 22¾ by 30¾, brought $7500. There has been a slight increase in prices since the year 1944, but the pre-depression level has not yet been reached.

While Rubens and van Dyck painted in much the same style and their works are in many ways comparable, as are their trends in general, Teniers is a different painter, and aside from the fact that he also is Flemish, his style and his price characteristics bear little in common with Rubens or van Dyck.

These three painters cannot be considered comparable either in style or in price with the remaining Flemish painters of the seventeenth century. The remaining large group of painters is similar to the Seventeenth Century Dutch School in many respects, including trend of prices, although as a general rule, Seventeenth Century Flemish art is less highly esteemed and thus usually lower priced than Seventeenth Century Dutch art of comparable quality.

PIETER BRUEGHEL, THE ELDER. *Temptation of St. Anthony.*
National Gallery, Washington, D.C. (Kress Collection)

The Sixteenth Century art of Flanders is highlighted by Pieter Brueghel, the painter of country folk and feasts with peasants wearing bright colors and dancing gayly in wild celebrations. During the next century Flemish painting became more subdued in color, and although country life and merrymaking were certainly still popular themes, the whole aspect of the paintings had changed. Brueghel started his own School of art with his very large family which eventually included a third as well as second generation of artists. His pictures often feature beautiful mountain landscapes, painted carefully with his typical greenish-blue hues.

Pieter's son, Jan Brueghel, too, had his own brand of blue, and while he was perhaps not the competent artist that his father was, his colorful landscapes and beautifully painted fruits, flowers and figures are very much in demand.

In 1952 Pieter Brueghel's very small picture of "Christ and the Woman taken in Adultery," 9½ by 13½, brought £11,025 ($30,870) in Christie's in London. In the same year his "View on the Rhine," which was not a painting but a pen, ink and sepia wash, 14 by 17½, still not large, brought £6510 ($18,230).

Too few genuine Pieter Brueghels come onto the market, and a price trend is difficult to establish. While other Sixteenth Century Flemish paintings appear, some of them very good, Sixteenth Century Flemish art is unfortunately not a large School marketwise.

Fifteenth Century Flemish paintings (or Flemish Primitives), particularly those done by artists who were born before the year 1450, form an entirely unique group in art history and in the art market. This group consists mainly of Hubert

148

and Jan van Eyck (the brothers who are credited with being the first to use "oil" as a medium in painting and who produced the famous Ghent altarpiece "The Adoration of the Lamb" in the Cathedral of St. Bavon), and the so-called and unnamed Master of Flémalle, Rogier van der Weyden, Hans Memling, and Gerard David.

These artists specialized in the reproduction of Biblical scenes, the subject matter of the day, and truly conveyed a deep religious feeling to the viewer. The quality of drawing and execution is superb, and comparable to any era—and we are talking about works completed in the early and middle 1400's. The portrayal of anatomical features and the rendering of fabrics are well developed, especially for this early date. The carefully glazed colors are jewel bright and well shaded,

VAN EYCK. *Annunciation.*
National Gallery, Washington, D.C.
(Mellon Collection)

and the composition of the paintings is well balanced and near perfect. The land-scapes which were usually painted as background material, and not as subject matter alone, show an excellent knowledge of perspective and a realistic and beau-tiful execution of detail. A great deal of care was used in blending the paint so that brush strokes are not evident; and it must be pointed out that if the Brothers Jan and Hubert van Eyck did not invent oil painting, they were at least the major pioneers in the use of this new medium for color.

On the negative side, the figures, particularly of the women, certainly do not have the beauty that appeared in later art, such as that of Boucher. But in defense of this peculiarity, it is reported that the women of Flanders at the time were in fact a plain looking group and obviously devoid of the more modern make-up. In all, there is surprisingly little stiffness and stylization of the figures when we consider the year, and what stylization there is does not detract but adds to the spiritual purity and timeless charm of these works.

As far as the market goes, no School has produced such a large proportion of painters who are now in the priceless category. A large and important altarpiece by any one of the leading Flemish Primitive painters mentioned above would today bring upwards of a million dollars. It is reported that the Frick Collection paid $750,000 several years ago for a small Flemish Primitive painting.

In June, 1938, the "Madonna and Child Enthroned," 28½ by 19½, by Hans Memling, brought £6510 ($26,235) and in April, 1939, the "Descent from the Cross," 21¼ by 15¼, brought $83,000 in New York, a most unusual price for an Old Master sold in New York in the year 1939. In 1945, a small "Portrait of a Youth" by Memling, 14 by 9, brought $21,500.

In June, 1938, the "Dream of Pope Sergius" by Rogier van der Weyden, from the Friedsam Collection, brought £14,700 ($59,315).

The unnamed Flemish Primitive Master called simply the "Master of the St. Lucy Legend," brought £1700 ($4760) in November, 1957, in London, and the "Master of the Magdalene Legend" brought £2310 ($6468). Both were medium sized paintings.

A third unnamed but good Flemish Primitive known as the "Master of the Embroidered Leaf" because he painted leaves which have the appearance of em-broidery sold for £8000 ($22,400) in 1959 in Sotheby's.

The price trend of Flemish Primitives, both major Masters and second-line painters, has been sharply up in the 1950's.

On a European trip last year we returned to the United States via Madrid just to look at some of our favorites among which is the unbelievably magnificent

"Descent from the Cross" by Rogier van der Weyden, which hangs in the Prado; and no trip will be made by us to Belgium which does not include a side trip to Ghent to take another look at the van Eyck "Adoration of the Lamb," one of the world's great art treasures.

SPANISH PAINTING

We go on now down the coast from Belgium, or what was Flanders, to Spain. There is a very close link between Spanish and Flemish painting. In the fifteenth century both countries produced Primitives and it is difficult to distinguish some Flemish Primitives from Spanish Primitives. While the great Primitives stand out and are easily identifiable, the minor ones of both countries are fairly plentiful, are not always identifiable, and are not in so great demand. This is particularly true in the case of Spanish Primitives. These have never been properly appreciated. Knowledge leads to appreciation, and these Spanish Primitives can be purchased fairly easily in Madrid in the shops of some small art dealers as well as in the larger galleries. Public taste has not turned sufficiently to this group, and probably this is due to the lack of information on the School, together with a lack of publication of it.

EL GRECO. *View of Toledo.*
The Metropolitan Museum of Art, New York
(Bequest, Mrs. H. O. Havemeyer, 1929,
Havemeyer Collection)

There are relatively few important Spanish artists from the point of view of high acceptance in the international world of art and in the international art market. These important artists are:

Velásquez	El Greco
Murillo	Ribera (also classified as Italian)
Zurbaran	Goya

There is little question that Velásquez is considered by the Spanish to be Spain's greatest artist. There is a great feeling throughout the entire art world that Velásquez occupies this position, and the great molder of art opinion, Bernard Berenson, who worked for decades with Lord Duveen establishing the importance of works of art throughout not only the United States but the world, states almost openly that Velásquez is not only Spain's greatest artist but that he may even be without rival in all of art, including the Italian in which Berenson specialized.

The great historical scenes and altarpieces of Velásquez have hardly any peers. They are characterized not only by a precision of painting, but by monumentality and a psychological insight into the characters represented.

VELÁSQUEZ. *Pope Innocent X.*
National Gallery, Washington, D.C.
(Mellon Collection)

A few Velásquez paintings have appeared at auction. In 1942 in New York his "Vintners," 28½ by 44½, brought $15,500. In 1945 his "Portrait of a Girl," 25½ by 22¾, brought $30,000, and in 1947 in London his "Duke of Alvarez," 79¼ by 41¼, brought £11,000 ($30,800). Rarely do his paintings appear, and those that do usually are not in the class of his great works. A few years ago a fairly good head and shoulders portrait by Velásquez was for sale in New York for $120,000. No price trend over the years can be established on the basis of these few paintings.

Velásquez lived from 1599 to 1660. Murillo lived from 1616 to 1682. He knew Velásquez, who was Court Painter to King Philip IV of Spain, and was assisted greatly in his artistic development by Velásquez and absorbed some of Velásquez' style. Murillo painted religious subjects beautifully. His Madonnas are symbols of sweetness and his "Virgin as the Immaculate Conception" is a delight to behold. Because of the fluid softness of his brush work and the beauty of his subjects he was known as the "Spanish Raphael."

In 1927 a "Madonna and Child," 49 by 37, a reproduced painting, brought $50,000 in a New York auction. The following year the small "Girl Lifting Her Veil," 20½ by 15, brought £5880 in London.

Our next bench mark is 1939 when the reproduced painting, "Ecce Homo," 22½ by 18½, sold for only $5000.

By 1956 it was clear that there was a comeback in the prices of Murillo. In that year, in November, the same "Girl Lifting Her Veil," which had previously sold for £5880, brought £25,000 at Sotheby's. Although the pound sterling was worth somewhat less by this time, it was clear that a good Murillo, even though small, had risen substantially in price. However, there are so few other examples of Murillo on the market that it is difficult to chart an accurate trend of prices.

The third artist whose prices we have traced is El Greco (1541 to 1614). At the beginning of the review period, "St. Martin Dividing His Cloak with the Beggar," a good sized picture, 54 by 42, brought £1365 ($6634). But let us go back a few years and note the prices of El Greco.

In 1882 the important El Greco, "Portrait of Ludovico Cornaro," was bought from the Hamilton Palace Collection by the National Gallery in London for £336 ($1532).

In 1886 an El Greco was sold for £304 and "Christ at Calvary" brought £995 in 1907.

No major auction gallery bothered to illustrate or even mention an El Greco sold in the peak seasons of 1929 and 1930.

An El Greco was sold in 1951 for 3,000,000 francs ($60,000).

By the year 1959 an El Greco of St. James, 27¾ by 21¼, not large, sold at Sotheby's for £72,000 ($200,000). In the same year the unrecorded, unknown El Greco labeled "Veronese" sold at auction in London for over $100,000.

Sixty years ago El Greco was virtually unknown and forgotten. Now he's a "must" for the museum collections and for those collectors who can afford him.

Besides illustrating the change in public taste, the rise of El Greco illustrates perhaps one of the main attributes of the work of an artist who gains public favor today—a strong, sure style easily distinguished from others. El Greco has such a style with his peculiarly elongated figures and his bright but limited color palette. Also, for example, van Gogh, Gauguin, Renoir, Cézanne, Braque, and Modigliani, to mention a few, have an unusual, readily identifiable style.

While El Greco was a generation before Velásquez and Murillo, Goya worked in the late eighteenth and early nineteenth century. Some of Goya's portraits have the majesty and restraint of the Eighteenth Century British artists and are comparable in quality, although many of his works are more "impressionistic." Of course the subjects are generally wearing the Spanish dress of the period which helps to identify the paintings as being by this artist. Goya does, however, have a style peculiarly his own, and his portraits of women, particularly those which are painted full length, sometimes have a stiffly posed, elongated, delicate, and wistful appearance not entirely in keeping with the subjects he painted. This stiffness was not true, however, in the case of his late works, which are quite strong, and surprisingly impressionistic.

Very few Goyas come onto the market. In 1942 a recorded, illustrated one— "Dr. Stafford," 27½ by 21½—sold in New York for $3500. In 1958 the Parke-Bernet Galleries sold "La Joven," 29 by 23, for $4500. The same painting had sold in 1938 for $6000. In June, 1961, a fine, recorded portrait brought $392,000 at Sotheby's.

Possibly the most beloved Goya in America is "Don Manuel Osorio de Zuñiga" —sometimes called the "Little Red Boy." Jules Bache purchased the painting about thirty years ago from the great salesman, Lord Duveen, for a price reported to be $160,000. The charming, signed painting now hangs in the Metropolitan, and because of its prime quality would probably bring an equally high price today.

The last Spanish painter we will consider is Sorolla y Bastida, who lived from 1863 to 1923. His painting shows little kinship with the earlier Spanish painters and falls more into the Modern Group which has already been discussed. He is not included there, however, because his style is not as experimental as the predominant modern Schools. His works are a vivid representation of nature. He was

ZURBARAN. *St. Francis*. Private Collection

excellently trained and uses a strong and bold stroke and bright, natural, pleasing colors. He specializes in out-of-doors scenes, especially those featuring seashores and boats. In April, 1960, his "Marine," 20 by 32, an exellent painting, brought $4350 in New York.

To summarize Spanish painting, Velásquez rarely appears on the market in the form of a good painting. If a prime example should appear it would bring a good price, well into six figures. El Greco brings a comparable price and is in even greater demand than Velásquez because his unusual style makes him somewhat akin to the Modern School which is now in vogue. While Murillo is scarce and brings high prices, his paintings would not be as high as in the case of these artists just mentioned and might even be at half the level. An important Goya would bring well into six figures, and few of these examples appear in London or New York. Sorolla is quite a different story. His history can be compared to that of the Moderns, a group to which, however, he does not belong. His prices trail those of the best Moderns, but are rising.

German Painting

Several years ago my wife purchased two altar paintings. She came home with them, very excited, and intimated that, while she was not 100 per cent sure, she had a feeling that the panels were Flemish Primitives and perhaps even by someone close to Rogier van der Weyden. The dealer had no idea what they were and she felt that she had made a great "discovery." Her enthusiasm was hard to share as the paintings appeared to be in quite poor condition—half of the surface being unpainstakingly overpainted. I had also made a purchase that day of a painting by Jakob de Wet. The de Wet was a pleasing purchase but the unknown altar panels appeared to be somewhat less than pleasing. A brief examination revealed that the panels were definitely not close to Rogier van der Weyden and were not Flemish Primitives, but were possibly German paintings of a later century. A magnifying glass would quickly prove the matter and show the poor quality and detail. At this point the tears were rising in my wife's eyes.

The magnifying glass test proved, however, to be somewhat surprising. Under the glass the paintings appeared to be of excellent quality. The entire subject was changed quickly and it seemed best at that point to go out to dinner. At dinner, after the tears were wiped away, my wife did admit that she had been over-optimistic and promised not to go making "discoveries" on her own without doing any research or consulting me.

Further research for the next few days determined that the paintings were not German, however, but were actually done by a leading member of the School of Sixteenth Century Flemish painters known as "Antwerp Mannerists." They are called "Mannerists" because of their extreme stylization. The artist is "The Master of 1518" who, while he is no Rogier van der Weyden, is represented in several prominent museum collections and is a fine discovery for anyone to make. When taken to the restorer, overpainting came off and revealed undamaged panels. It was then time for me to apologize to her and take her out again to dinner—this time for a celebration.

This story illustrates the relationships between Dutch and Flemish painting on the one hand, and German painting on the other. The Flemish authority, Max Friedlaender, has stated in *From van Eyck to Brueghel,* "In the fifteenth century the Netherlands were more of an entity with a uniform culture and the Germanic essence . . . flowed through the entire land.

"Holland, the influence of which in the structure of South Netherlandish art was demonstrably strong, may be regarded as a Germanic area. . . . The area of

VAN DER WEYDEN. *Portrait of a Lady.*
National Gallery, Washington, D.C.
(Mellon Collection)

WOLF TRAUT. *Portrait of a Woman.*
College of the City of New York
Photograph by John D. Schiff

Northern Brabant . . . must be described as predominantly German in the wider sense, so that not only Geertgen, Jan Mostaert, Lucas van Leyden, Jacob van Amsterdam but also Jerome Bosch and Pieter Brueghel of the later artists . . . and the brothers Hubert and Jan van Eyck may be accepted with some degree of probation as painters of Germanic extraction."

Stephan Lochner and Konrad Witz, the two leading German Primitives, are very close in style to the great Flemish Primitives. The North Carolina Art Museum in its original collection paid more for a Stephan Lochner than for any other painting, including Rembrandt and Rubens. Good examples of this period in German art history rarely come onto the auction market or onto the art market generally.

One of the greatest if not *the* greatest of German artists was Albrecht Dürer, who lived from 1471 to 1528. A prime Dürer would bring in the neighborhood of $500,000 or more at the end of the decade of the '50's, and needless to say, such a painting has not appeared. A small pen drawing on paper, a sketch of two horsemen, was sold at Christie's in 1958 for £4200 ($11,760). This price in-

DÜRER. *Madonna and Child.*
National Gallery, Washington, D.C.
(Kress Collection)

DÜRER. *Self-Portrait*. The Prado

dicates what an important painting by Dürer would sell for. Dürer was not only one of the few really great German artists; he is considered one of the greatest artists of all time. He had the technique and training to draw or paint almost anything, from great altarpieces and panel portraits, to flowers, hands and rabbits, and while his paintings have a slightly stylized quality and his women are not the most beautiful, they represent the predominant German types.

The other German Master of great importance is Hans Holbein who was born twenty-six years after Dürer. As a portraitist no one exceeded him. He skillfully portrayed elegance and majesty. His bright, jewel-like coloring of robes and draperies dispels the somberness later to become evident in many German and Dutch portraits. He, like Dürer, also painted religious pictures, including altarpieces.

In July, 1929, one of the finest paintings to come onto the auction market in recent years was offered at Christie's in London, the Holbein "Portrait of Edward VI as a Child," a masterpiece of portraiture. It was relatively small, 22½ by 17, and brought £9975 (about $50,000).

HOLBEIN. *Sir Thomas More.*
The Frick Collection, New York

Like Dürer, paintings by Holbein seldom come onto the market, and good Holbeins have hardly ever changed hands in recent years. It is expected that his prices would be about at the level of Dürer. From Holbein and Dürer it is a step down quality-wise and price-wise to the other painters of the time.

Lucas Cranach painted at about the time of Holbein, and his stylized paintings, particularly those of rather unshapely slant-eyed nudes, hang in most museums of the world. Cranach was a skilled craftsman and no doubt a master, but his workshop pieces hurt his value on the market. He maintained a large workshop, and it is difficult in some cases to determine what he himself painted and what the workshop painted. The level of his prices at the end of the decade of the '50's was about $20,000 for a good painting. In March, 1959, "Adam and Eve" was offered for sale in London and brought 6200 guineas ($18,600).

In 1947 a portrait by Hans Burgkmair, 16 by 11¾, brought $13,000, and in 1953 two religious scenes by the same artist brought £3600 and £5500 ($10,000 and $15,400). Herman Tom Ring brought £10,000 ($28,000) and in 1959

Hans von Kulmbach, also a lesser master, brought at auction £6500 ($18,200). The subject was a "Portrait of a Man," 16 by 12¼. This is about the auction level of the lesser German artists of the century, with retail prices, of course, higher, and with prices somewhat higher for Grunewald, Altdorfer and Baldung.

From this point on there is little significant painting, with a few exceptions, before the nineteenth century, when we have Caspar David Friedrich, Moritz Schwind, Alfred Rethel, Karl Spitzweg, Ferdinand Waldmueller, Adolf Menzel, Franz von Lenbach (the great portraitist of Bismarck), Wilhelm Leibl, Wilhelm Truebner, Hans Thoma, Anselm Feuerbach, Arnold Boecklin and Fritz Uhde.

Today this School is fairly closely confined to the markets of Germany. Its many pictures and their popularity parallel those of nineteenth century England and nineteenth century Holland. Locally they form an important part of the market, although these masters, some of them once important internationally, are now generally sold at relatively low prices. There is some prospect that some of the artists may grow in international importance, artists such as Spitzweg and Feuerbach. It is interesting to note that early in the twentieth century an entire volume of the Classics in Art series (*Klassiker der Kunst*) was devoted to Thoma, Uhde, and Feuerbach. Times and tastes change, and at present these artists do not form a large part of the International Market.

In summary, early German art because of its scarcity does not form a large part of the market although high prices are reached, particularly by the near-priceless Masters, Holbein, and Dürer. Strong buyer interest in the later German Schools (with the exception of the German Expressionists who were considered in the chapter on Modern Art) is confined somewhat to the local European markets and has not been significantly high here in the American auctions.

VIII

Italian Art

HE ONE NATIONAL SCHOOL OF ART WHICH IS PRESERVED IN THE museums of the world more than any other is Italian art. It is not necessarily the finest art that has been produced in the world, but it very well may be, taken as a whole. In Italian art all of the forward strides made in painting up until the time of the late nineteenth century are represented, if not actually pioneered. Italian painting encompasses many Greats—Leonardo da Vinci, Raphael, Michelangelo, Botticelli, Giotto, Bellini, Giorgione, Titian, and Fra Angelico, to gather a bouquet of important names.

In the history of Italian painting we find two important answers to questions that must be in the minds of everyone who has even a remote interest in art: (1) What is the point in painting, and what has been the position of painting in the lives of people down through the centuries? and (2) What constitutes a good painting, if anything? Unless we have a complete understanding of the latter we must always sit and look at the paintings of some of the newer Schools and ask ourselves vaguely, "What is all this? I wonder if it's good or bad or if I am just too unenlightened to understand how fine it really is?"

Duccio (1255 to 1319) represents the type painting that existed for 500 years, starting in the ninth century and ending in the fourteenth. In that time there was no printing, and there was a woeful lack of education among the great masses of the people. The two effective ways in which the populace as a whole could be

162

communicated with were word of mouth and the painted picture. It is difficult in the 1960's to conceive of such times, with our host of media for communication.

In the Middle Ages, which preceded the Renaissance (and the Renaissance began in the fourteenth century and continued through the sixteenth), art was an integral part of and a vehicle of expression for the Church. The effect of seeing the Saviour on the Cross or the Virgin and Child surrounded by angels was at least as effective as the proscriptions of the priests to live a Christian life.

The artist was asked by the church officials to paint these religious scenes on the walls of the Church, and between the ninth and fourteenth centuries this activity was carried on primarily in Byzantium (what is now Turkey), and is consequently called generically Byzantine art even though a great deal of art of this type was done in Italy. It was obviously under the direct influence of Byzantium.

In time churches developed windows, and the development of glass made windows more practical. Wall space consequently became smaller and the artists started to paint on detachable panels that could be moved from place to place in the church. This is the origin of our modern picture which is hung on the wall, not painted directly on the wall.

From the fourteenth to sixteenth century Italy was a group of individual states, not one country as at present. Florence and Venice were the leaders, not only in

DUCCIO. *Prophets Isaiah and Ezekiel.* National Gallery, Washington, D.C. (Mellon Collection)

art, but in military power as well. By the early sixteenth century the general prosperity and military success led to a glorification of each of these separate states
and a love of ease and splendor. The officials of the country took over art and
the leading artists in order to use them as tools of the state. The Doge's palace in
Venice seems almost designed for the display of large paintings, and if it was not
so designed originally, it was shortly thereafter covered with monumental paintings prepared in the interest of furthering the policy of the state, as, for instance,
the painting depicting the Doge bringing about a reconciliation between the Pope
and the Emperor Barbarossa. During this period it was the policy of Venice to
hold the balance of power in Italy by supporting and strengthening both the Pope
and his supporters and his enemies.

The state used art not just to convey messages indicating its importance and
power, but it used the artists to record scenes of carnivals, feasts and pageants,
everything grand, fine, glittering and important connected with the state; in this
case, Venice. Venice pioneered successfully in this type of painting.

In Venice there were a number of social clubs or fraternal organizations known
as Mutual Aid Societies. It was not long before these societies conceived the idea
of employing the artists who worked in the Doge's palace to paint pictures to
hang on their walls, pictures not so much of the power and majesty of the state,
but of pleasant scenes of the pageant type. Gradually the subject of the pictures
changed from ceremonies to pleasing scenes which could be hung in a person's
home. This is primarily the place and purpose of paintings today, and this stage
was arrived at through the process of working down in painting from the Church,
to the Council Chambers, to the Fraternal groups, to private homes. The location
of the pictures in the homes was accomplished after the middle of the sixteenth
century.

Simultaneously the portrait was developed, along about the end of the fifteenth
century, and at this time it was generally used to glorify the head of the state by
making him appear noble and important. The painting was a monument to him
that would be passed down through the ages and, to a certain extent, the painting
took its place among other monuments which he erected to himself, such as palaces,
public edifices and statues.

I. *Primitives*

The paintings of Duccio and the other Primitives of first rank, such as Cimabue,
have two important qualities: the *drawing* is well developed for the time and the
color is pleasing. These are the primary elements of painting: (1) drawing and

(2) color. The greatest collection of Italian Primitives is in the Siena Gallery in Italy. There is a certain sameness about all Italian Primitives, and it takes a real expert to distinguish among the various Masters of this School.

A weakness of Italian Primitive art is that it is flat and for that reason is somewhat monotonous. Yet Primitives are some of the most sought after paintings on the international art market.

In the Primitive Italian School, which includes the painters prior to the coming of Giotto and the type of more advanced painting he was responsible for developing, important masters such as Cimabue and Duccio seldom appear on the auction market.

Since these first rank artists appear on the market so infrequently as to be for all practical purposes nonexistent, we have traced the prices of the second rank artists who, although not of the rarity and perfection of Duccio, are, nevertheless, of excellent quality.

In 1926 a Sano di Pietro, a Sienese painting, sold in London for £220 ($1069).

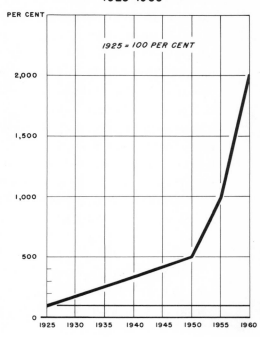

ITALIAN PRIMITIVES
PRICE HISTORY IN PERCENTAGE
1926-1960

1926 = 100 PER CENT

ITALIAN PAINTING TO 1450
PRICE HISTORY IN PERCENTAGE
1925-1960

1925 = 100 PER CENT

In 1931 another Sienese Primitive, Bartolo di Fredi, sold for £462 ($2093).

In 1949 Giovanni di Paolo, 10¼ by 9, brought $11,000 in New York. The following year Taddeo di Bartolo, a Sienese Primitive, brought £2835 ($7938).

In 1953 a painting labeled simply "School of Rimini" brought £10,000 ($28,000) in London and a Sassetta went for £9,000 ($25,200). A small Sano di Pietro brought £3000 ($8,400).

In 1959 two altar panels by Sassetta were offered for sale by a secondary dealer in Florence for $80,000. They were medium sized panels, but it was not clear that they were by Sassetta himself.

The rise in the price of Primitives from 1926 to the end of the '50's was in the neighborhood of a rise from 100 per cent in 1926 to 4000 per cent in 1960.

II. *Painting to 1450*

Duccio and Cimabue were Primitives who painted in the style of the Byzantines, and Byzantine art was the same for 500 years. There were no innovations of a major character in five centuries.

The relationship between Cimabue and Giotto was a close one. There is a little legend about the relationship between the two artists which is worth repeating simply because it is interesting, whether or not it is strictly accurate historically. Cimabue (1240 to 1302) was a great artist of the period. Giotto, who was a shepherd boy with some inclination toward art, was busy in the fields drawing pictures of his sheep on a slate. Cimabue happened to pass by at this time and was so impressed by the boy's talent that he took Giotto with him to Florence as his apprentice. This was the prologue to modern painting.

Let us look at a Cimabue alongside a Giotto. We can compare the same subject as represented by each artist.

While both paintings look primitive from the viewpoint of the middle twentieth century, there is a striking difference in effect between the Cimabue and the Giotto. Cimabue's faces do not give the impression of roundness. They look flat, and this is so because it is obvious that he could not use shading in the way that Giotto could. The folds of Cimabue's garments on the Virgin are indicated by gold lines. They hardly look like folds at all. Giotto's folds, on the other hand, are so realistic as to give the viewer the impression that he is looking at an actual garment.

Cimabue's Virgin looks emaciated and generally flat. Under the folds there does not seem to be any body. Giotto's Virgin looks like a person. Under the garment there appears to be a body and the garment appears to be draped on the

CIMABUE. *Madonna and Child Enthroned.*
The Uffizi Gallery, Florence

GIOTTO. *Madonna and Child Enthroned.*
The Uffizi Gallery, Florence

body. One can see the form of the right knee of the Virgin and imagine that he could reach out and touch it.

On either side of the Virgin are groupings of saints in both the Cimabue and the Giotto. The saints in the Giotto fit into the picture from the front to the back, so that there is a third dimension. In the Cimabue picture the saints seem to be piled on top of each other in the same plane, so that there is little or no third dimension.

When one looks at the arch over the two saints at the bottom of the Cimabue picture it is not immediately clear whether the arch goes up or whether it goes back, and the perspective is poor. The curve above this arch on which the Virgin rests her feet clearly seems to go back, not up; but if this is so, then does the arch under it (the one over the heads of the saints that we looked at first) go up or back? The painting technique falls down at this point.

Finally, the columns to the right and left of the Cimabue Virgin, which the saints are holding onto, are a little unclear. One must look closely and then come to the conclusion, "Oh yes, I see. They are supposed to have depth, but I didn't see that right away." The depth of the altar panels and the base of the Giotto piece are much better (from the point of view of perspective).

Giotto, who lived from 1266 to 1336, gave *form* to paintings, thereby releasing painting from the stiffness of Byzantine art. He did this through clever use of line, through shading, through good grouping of his figures and through a sense of what is important and what is not concerning the things he was representing. A more artistic term than simply form for what he developed is *Tactile Values,* and this is painting quality No. 3. This goes along with No. 1, *Drawing* and No. 2, *Color,* which were in existence earlier.

Tactile values, or form, include not only the feeling that there is a third dimension, that you are looking at something solid and as it really exists, but it includes the sensation of contact that one gets just from looking, the illusion that what you see has weight, volume, bulk, inner substance and texture. This is what Giotto gave to art, and in Giotto's works we discover the beginning of naturalistic painting.

It took 135 years after the birth of Giotto for another artist to come onto the Italian scene who would make any significant advance in painting after Giotto: Masaccio, who lived from 1401 to 1428. In Masaccio, even more than in Giotto, you feel as though you can reach out and touch the figures and objects painted. Masaccio had an even greater sense of the significant in painting—which objects to stress and which to play down. His paintings give the viewer an even surer sense of reality, and are further along in the evolutionary scale of painting.

MASACCIO. *The Tribute Money.* Santa Maria del Carmine, Florence

In this same era Fra Angelico, the pious monk, painted his exquisite masterpieces. One of his great contributions to art was the true landscape. There was no
landscape in either Giotto or Masaccio. Fra Angelico was the teacher of Fra Filippo
Lippi.

To the author's knowledge no paintings by Giotto or Masaccio have appeared
on the auction market in the entire period studied, 1925 to 1960, at least paintings
that appeared to be genuine works of these masters. In fact, the only unquestioned,
typical, good works of the major artists of this period of Italian art to come onto
the auction market in the 35 year period studied can be counted on one's fingers.

One of the finest paintings of this school, or of any school, did, however,
appear in New York on November 3, 1944, a "Madonna and Child," by Fra
Filippo Lippi, 32¾ by 24¾. This was a typical work of the Master, in fine condition and about as well documented and authenticated as is possible. The price was
$30,000, very low for a work of this quality.

In 1955 a Masolino di Panicale, 20 by 12¼, brought £3500 ($9800), and
in June, 1957, two rather small saints on panels (14¼ by 5½, two paintings)

FRA FILIPPO LIPPI. *Madonna and Child.*
Parke-Bernet Galleries, Inc.

brought £7800 ($21,840). These were by Fra Angelico, as was another small saint on a panel which was offered by a dealer a few years ago for $80,000.

It is hardly possible to establish a price trend for this School and era, so rare are *any* paintings by the leaders, much less fairly large, typical paintings. The graph would be about like that of the Primitives, but less steep, since good paintings in this period have been in demand throughout the period.

III. *1450 to the Early Sixteenth Century*

The greatest single contribution to mature painting in this era was made by Antonio Pollaiuolo (1429 to 1498). From his paintings for the first time in the history of Italian art, one receives the impression of *movement,* and this is a fourth characteristic of modern painting, along with drawing, color and form. By movement is meant the feeling, on looking at the painting, that something is going on, that forms are in motion, that there is action and that the artist caught what was

FRA ANGELICO. *The Entombment.*
National Gallery, Washington, D.C.
(Kress Collection)

POLLAIUOLO. *Martyrdom of St. Sebastian.*
National Gallery, London

going on as a camera catches a photo finish at a horse race. In Giotto and Masaccio, the prior innovators, there was *no movement*. It remained for Pollaiuolo to make this contribution.

Landscape painting was developed by Fra Angelico (1387 to 1455), but it was further developed in this 1450-to-early-sixteenth-century period by Verrocchio (1435 to 1488), who operated the School reportedly attended by Leonardo da Vinci, Perugino and Lorenzo di Credi, if we can conceive of such an illustrious group of art students. (The opinion that Perugino attended Verrocchio's School is disputed by some art authorities.) Verrocchio made an important contribution through a well developed technique of portraying light and shadow.

In this period also the first Italian genre paintings were produced (depiction of ordinary people either inside or outside), which genre paintings now represent such a large proportion of those which hang in the homes of private individuals. Prior to this time religious themes had been everything. The modern portrait started at the beginning of the sixteenth century.

LEONARDO DA VINCI. *Madonna of the Rocks.*
The Louvre, Paris

During this same period Michelangelo lived, and his major contribution to art was his monumental depiction of the figure, both male and female. These forms cover the ceiling of the Sistine Chapel in the Vatican in Rome, where he himself labored for years painting while lying on his back on scaffolding close to the ceiling. Michelangelo, who lived from 1475 to 1564, featured the nude as a subject in painting. Now nearly every art class, as soon as the students learn the primary techniques, goes to the painting of the human body, which offers the most difficult study subject.

One further major contribution was to be made to mature art, and it was made in this era: space composition. This was made in the Umbrian School of art by Perugino and still more by his pupil Raphael. While Giotto and Masaccio gave form to art, you could not look deeply into a picture and feel as though you were actually there. It remained for Perugino and Raphael to achieve this stride in painting technique. Your eye runs from the Madonna and Child to the field with its grass and flowers in which the Holy Family sits, to the hills behind, spotted with Umbrian trees, and perhaps crowned by a castle or town. It was a difficult illusion to achieve, but when we have it, all of the major elements of realistic painting have been developed. What Perugino and Raphael achieved has been, in a fashion, put to work in the kind of mural painting so popular today which gives the impression that one is looking not at a painted wall, but is looking out on the sea or at a forest or a distant village.

This was not only the era of Bellini, Botticelli, Mantegna, and Piero della Francesca, but also of that universal genius who takes second place to no one in the field of art: Leonardo da Vinci. Only with an understanding of the history of art, of how long it took to develop the techniques of modern painting and how hard it was to make these developments can we appreciate what Leonardo was. He lived from 1452 to 1519 and died one year before Raphael.

Leonardo embodied all of the achievements of Giotto and Masaccio in form and tactile values, all of Pollaiuolo's movement, and Verrocchio's use of light and shade. In Leonardo's "Madonna of the Rocks," now in the Louvre, he clearly portrays space within the grotto and, although perhaps not the master of space composition that Raphael was, his space composition is entirely adequate. Most important, his forms have a restrained beauty, and the human features, particularly the hands, are near to perfection. Leonardo sketched many experimental pictures of garments until he developed a superb technique for presenting the folds not

GIOVANNI BELLINI.
Portrait of a Young Man in Red.
National Gallery, Washington, D.C.
(Mellon Collection)

only accurately but beautifully. His landscapes, while of a mysterious quality, are first class.

The Italian School, from 1450 to the early sixteenth century, is one of the most revered and desired Schools in all art. Possibly the only major Master of this period who can be traced through public price records is Giovanni Bellini, Venice's leading fifteenth century painter, the teacher of Titian and Giorgione.

At the beginning of the review period, in the year 1927, a "Portrait of a Boy," 15 by 9, not a large portrait, a little over the size of a piece of typing paper, brought £6510 ($31,639).

In 1945 his "Madonna and Child," 29¾ by 23¼, brought $21,000.

In 1946 Bellini's "Pieta" was purchased for £3360 ($13,540), a fairly small painting 16¾ by 12¾.

Bellini's prices were down as compared with the 1920's.

In 1948 "St. Jerome in the Wilderness," 14 by 17, brought £4830 ($19,465).

Now prices change: In November, 1958, "Christ at the Column," a tiny pen and ink drawing, 9⅜ by 5¾, came onto the market. It is the kind of sketch an artist would make many times in order to organize his ideas before starting on a painting. It might have taken 20 minutes to make this sketch. The price was £15,750 ($44,100).

In the same season two wings of an altarpiece (triptych), with no central part, brought £22,000 ($62,384). Each wing measured 31½ by 11¾.

In July, 1955, three studies of an apostle, also a sketch, brought £15,540 ($43,512).

With limited public sales it is hard to draw a price line for this School in this period, and reliance must be placed on prices of different masters during the period.

Raphael in the 1920's was higher in price than Bellini. In the latter part of the decade Andrew Mellon purchased the famous "Alba Madonna" from the Hermitage in Leningrad, for $1,166,000, and Raphael's small "St. George and the Dragon" for $747,000. Both paintings are now in the National Gallery in Washington and both are, and were in the 1920's, museum paintings and thus in a different price category from the usual market items.

In 1939 Raphael's small "Madonna of the Pinks," 11 by 8½ (just the size of a sheet of typing paper), brought $60,000.

Today an important Raphael would bring over a million dollars.

As mentioned earlier in this book, there is one painting by Leonardo known to be in private hands—"Genevra di Benci" in the Liechtenstein Collection. At

RAPHAEL. *Alba Madonna.*
National Gallery, Washington, D.C.
(Mellon Collection)

least one organization has offered $1,000,000 for this painting, and the offer was refused. It is reported that another organization offered $2,000,000 and this offer also was refused.

In 1951 a small "Head of the Virgin," 7¾ by 6, a drawing by Leonardo, brought £8000 ($22,400).

It is recognized that a number of other paintings attributed to Leonardo have been on the market from time to time. Over the past five years several of them have been examined, and their backgrounds studied and discussed with several art experts, notably Dr. W. E. Suida who, at the time of his passing, was the world's leading authority on Leonardo.

Some of these paintings were unfinished, some damaged, some only in part, if at all, by Leonardo and some reattributed from lesser artists to Leonardo. These latter suffer in price because at some time in the past someone said they were painted not by the Master but by a lesser artist.

On a level just below Leonardo and Raphael there is Raphael's teacher, Pietro Perugino, and his associate, Bernardino Pinturicchio. In 1944 the Thompson Collection was sold in New York. In this collection there was a "Madonna and Child and Saint Jerome" by Perugino which brought $12,000 and a "Madonna and Child" by Pinturicchio which went for $16,500. In November, 1945, another Perugino, "Madonna and Child," brought $11,000.

GIAMPIETRINO.
Madonna and Child and St. Jerome.
Private Collection

At the end of the decade of the 1950's these paintings would have been in the low six figure class, and an important Perugino was offered for $250,000.

Around Leonardo was a group of painters very close in style to the Master but of lesser quality. In some of these artists the design and even the hand of the Master appear. In the group are Luini, Boltraffio, Solario, Giampietrino, da Sesto, da Predis, and d'Oggiono. Luini commands the highest prices with Boltraffio probably next.

Francia is an excellent artist close in style to Raphael; but Raphael, too, had a group of lesser artists as followers.

In 1927 Giampietrino of the Leonardo School brought $11,000 and Francia, close to Raphael, went for $21,000.

In 1944 Francia sold for $12,000 and Luini of the Leonardo School brought $6000. Prices were down from the 1920's.

In 1940 Solario of the Leonardo School brought $16,000. In 1939 Giampietrino brought $6,200.

In 1957 Marco d'Oggiono, a Leonardo School member, was sold for £3000 ($8,400).

At the end of the decade Marco d'Oggiono and Giampietrino were in the "under $35,000" class, comparable with what they had been in the 1920's. Luini and Boltraffio were just under six figures. Francia of the Raphael group (not a follower, but similar in style) was in the "under $35,000" class.

IV. *Middle Sixteenth Century*

By the early sixteenth century all of the major techniques of painting had been developed, and with these the great Venetians went to work in the middle part of the century. Venetian painting dominates this period, and this group of artists is best represented by Titian, whose life span covered the long period from 1477 to 1576 (99 years). Although he was born six years before Raphael he lived into another and newer era in Italian painting.

The characteristics of Venetian painting of the middle sixteenth century were harmony of color and splendor. The painters of the period worked on big canvases or painted directly on walls, first at the instigation of the Doge and his Council, later for the Confraternities, and, finally, for private individuals.

Giorgione died at the early age of 32, but even though he lived these few years he took his place in the forefront of Venetian painters. The work of all of these four artists really stems from Giovanni Bellini.

TITIAN. *Cardinal Pietro Bembo.*
National Gallery, Washington, D.C.
(Kress Collection)

MIDDLE SIXTEENTH CENTURY VENETIANS
PRICE HISTORY IN PERCENTAGE AND DOLLARS
1927 - 1960

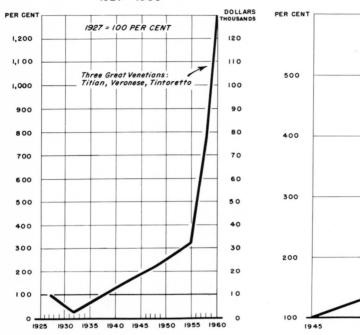

ITALIAN BAROQUE PAINTERS (1550-1700)
PRICE HISTORY IN PERCENTAGE
1945 - 1960

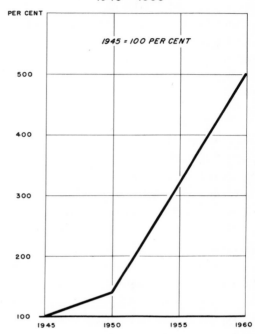

Possibly Venice added one more element to modern painting—pleasant associations—for we like to look at paintings which depict enjoyable things, such as sumptuous feasts, beautiful women, fine clothes, flowers and pleasant landscapes. Few normal people like to look at morbid or unhappy things over a long period when a painting hangs on one's wall.

At this point, then, we have all of the elements of mature painting developed:

1. Drawing   4. Movement
2. Color   5. Space composition.
3. Form or tactile values

We also have these collateral developments which, although not of the essence in the development of mature art, are, nevertheless, antecedents of modern subject matter for paintings:

A. Landscape   D. Pleasant associations as a goal of
B. Genre   the artist in producing the paint-
C. The nude   ing.

The other major artists of this time were Correggio, Pontormo and Bronzino; the latter two being known as Mannerists, following the great period of the middle sixteenth century in Venice.

On July 15, 1927, two Veronese paintings, each 10 by 43, one of "Diana and Actaeon," the other of a "Caledonian Bear Hunt," sold for £1470 and £1785 respectively ($7144 and $8675). These prices were probably somewhat below what Titian would have brought in the same year.

In 1932 and 1933, at the bottom of the depression, two Veroneses brought £480 and £540 ($1680 and $1890). Prices were down from the 1920's.

In 1946 a Veronese went for £1995 ($8040). In 1947 a Tintoretto sold for £4830 ($19,465) and in 1948 a Titian, "Virgin and Infant Saviour," brought £3990 ($16,080).

In 1955 a Titian brought £11,550 ($32,340).

Two years later a Veronese brought £9800 ($27,440), and in the 1958-1959 season a Titian portrait went for £24,000 ($67,200).

The prices of the three great Venetians of this period are now in six figures.

It is interesting to note that the Mannerist Pontormo in 1927 sold for $37,000, exceeding the price of Veronese in the same period. This same price for Pontormo in 1959 or 1960 would be about the market. The three leaders rose to perhaps 1300 per cent of the 1927 price while the Mannerists are about at the 1927 level.

V. *Baroque Period—Late Sixteenth and Seventeenth Century*

In the middle of the sixteenth century in Venice, painting hit a high point of perfection and monumentality. The paintings were large, extremely colorful, and filled with well drawn figures, well placed within the confines of the borders.

When art moved from the Doge's palace to the fraternal organizations and finally to the homes, a new demand was felt, the demand of homes suitable for hanging attractive paintings on the walls to enhance the pleasure of living. To meet the growing demand which had now reached down to the wealthier people, a new and larger group of artists arose, not only in Venice, but in other of the cities of what is now Italy: in Bologna, in Genoa, in Ferrara, in Rome, in Naples. This represents a great geographic spread of art induced by a more popular and generalized demand than had heretofore confined the principal Schools of art to Florence (Giotto, Fra Angelico, Botticelli, and Leonardo), Umbria (Perugino, Pinturicchio, Piero della Francesca and Raphael), and Venice (Bellini, Titian, Veronese, and Tintoretto).

The paintings of the Italian Baroque period are characterized by an excellence of drawing and color and by good rendition of the feeling of movement. However, the flowing robes, trickling water, waving flags and gestures with upraised hands make a person feel a little fatigued looking at them hanging on the wall over a period of time.

We could consider a sample of the artists by School (Genoese, Ferrarese, etc.) within the general Italian School of this Baroque period, but little would be accomplished by this breakdown. The generally leading artists of all Italy will be taken up briefly instead.

Francesco Albani (1578-1660) was a member of the famous Bolognese Academy of the Carracci family and in his own right was an excellent artist of altarpieces, many of them large, as well as mythological paintings. He had a workshop of good size and produced some fine paintings of nudes that influenced the later French painters.

Jacopo Bassano and his sons, Francesco, Girolamo, and Leandro, turned out a large number of paintings which combined landscapes with peasants and religious subjects, such as the rising of Christ from the tomb while peasants with animals watched nearby. The Bassano family of which the father, Jacopo, was the best artist, were Venetians in the fine Venetian tradition.

The Genoese painter, Luca Cambiaso, although he barely gets into this period (1527-1585), was characterized by dark colors and a very subtle use of light. He was the leading painter of Genoa at one time, and from here went to Spain where he became Court painter to Philip II.

The Carracci family (Ludovico, Annibale, and Agostino) founded the Bolognese Academy, a School of far reaching influence. It was founded upon the principle that the best art is that which combines the best elements of the past: Raphael, Michelangelo, Correggio, and others. While the paintings of the Carraccis were good, they do not approach the greatness of those painters to whom they chose to aspire.

In recent years it has been considered that the Carracci Institute in some ways was related to twentieth century painting, and was a forerunner of modern Schools. For this reason the Carracci family has been undergoing a revival of interest.

The Milanese painter Caravaggio (1573 to 1609) was one of the most influential of all Italian artists on the Schools and artists who came later. He brought a realism into his art that had not been achieved earlier, and he developed the use of light and shadow to a degree never used prior to this time. In this development he influenced Rembrandt, Rubens, and Velàsquez, each one of these painters having no superior in his entire School of art.

CARAVAGGIO. *The Musicians.*
The Metropolitan Museum of Art, New York
(Rogers Fund, 1952)

Caravaggio's life was one of disorder and brawling. In one fight he killed a man and had to flee to Naples. From Naples he had to take flight to Sicily for the same type of offense.

The Genoese artist Castiglione was one of the few universal geniuses of any era. His skill in drawing was limitless, and while he is typified by his paintings of sheep in landscapes, he at the same time was a master in painting flowers, armor, figures and almost all other objects.

Pietro da Cortona was a Roman artist who lived from 1596 to 1669. He died the same year that Rembrandt did. While this topnotch painter was commissioned to do wall and ceiling paintings all over Europe, and some of his work is found in the great edifices, he is scarcely known in the United States, and few American museums have samples of his work.

The Bolognese painter Domenichino was a follower of the Carracci family and their assistant. While he was not up to them in quality of painting, he carries their advances in painting into the seventeenth century. His work is becoming better and better recognized in the twentieth century and more museums are seeking it.

The Neapolitan painter Luca Giordano (1632 to 1705) was known for his immense production of paintings, most of them altarpieces and other religious works. In all he produced perhaps 5000 paintings, and while he is highly respected as a painter, he copied the style of other artists so well that to some extent he can be considered a plagiarist.

Luca Giordano. *Holy Family.*
College of the City of New York

The Ferrarese painter Guercino combines the bright color of the Venetians with Caravaggio's use of light. He was a painter of many large pictures and, while for a time his paintings were not thought much of, in the middle of the twentieth century his works were again sought after.

Guido Reni is best known for his painting "Aurora." This is, or was, one of the most publicized of all paintings, especially in the early years of the twentieth century and during the 1920's. It was copied and reproduced again and again, and there was hardly a schoolboy of that period who was not familiar with it. Reni was a follower of the Carracci family and, at the time he painted, was considered a good painter and typical of the gracious spirit of his times. Later the spirit of the times changed, and he was considered over-sweet and sentimental.

Ribera, although a Spaniard and although patronized by Spain, was more of a Neapolitan painter than Spanish. He was a follower of Caravaggio. He painted religious subjects which inspired a feeling of devotion, especially saints on which the light fell in a most effective and well developed manner. This he learned from Caravaggio.

Salvator Rosa (1615 to 1673) was the Neapolitan painter of battle scenes and bright and action-filled landscapes. The colorful, dynamic landscapes that he produced have found adherents in the twentieth century, and particularly toward the middle of the century.

Bernardo Strozzi is one of the distinctly more important painters of the Italian Baroque. He was a Genoese painter, and is characterized by his portrayal of peasants and old men. His paintings are large, sometimes over life-size, with dramatic use of light and strong but restrained color. Most of his paintings are of a monumental size more suited to public display in museums and large halls than to private homes.

In the early 1800's, at the turn into the nineteenth century, Italian Baroque was the School to have, and large numbers of paintings of this School came into England. Later there was a decline in the popularity of this School, and only in the middle twentieth century has the School increased again in popularity. There are many artists in this School, and many of them are outstanding. Their quality does not vary as greatly as did the quality of the earlier artists, where the "greats" were a long way above the rest. In this period there was a tendency for art to seek a norm of ability, and while the era in general did not equal, even at its best, those earlier eras of Italian art, there were many very good artists who responded to the demand by more and more people for more paintings for their public buildings, their churches, and their homes.

The heyday of the Italian Baroque was about 1800. From that time until the Post-World War II period they were not in favor. Then a steady and rapid rise took place in their prices.

So many artists have been mentioned in this School because here more than in any other *quality* is what determines price, more so than name. It is difficult to tell in this period just who is best from a price point of view.

Only in the last few years of the decade of the 1950's have Baroque Italian paintings come to be featured by American auctions, and only recently have American auctions favored Baroque paintings and provided a good market for them. The English market recognized them a decade earlier and established a definite price differential for them which was above the American market.

In 1946 a Carracci (Agostino) brought £380, and in 1947 an Annibale Carracci brought £420 ($1531 and $1693 respectively).

In 1953 a Ludovico Carracci brought £1300 ($3640) and prices of the paintings of this family have risen steadily since that time.

During the war Salvator Rosa was not in demand. In 1948 one of his paintings sold for £94/10s. ($380). In the decade of the 1950's his prices rose to over £3000 ($8400).

In 1948 a Castiglione was sold for £540 ($2176). In 1958 one brought £3200 ($8960).

Guercino in 1950 sold for £52 and $150 in London and New York, respectively. In 1953 one brought £1900 ($5320) and Guercino prices have been rising.

In 1946 a Luca Giordano brought £147 ($592) and in 1957 £2100 ($5880).

This is the history of this School of art since World War II. It is characterized by a steady, rapid rise, with Baroque paintings beginning to be featured both by dealers and by the auction market, particularly toward the end of the decade of the 1950's. Baroque paintings, unlike the paintings of the earlier Italian Schools, are not scarce, but the more important paintings are rapidly disappearing from the market.

VI. *Eighteenth Century Painting*

First of all, the eighteenth century is the period of the great Canal painters, Canaletto, his pupil Guardi, and Bernardo Bellotto. While Canaletto painted beautiful pictures of Venice, its canals, its harbor and its churches and squares which make these paintings assets in the home, Guardi achieved a certain sketchy quality, which to a small degree relates his painting to the modern Schools. In a

FRANCESCO GUARDI. *View on the Cannaregio, Venice.*
National Gallery, Washington, D.C. (Kress Collection)

way these modern Schools refer back to this master and say, "See, he painted this way, and he was a Master."

Bernardo Bellotto painted with almost photographic accuracy, but whereas he portrayed detail as well as the camera, Guardi achieved something more—an individuality and the power to stimulate in the viewer the feeling, "How beautiful! Look at those little figures, at their strength."

Pannini painted at the same time and in the same vein, but his subject matter was architecture, and especially ruins. He was from Piacenza rather than from Venice, the home of the Canal painters, and he influenced the development of the style of these painters.

Let us go back to Venice to three painters who produced works in a similar style: Sebastiano Ricci, his nephew Marco Ricci, and Giovanni Battista Pittoni. These painters of altarpieces as well as other subjects are characterized by a certain peculiar stylized strength that gives their paintings an individual quality which makes them easily recognizable. The combination of uncle and nephew in the Ricci family was a good one, with Marco painting the landscapes into the paintings of Sebastiano. This uncle and nephew combination spread the Venetian style of the Baroque throughout the world and led to the Rococo or decorative, light-colored style of Tiepolo, a Venetian painter who lived from 1696 to 1770.

While Tiepolo seemed to concentrate on the same type composition of the Holy Family that the Ricci family and Pittoni produced, with figures on the ground and others in the heavens higher up in the picture, he has a strength and a force that placed him at the top of the painters of Venice of the eighteenth century. He also painted in light colors which offered a welcome contrast to the earlier predominantly dark Baroque backgrounds.

The Genoese painter Magnasco has an impressionistic quality which relates him to modern painting. His figures and landscapes, especially marine landscapes, are more fantastic than real. The skies seem to explode, belching forth storms. The sea consists of sparkling, mountainous waves, and the peculiarly drawn little figures often are depicted either straining at fishing nets or in devout prayer.

Some of the other important names of the eighteenth century are Francesco Solimena, Giovanni Battista Piazzetta and Pietro Longhi.

The eighteenth century is comparable with the Baroque period. It is not a period of major development in art. It rather represents a consolidation of the strides and innovations which were made up through the middle sixteenth century in Venice. Neither the Baroque nor the eighteenth century produced a genius like Leonardo or Michelangelo, although in many ways Caravaggio was a great pioneer.

TIEPOLO. *Apollo Pursuing Daphne.* National Gallery, Washington, D.C. (Kress Collection)

The outlines of quality painting had been laid down and the task was one of spreading what good had been developed. Painting was no longer the primary instrument of the Church or of the rulers of the various cities the way it once was. The patronage of the artists by these two groups fell off, and the honor in which artists were held declined. Under these conditions a certain mediocrity developed which was felt strongly after the eighteenth century in Italy.

The Eighteenth Century School can be broken down into two parts from a market and price point of view: (1) The Canal painters (Guardi and Canaletto) and (2) all the rest.

The Canal painters have long been in demand, primarily in England, but also in America. Some excellent Canalettos sold in 1928 for about $30,000 each. Thereafter their price fell to under $10,000 in the depression, then rose gradually until in 1955 the $30,000 pre-depression level was approximated. By the end of the decade the price of an important Canaletto was between $50,000 and six figures.

At the beginning of the period Guardi sold for about $7500. In the depression a fair price was $2500. Up to the war prices had reached the pre-depression level and by 1946 had excelled it, until 1955 when prices began to shoot up to the level of $50,000 at the end of the decade.

The rest of the Eighteenth Century Italian artists resemble the Baroque Italian painters of a century earlier both in price level and price behavior more than do the Canal painters. These other painters were generally not favored by the pre-war market either in America or in England. After the war, however, they came into favor, and even more so than the Baroque painters.

In 1939 a fair price for a Magnasco was $150 to $210, and in 1940 it rose to $400.

In 1954 £2300 was a fair price ($6440) and the level at the end of the decade was close to $10,000.

Sebastiano and Marco Ricci and Pittoni have a comparable price history, and in 1958 three Riccis sold for £3930, £6825 and £8400 ($11,172, $19,110 and $24,500 respectively).

In 1957 a Pittoni brought £6000 ($16,800), in 1958 £7200 ($20,160) and in 1960 £8200 ($22,960).

Like the Baroque artists, prices before the war are hard to obtain because the paintings of the eighteenth century were not enough featured by auctions to war-

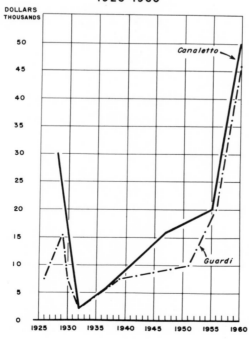

EIGHTEENTH CENTURY CANAL PAINTERS
PRICE HISTORY IN DOLLARS
1926-1960

rant photographs in the catalogues, and unless we have examined photographs of the paintings we have usually not recorded their price.

As with the Baroque School, there are also a number of eighteenth century Italian paintings on the market.

In the nineteenth century Italian art lost its outstanding, monumental and pioneering quality, and it is not until the twentieth century that Italian artists become prominent again, but then as members of the group of contemporary artists of the world rather than as distinctly Italian artists.

IX

American Art

I. *Portraitists*

SIDE FROM PRIMITIVE AMERICAN PAINTING, WHICH CONSISTED largely of portraits by unknown, itinerant "limners" who painted these portraits of the family for from twenty-five cents to two dollars each, the first American artist of real merit was Benjamin West (1738-1820). Prior to West's time the archaic style of art went along with the primitive farm furniture which is found so plentifully in New England and which has now become many a collector's choice. The furniture as well as the art was simple and sturdy and lacking in refinements. Our ancestors were concerned with mere existence in the early days. Art was a minor matter until they became more settled and prosperous and could find time for such luxuries. Still, these early paintings are America's primitive art and, being part of our heritage, today are growing in demand, particularly for decorative purposes, along with early American furniture. Examples can still be picked up for low prices.

In the 1560's, some 170 years before Benjamin West was born, the French artist Jacques Le Moyne, came to Florida to paint, and some years later the English artist, John White, became Governor of Sir Walter Raleigh's Virginia colony. The Swedish immigrant, Gustavus Hesselius (1682-1755), started painting in America in 1712. John Smibert (1688-1751) is a step ahead of these other artists in professional quality as was his follower, Robert Feke (c. 1705-1750). The house painter Joseph Badger (1708-1765) was a contemporary and competitor of Feke.

189

BENJAMIN WEST. *The Battle of La Hogue.* National Gallery, Washington, D.C.
(Purchase Fund Andrew W. Mellon Gift)

Benjamin West, born in 1738 in Pennsylvania, died in London in 1820 after spending most of his painting career in England where he taught many of our American artists, including Gilbert Stuart, Thomas Sully, Washington Allston, Charles Willson Peale, Rembrandt Peale, John Trumbull, and Samuel Morse, the last being a first-class artist in addition to being famous for the invention of the telegraph.

Although Benjamin West was an American, most of his painting life was spent in England; so we must go to another painter to find the more truly American artist: John Singleton Copley (1737-1815). As a portrait artist Copley was probably excelled by no one in this country. His subjects (in keeping with his aristocratic name) are usually of the socially prominent of Boston, Philadelphia, and New York. His style is conservative, and he was very popular up until the year 1774 when he left, on the eve of the American Revolution, for England. He felt the need to study abroad, possibly because he knew of the success of West in London. But this was a period of frustration for Copley, and he died a lonely old man in London with his work declining in quality, popularity, and vogue. His prices today, however, are about comparable to those of Stuart.

That brings us to the most famous name in American portraiture, Gilbert Stuart (1755-1828). When we think of George Washington we almost invariably think of Gilbert Stuart's portrait of Washington. Mark Twain once stated, "If Washington should rise from the dead, and not resemble the Stuart portrait, he would be denounced as an impostor."

CHARLES WILLSON PEALE.
Portrait of William H. Crawford.
Atlanta Art Association

GILBERT STUART. *Mrs. Richard Yates.*
National Gallery, Washington, D.C.
(Mellon Collection)

Stuart first tried his success in London, but over-drinking and an undisciplined life did not bring him fortune. He went to Ireland to paint in 1787, returning to America in 1793, where he accomplished what has made him immortal in American art: the portraits of George Washington. He made three Washington portraits from life. The third portrait, the Athenaeum portrait, is the most famous portrait of the President. He kept the unfinished original of this portrait and made many replicas from it. Some sources say there were 70 replicas made by Stuart of this portrait and 121 variations from the three originals.

"It was whispered about," Stuart explained, "that I fixed on Washington because I needed the money. How true! I was as broke as last year's bird's nest, but that isn't all. I believed that Washington was the greatest man in history, and I'm not too modest to say that I was the only artist capable of doing him justice."

These paintings have not only immortalized Stuart, but to some extent, have immortalized even the "Father of our Country."

In December, 1934, "Lady Liston" by Stuart, 29 by 24 inches, brought $20,000 and "Lord Liston," the companion portrait of the same size, brought $10,500. In February, 1945, "Sir Robert Liston" brought exactly $5,500, about half the price of 1934.

In October, 1949, a large Gilbert Stuart of George Washington, 94 by 58 inches, brought $17,500, and in April, 1952, a small George Washington, 30 by 25 inches, brought $12,000. Another George Washington, 25½ by 21½ inches, brought $4,300 in 1953 and still another, 27½ by 23 inches, brought £800 in 1957 ($2,240).

The trend of Gilbert Stuart has been down, and of all the Gilbert Stuarts the most generally favored are the George Washingtons. If a Stuart of George Washington is not thoroughly authenticated, it is of doubtful value. There were a number of fine replicas by Stuart, and many other artists had a chance to see and copy them over the years.

Thomas Sully (1783-1872), another student of West and another important name in American portraiture, lived a little later than Stuart and succeeded him as the most popular painter in America. While he was a good painter, he never achieved an individual style or skill sufficient to place him among the greatest of the world or even of the period.

Charles Willson Peale (1741-1827) was not only an eminent portrait artist himself, but so were his sons, Raphaelle and Rembrandt Peale. Charles Willson Peale's general admiration for art is indicated by the names of his children to whom he also taught art: Raphaelle, Rembrandt, Titian, Rubens and Angelica Kaufmann

THOMAS SULLY. *Lady with a Harp, Eliza Ridgely.*
National Gallery, Washington, D.C.
(Gift, Maude M. Vetleson)

CHARLES WILLSON PEALE. *Timothy Matlack.*
National Gallery, Washington, D.C.
(Mellon Collection)

Peale. He also taught his brother, James, to paint, and James had four children who were artists. Rubens Peale had a daughter who became an artist.

We go now to the Reconstruction Period for our next portraitist, Thomas Eakins, who lived from 1844 to 1916. He was one of our great American portraitists, a fine American genre painter and one of the most sought after American artists today. His paintings often bring over $15,000.

While all of the American portraitists up to this point in American history were influenced by the British School, Eakins studied in France and Spain, and represents a departure in painting from what might be considered American painting in the British style.

II. *Whistler and Sargent*

We now come to our two expatriates, Whistler and Sargent. James Abbott McNeill Whistler was born in Massachusetts in 1834 and died in 1903. Whistler was the great American experimental artist of this time. He not only influenced American art, but even opened the way for Impressionism and abstraction. Such an international influence cannot be claimed by very many American artists.

If any single painting is famous in America it is "Whistler's Mother." Strangely enough, although this painting is almost never referred to as anything but "Whistler's Mother" this was not the title Whistler gave it. It was "Arrangement in Grey and Black No. 1." Although it typifies American art of the period, it does not hang in an American gallery, but in the Louvre. The Louvre did loan the painting to the Metropolitan several years ago and many people enjoyed viewing it in the Metropolitan's entrance hall.

A few years ago a small New York auction house put up a Whistler drawing for sale. It was charcoal on brown paper, signed with Whistler's characteristic butterfly, and along with the sketch went a written attribution by the great authority on Whistler, Joseph Pennell. No one seemed interested in starting the bidding, and the auctioneer kept offering it at a lower and lower starting price. Finally he arrived at the point where he said, "Will anybody *have* it for ten dollars?" I gladly took it. How different this situation was from the 1920's when to many Americans the name Whistler was synonymous with "Art."

In the 1920's Whistler could generally be purchased for a few thousand dollars. In 1932 three Whistlers went for under $500. In 1935, "Nocturne; the Solent," 19¾ by 36¼, brought $12,000 and, in 1940, "Nocturne: in Black and Gold" brought $7,000. By 1945, and for the few succeeding years, the price level of Whistler was about $2,500. By 1958, "The Thames from Battersea Bridge"

SARGENT. *The Wyndham Sisters.*
The Metropolitan Museum of Art, New York
(Wolfe Fund)

WHISTLER. *The White Girl.*
National Gallery, Washington, D.C.
(Whittemore Collection)

brought $4,500. This same picture had sold in 1945 for $2,700. Whistler is experiencing a rise which, although it does not place him in the higher levels price-wise, may possibly be the beginning of a trend.

With John Singer Sargent (1856-1925) we arrive at an artist who has some present impact on the world market, although even in his case, not a really significant impact. His portraits of the great and near great of his time are brilliant pieces of painting. While he was under the influence of artists of the French School and studied the Old Masters of Spain, primarily El Greco and Velásquez, his style was his own. There is nothing dead or passive about his work. He enjoyed great popularity during his lifetime, but declined in favor in the '30's and '40's.

In 1929 the Metropolitan Museum purchased his large canvas, a portrait entitled "The Wyndham Sisters," for a reported $90,000. His prices plummeted in

1932 and 1933. By 1935, "Under the Willows," 27 by 22, brought $1,400 and "The Lady in Black," 31¾ by 23¼, brought $4300. From that time his prices were sporadically up and down and by 1945, "John Townsend, Esq.," 51 by 34½, reportedly once sold by Knoedler, brought $375 at auction.

In October, 1956, "Mlle. Dettan" brought $3,000; in 1958, "Pomegranites, Majorca" brought $2750 and in November, 1959, Sargent's "Monet's Garden at Giverney," a beautiful impressionist painting, brought $6250. Sargent's prices seem to have turned upwards, probably because of the affinity of Sargent at certain points in his painting history with Impressionism.

How different are these more recent prices from those brought back in July, 1925, in London, to liquidate his estate. Listed below are some of the auction prices:

	Pounds	Dollars
Side Canal in Venice (watercolor)	4830	23,329
Salute (watercolor)	3360	16,229
Doge's Palace (watercolor)	2415	11,664
Boats at Anchor (watercolor)	2100	10,143
San Vigilio	7350	35,500
Window in the Vatican	3150	15,215 bought by Sir Joseph Duveen
Church of the Jesuiti	3570	17,243 bought by Sir Joseph Duveen
Carmencita	5040	24,343
Simplon	4410	21,300

Sargent's paintings in this sale brought £182,585 ($881,885). The gem of the show and sale, "Mme. Gautreau," was withdrawn just before the sale, having been bought privately by Sir Joseph Duveen for the new wing which he was building for the Tate Gallery in London. This was the esteem in which Sargent was held.

III. *American Impressionists*

The leading American Impressionist is Mary Cassatt and while she came from a prominent Philadelphia family and her father was no less a typical American than a president of the Pennsylvania Railroad, she has been included with the French Impressionists. She lived and painted in France and was in most respects a product of French Impressionism except for some of her subject matter. She was fond of painting mothers and children, or children alone, and these were more American than the outdoor scenes usually chosen by the Impressionists.

Mary Cassatt's prices were about $2000 to $2500 in 1926. They did not drop during the depression. In 1930 five of her paintings brought at auction $4300, $4600, $5500, $8500, and $4800. By 1959 two of her paintings brought $26,000 and $39,000.

The next prominent American Impressionist is Childe Hassam. His paintings that appear on the market now, and command the highest prices, are landscapes of rural New York and New England, although he did a great many pictures of New York City that typify his era. He uses a bright pastel palette and has a delicate, typically impressionistic style.

From a price level of about $2500 in the 1920's, toward the end of the decade his prices dropped to $500. By 1935 his prices were again over $2000, but the war saw a slip in Hassam prices again to about the $1000 level, and only after 1950 did he show a marked rise.

After 1957 his prices rose from the $2500 level to $5500 for the "Stewart Mansion" in New York in 1959 and $8750 for "Brittany Cottage" in the same year. His fortunes price-wise in the 1950's were tied to the Impressionists.

Hassam studied in Paris at the Ecole des Beaux Arts under Boulanger and Lefebvre. Later he turned to Impressionism. Several other artists of American origin follow a similar line of artistic development:

1. Frank W. Benson   3. Gari Melchers, whose "Mother and Child"
2. Thomas W. Dewing   is on a par in excellence with Mary Cassatt.

MARY CASSATT. *Caresse Enfantine.*   CHILDE HASSAM. *Sunny Blue Sea.*
Smithsonian Institution   Smithsonian Institution

All of these three artists studied under the same Ecole des Beaux Arts teachers in Paris. Their similar training is responsible in some measure for their general similarity of style.

It is not stretching things too far to classify all these artists as American Impressionists, and in addition, the following:

4. Robert Reid whose "Violet Kimono" is an unusual and extremely pleasing figure painting in the Impressionist style.
5. Max Bohm.
6. John Henry Twachtman who painted landscapes vaguely reminiscent of Monet, as if the scene were viewed through a mist.
7. Henry Golden Dearth, a combination Impressionist and Post-Impressionist, who uses forms and bright contrasting colors to give a result that is something of a cross between Gauguin and Redon.
8. Frank Duveneck, the teacher of Twachtman. Although it is stretching a number of points to call Duveneck an Impressionist, he painted with a bold, firm style reminiscent of Manet and Cézanne. He attempted to produce a strong stroke, yet keep his modeling and clarity of line, like Hals, Rembrandt, and Velásquez.

In 1898 an exhibition was held entitled "Ten American Painters." These thereafter were known as "The Ten" and composed a kind of School. They were

GARI MELCHERS. *Mother and Child.*
Smithsonian Institution

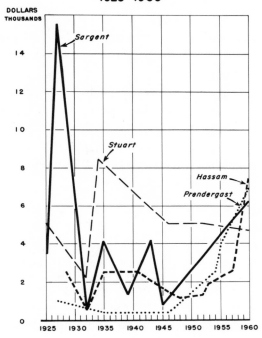

FOUR AMERICAN ARTISTS
PRICE HISTORY IN DOLLARS
1925-1960

Hassam, Benson, Dewing, Reid, and Twachtman, and in addition Joseph R. De Camp, Millard L. Metcalf, Edward Simmons, Edmund C. Tarbell, and J. Alden Weir.

It is interesting to note the report, *Christie's, 1766 to 1925,* prepared by H. C. Marillier, published in 1926. He says (page 249), "Nor does one hear much today of the later, 'Impressionist' Schools of England, France or Holland, with their 'Futurist' descendants. These still exist, but one seldom sees a concerted grouping of their works such as used to prevail at the Grafton Gallery."

How impossible this statement seems today when one of the "signs of the times" is the enormous prices of Impressionist paintings.

But one wonders when he looks at the many American Impressionists simply covering wall space of "The National Collection of Fine Arts" in the Smithsonian in Washington, with relatively few viewers, whether these will soon come back and perhaps be tied to the rising popularity of the European Impressionists. The American Impressionists are not distinctly inferior painters to the Frenchmen and other continentals.

IV. *The Ash Can School*

In 1907 a canvas by George Luks was rejected by the National Academy. This affront solidified a group of American painters, a dissident group who wanted to experiment with new styles of painting and new subject matter. They formed themselves into "The Eight."

When they were denounced because of the dreary subject matter that they used, alleys, pool halls, etc., one of them, John Sloan, replied, "You are right; we are the charter members of the Ash Can School of Art." This name has stuck with them ever since. Their opponents, however, tagged the group with an even more extreme name, "The Revolutionary Black Gang." Feeling at the time against them ran high, to say the least. The group included:

Maurice Prendergast	Ernest Lawson
William Glackens	Everett Shinn
Robert Henri	George Luks
John Sloan	Arthur B. Davies

The above are arranged in the order of market price as of the beginning of the decade of the 1960's. While $30,000 is not out of line for a Prendergast, Henri might range from $3500 to $8000, and $1000 might be a fair price for a Davies.

GEORGE LUKS. *The Miner.*
National Gallery, Washington, D.C.
(Dale Collection)

MAURICE B. PRENDERGAST. *Landscape with Figures.* Corcoran Gallery, Washington, D.C.

These eight were distinctly American painters. They were not imitators of the Europeans, or poor followers or hangers-on who could not quite make the grade. They painted American subjects as an American would paint them, and they captured the spirit of the country and of its bustling city life. Their locale was mainly New York.

Luks is known for his excellent action pictures, one of the most notable being "The Wrestlers," done in 1905. In all of his ringside pictures he gets the intense movement of the contestants, the struggle to win, and the spirit and kindred feelings of the ringsiders whose facial expressions and attitudes he caricatures. He painted life on the East Side of New York. For New Yorkers he captures the exact mood and feeling of the city, and particularly the feeling of the time.

In the George Luks sale at the Parke-Bernet Galleries in October, 1951, his paintings generally brought under $1000, and many brought under $500. In the years 1959 and 1960 prices were more realistically at the $5000 level.

About three years ago a drawing by Everett Shinn, one of his typical scenes of ballet dancers, could be bought at the sales office of a large Eastern museum for $200. For $200 or less one could have his choice of several sketches offered for sale. This price level is now long since past.

In 1959, "Trapeze Performer," a pastel, 17 by 20, brought $1500, and "Tightrope Walker," 24 by 18½, brought $2750. One of his paintings sold at auction for $4100.

While Luks gravitated to lowly and sordid scenes of the city, John Sloan painted in addition to the landmarks of Greenwich Village, views of New York's elevated trains, the famous old High Bridge from Manhattan to the Bronx (one of the only foot bridges left anywhere around the city) and other scenes, not only beautiful from an impressionistic point of view, but so much a part of the tradition of Big City life in the growing, onward-pushing America.

Of this group the most active artist in the art market today is Maurice Prendergast, known primarily for his watercolors, but also as an oil painter. Prendergast is usually classified as an Impressionist, and at one period of his productive life he did paint delicate, light-filled scenes reminiscent of the Impressionists. Later, however, he tended to flatten his pictures and painted characteristic little figures with heavy outlines which are less Impressionistic. It is this group of tapestry-like paintings that appears regularly on the market.

In 1927 "The Beach" and "Promenade" brought $1050 and $1400 respectively. By 1935 one of his pictures brought $625 and by 1937, $350. In 1942 one was sold for $250, and in 1944 two brought $500 and $350 respectively. As late as 1946, "Promenade," 13 by 19½, went for only $200, but by 1954, "Montparnasse," a watercolor, brought $1400, a relatively small picture, 13½ by 19¼. By 1955 "Sunset and Sea Fog," 18 by 29½, sold for $4400. In April, 1960, the Parke-Bernet Galleries sold a Prendergast for $7000. It must be pointed out that Prendergast has the distinctive style that makes his paintings easily recognized, and this recognition tends to raise prices. It is clear that Prendergast has been rising rapidly, unlike a good many others in the American School, and now will bring at retail over $30,000.

V. *The Landscapists*

Among the first names we think about when American art is mentioned is Winslow Homer. He is best known to us for his scenes of fishermen on the Grand Banks from his Maine period in art and for his West Indies scenes, as, for example "The Gulf Stream," the painting of the broken fishing boat, sailless and mastless, manned by a tattered Negro lying on deck, the boat in churning seas surrounded by sharks. The subject matter and painting quality represent the strength of the natural elements which Homer depicted so well.

In the late 1920's Homer's paintings were in the low four figure range, and from here declined to the under-$1000 level in the early '30's. In 1949, a watercolor, 20¾ by 29¾, entitled "A Voice from the Cliffs," brought at auction $12,000. In 1953, a small painting entitled "School Time," 13 by 19¼, brought $5400, but as of 1960, $35,000 for his bright, small, typically American scenes, was about the retail market. It is known that $125,000 was refused for an im-

WINSLOW HOMER. *Breezing Up*. National Gallery, Washington, D.C.
(Gift, W. L. and May T. Mellon Foundation)

portant, large Homer. Homer was the highest priced American artist at the end
of the '50's, his water scenes bringing the top figures.

The second landscapist we will look at is George Inness. A painting that
typifies most of Inness's work is the large canvas in our National Gallery entitled
"The Lackawanna Valley." The Pennsylvania countryside and that of New York
State were typical of the subjects Inness chose for rendering. It is a beautiful,
natural landscape with a train puffing up the hill, done in a realistic style.

As Inness progressed in his art he took on elements of the Barbizon School of
France and especially the tonality and ethereal qualities of Corot. This type of
landscape is obviously not the realistic landscape of "The Lackawanna Valley."
Both types of landscape appear on the market, and this decided difference in

GEORGE INNESS. *The Lackawanna Valley*. National Gallery, Washington, D.C.
(Gift, Mrs. Huttleston Rogers)

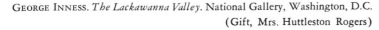

style would be unusual in one artist were it not for the fact that the possibly greatest British landscapist, John Constable (1776 to 1837), also painted two distinct
types of landscape: one extremely realistic and the other sketchy and decidedly
impressionistic in style, although of course, Constable much preceded the Impressionists.

In the 1920's, Inness's paintings brought prices in the medium four figure
range. They could be bought for as low as $1000, but in 1929 "The Coming
Shower" brought $8100.

Although in 1932 and 1933 his paintings were at the $500 level, "St. An-
drew's," 32 by 42, brought $4100. In the '30's many of his paintings still brought
under $1000, but in 1943 the level of the 1920's was apparently again achieved,
when three of his paintings brought $10,000, $8000 and $4700. From this point
on, there was a general lack of interest by the art market in his paintings, and
fine examples have gone for under $1000. In October, 1959, "Medfield Oak"
brought $3300. This price was high for Inness as of that time, and possibly rep-
resented a strengthening in his prices.

Albert Bierstadt was one of the popular painters of nineteenth century America. His was a characteristic locale: Yosemite Park, the Rocky Mountains, the
California Redwoods. A typical scene is of a mountain forest with tall trees, a
pool, and a bear drinking in the pool. These typically American scenes brought in
the late 1800's sums in five figures. Bierstadt then went out of style, and only in
the last ten years has there been a revival of interest in him. Whereas he was out
of favor in the first half of this century, toward the end of the 1950's he again
rose to the four-figure level, although not to the five-figure level. His quality,
particularly in his small paintings, is excellent.

ALBERT BIERSTADT. *The Buffalo Trail*. Corcoran Gallery, Washington, D.C.
(Gift, Mr. and Mrs. Lansdell K. Christie)

Thomas Moran used as his locale almost the same area that Bierstadt did, Yellowstone, the Grand Canyon, and Yosemite Park. Like Bierstadt he painted large canvases exhibiting considerable skill in rendering subjects realistically.

The Encyclopedia of Painting describes the paintings of Moran in this way: "His later huge canvases . . . achieved, like those of Bierstadt, a monumental dullness."

This was the feeling in the early twentieth century about both Bierstadt and Moran and about the so-called Hudson River School which painted views of the Hudson River and the nearby Catskill Mountains. The group fell into disfavor. But times change, and art opinion likewise changes, and these artists are now showing some strength in the market. Large Bierstadts are no longer a drug on the market, and art critics are wiping their glasses for a new look.

VI. *The Prairie Painters*

Frederic Remington (1861 to 1909) is the great painter of the American West with its pioneering spirit and its action, including Indian warfare. Remington himself went West as a cowboy and later became a rancher. He knew the life and everything that it involved in the way of toil, strife, and struggle, and these scenes become alive on his canvases. His paintings bring in the neighborhood of $8,000 to $30,000, and there is a preference and an active and rising demand for them in the market of the late 1950's and early 1960's.

REMINGTON. *An Indian Scout.*

Charles M. Russell lived in the same era of American history—the development of the Frontier (1865 to 1926). Russell's paintings are in the same vein, employ the same subjects, and are in a similar, precise style. Russell brings prices nearer the $5000 level, but he too has shown an increase in prices in the last five years of the decade of the 1950's.

VII. *American Scene Painters*

This is the usual descriptive title used in connection with those American classic painters of the 1930's who depicted the American scenes and life at about this period.

Thomas H. Benton started to paint the American countryside after World War I, and developed the movement toward mural painting of American scenery. This period followed his experimentation with Cubism and with other forms of modern art at the time. He painted in the East, but in the 1930's left for the West and pictured beautifully the wide open spaces on his canvases.

Grant Wood is best known for his typically American, somewhat amusing painting entitled, "The Daughters of the American Revolution." Although the ladies have a certain dogmatism in their demeanor, they are quaint and heartwarming rather than the object of any biting satire on the part of the artist. Grant Wood's "American Gothic" is another picture well known to most of us, of an

GRANT WOOD. *Hired Girl.*
Parke-Bernet Galleries, Inc.

MOSES. *The Picnic.* Courtesy Parke-Bernet Galleries, Inc.

old-time American farmer with pitchfork in hand standing by his wife. Both are middle-aged, solid, honest, puritanical-looking people. These pictures, while a commentary on life in America, are representative of the solid American heritage and typify a new era of homespun American art.

In 1952 Grant Wood's "The Radical," a crayon drawing, brought $900, and "The Good Influence" brought $1400. In 1959 "Spilt Milk" brought $3750 and "Hired Girl" was sold for $4250. His prices in the decade had risen substantially. This is a distinctive artist painting in his characteristic and typically American style.

John Steuart Curry was a third member of this "American Scene Painter" group. He became famous for the painting done in his locale entitled "Baptism in Kansas." Curry was born on a Kansas stock farm and he depicted the life around him with considerable insight into the spirit of the times.

Anna Mary Robertson Moses (Grandma Moses) is one of the phenomena of our times. She started to paint at age seventy-six when most people have long since retired. In 1938 three of her paintings were displayed in the Museum of Modern Art, and in 1939 she had her first One-Man Show. She was born in the year 1860 and since her seventy-sixth birthday has produced two thousand paintings. These are in the primitive American tradition, and although she is certainly not formally included in the "American Scene Painters," she paints the American scene as few people ever could. Her paintings being primitive in quality are decidedly lacking in perspective, but they are heart-warming, bright, and cheery. The titles of some of her works sold in the past ten years indicate her subject matter as well as her unique spirit: "School Days," "Sugaring Off," "Whoa, There," "Winter is Here," and "Horses, Horses."

207

RYDER. *Pastoral Study.*
Smithsonian Institution

In 1950 the "Village of Hoosick Falls" sold for $1300, and in 1953 "School Days" brought $925. There was a general increase in her prices until in 1960 "The Picnic" sold for $4100.

Grandma Moses is a factor in the market. There is a substantial demand for her paintings, and there are enough of them to give some liquidity to the market and at the same time provide a reasonably stable price level.

One final artist should be mentioned before we leave the American School, and he does not seem to fit into any category: Albert Pinkham Ryder. Ryder lived from 1847 to 1917. He produced interpretations of romantic literary themes, moonlit seascapes, and landscapes. Some of his religious themes have a strange quality about them. The painting of the figures is not precise, but it is done masterfully. While he does not use bright colors, he gets strength into his themes through the use of contrasting quiet tones and a unique enamel-like quality which was apparently the result of careful painting and repainting of the surface plus many coats of varnish. Probably the best collection of Ryder's paintings is in the National Collection of Fine Arts in Washington. Some of these paintings have gone beyond the normal stage of delicate cracking in fine lines (these lines are known as "crackle") Various parts of Ryder's paintings seem to have separated in abnormally large cracks almost as though they had exploded.

Ryder's "Death on a Pale Horse" is in the Cleveland Museum and is an example of the eerie quality of his paintings. It is an "in memoriam" painting to a friend of his, a waiter, who bet all his savings on a pale horse which did not win, with the result that the waiter committed suicide.

His "Forest of Arden" causes one much pause. The painting has excellent quality as far as composition goes, excellent colors, fine rendition of light, good perspective, and a feeling of space (the space composition that the Renaissance Italians strove so hard to achieve). It has certain indistinct qualities, such as the Impressionists produced, but it is not an Impressionist picture. It has the monumentality and indistinct brushwork of some of Bassano's work done almost 400 years before in the great Middle Sixteenth Century Venetian School, yet the colors are fairly bright and may have been influenced by the Impressionists.

Although Ryder left about 150 paintings, he was copied more than any artist with the exception of Corot. It is reported that one collector possessed no fewer than 2400 Corots, all fakes. One sees many so-called Ryders in the smaller auctions in New York, but it is difficult to be sure of the genuineness of these without great detailed study of each painting offered for sale.

Time has dulled the paintings of Ryder, but under the old varnish there may well be the art of one of the great modern geniuses.

In 1946 Ryder's "Siegfried and the Rhine Maidens" brought $23,500. This was very high for Ryder at the time, but the painting was of museum quality and was destined for a museum. Since that time he has appeared rarely, if at all, on the market, and the existence of so many fakes has made a Ryder painting a questionable commodity.

RYDER. *Siegfried and the Rhine Maidens.*
National Gallery, Washington, D.C.
(Mellon Collection)

American Painting in Summary

The spirit of every country is reflected in all of its aspects, including its artistic productions. This statement is as true of America as it is of any other country. Ever since its founding America has been a pioneering land.

We have been intent, since the unification of the country under the Constitution in 1789, on developing our resources and building the Number One industrial machine in the world.

It must also be remembered that the Industrial or Economic Revolution began in about 1795, not only in the United States, but throughout Western civilization. The emphasis has been on material things, on the increase of wealth through capitalistic methods of production.

With this background let us remember that the first American artists of note were Benjamin West who lived from 1738 to 1820, and John Singleton Copley who lived from 1737 to 1815.

Art in America began at a time when the American economic machine was just starting, as were the economic systems of the other major industrial countries. The premium was on work, innovation, invention, new forms of business organization to enable the resources of the country to be developed. Art was somewhat out of tune with the aims and objectives of the times. By many Americans of pioneering spirit art was considered a kind of play and not real work at all, a sort of pastime for somewhat idle people. Certainly public attention was not focused on the development of art as a major or even a minor American goal.

By the time Benjamin West and John Singleton Copley were born, the development of the Italian art of the Renaissance had run its course. Even the great Venetian School of Titian, Veronese and Tintoretto was nearly two centuries old. The Seventeenth Century Dutch art of Rembrandt and Hals was nearly a century old.

There was no foundation of painting in America on which our artists could build, and there was no tradition and no standard of excellence. We could only look to Europe for our pattern. Whereas the pre-Revolutionary well-to-do American families often patterned their lives and appearance after the British aristocrats, the post-Revolutionary Americans became hard working, rugged individualists, and "British style" portraits did not so much appeal to this type of person.

Then, too, America was far from Europe. It took a great deal of time and money for the young student to go abroad to study, and there was little means of earning a livelihood when the artist arrived in Paris or London and wanted to pursue his studies.

Although many of our young artists did go abroad to study, as was considered necessary until recently, we did not develop a new School of art until our artists "discovered" America. When they turned for their inspiration and subject matter to our city streets, our Western plains and our American heritage, the canvases came alive with their sincerity and our American Art Renaissance was inaugurated.

Today we have more museums than any other nation, and the artist, whose profession was not held in such high esteem in this country some years back, is now respected and lauded. We sincerely want to understand his aims.

Without this support, so prevalent today, our American art could not figure importantly in the world art markets, even with such able artists as Stuart, Sargent, and Ryder. In the past it has lacked the backing and milieu to develop properly, but today's new interest in art has developed along with new forms of art, new techniques, and new Schools of which Americans are becoming a part. American art, past and present, is increasing in importance, a fact which should not be overlooked by the collector.

X

Why the Uptrend in Art

HERE IS NO DOUBT THAT THE DEMAND FOR ART IS GROWING RAP-idly, and that prices are on a rising curve. We must look for an explanation for the increase in both sales and prices to the two sides of the market: demand and supply. This is the standard analysis of any product or industry.

Every so often over the past decade the sale of a painting has been written up in the newspapers. The reason for the write-up is generally the high price at which the painting sold, especially compared with what the paintings of the particular artist sold for in the past. Each news item has shown the rise which took place in the prices of the artist's works or in his School of painting over the past several years, and to a considerable extent the tone of the articles has been the same as those relating to the spectacular rise in some security traded on the Stock Exchange.

The basic factor on the demand side of the painting market is a consciousness of art which is penetrating deeper and deeper into the public mind and becoming more and more a part of our life and culture. A great factor responsible for this consciousness is the increasing volume of books on art, all the way from $.39 books to one volume for $35. Art stores now usually have a counter or section devoted to art books, and there is hardly a Sunday paper which comes out without a Supplement, Magazine Section or Book Review Section that does not feature art. More and more people are becoming aware of paintings, artists, Schools of art, and what Schools are in vogue.

Art is becoming an ever more important part of our intellectual life. There is a definite movement toward art and antiquities. The great sales increase of art shops, antique stores, second hand stores and art auctions since the war testify to this fact. When one traces the publications in the home and decoration fields for the last decade he cannot help but be impressed by the increasing employment of paintings, especially Old Master paintings, and genuine European antiques, including those of the Renaissance period.

It is only necessary to go back to the depression years of the thirties and the immediate post-depression years to see the greatly changed attitude toward art and antiquities.

In the United States the Roosevelt Administration, and the forces behind it which put it into office and which gave it its strength, emphasized reform. It attempted to raise the living standard of the poor and limit the income of the rich. What the rich stood for and their attributes went out of favor in this era, and one of the attributes of wealth to go out of fashion first was the use in the home of old paintings in gold frames.

One of the most sought after items in the art trade today is the tabernacle frame, which was often put on Italian paintings of the early fifteenth and sixteenth centuries. To some extent a tabernacle frame looks like a miniature carved wood mantlepiece with side columns. A genuine period tabernacle frame in excellent condition can command a price in four figures at the present time.

One of the art dealers in lower New York remembers the time when this type frame had to be thrown away since no one wanted it. He also remembers in the depression when he could purchase whole collections of antique paintings at a cost of just a little more than nothing, so that almost anything he sold them for was profit.

In the depression and post-depression years "functionalism" was in vogue, an attitude toward art and decoration that emphasized simple line, simple form and no ornamentation. In automobiles chrome trim, radiator ornaments, Continental spare wheels, tires on the outside and elaborate bumpers were out. One proud occupant of a small apartment pointed out that the vogue was large flat surfaces of wall completely unbroken by paintings, or by anything else, for that matter, and his apartment met these standards.

With this emphasis on lack of decoration, and since art objects were an attribute of the rich and consequently taboo, the art market was relatively limited.

All through history there are alternate periods of art consciousness and periods in which art is very nearly dead.

King Charles I of England, who reigned from 1625 to 1649, did more to promote art than any other British king, before or since. He established art in England. Prior to his reign there were no good collections. His own collection was one of the finest the world has ever seen.

When Charles I was beheaded, Oliver Cromwell, who took over the British government, disposed of Charles' collection. It glutted the market for years, and since it was the only collection of real note in the country and was dispersed, the result was a deadening effect on art collecting in England and possibly in the entire Western world. In England collecting lay dormant for 100 years, and what little collecting was done was confined to Dutch and Flemish paintings, there being little market for Italian paintings. It is ironical that in the London of today there is little trading in Old Master Italian paintings either, and the emphasis is on Dutch. But the difference is that early Italian pictures today are in such great demand that there are very few on the market.

During the Napoleonic conquests, from 1795 to 1815, there was a tremendous influx of French paintings into England to escape the pillage and destruction which went along with the establishment of the new order. As Napoleon's ambitions grew and extended to other countries, the noble families of Italy began to send their paintings to England, partly through fear, partly in the interest of economy.

The newly built princely mansions of the British nobles were in that era just being completed, and to the Gainsboroughs, Reynolds, and Romneys which were finding a place as decorations for these mansions by a newly enlightened Britain, there were added splendid Dutch and Italian paintings. England's isolation from possible invasion, and the new interest in purchase of art resulted in an influx of art works which provide much of the stock of art now appearing on the international art market.

This demand for paintings to decorate the homes of the wealthy British families spread, after the turn of the twentieth century, to America, whose industrialists and financiers, including Mellon, Frick, Morgan, Widener and Kress, primed with the profits obtained in new industries in a new land, were able to outdo the European collectors in their pursuit of works of art.

The truly modern home today is a home of elegance, and a part of the elegance is becoming more and more the province of antiques and paintings, both of the new Schools and Old Masters.

A study of interior views of modern homes year by year since the war reveals a distinct trend to art and art objects as decor. The demand for these objects comes either directly from the home owner or from the interior decorator, or from the home magazines through their influence on the homemaker who reads them to find out the latest thing to do to be in style.

The next major factor on the demand side of the art market is the influence of the increasing importance of the Schools of art in greatest vogue at the present time—the Impressionists and French Moderns. The spectacular rise in prices of these Schools has led to the idea that such paintings might be a good investment. The news does not fall on unseeing eyes that Paul Mellon, the Pittsburgh banker, purchased a painting for over $600,000, or that Henry Ford II purchased a Renoir for $200,000, or that Nelson Rockefeller sold a Braque for $145,000.

"These are the wealthiest families of the country. They must know what they are doing financially. They have an eye on the investment value of anything."

So the thinking of those watching these transactions goes. "Why then don't I do the same thing, and maybe it will be a smart investment for me too?"

More and more of the purchasers of art have an eye on the investment value of art. There is a good deal of evidence that at times art objects move beyond investment to pure speculation. One successful industrialist from the South purchased over $150,000 worth of paintings on credit, giving notes due within a year in payment, with the idea that he could sell the paintings at a profit before the notes came due, thus realizing a fine return on a minimum of invested capital.

There is also evidence that syndicates have been formed to buy up the paintings of a particular artist, then publicize the artist, show collections of his paintings in various places and sell the paintings when the prices of the particular artist rise far enough.

Paintings have long been symbols of the rich, and their ownership identifies the possessor with the rich to some extent. This is a very strong motive for the purchase of paintings and a factor in the market not to be ignored.

Behind the desire to purchase a painting and behind the many and varied motives for its purchase in the art market there must be the wherewithal to purchase, the economic power to make the desire effective.

The decade of the '50's represented a period not just of prosperity but of economic boom. Such an era creates a surplus of income over outgo for an ever-increasing segment of the population, a fund of free investable cash. As individual income goes up, and after the primary needs of life for food, clothing, shelter, and necessary recreation have been met, investable funds grow disproportionately.

The effect of these funds on the stock market in the fifties was obvious, when prices were driven so high by the pressure of investable dollars that yields were ridiculously low. The only justification for buying stocks became a further appreciation which would result in a capital gain.

As yields drop and the level of the stock market rises this market becomes progressively less attractive to funds seeking outlets. One of the possible investments for these funds is paintings, and this aspect of paintings has not been overlooked by the intelligent investor. At least one foreign corporation invested its free funds in paintings while waiting for other normal business uses for the funds. There is a little evidence that corporate collections of paintings in the United States may have been accumulated at least with a corner of the corporate eye on the value of the collection from an investment point of view, and this corporate collecting program will be gone into in detail later.

When the pressure of inflation grows, and the dollar is worth progressively less, the pressure grows on the individual to put his funds into something which will not go down in value as prices rise. Paintings are one possibility, and in the 1950's the painting market rose considerably faster than the price level.

A final factor in the demand for paintings is "Goldmining." The news of great discoveries, whether real or fancied, has had its effect on many people, and there is a certain segment of buyers intent on discovering a Rembrandt or a Leonardo. One of the dealers on Third Avenue in New York reports that after every piece of news of the discovery of an Old Master painting he immediately experiences an increased interest in the wares of his shop. He states that it is not at all unusual for someone to come into his place of business and ask in all seriousness if he has a Leonardo da Vinci for sale. As we will see, however, some genuine discoveries of lost works of art have been made that are almost unbelievable.

The other side of the art market is the supply of paintings, and the interaction of the available supply with the demand is responsible for the present level of prices. It will immediately become obvious why the supply side of the market for paintings is like the supply side of no other commodity and has a most peculiar long run effect on price. The supply of the product of the art industry is *absolutely* limited. There is a fixed supply, and as more of this fixed supply is purchased, there remains progressively less to be purchased. The remaining demand must be satisfied out of this absolutely limited *and* decreased supply. The only segment of the art market which is an exception to this rule is the Contemporary and living artist segment which is producing now. This market will be discussed separately.

In the year 1939 the new building of the Museum of Modern Art was opened. Since that recent date literally hundreds of museums have been established throughout the United States and throughout the world. In the year 1959 the Frank Lloyd Wright-designed Guggenheim Museum in New York was opened, and to some extent this collection is of the same Schools as the Museum of Modern Art. In April, 1956, the North Carolina Museum was opened. In 1959 the Birmingham, Alabama Museum completed its own building and moved out of its shared quarters. These are only a few examples of the tremendous postwar growth in museums, not only in the United States but world-wide.

Throughout a significant part of the postwar period the Kress Foundation, established by S. H. Kress—an excellent collector—purchased paintings in the market and was engaged in the establishment of collections of paintings in various museums throughout the country. It is possible that the Foundation has invested as much as $75,000,000 in paintings, including Mr. Kress's original collection, and most of these paintings have been distributed to 20 museums around the United States, including Washington's National Gallery.

The significant thing about the growth of museums in every part of the land and the world, and the increased activities of already existing museums, is not alone that they purchase paintings in the market, but that they remove forever from the art market the paintings that they purchase. As a rule with very few exceptions, when a museum buys a painting, that painting seldom leaves the museum's collection. It is off the market forever. The extent of this purchase and permanent removal is great.

To cite one example of museum purchases, the National Gallery of Victoria in Melbourne, Australia between July, 1958, and July, 1959, purchased 21 oil paintings, including "Calvary" by Jan Brueghel, and the "Finding of Moses" by Sebastiano Ricci, both important paintings by anyone's standards. During the same period there were five oil paintings donated to the museum, including a valuable marine painting by Willem van de Velde (Seventeenth Century Dutch artist), "The Quarters, Alresford Park" and "Three Cloud Studies," both by Constable.

For the year 1959 the Montreal Museum of Fine Arts purchased seven eighteenth century or earlier paintings and drawings, two Contemporary European paintings, and 24 Canadian items, mostly oil paintings, a very sizable purchase in any one year.

The Manchester City Art Galleries in England in the year 1956 bought five oil paintings and received as gifts and bequests three oil paintings.

For the year 1957-1958 the Los Angeles County Museum listed among its important acquisitions the following:

Delacroix: "Henry IV Giving the Regency to Marie de Medici"—purchased.

Orozco: "Mexican Landscape"—gift of Mr. Feldman.

Pissarro: "Shepherds in the Field"—gift of Arnold S. Kirkeby.

Lorenzetti: "Madonna Enthroned with the Christ Child"—gift of the art firm of Rosenberg and Stiebel.

Corot: "Wooded Landscape"—gift of Count C. C. Pecci-Blunt.

Goya: "Portrait of la Marquesa de Santa Cruz"—purchased.

Bernard Buffet: 7 paintings—gift of Julian J. and Jean Aberbach.

London's Tate Gallery for the year 1958-1959 acquired no fewer than 60 works. A gift of Mrs. A. F. Kessler included a Daumier, a Degas, three Dufys, a Matisse, two Modiglianis, two Picassos, two Renoirs, and a Toulouse-Lautrec.

Another way to determine the influence on the art market of purchases of paintings by museums is to see where the best auction items went.

A Romney portrait group of the Leigh family is now in the National Gallery of Victoria, Melbourne, Australia and Picasso's "La Belle Hollandaise," the highest priced painting by a living master sold at auction, went to the Queensland Museum. These items were both highlights of the 1958-1959 Sotheby's season. The Picasso brought the huge price of £55,000 ($155,100).

In the Sotheby 1957-1958 season a Pittoni "Rest on the Flight into Egypt" went to the National Gallery in London, and Rubens' "Meeting of Abraham and Melchizedek" is now in the National Gallery in Washington.

At Christie's London auction after the war and up to the year 1958 no fewer than 21 of the most important paintings sold went to museums, and this represents a large proportion of the total number of all important works sold to both museums and private purchasers. This group of museum purchases includes:

Batoni—"Portrait of Peter Beckford"—Statens Museum, Copenhagen ....$ 4,116
Crespi—"Rest on the Flight into Egypt"—City Art Gallery, Bristol 5,000
M. le Nain—"Family Dinner"—Toledo, Ohio Museum of Art 11,848
Murillo—"Rest on the Flight into Egypt"—Art Institute, Detroit 13,541
Gainsborough—"Harvest Wagon"—Barber Institute, Birmingham 82,514
Rembrandt—"Self Portrait"—Glasgow Art Gallery and Museum 52,894
O. Gentilleschi—"Rest on the Flight into Egypt"—City Museum, Birmingham.... 2,116
van Dyck—"Rinaldo and Armida"—County Museum, Los Angeles 19,465
Bellini—"St. Jerome"—Barber Institute 19,465
Rembrandt—Sheet of Studies—Barber Institute 15,456
Winston Churchill—"Blue Sitting Room"—Sao Paulo Fine Arts Museum 4,828
William Blake—"Job Confessing"—National Gallery of Art, Edinburgh 28,593
Pieter Brueghel the Elder—"View on Rhine"—Pierpont Morgan Library 18,228
Constable—"Salisbury Cathedral"—Huntington Library and Art Gallery 60,270
Richard Wilson—"Ponte Mario"—Huntington Library 1,411
van Dyck—"Ecce Homo"—Barber Institute 23,520

Matisse—"Portrait of André Derain"—Tate Gallery 19,693
Sickert—"Old Heffel, the Fiddler"—Dunedin Art Gallery, Auckland, N.Z. 3,234
Romney—"Maj. Gen. James Stuart"—Scottish Nat. Portrait Gallery, Edin. 8,820
Salvator Rosa—"L'Umana Fragilita"—Fitzwilliam Museum, Cambridge 9,408
Castiglione—"Angel Appearing to Shepherds"—City Museum, Birmingham 9,408

In a later chapter we will look at the results of a broad survey of what the American art museums have been purchasing in recent years.

Let us next look at the total number of paintings by a particular artist either actively on the market or potentially on the market, and by potentially is meant those paintings which are in private hands but which a high enough price might bring onto the market.

Jan Vermeer of Delft is an excellent example. There are 36 Vermeers in existence, more or less. There may be others which are unrecorded in private collections, and there may be added to the total some that hang in museums which are not recognized by all authorities as Vermeers, but there are 36 which are generally recognized as being by the Master.

The painter died in 1675. In 1741, 36 of his paintings were in private hands. None was in a museum. Not all of these were known, and not all by any means were labeled Vermeer. Nevertheless, all of them were in private hands.

In the year 1742 one painting went into a museum—"Lady Reading a Letter at an Open Window." It was bought in Paris for the Dresden Picture Gallery by the Legation Secretary of Saxony. It has been catalogued as a Vermeer, however, only since 1862. Prior to that time its true authorship was unknown.

Twenty more years passed before another Vermeer went into a public gallery.

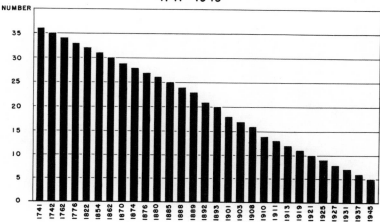

PAINTINGS BY VERMEER STILL IN PRIVATE HANDS
1741 - 1945

The "Lady and Gentleman at the Virginals" was bought by Richard Dalton for King George III as a Frans Mieris and went into Buckingham Palace.

The third Vermeer went into a gallery in 1776, 15 years later.

Forty-six years went by before another Vermeer went into a museum—in 1822. This was the great "View of Delft" bought by the Dutch government and now in the Mauritshuis in the Hague. The price was a pittance—2900 florins.

Thirty-two years later, in 1854, the "Woman in Blue Reading a Letter" was bequeathed to the City of Amsterdam and is now in the Rijksmuseum in that city.

In 1862 a painting that had been bought in a lot of 268 pictures in 1741 and identified as a Vermeer of Utrecht, rather than a Vermeer of Delft, was correctly identified by the Dresden Picture Gallery.

One hundred and eighty-seven years after the death of the painter, and just 100 years ago, 30 Vermeers were still in private hands and only six in museums.

By the turn of the century 18 Vermeers were still in private hands. By the post-war period only five paintings out of the total of 36 were still in private hands. All the rest were in museums. All of the demand for Vermeers had to be satisfied, and still has to be satisfied, out of this total of five paintings, and it is not at all certain that any substantial portion of these, if any at all, are for sale.

The tightness of the market for Vermeers and their ever-climbing prices led to the greatest of all art swindles—the van Meegeren forgeries that focused the attention of the world on art and threw a bombshell into the center of the world of art experts. The story will be told later.

Vermeer illustrates the phenomenon of the change in popularity in the Schools of art. The great Seventeenth Century Dutch artists are nearly priceless. So are the

JAN VERMEER. *View of Delft.* (Detail) Maurithuis, The Hague

great names in fifteenth and early and middle sixteenth century Italian art. The Flemish Primitives are even higher, if that is possible, and they are so rare as to be virtually nonexistent.

The buying public must thus turn to other Schools of art, at least to those in which there are paintings available for purchase. This is at least a partial explanation of the change in public taste and the boom in Impressionists, Post-Impressionists, French Moderns and Central European Expressionists.

The art industry, especially the nonliving Masters segment, can never be like the steel industry with its periods of under-capacity operations or like the railroad industry with its permanent decline in demand. The supply of paintings is almost a fixed supply, and each year a sizable portion of this fixed supply goes permanently off the market into museums.

Several countries have devised ways to see that this situation continues. Italy requires an export permit from the Fine Arts Commission, and every painting for which an export permit is required is examined by a group of experts. If the experts decide the painting is a national treasure the Fine Arts Commission may purchase it from the person desiring the export permit for the price he paid for it.

I bought a painting in Rome in the fall of 1959. Finally, after much official study, an export permit was granted, but the Commission raised the value of the painting to two-and-one-half times the actual purchase price before applying the export tax, which tax in itself is a deterrent to the export of these art treasures. Similarly France has an export control system, and England applies controls to the more expensive paintings.

In the United States a tax inducement is offered to get good paintings into our museums. The donor of a painting to a museum is allowed to deduct the present appraised value of his painting or other work of art up to a total of 20 per cent of his income before application of the Federal income tax. If his income against which the tax is applied is $100,000, he can deduct a painting or other work of art up to an appraised value of $20,000 (20 per cent of the $100,000). He then pays tax on only 80 per cent of his income or $80,000, an obviously lower tax than he would have to pay on $100,000.

There are no doubt many owners of art objects who paid under $5000 for French Modern or Impressionist paintings who can now have their paintings appraised at much over this figure—say $50,000. If they ran the risk of auctioning the painting they might not get $50,000 less the auction fee, but let us assume that their net was $40,000. If they paid $5000 for the painting their net profit on the transaction would be $35,000, on which they would pay roughly 25 per cent capital gains tax, or $8750, leaving $26,250, the net in-pocket on the transaction.

If the donor is in the 90 per cent tax bracket he can donate the $50,000 painting and instead of paying the 90 per cent tax of $45,000 on his last $50,000 of income, he saves this tax of $45,000 and is thus better off. In the same way many states have made provisions for allowances in their personal income tax structure for such contributions.

Finally, in order to encourage art collecting, there is a provision that antique works of art may be brought into the country duty-free, and this provision is a tremendous stimulus to the growth of art museums as well as private collections in this country.

The growing consciousness on the part of the public in regard to art, the use of art as decor, and the prestige value of art have been responsible for the increased demand for paintings, with increased incomes and a supply of savings to back up the demand.

But this same demand, plus a growing demand by the ever-increasing number of art museums in the country and in the world, results in fewer and fewer paintings available on the market for purchase.

The situation might seem to be one that is perfect from an investment point of view: an increasing demand together with the permanent removal of a large part of the supply to museums, plus an absolutely limited supply; but as we will see, paintings, although a good investment, do not provide any such thing as absolute security against a price drop, particularly against the effect of a major business recession.

XI

Over-all Price Trend and the Investor

O SAY THAT THERE WAS A RISE IN THE ART MARKET IN THE POST-war period is a gross understatement. The rise was apparent immediately after the war, but by the turn of the decade into the sixties, the only descriptive word that could properly be applied was "boom." Headlines were made primarily by the Impressionists and Post-Impressionists, particularly by Cézanne, van Gogh, Gauguin and Renoir. The French Moderns, particularly Matisse, Picasso, Braque and Léger were not far behind. Finally, the event of a prime Old Master coming onto the market, such as Rembrandt, Rubens or Gainsborough, brought forth bidders willing to raise the price even higher.

The conclusion then would seem to be a simple one: invest in art, especially in Impressionists and Moderns, and ride the market up. Very many people did just that and saw their art acquisitions appreciate rapidly in value.

The Arnold Kirkeby Sale of November, 1958, at the Parke-Bernet Galleries in New York was a record sale for total amount received and for prices of individual paintings, and 29 paintings sold brought in $1,548,500—the second highest total for any art auction up to that time. There is little question that the collection sold for far more than it cost the owner when he collected it in the postwar period.

Yet at this sale a Picasso "Mother and Child" sold for $152,000. The painting was purchased for the collection in 1957 for $185,000. The loss was $33,000 on this one painting.

Parke-Bernet on August 4, 1959, sold Item No. 86, a painting entitled "Le Potager" by Maurice Vlaminck for $15,000. This same painting was sold from the Georges Lurcy Collection on November 7, 1957, for $17,000. The loss on this particular transaction was $2000—plus the commission paid to the auction house.

For the Picasso $185,000 is not a small sum for anyone to invest. For the Vlaminck $17,000 is small by comparison, but it is certainly not "pin money."

You can lose money on the School of paintings in vogue, and at the beginning of the sixties the vogue is Impressionists and Post-Impressionists, at least as far as costly paintings go. It is possible to lose money on paintings even though the School is characterized by an extremely rapid rise in prices.

In October, 1951, New York's then existing Kende Galleries sold the collection of a Swiss. Included in the sale was a painting attributed to Murillo entitled "The Geometrician," a fairly large painting of the figure of a man. The painting brought $6500.

In April, 1960, the Parke-Bernet Galleries sold the same painting, this time reattributed to Luca Giordano, for $900. The loss was $5600.

In January, 1945, the John Bass Collection of paintings was sold in New York. In the collection was a beautiful painting entitled "Portrait of a Lady with Amors." The composition and quality of painting were excellent. It was a good size—25 by 29½—and was a typical work of the Dutch artist Daniel Mytens who lived and painted in the early part of the seventeenth century. He painted in England under James I and Charles I and was a leader in portraiture prior to the time van Dyck arrived in England. The painting brought $2000, a fair price.

In April, 1960, the same painting sold in the same gallery for $1300. In 15 years the price had declined.

In the same John Bass Collection there was an unusual and good portrait of a lady entitled "Hagar" by Govaert Flinck, a pupil of Rembrandt. This painting was also of a good size—30 by 27. It brought $1600.

When this same painting was resold at the end of 1950—five years later—it brought $850, about half the original price.

One of the fine Italian masters of the early sixteenth century is Lorenzo Costa. In November, 1945, a Costa of the "Descent from the Cross with Two Angels," 22 by 28½, was sold for $6600.

In May, 1951, the same painting brought $1050.

The original prices of all of these paintings were not up in the clouds and unreasonable, and a knowledgeable collector who was also a prudent investor might well have bought any of them or all of them at the original sales price. Yet all of the paintings went down in value.

VINCENT VAN GOGH. *Public Gardens at Arles*.
Phillips Collection, Washington, D.C.

The question immediately springs to mind as to whether it might not be wise to buy in the School of art in the greatest vogue at the time—the Impressionists and French Moderns at the present time—but pick out an absolutely prime, high priced master in this School and keep looking until one such painting can be picked up at not too high a price.

In the famous Goldschmidt seven-paintings-for-$2,186,000 sale of October 15, 1958, a van Gogh landscape with two figures entitled "Public Garden at Arles" was sold for $369,000. The buyer was Henry Ford II.

VINCENT VAN GOGH. *A Canal Near Nuenen*.
Parke-Bernet Galleries, Inc.

In the April 15, 1959, sale of modern paintings held at the Parke-Bernet Galleries, a van Gogh entitled "Canal Near Nuenen" was sold for $4250.

Why did one van Gogh sell for $369,000 and another for $4250? The latter painting was long known in New York art circles. It had been offered for sale over a long period. No one was known to have questioned its authenticity as a van Gogh. It is recorded and illustrated in J. B. de la Faille's book on van Gogh, and de la Faille supplied a signed certificate stating that this was the picture that appeared in his book.

The $369,000 van Gogh is also listed and reproduced in de la Faille. The $369,000 painting appears on page 358 and the $4250 picture on page 167.

Whereas only half a page is used for the reproduction of the expensive van Gogh, an entire page is used to illustrate the inexpensive one. Both paintings are typical van Goghs.

The differences are these: the low priced painting is typical of a period in which van Gogh painted in dark colors, mostly greens. The van Goghs that everyone thinks of as being van Goghs are bright, and the paint stands out in bold, short strokes. What is most wanted by the public is this typical, bright period van Gogh.

On the "Canal Near Nuenen" there is little background, but a page and a half of background goes with the "Public Garden at Arles." The latter painting is reproduced in the books of six authorities on van Gogh. It has been exhibited by five leading art dealers of the world, including Knoedler, Durand-Ruel, Wildenstein, and Rosenberg.

Finally "Public Garden at Arles" came from the obviously outstanding collection of Jakob Goldschmidt and from the collection of the Prince de Wagram.

Cézanne was a great copyist of Old Masters. One of his main objectives in life was to dignify his paintings by identifying them with the Old Masters—in quality of painting. Whether he achieved this result is problematical, but we do know that in the year in which his "Boy in a Red Vest" was sold it brought the highest auction price up to that time of any Impressionist or Post-Impressionist sold—$616,000.

Yet recently one of these Old Master copies by Cézanne was auctioned for a few thousand dollars. It was fully signed and not questioned as to authenticity.

For various reasons, some technical and some not, certain paintings by fine artists bring high prices and others do not, but the point to be made here is that while the Schools of art in particular favor may be rising, the price of a particular painting may be declining, and while a painting by a big-name artist may bring a big price, the big name is no guarantee that the painting must of necessity bring a big price.

It is hardly possible to emphasize the foolishness of investing a great deal of money in just one painting and considering this one painting as an investment which may one day be liquidated at a good profit. Yet this is a prevalent view of the investment value of art among some art owners who are otherwise good businessmen.

To own just one painting is like investing all of one's assets in one stock. Standard Oil Company of New Jersey is certainly a fine company and its stock is good, but there is merit to the attitude that it might not rise as surely as would a portfolio of selected stocks. There is the additional disadvantage in owning just one painting as against owning just one kind of stock: one always knows the value of the one stock, but he doesn't know the value of the one painting until he offers it for sale.

If one invests in paintings of any School he should invest in a collection—say a dozen paintings rather than one, and these purchases should be divided among several artists. The chance is very good that one or more of the paintings will go down in value just as one stock in a portfolio may go down. Yet the performance of the collection (like the stock portfolio) might be excellent. Later in this book a series of possible collections are listed which might be built up in the present art market. The possible prices of these paintings will be listed.

It is very interesting to study the prices of the same painting offered at auction more than once so that two prices have been established at two different points in time. There are weaknesses in this price comparison which should be mentioned in advance: a sale may not actually have taken place and the owner may have bid in the painting himself either at the first sale or at the second sale. Or a group of dealers bidding together may have manipulated the price in either the first or the second sale. While they can do this, and often do, at any sale and in the purchase of any picture, it is mentioned here because we are trying to draw conclusions from a relatively few pictures which have been sold twice through auction, and the operation of a ring could seriously vitiate the conclusions which we may draw. The paintings which we have chosen for this price comparison are those which have been sold on dates which are close together.

In October, 1943, a painting entitled "Chrysanthemums" by the American artist Eugene Speicher was sold for $800. In May, 1946, the same painting was resold for $475, a loss of nearly 50 per cent.

In March, 1945, "Arab Encampment" by Eugene Delacroix was sold for $750.

In January, 1946, the same painting was resold for the same price—$750.

The French Modern painter, André Derain, realized $1800 in March, 1956 for his portrait "Young Man in a Felt Hat." In November of the same year the same painting brought $1400.

Another Derain, "Head of a Woman," brought $550 in April, 1946. In April, 1950, it was resold for $500.

A third Derain was sold in 1948 for $750, and again in 1952 for $800. With the commission to the auction house considered the result was certainly a loss.

A Diaz "Nymph et Amor" sold for $2100 in March, 1928, and for $1100 in April, 1929—in the middle of the boom months!

The Seventeenth Century Dutch landscapist, Jan van Goyen, brought £1400 in March, 1952—"River Scene with View of the Maria Kerk." The same picture brought £787 in June, 1954—a drop of almost 50 per cent.

The modern Kisling "Young Provincial Girl" brought $500 in January, 1944. One year later the same painting brought only $50 above this figure.

One of the leading Expressionists, Oskar Kokoschka, sold for $1100 in January, 1950—"The Hunters." The next April it brought $725, a loss of one third of the first price.

Finally, let us look at the price experience in these close-together double sales of two moderns: Utrillo and Vuillard:

Sotheby's in London in July, 1957, sold Utrillo's "Aubervilliers" for £9200. The next July they sold the same painting for £7000—a loss of over $6000.

"Woman with a Blue Apron" by Vuillard was sold in March, 1949, for $1000 by the Parke-Bernet Galleries. Just one year later the same painting brought $625 —a loss of almost 40 per cent.

Between most of these pairs of dates the trend of the painting market was definitely up. In many cases the painter was in a School of art coming into favor and generally rising in price.

All of these examples should raise a red flag to the person who wants to speculate by buying a painting in the hope of realizing a quick profit through a fairly short term investment.

Even more important is the rise and ebb of the art buying public's interest in a particular School or artist, and we will shortly trace this change in popularity.

XII

The Impermanence of Public Acceptance of Art

F ALL OF THE PEOPLE IN OUR WESTERN CIVILIZATION WITH ANY knowledge of art, whether profound or slight, were asked the question, "If you could have one genuine work by any Master, and if this work were given to you free, whose work would you choose?" the name of the artist who would in all likelihood appear the greatest number of times is Rembrandt.

Early in 1960 the National Gallery in London purchased a Rembrandt, "Horse and Rider," for a reported $1,500,000. Many experts wondered why it brought so little! The answer is that while overseas buyers would have been willing to pay more, the owner, being a Britisher, was willing to take less provided the painting remained in England.

The criticisms of Rembrandt and his style of painting since his death in 1669 show a remarkable trend. At the time of his death Rembrandt had long since been through bankruptcy. During his lifetime his trend of public acceptance was not very favorable.

The popular Seventeenth Century Dutch style was a tight style of extreme precision, with considerable use of muted color and black. Rembrandt, although he started out in this traditional style of his country and period, gradually changed to the use of heavy brushwork (*impasto*) as well as to the use of many colors to blend into an effect of richness, and finally to the unique representation of lighting

229

REMBRANDT. *A Lady and Gentleman in Black.*
Isabella Gardner Museum

REMBRANDT. *Self-Portrait.*
National Gallery, Washington, D.C.
(Mellon Collection)

which, together with his use of brown glazes, gave a warmth to his paintings. His late style was not precise. The later in his life he painted, the freer his style became and the more sketchy and dramatic his compositions.

His masterpiece in the Amsterdam Rijksmuseum, "The Night Watch," was a contract work to be paid for by the various citizens whose likenesses appear in the large canvas. The painting was supposed to be a group portrait of a company of Amsterdam Musketeers. The Musketeers were disappointed because of the sketchy, unorthodox style of painting and the fact that the canvas was not a grouping of flattering portraits of each, but rather a moving, dramatic composition with many of the members of the group placed in the background or otherwise subordinated to the effect of the whole painting. Many refused to pay their proportionate share of the cost. Probably this work was the beginning of his end as a popular sought-after and prosperous painter of seventeenth century Holland, but at the same time it was the milestone in his rise to greatness.

These are the changing opinions of Rembrandt over the years as viewed by the critics of each period:

Roger de Piles, 1706: "He has sometimes enriched the poverty of his subjects by a happy motion of his genius, but having no certain knowledge of beautiful proportion, he easily relapsed into the bad taste to which he had accustomed himself."

Jean Auguste Dominique Ingres, 1821: "Let us not admire Rembrandt and the others through thick and thin; let us not compare them, either the men or their art, to the divine Raphael and the Italian school: that would be blaspheming."

Eugene Delacroix, 1851: "It may sound like blasphemy, but people will perhaps discover one day that Rembrandt was as great a painter as Raphael."

Eugene Fromentin, 1876: ". . . this so-called materialist, this *trivial, ugly* man was a pure spiritualist. . . . If we take him thus, Rembrandt is quite explained— his life, his work, his tendencies, his conceptions, his poetry, his method, his processes, even to the varnish of his paint, which is nothing but a daring and carefully sought out spiritualization of the material elements of his craft."

Vincent van Gogh, 1888: "And so Rembrandt has alone or almost alone among painters, that tenderness in the gaze . . . that heartbroken tenderness, that glimpse of a superhuman infinite that seems so natural there."

In this series of comments we find Rembrandt changing in public favor from almost complete rejection to a painter greatly revered.

Next let us look at the public attitude toward Vermeer.

Philip L. Hale, in his book, *Jan Vermeer of Delft,* Maynard and Company, Boston, published in 1913, in the preface states: "This book is written to make

VERMEER. *Girl with a Red Hat.*
National Gallery, Washington, D.C.
(Mellon Collection)

the name and work of Jan Vermeer of Delft better known to Americans. Although he is now well-known to artists and connoisseurs he still remains quite unheeded by very many intelligent and cultivated people."

It is difficult to conceive of Vermeer as ever being anything but the élite of painters commanding enormous prices.

A. B. de Vries, in his book, *Jan Vermeer van Delft,* B. T. Batsford, Ltd., London, 1948, states (page 12): "Until the middle of the nineteenth century the name of Vermeer or van der Meer—there is no unanimously accepted form—if not altogether forgotten, is only mentioned *en passant* in connection with one painting or another, which, however, seldom awakened any particular interest."

As far as can be determined, Vermeer during his lifetime was mentioned only three times in print.

About 1803 there was published in Belgium a *Catalogue of Paintings Sold in Brussels Since the Year 1773* (ending around 1803). Despite the fact that the catalogue quotes such relatively minor painters as Daniel Vertangen, Henry Verschuring, Jan de Vinck and Jan Worst, no mention whatever is made of Vermeer in the entire catalogue. Yet surely at least one Vermeer was sold or could have been sold in this period.

The truly great Vermeer painting, "Soldier and Laughing Girl," in the Frick Collection in New York, was purchased in the middle eighteen-hundreds by Leopold Double in Paris, but purchased not as a Vermeer but as by the artist Pieter de Hooch. The price was £246/15 *s.*

The Vermeer "Lady and Gentleman at the Virginals" now in Buckingham Palace, was bought in 1762 by Richard Dalton on behalf of King George III of England as a Frans van Mieris.

Vermeer's "Painter in His Studio" in the Kunsthistorisches Museum in Vienna, was purchased in 1813 by Count Czernin from a saddler as being by Pieter de Hooch.

"The Maid Handing a Letter to her Mistress" by Vermeer, and now in the Frick Collection, New York, sold in Paris in 1776 as a work of Gerard Ter Borch. It was sold again in 1837 as a Ter Borch—for 460 francs.

Vermeer's "Allegory of Faith," now in the Metropolitan Museum of Art, New York, sold in 1899 as a work by Eglon van der Neer.

In 1866 the art authority Buerger-Thoré wrote three illustrated articles about Vermeer in the *Gazette de Beaux Arts*. This was the beginning of Vermeer's fame as a painter.

Yet as late as 1877 Vermeer's countryman, Vincent van Gogh, wrote to Bernard, his friend, "Do you know a painter called Jan van der Meer?"

In December, 1955, *Fortune* published the first of a series of two scholarly articles entitled "The Great International Art Market." The illustration above the title of the article is "Portrait of a Young Girl" by Jan Vermeer, owned by Mr. and Mrs. Charles B. Wrightsman. The Wrightsmans reportedly paid $350,000 for the painting. The *Fortune* article states, "The only thing likely to happen to the Vermeer's value in the foreseeable future is that it will increase until, sometime not too far distant, it will be altogether priceless."

VERMEER. *Blue Girl.*
Collection Charles B. Wrightsman

In London in the fall of 1959 a major dealer asked me whether I knew the Wrightsmans. While the reply was in the negative, the Wrightsman Vermeer had been seen many times. The dealer then asked what a fair estimate of the price the owner might sell it for would be. Out of the air a "guesstimate" of $1,000,000 was pulled. This would be a fair market price. Surprisingly enough the dealer showed considerable interest and stated that he would see whether his client (and he had one particular one in mind) might be willing to offer $1,000,000!

Such is the history of Jan Vermeer of Delft.

The greatest of the Seventeenth Century Dutch artists bring high prices indeed —Rembrandt, Hals, Ter Borch, Vermeer. In December, 1960, a Hals "Portrait of a Cavalier," a fine typical work of the artist, sold at auction in London for the equivalent of $509,600 (£182,000).

The review of *Christie's Season, 1931,* Constable and Company, Ltd., states (page 37), "When Mr. Lewis paid 550 guineas ($3,025) on July 17 for a small portrait of a gentleman by Frans Hals, I was reminded that the day has long since passed when a Hals portrait could be picked up for a five-pound note ($25) in the Strand. This actually happened in 1884, and another picture had to be thrown in to effect a sale."

This small portrait could even be the same one which is being offered in New York for the very reasonable price (by today's standards) of $80,000.

What the report of 1931 considered a big price ($3025) as compared with the past was still only a fraction of the prices of Frans Hals today.

This same report on the 1931 season says on page 22, "The season was not to be deprived of a Fantin-Latour flower piece even if the subject was not of a cluster of roses for which the market has shown a decided preference since the auction fervour for Fantin's work began some years ago. The picture sold for 390 guineas ($2145) to Messrs. Williams and Sutch on March 6 was of scarlet, pink, and white hollyhocks, and many lovers of Fantin's works were careful to explain to me that, generally, they preferred rose themes for buying or selling. Yet if the hollyhock price is moderate compared with such a sum as 2,600 guineas ($14,300) given in 1924 for a triumphant 'Bourriche de Roses,' the true comparison is with earlier prices. I remember well the days when his beautiful renderings of flowers could be bought at Christie's for 20 guineas ($110) or less, and I once tried to persuade a friend to buy half-a-dozen and impanel them in a white room of his house on the river. He then decided to buy the expensive etchings after Meissonier, now almost unmarketable. In the second of these annuals, mention was made of a dealer placing in his window (near Christie's) three Fantin rose pictures

FANTIN-LATOUR. *Still Life.*
National Gallery, Washington, D.C.
(Dale Collection)

at 20 guineas apiece in 1896 and having to take them home as nobody wanted them."

The previous issue (1930) of the report on Christie's season (page xvi) states, "In 1892 no picture by him (Fantin) had yet attained 50 pounds at Christie's, but people were ready to pay thousands for Rosa Bonheur's works. Time avenges. As stated on page twelve of last year's volume, there was the spectacle in 1929 of a huge canvas by this countrywoman . . . bringing only 46 guineas ($253) after having realized 4,200 guineas ($23,100) in 1888."

The huge canvas, "The Horse Fair," by Rosa Bonheur was for years one of the great drawing cards of the Metropolitan Museum of Art in New York. This painting was possibly the prize exhibit for the lecturers and teachers who explained the objectives and techniques of painting by reference to the effectively portrayed animals. Public taste then changed and the great work was put in storage and remained there until the late 1950's.

Today, however, "The Horse Fair" once again hangs on the wall of the Metropolitan. It has returned to public favor.

Let us trace the history of two artists who didn't fare so well. The first is William Clarkson Stanfield, a British painter of seascapes and rural scenes, who lived from 1793 to 1867.

The Art Sales summary by Algernon Graves, published in 1921, lists one Stanfield sold in 1837, one sold in 1838, five sold in 1845, and two sold in 1848. The demand for Stanfield's paintings was not great, and the prices were not high. The year 1860 saw six of his paintings sold at auction. Nine went in 1863, four years before his death. The prices of four of those paintings were: £2,677, £1,575, £1,282, and £861. At roughly five dollars to the pound, the prices in dollars were $13,385, $7,875, $6,410, and $4,305.

For the next thirty years this high level of prices was maintained.

In the year 1881 two of his paintings sold for £3,465 and £2,677 (about $17,000 and $13,000 respectively). In 1892 one sold for £3,150.

In the period of 1901 to 1913, twenty paintings were reported sold. The top price was £514/10s. In 1913 one sold for £168.

In 1824 Stanfield was made a member of the Society of British Artists. He sent his first piece to the Academy in 1829. In all he exhibited one hundred and thirty-two works at the Academy exhibitions. At one time, at least, the National Gallery in London owned four of his works. During his lifetime he was by no means a minor artist.

Now let us see how he is described in Bryan's *Dictionary of Painters and Engravers,* Volume V, by George C. Williamson, Macmillan Company, 1905. The *Dictionary* states (page 114), "In his easel pictures he could never entirely free himself from the influence of the theatre, and his best landscapes are marred by a cold staginess of effect and of treatment. His pictures were greatly admired in their day, but their reputation has waned, and is not likely to revive."

The Art Trade Journal publication of Art Prices Current for 1921-1922 season of Christie's London Auction reports ten Stanfields sold. The top price was £81/10s. Although the pound sterling was a little different in value, the huge drop in Stanfield's popularity is clear. His low price in these ten paintings was £5!

The 1956-1957 season saw little revival in prices. Two were reported sold, by the same publication, at £80 and £50, and only in the year 1958 do we see any sign of revival.

The Encyclopedia of Painting, Bernard Myers Editor, Crown Publishers, Inc., New York, 1955, writes up Stanfield thus: "British marine painter and friend of Turner. He was popular in his time for seascapes and lake scenes in oil and watercolor." There is no further description. Stanfield hardly rises to the level of being damned by faint praise.

Constant Troyon is another painter with whom the years have not dealt kindly. He was an outstanding landscapist of the French Barbizon School who lived from 1810 to 1865. Bryan's *Dictionary* of 1905 describes him as, "A prominent member of the modern French landscape school. . . ." Troyon had a Salon exhibition in 1883. He was made a Chevalier of the Legion of Honor. Bryan's *Dictionary* adds, "Honors flowed upon him, and after the Universal Exhibition of 1855 the tide of public opinion turned enthusiastically in his favour."

Troyon was made a member of the Amsterdam Academy in 1847 and received the Cross of the Belgian Order of Leopold. Two of his paintings were placed in the Louvre. Many others were placed in other prominent museums.

CONSTANT TROYON. *Road in the Woods.*
The Metropolitan Museum of Art, New York
(Bequest, Collis P. Huntington, 1925)

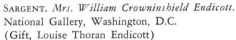

SARGENT. *Mrs. William Crowninshield Endicott.*
National Gallery, Washington, D.C.
(Gift, Louise Thoran Endicott)

In 1875 one Troyon sold for £1008 (about $5,000). By the year 1888 one of his paintings brought £3,675 ($18,375), and by 1910 one brought £6,090 (about $30,000).

For the season 1921-1922 Art Prices Current reported six of his paintings sold. The top price brought was £126, and the low price £16/6s.

In the 1946-1947 season three Troyons were sold in the number one American auction house—for $150, $150, and $200.

Ten years later prices were a little better, but one Troyon at a secondary New York auction brought exactly $17.50!

The 1931 Christie's Report (page 25) says, "That the highest prices can be given for modern art was proved in the amazing dispersal after the death of Sargent six years ago. Then, in a single day's sale on July 24, 1928, 163 water color drawings and studies in oil amassed a total of £145,984 ($749,200), a gigantic sum exceeding the combined totals of the dispersals which followed the passing of Reynolds, Landseer, Leighton, Millais, and Burne-Jones."

It is of considerable interest that the report calls Sargent a modern. No doubt he was then, and everything that was not modern like Sargent had to work hard to justify its existence. In 1959, after a thirty year period of almost complete neglect, two of Sargent's works sold at Parke-Bernet brought $2,250 and $6,250 respectively, sums far and away higher than possibly any of Sargent's prices in the preceding twenty years.

One of the debacles in art price history occurred to the paintings of one of the most fêted of England's painters. The 1931 Christie report (page 24) states, "The appearance for example of two pictures by Alma-Tadema aroused memories of the Ernest Gambart sale on Academy Banquet day twenty-eight years ago. This famous Academician was then alive to enjoy the tidings that his 'Dedication to Bacchus' had been bought by Lockett Agnew for 5,600 guineas ($30,800). 1903 was indeed a great year for him as in the Marquand sale, New York, his 'Reading from Homer' brought £6,060 ($33,000). To mention Ernest Gambart is to recollect that he once offered 12,000 guineas ($66,000) to Alma-Tadema for a picture, which was refused because the painter demanded 15,000 guineas ($82,500).

"The two pictures, on small oval panels, offered on May 1, were especially painted for Sir John Aird in 1907. This 'Oriente' and this 'Bacchante' were bought by Mr. Nathan Mitchell at 150 guineas ($825)."

In early 1945 "Going Down to the River" by Alma-Tadema, a fairly large painting, sold at auction in New York for $800, and "The Sculpture Gallery" sold for $850. Both of these paintings had been significant enough to have been on loan to New York's Metropolitan Museum of Art. A watercolor, "After the Bath," had been on loan to the Metropolitan also. It brought $200. Two other Alma-Tademas brought $1,300 and $1,000.

ROSA BONHEUR. *The Horse Fair.*
The Metropolitan Museum of Art, New York
(Gift, Cornelius Vanderbilt, 1887)

EL GRECO. *Portrati of Ludovico Cornaro.*
National Gallery, London

Few of the paintings of Alma-Tadema have appeared on the market in recent years, and there is no general demand for them.

In 1882 the National Gallery in London bought the portrait of Ludovico Cornaro for £336 ($1,630).

That the National Gallery was daring in purchasing an El Greco is indicated by the opinion of the art authority R. A. M. Stevenson in his book on *Velásquez,* published in 1902. He refers to El Greco in the following way, "While El Greco certainly adopted a Spanish gravity of colouring, neither that nor his modeling was ever subtle or thoroughly natural. . . . While one admits Greco's superior freedom and ease of style, one perhaps admires still more the inborn power of seeing shown by Velásquez. While Velásquez ripened with age and practice, Greco was inclined to get rotten with facility."

An art critic could hardly have been less complimentary in regard to the painting of El Greco.

Until the turn of the century El Greco was practically unknown outside of Spain, where he painted most of his pictures. In the eighteenth century Murillo was the most famous and widely known Spanish artist. In the nineteenth century tastes changed and Velásquez replaced Murillo in favor. Goya followed along behind Velásquez in the Spanish School, but El Greco remained obscure. Because of his great versatility, some of his paintings were not always easy to recognize, and few paintings were attributed to him, the rest by his hand being attributed to one or another sixteenth century artist. While it is true that the Prado in Madrid owned paintings by El Greco, they were relegated to the cellar.

Around the turn of the century the American, John Singer Sargent, visited Madrid and studied the paintings of El Greco in the Prado's cellar, where many of these works were badly in need of repair and cleaning.

Cézanne, who is the highest priced of all Post-Impressionist artists today, was perhaps the main instrument in securing recognition for El Greco. Cézanne, anxious to tie his art in with the "museum art" of the past, called attention to El Greco, probably because of El Greco's unique departure from photographic fidelity, so very much in keeping with the spirit of the moderns.

What helped the rediscovery and recognition of El Greco was the simple fact that he signed many of his paintings. The signatures were sometimes overpainted by restorers attempting to pass the paintings off as being by a more prominent artist, or the signatures were hidden by accumulations of dirt and aged varnish or covered by the edge of the picture frame. Later, removal from the frame, cleaning and close examination revealed the signatures and thus resulted in the positive identification and establishment of a group of true El Greco masterworks.

Four years after the National Gallery in London took the bold step of investing £336 in an El Greco in 1882, another El Greco was sold for £304. In 1907, "Christ at Calvary" was sold for £1,995 ($9,735).

Even in the pre-depression boom seasons of 1929 and 1930 no one of the three major auction houses in England or America either illustrated or mentioned an El Greco in its sales publications.

However, in 1959, an El Greco of St. James, not large (27¾ by 21¼) was sold at Sotheby's for £72,000 ($200,000). In the same year an unrecorded hitherto unknown El Greco labeled "Veronese" instead of "El Greco" sold for over $100,000. This fine painting, now in the Wrightsmans' collection, has been on loan to the Metropolitan.

The tanker tycoon Niarchos in 1955 purchased the "Descent from the Cross" for a price reported to be well into six figures, and the Metropolitan Museum in New York purchased an El Greco for a comparable price shortly thereafter.

Art dictionary definitions reflect the esteem in which particular artists are held at the time of publication of the dictionary. *The Encyclopedia of Painting,* Crown Publishers, New York, 1955, identifies El Greco as the, "Most stirring of Spain's religious painters. An unusual personal genius in whom the divergent tendencies of Spanish Mannerism, Venetian colorism, and late Byzantine icon-painting reach their apogee."

This definition is sharply in contrast with R. A. M. Stevenson's 1902 description of El Greco, that, ". . . Greco was inclined to get rotten with facility."

It will be seen later how certain collectors had an absolute genius for collecting those artists when their prices were low who would later be at the very pinnacle of desirability, while other collectors had a peculiar faculty for collecting the paintings of artists who would uniformly fall into oblivion.

This analysis of changing public acceptance of art has cited three of the greatest artists in history and traced them from near oblivion to the pinnacle of public acceptance—Rembrandt, Vermeer, and El Greco. To this group we might add Hals.

Is there any general explanation of (1) why these artists were early not accepted, and (2) why they later received such general public acclaim?

In the first place, in their time they departed sharply from the group of painters of the period to which they belonged. Rembrandt started out like the rest of the Seventeenth Century Dutch painters—van der Helst, Moreelse, and de Keyser—with a tight, elegant, near-photographic style.

But then he departed from this exactness, and more and more as time went on. He used *impasto,* painted more sketchily, and through the use of unusual lighting and rich brown glazes created an impression of depth and strength.

Vermeer used bright, vibrant colors and employed unusual lighting effects, this light often streaming dramatically through an open window. Although Pieter de Hooch and some other of the Seventeenth Century Dutch painters also used window lighting, Vermeer is unquestionably its master. In his "View of Delft" in the Mauritshuis, The Hague, Holland, Vermeer achieves an effect which is almost impressionism. He suggests, with shimmering dots of light and color sparkling across his canvas, the Pointillist technique developed later by Seurat and Signac in the late nineteenth century. The surfaces of his paintings are, unlike the Impressionists, almost glass-like. His skill as a craftsman is apparent and sometimes almost breathtaking. His impressionism is combined with a background of rigorous training and a top standard of workmanship. His jewel-like paintings cannot be overpraised.

The style of Hals that is the most admired today is again not the precise, photographic style characteristic of his contemporaries, but is his later, free-brush-stroke style, displaying cavaliers and ladies with bright cheeks, rich natural flesh tones, smiles, and sparkling eyes, in casual natural poses.

Finally, El Greco did not paint in his later period with the excellence and natural life-like perfection of Velásquez or the traditional Sixteenth Century Spanish style. He, even more than Rembrandt and Hals, departed from the style of his contemporaries and developed a unique figure elongation which makes his canvases instantly recognizable to the gallery visitor today. His technique of elongation gives his figures an almost unworldly, spiritual quality. This, together with his contrast of a few strong colors, his good composition and strong, sure brush work, contributed to his rediscovery and new popularity.

All of these late accepted painters departed from their School and times through a daring quality which expressed itself in an inexactness which is akin to and foreshadows Impressionism as well as other late related Schools of art.

It might follow that other art rebels of their time would have a similar history of late acceptance, particularly if their rebellion is in the direction of the recent, accepted Schools.

Two little incidents in the history of art dealership illustrate non-acceptance of new styles of art followed by general public acclaim.

After the First World War the New York art dealer Leon Medina lived and operated for a number of years in Paris. A part of his trade consisted in selling his purchases of objects of art to the large Paris dealer Demotte. One day in 1920 while Medina was delivering an art object to Demotte the latter asked him for a

MODIGLIANI. *Adrienne.*
National Gallery, Washington, D.C.
(Dale Collection, Loan)

favor. The favor was to buy eight or ten paintings for £50 ($240) from an artist who was sick in the hospital so that the artist could pay his hospital bill.

Medina examined the paintings, then told Demotte, "I'm returning to London and I frankly don't care to bring those paintings of nudes with me. They may be denied admission. Anyway, the paintings are ugly. They have no form. The eyes slant, and I just don't think they are good art. But here is £50. I have placed my initials on ten of the canvases. You sell these, and donate the proceeds along with my £50 to the artist to help him out."

The artist's name was Amedeo Modigliani.

Medina was still in Paris in 1931. A dealer on the Rue de la Boetie offered him thirteen canvases by one artist for $10,000. Medina refused the deal. The paintings were by Paul Gauguin! One of the paintings offered him was reported to have been sold later to one of the leading American museums for a sum in six figures.

XIII

The Changing Price Tag on Art Collections

HE VERY HIGHEST PRICED GROUP OF PAINTINGS SOLD IN RECENT years was the Jakob Goldschmidt "Seven Paintings for $2,186,000." These paintings were the cream of the excellent Goldschmidt Collection. The seven were:

Cézanne	"Boy in a Red Vest"	$ 616,000
Manet	"Self Portrait"	182,000
Manet	"Promenade—Portrait of Mme. Gamby"....	249,200
Manet	"Rue Mosnier with Flags"	316,400
van Gogh	"Public Garden at Arles"	369,600
Cézanne	"Still Life with Large Apples"	252,000
Renoir	"La Pensée"	201,000
		$2,186,200

The van Gogh "Public Garden at Arles" was formerly in the collection of the Prince de Wagram and in the Fayet Collection. Mr. Goldschmidt is reported to have purchased this painting thirty years prior to the sale for $15,000. The profit on this one painting was $354,000. The painting sold for almost twenty-five times its purchase price.

Manet's "Rue Mosnier" was sold for $316,400. The painting was in the August Pellerin Collection and in the Collection of Baron Herzog of Budapest. In 1931 Mr. Goldschmidt is reported to have paid $64,000 for the picture. The sale price was nearly five times the purchase price.

244

Manet's "Portrait of Madame Gamby" was also in the August Pellerin Collection and had been bought in 1884 in the Manet Sale by the actor Faure for 1500 gold francs. Mr. Goldschmidt owned the painting twenty-five years and had paid $35,000 for it. The selling price of $249,200 was seven times the purchase price.

The selling price of these three paintings was $935,000. The cost was $114,000 or 12 per cent of the selling price. Under the assumption that Mr. Goldschmidt paid 12 per cent of the selling price for all the paintings, his cost on the $2,186,000 sale would have been $266,000, and the profit to his estate $1,920,000.

In this transaction two facts stand out: (1) Mr. Goldschmidt collected an absolutely topnotch group of seven paintings by the leading Impressionists and Post-Impressionists for which he paid a good price, not a low price, considering the years in which he bought. He may have paid dearly at the time, but in this group of paintings he bought the best.

The second fact is that he had owned the paintings a long time.

As far as price goes, we now move from the expensive to the inexpensive: Lucius O'Callaghan was a Dublin architect and at one time Director of the Dublin National Gallery. Over the years he purchased Seventeenth Century Dutch and Flemish art, rarely spending over $25 or $50 for a painting. In all, he probably invested between $4200 and $5600.

In 1957 Christie's sold this collection for just under $37,500. The selling price was seven and a half times the cost. The cost of 13.3 per cent of the selling price is just a little higher in ratio than that of the Goldschmidt Collection.

The third collection to be sold in recent years in which prices as well as costs are available is the Rees Jeffries Collection sold in November, 1954, at Christie's in London. This sale was mentioned earlier as a milestone in the price history of modern paintings.

A Matisse which realized $19,700 in 1954 cost $1700 when purchased in 1928. A Bonnard which sold for $11,760 cost $750 in the same year, 1928, and a Braque which brought $3400 cost $210 in 1935.

The entire collection realized £44,320 ($124,000). It cost the seller £3332. The selling price was over thirteen times the cost. Alternatively, the cost was 7½ per cent of the selling price. Although the profit was certainly handsome, one wonders where he could get a Braque today for $3400.

On November 6, 1959, a totally different School of paintings was sold at auction—The H. L. Fisson Collection of fifteen Constables. All were landscapes by this English master who lived from 1776 to 1837. The total price received in London for the fifteen paintings was £85,900 ($240,800). This sum is exactly ten times the cost of the Constables to Mr. Fisson in the late 1920's.

Not all purchased paintings are sold so favorably, however. In 1944 the Edward Stotesbury Collection was sold, and we are able to compare the sales prices on a number of the British portraits with what Mr. Stotesbury paid for them:

		Cost	Selling Price	Loss
Romney	"Portrait of Captain Stables"	$ 50,000	$ 5,500	$ 44,500
Lawrence	"Hon. Caroline Upton"	50,000	9,000	41,000
Romney	"Sir William Lemon"	38,000	4,200	33,800
Romney	"Master Day"	140,000	8,500	131,500
Romney	"William Beckford"	140,000	9,500	130,500
Hoppner	"Tambourine Girl"	300,000	10,000	290,000
Romney	"The Vernon Children"	134,713	22,000	112,713
		$852,713	$68,700	$784,013

The loss on these seven paintings is staggering. The selling price was 8 per cent of the cost to Mr. Stotesbury, and out of an investment of $852,713 only $68,700 was salvaged.

Although paintings are bought because of (1) their beauty and (2) the excellence of the painting, either or both of which factors give the painting (3) value expressed in terms of money, one wonders whether Mr. Stotesbury shouldn't have been aware of the fact that public taste was changing, that the Eighteenth Century British portraitists were going out of vogue, and that to ignore this trend was like looking at a portfolio of stocks which was declining and say, "I'm not worried. I'll just wait, and they will come back!"

On the other side of the argument is the fact that Mr. Stotesbury received his value from the paintings through their beauty and quality. He didn't need to worry about money, and, in any event, he could take neither paintings nor money with him.

All of us are not as wealthy as Mr. Stotesbury was, however, and to use the above arguments to justify keeping the British portraits until their value had all but disappeared completely leaves out any element of investment value in paintings, and as what we are talking about in this book is investment, it is well to note that in Mr. Stotesbury's case art was a bad investment.

No one knows exactly what J. Pierpont Morgan, Sr., the great prototype of all American investors, put into art and antiquities. One estimate is $60,000,000, and Mr. Mitchell Samuels, late Chairman of the Board of French and Company, who knew Mr. Morgan and sold him many works of art, thought this figure not unreasonable.

At any rate, Mr. Morgan did not have the reputation of throwing money around or making imprudent investments. But let us note one of his purchases: a portrait by Sir Thomas Raeburn. Mr. Morgan bought this painting in 1928 at a cost of $150,000. It was sold in 1944, just sixteen years later, for $14,000. The loss was over 90 per cent of the cost.

In February, 1935, J. Pierpont Morgan, Jr. sold a group of paintings that he had inherited from the elder Morgan. The reason which Mr. Morgan, Jr. gave for the sale was simply that he understood "the market for good paintings to be favorable." This was the group of paintings sold:

		Approximate Price
Ghirlandaio	"Portrait of Giovanna Tornabuoni"	$ 500,000
Frans Hals	"Portrait of a Man" and "Portrait of a Woman"	300,000
Sir Thomas Lawrence	"Miss Farren, Countess of Derby"	200,000
Fra Filippo Lippi	"St. Lawrence Enthroned"	500,000
Peter Paul Rubens	"Anne of Austria"	
	Approximate Total	$1,500,000

Mr. Morgan, Sr. paid about $250,000 for the Ghirlandaio portrait in 1907 when he bought it from the Rudolph Kann Collection. In the 1860's Henry Willett had purchased the picture for £600 (about $3000) from Madame de Sagen, and, after having held it for thirty years, sold it in the 1890's for £12,000 (about $60,000).

Within twenty-four hours after Knoedler's received the paintings for sale, bids began to pour in, many from European museums. Within this twenty-four hour period the Ghirlandaio portrait was sold after a private buyer had sent a special plane to New York to get a photograph of the painting. After inspecting the photo he purchased it by a long distance call, just ahead of a competitor.

The New York Metropolitan Museum of Art bought the Fra Filippo Lippi and the Rubens.

In June of the same year Mr. Morgan sold a Holbein portrait of a young woman painted on the back of a playing card for $30,306. Mr. Morgan had purchased the painting thirty-one years earlier from Joseph Duveen for $14,264. Now Lord Duveen bought it back for over twice the original price.

At the same time Mr. Morgan sold a group of miniatures for $340,651, a little over one-third of their cost.

Fine pictures bring fine prices, and almost always have a market; but tastes change, and if Mr. Morgan had held his Lawrence for ten more years he might have realized only $20,000 instead of $200,000.

Jules Bache, another top level investment banker, purchased a Madonna and

Child, presumably by the great Fifteenth Century Venetian painter Giovanni Bellini, for about $150,000. This same picture was sold in 1945 by the Kende Galleries in New York for $5500, about 3 per cent of the purchase price. The loss to Mr. Bache was caused by entirely different factors than have been responsible for the losses discussed so far in this chapter. The price of $150,000 should have been achieved in 1945 since it was a fair price for a Bellini Madonna. The Bache estate should hardly have taken a loss, but unfortunately something happened which can overnight destroy the value of any painting. Critical reservations were made about the painting by the art experts. The implications were that the painting was really not a Bellini. Very little doubt on the part of the experts has to be expressed about any painting before its value plummets. Sir Joseph Duveen found out this fact to his sadness in the case of a painting, presumably a Leonardo da Vinci, which was being offered for sale to a museum. When the museum refused to complete the deal because of Sir Joseph's "critical reservations" the seller brought suit against Sir Joseph, who settled out of court for a sum reported to be well into five figures.

Another lesson can be learned from these sales: (1) Public taste changes, and paintings once avidly sought after go out of style and lose their value; (2) to have value and to hold it a painting must be authentic and not subject to reservations on the part of the art experts.

The third lesson is that when the price of paintings is high, and by high we can arbitrarily establish the figure of $100,000 or more, the risk of losing is great. It is great for two reasons: first, the painting is expensive in terms of dollars by almost anyone's standards; second, if a loss is taken, even a very small loss percentage-wise, the actual number of dollars lost is great.

To go back to the happier side of collecting for resale, a collection of top quality Impressionist and Modern paintings was sold by Mr. and Mrs. Edward G. Robinson in 1957. For twenty-five years Mr. Robinson purchased paintings of these Schools, presumably starting in earnest after *Little Caesar,* the film that established Mr. Robinson for all time. The film came out in 1932.

The buyer, Stavros Niarchos, purchased the collection through Knoedler and Company for $3,250,000—fifty-eight paintings, and one sculpture by Edgar Degas. Included in this group are paintings listed on the following page.

Out of the total group of fifty-eight paintings sold, Mr. Robinson repurchased fourteen of the lesser paintings so that the net price of the remainder to Mr. Niarchos was $2,500,000. It is reported that the entire collection cost Mr. Robinson about $1,000,000. The investment was a good one!

1957 Valuation

Gauguin	"Horsemen on the Beach"	$200,000
Renoir	"After the Bath"	60,000
Matisse	"Dinner Table"	75,000
Cézanne	"Black Clock"	200,000
Corot	"Italian Woman"	200,000
Seurat	"Le Crotoy"	185,000

In the same category was the Georges Lurcy Collection which was sold by the Parke-Bernet Galleries in November, 1957. It was reported that one hundred and fifty millionaires were present at the sale. Some of the buyers and their purchases were:

Henry Ford II	Renoir "La Serre"	$200,000
Alex Goulandris	Gauguin "Mao Taporo"	180,000
	Bonnard "Still Life with Cat"	70,000
	Matisse "Dans le Boudoir"	25,000
Douglas Dillon	Monet "Woman in a Garden"	92,500
Mrs. David Rockefeller	Signac "Beach Scene"	31,000
Edward G. Robinson	Derain "Vase of Flowers"	5,500
	Braque "Sausage"	12,000

The sixty-five paintings brought in a total of $1,708,550, or $26,285 per painting. Mr. Lurcy was an extremely shrewd businessman and is reported rarely to have paid over $10,000 for a painting. The increase in value of the collection, much of which was purchased during the years of World War II, was excellent.

Let us now compare three collections of paintings sold toward the end of World War II:

1. The Stanley N. Barbee Collection sold on April 20, 1944.
2. The William H. Vanderbilt Collection sold on April 18 and 19, 1945.
3. The Edward T. Stotesbury Collection sold on November 18, 1944.

These three collections were sold by the Parke-Bernet Galleries in New York within a twelve-month period.

The Barbee Collection was primarily of Impressionists, French Moderns and Americans. The entire sale brought in $114,500.

In this sale we have studied only the paintings which were illustrated in the catalogue. Only from looking at an illustration of the painting can we get some idea of the nature of the picture and the quality of the painting. We want to know these things so that we can estimate, picture by picture, what the collection would possibly bring if sold in the early part of the 1960's.

The illustrated paintings alone brought in $112,525, and this total included a large Manet portrait entitled "Le Clairon," 39¾ by 32; Renoir's "Gabrielle au Collier Vert," 21¾ by 18; Seurat's "L'Ile de la Grande Jatte," 6 by 9¾; Cézanne's "Satyrs and Nymphs," 9½ by 12; and Gauguin's "Tahiti," 15 by 11¾.

The thirty-four paintings which brought in $112,525 in 1944 would have brought in at the most conservative estimate $689,500 in the early 1960's. This is six times the figure for which the collection was sold in 1944.

The second collection, that of William H. Vanderbilt, is as characteristic as the Barbee Collection, but whereas the Barbee Collection was almost solely an Impressionist and Modern Collection, the Vanderbilt Collection was a Nineteenth Century Naturalistic Collection. It was sold in April, 1945.

In the nineteenth century, when the collection was probably built, it contained some of the then priceless names—Constant Troyon, Jean Francois Millet and Sir Lawrence Alma-Tadema. In addition it had some smaller artists, but nonetheless "names to have." Some of these were Leon Bonnat, Emil van Marcke, Baron Hendrik Leys and Paul Jean Clays.

The illustrated paintings in the collection brought in $284,500. In the early 1960's these same paintings could not have realized over $112,500, and the appraisals were made picture by picture for all ninety-eight illustrated paintings. This appraised sum averages $1000 a painting, 40 per cent of what they sold for in 1945.

The third collection has already been touched on briefly: the Edward T. Stotesbury Collection of British portraits. Out of an investment by Mr. Stotesbury of $852,713 in seven paintings, his estate salvaged $68,700, 8 per cent of the purchase price. This ratio of selling price to cost on the seven paintings suggests that the total of the eighteen paintings on which $127,000 was realized cost nearly $1,600,000 and that the loss was close to $1,500,000.

Now, whereas the Barbee Collection of French paintings sold in the 1944-1945 period would have sold for at least six times the price if sold in the 1959-1960 period, and the Vanderbilt Collection of nineteenth century, traditional paintings would in 1959 to 1960 have brought only 40 per cent of the price actually realized in the 1944-1945 period, the Stotesbury Collection probably would have realized *the same sum* in 1959-1960 that it did in the 1944-1945 period. The British portraits as a group dropped in value after 1945, but later recovered to the 1944-1945 level. If Mr. Stotesbury had owned eighteen Gainsborough portraits instead of Romneys, Lawrences, Hoppners and Raeburns, however, the collection would have brought far higher prices in the 1959-1960 period than it did in 1944-1945.

So here we have three collections sold at the end of the war. One, the Barbee Collection, would have gone up tremendously if held fifteen years longer. The second, the Vanderbilt Collection, would have lost over 50 per cent of its 1944-1945 value; and the third, the Stotesbury Collection, would have sold for about the same amount.

STANLEY N. BARBEE COLLECTION
Sold April 20, 1944, Parke-Bernet Galleries

Artist	Title of Painting	Size (Inches)	Sale Price	Estimated 1960 Price
Raoul Dufy	Ascot (watercolor)	19¼ x 25¼	$ 800	$ 2,500
Raoul Dufy	Regate: Le Bassin a Deauville	15 x 18¼	750	2,500
Max Liebermann	Picnic in the Woods	19½ x 14	800	2,500
Paul Gauguin	Tahiti	15 x 11¼	3,800	50,000
Cézanne	Pont au Aqueduc (water color)	12½ x 18½	1,100	12,000
Cézanne	Satyrs et Nymphs	9½ x 12	2,250	15,000
Cornelis de Heem	Still Life with Fruit	11 x 15¾	600	2,500
Greuze	L'Innocence	15¾ x 12¼	1,800	3,000
Rouault	Fille de Cirque	23¼ x 15¼	3,700	25,000
Daumier	Don Quixote	10 x 8	5,500	15,000
Seurat	L'Ile de la Grande Jatte	6 x 9¾	6,400	30,000
Renoir	Femme Assise	15 x 11½	8,000	25,000
Raoul Dufy	Fenetre Ouverte	14¾ x 18¼	1,700	4,000
Braque	Nature Morte	18¼ x 27	3,200	32,000
Daumier	Charles Deburan	13½ x 9¼	6,000	15,000
Renoir	Abricots et Figues	12¾ x 16¼	4,250	18,000
Sisley	Junction-Loing and Seine	19¾ x 26	4,100	25,000
Vuillard	Intimacy	25 x 24½	4,900	25,000
Degas	Femme à sa Toilette	32¾ x 24½	4,000	18,000
Manet	Chanteuse de Cafe Concert	32 x 25¾	6,000	60,000
Renoir	Gabrielle au Collier Vert	21¾ x 18	9,250	50,000
Degas	Trois Danseuses (pastel)	27¾ x 22¾	9,500	25,000
Manet	Le Clairon	39¾ x 32	8,000	125,000
Boudin	Sortie du Port du Havre	47 x 64½	3,600	50,000
van Dongen	Lilacs	51½ x 38½	3,600	20,000
Hartley	Sea Window: Summer	28 x 22	1,500	5,000
Joe Jones	Water Hole	26½ x 36	300	3,000
Darrell Austin	The Tigress	30 x 36	3,000	10,000
George Schreiber	Going Home	28 x 36	850	5,000
Eilshemius	Green Valley	13½ x 18½	350	2,500
George B. Luks	Flower Venders	16 x 20	750	5,000
John Sloan	Roof Gossips	20 x 24	925	2,000
Moise Kisling	Girl with Braids	16¼ x 13	500	2,500
Raphael Soyer	In the Studio	36¼ x 22	750	2,500
TOTAL OF 34 PAINTINGS			$112,525	$689,500

William H. Vanderbilt Collection
Sold April 18-19, 1945, Parke-Bernet Galleries

Artist	Title of Painting	Size (Inches)	1945 Sale Price	Estimated 1960 Price
Domingo y Munoz	Interior of a Stable	5 x 6¾	$ 850	$ 500
August Pettenkofen	Hungarian Volunteers	11 x 14	800	500
Mariano Fortuny	A Court Fool	7½ x 5¼	1,050	500
Ludwig Knaus	The Rag Baby	23½ x 17½	1,350	1,000
Rosa Bonheur	Bulls Fighting (pastel)	23 x 32	500	750
Eastman Johnson	The Horse Trade	17 x 21¾	1,400	1,400
Arthur F. Tait	In the Woods	20¼ x 30¼	3,000	1,000
Charles Jacque	The Sheep Stable	12½ x 18¼	425	425
Constant Troyon	Autumn Woods with Cattle	15¼ x 22	600	600
Alex. Decamps	An Italian Family	15½ x 12¼	400	400
Thos. Couture	The Realist	18 x 14¾	2,500	1,250
Charles Bargue	Artist and his Model	11 x 8	5,700	1,000
Jean Meissonier	Liseur	8¾ x 6½	1,800	1,000
Mariano Fortuny	Arab Fantasia	20 x 24½	2,900	750
Adolf Schreyer	Arabs Resting	17¾ x 30	1,100	1,100
Narcisse Diaz	Colin-Maillard	15½ x 18¼	1,250	650
Pierre Rousseau	River Scene	16½ x 25¼	3,200	2,500
Narcisse Diaz	Forest of Fontainebleau	33 x 44	2,500	1,000
Jules Dupre	River Scene—Boats	11 x 15¾	1,600	2,000
Pierre Rousseau	Farm on Banks of the Oise	16 x 25	2,700	1,500
Rosa Bonheur	Flock of Sheep	26½ x 35¾	2,700	1,200
Constant Troyon	On the Road	32¾ x 46½	1,400	1,000
Pierre Rousseau	Gorges D'Apremont	26 x 39½	2,700	1,200
Jean Boldini	Parisiennes	12¼ x 9½	6,000	1,000
Jean Meissonier	Artist at Easel	13 x 9¾	3,250	1,000
Jean Francois Millet	Paysanne	39½ x 31¾	30,000	5,000
Rosa Bonheur	En Foret	(not listed)	8,000	2,000
Eugene Fromentin	Crossing a Ford	40¾ x 55½	2,000	2,000
Jules Dupre	Autumn Sunset	31¾ x 51½	2,100	2,100
Josef Israels	The Peasant's Home	37½ x 52	3,500	750
Jean Millet	Le Semeur	41¼ x 33	26,000	5,000
Mihaly Munkacsy	The Two Families	42 x 59¼	3,600	600
Alma-Tadema	Going Down to the River	32½ x 68	800	600
Jean Gerome	Sword Dance at the Pasha's	26¼ x 42¼	1,800	800
Raimundo Madrazo	Fete During the Carnival	26 x 44	4,200	600
Edouard Detaille	Ambulance Corps	31½ x 51¼	1,200	600
Alma-Tadema	Sculpture Gallery	30¼ x 23¼	850	650

Artist	Title of Painting	Size (Inches)	1945 Sale Price	Estimated 1960 Price
Alma-Tadema	Picture Gallery	30¼ x 23¼	1,000	650
Ludwig Knaus	German Village Fete	41 x 58	2,500	1,000
Alfred Stevens	Ready for the Ball	35½ x 45¾	1,900	500
Louis Breton	The Rainbow	43½ x 61	900	900
Emile van Marcke	Pasture at Soreng	47 x 63¼	1,200	500
Ferdinand Roybet	A Musical Party	57½ x 47½	3,100	750
Florent Willems	The Dance	43 x 29¾	1,000	400
Ignacio Escosura	The Heir	23¾ x 36	1,500	400
Louis Leloir	The Portrait	24½ x 39½	1,150	400
Baron Hendrik Leys	Lucas Cranach Painting	22½ x 36¼	1,150	400
Baron Hendrik Leys	Rights of the City Accorded	43 x 79	1,050	400
Fred. Kaemmerer	Ladies of the Directory	24 x 19¾	700	300
Francis Grison	The Happy Omen	25¼ x 26½	1,250	350
Ludwig Knaus	Ideal Head	10¼ x 7¾	750	350
Jules Dupre	Shepherd Boy	11¾ x 15½	400	800
Pierre Rousseau	Village of Barbizon	8½ x 18	500	500
Alma-Tadema	After the Bath (water color)	11 x 6¼	200	400
Chas. Bargue	The Almee	16 x 9½	2,000	300
Jose Munoz	Halt at the Inn	26½ x 22¼	2,550	400
Edouardo Zamacois	The King's Favorite	22 x 17½	800	350
Rosa Bonheur	Old Monarch	36½ x 30½	2,000	600
Pierre Rousseau	Morning	11¾ x 21¼	1,400	600
Eug. Fromentin	Arabs Watering Horses	23¾ x 28¾	2,700	600
Narcisse Diaz	Eastern Bazaar	16½ x 11	650	650
Jean Millet	Hunting in Winter	18 x 15½	1,800	800
Jean Meissonier	Le Peintre	15½ x 19	3,100	700
Jean Boldini	Ladies of First Empire	13¼ x 10¾	11,000	1,100
Jean Millet	Shepherdess	15 x 10¾	11,000	1,500
Jean Millet	Knitting Lesson	16¼ x 12½	12,500	2,500
J. B. Corot	La Route au Bord	16 x 23¾	8,900	8,900
Pierre Rousseau	Study from Nature	13¼ x 19½	1,800	1,800
Rosa Bonheur	Noonday Repose	17½ x 24	850	600
Jean Meissonier	Arrival at the Chateau	20¼ x 26	4,200	700
Chas. Bargue	Chess on the Terrace	11¼ x 17¼	6,100	800
Oreste Cortazzo	Judgment of Paris	20¾ x 32½	2,500	600
Jean Vibert	Committee on Moral Books	26 x 19	2,700	1,200
J. B. Corot	Orphee Charme les Humains	16½ x 24	8,500	8,500
Charles Daubigny	Landscape: Sunset	32 x 57½	1,900	5,000
Jean Gerome	Reception of the Prince	38 x 55	5,100	1,000
Adolph Schreyer	Retreating Arab Horsemen	45½ x 68½	2,800	2,800

Artist	Title of Painting	Size (Inches)	1945 Sale Price	Estimated 1960 Price
Wm. Bouguereau	Going to the Bath	39 x 29½	1,800	1,500
Narcisse Diaz	Cupid's Whisper	Circular 36¼	700	600
Jules Breton	Brittany Girl	62 x 41½	1,000	1,000
Ludwig Knaus	Road to Ruin	32½ x 43¼	1,600	600
Mihaly Munkacsy	Gypsies Camping	26¾ x 41	4,100	800
Felix Ziem	Doge's Palace, Venice	27¼ x 40¼	1,500	1,500
Jose Cordero	Spanish Christening	36½ x 65½	4,500	800
Raimundo Madrazo	Masqueraders	40 x 26½	1,250	500
Alfred Stevens	Morning Call	25¾ x 18¼	2,200	600
Alma-Tadema	Roman Theater Entrance	27¾ x 38¾	1,300	600
Eug. Isabey	French Hospitality	28½ x 36½	1,400	1,000
Baron Leys	Soldiers' Amusements	26¼ x 35	1,200	500
Leon Bonnat	Arab Plucking Thorn	55 x 41½	550	400
Jules Lefebvre	Girl Standing on Beach	62 x 36½	500	750
Paul Jean Clays	City of Antwerp	30 x 43½	1,350	600
Emile van Marcke	Cows in a Pool	23 x 33	650	500
Franz Defregger	Tourists in Tyrol	39¼ x 54	2,000	1,200
Constant Troyon	Cows and Landscape	20½ x 28½	575	750
Emile van Marcke	White Cow	22¾ x 26¾	500	400
Francesca Vinea	Italian Dance Party	30 x 56	1,650	400
Baron Leys	Education of Chas. V	36½ x 46	1,350	600

TOTAL OF 98 PAINTINGS $284,500 $112,525

EDWARD T. STOTESBURY COLLECTION
Sold Nov. 18, 1944, Parke-Bernet Galleries

Estimated 1960 over-all price total approximately the same in 1960 as in 1944.

Artist	Title of Painting	Size (Inches)	1944 Sale Price
Raeburn	Mrs. David Monypenny	30 x 25	$ 3,500
Romney	Charlotte Margaret Gunning	30 x 25	9,500
Hoppner	Samuel Brandram, Esq.	30 x 25	2,500
Lawrence	Miss Glover of Bath	30 x 25	3,200
Romney	Captain Stables	50 x 40	5,500
Lawrence	Hon. Caroline Upton	30 x 25	9,000
Lawrence	Hon. Sophia Upton	30 x 25	4,600
Romney	Lady Lemon	50 x 40	9,500
Romney	Sir William Lemon	50 x 40	4,200
Romney	Master Day	66 x 38½	8,500
Hoppner	Mrs. Jordan	50 x 40	4,000

Artist	Title of Painting	Size (Inches)	1944 Sale Price
Romney	William Beckford as a Boy	65 x 53	9,500
Hoppner	The Tambourine Girl	94 x 58½	10,000
Romney	Mrs. Bracebridge and Daughter	62 x 48½	4,500
Lawrence	Mrs. Thompson and her Son	88¼ x 58	6,750
Romney	Miss Clavering	49 x 39	6,500
Romney	The Vernon Children	59½ x 46	22,000
Hoppner	Sir Humphrey Davy	30 x 25	3,750
	TOTAL OF 18 PAINTINGS		$127,000

The late Andrew Mellon not only financed the construction of the National Gallery of Art in Washington but gave it a superb collection of art. For the group of paintings listed below he paid $18,778,560, most of them bought in the era of the 1920's and 1930's, many from Sir Joseph Duveen. This sum is almost identical with the sum total of the "Target" Collection.* Let us see what Mr. Mellon was able to purchase for about the same sum:

Raphael	Alba Madonna	$1,166,400
Raphael	Niccolini-Cowper Madonna	836,000
Botticelli	Adoration of the Magi	838,350
Titian	Venus with Mirror	544,320
van Eyck	Annunciation	503,010
Perugino	Crucifixion	195,615
Reynolds	Lady Compton	500,000
Gainsborough	Duchess of Devonshire	410,000
Lawrence	Lady Templeton and Child	250,000
Rembrandt	Young Men at Table	375,000
van Dyck	Marchese Balbi	450,000
Rembrandt	Elderly Lady	200,000
Rembrandt	Self Portrait	575,000
Rembrandt	Lucretia	175,000
Goya	Marquesa de Pontejos	212,700
Raeburn	John Tait and Grandson	125,000
Ter Borch	Interior	175,000
Raeburn	Miss Eleanor Urquhart	64,350
Gainsborough	Mrs. Catherine Felton	225,000
Romney	Mrs. Davenport	230,000
Romney	Mrs. Willoughby	50,000
Hoppner	The Frankland Sisters	198,000
Gainsborough	George IV	55,000

* See page 401.

Gainsborough	Mrs. John Taylor	115,000
Hobbema	Village Scene	250,000
Turner	Mortlake Terrace	110,000
Cuyp	Men and Cows	62,000
Turner	Venetian Scene	99,000
Hals	Portrait of a Young Man	350,000
Constable	Salisbury Cathedral	75,000
de Hooch	Courtyard	200,000
Goya	Portrait of a Girl	150,000
Hobbema	La Ferme au Soleil	108,815
Velásquez	The Needle Woman	275,000
El Greco	St. Martin and the Beggar	120,000
Hals	Portrait of an Old Lady	250,000
Hals	Portrait of Nicholas Berchem	170,000
Reynolds	Lady Caroline Howard	300,000
Titian	Madonna and Child with St. John	350,000
Titian	Portrait of a Man	135,000
Moro	Man and Dog	320,000
Metsu	The Intruder	225,000
Bellini	Young Man in a Red Coat	280,000
Michael	Man in a Fur Coat	60,000
Titian	Portrait of a Lady	550,000
Stuart	George Washington	50,000
El Greco	St. Ildefonso of Toledo	35,000
Rembrandt	Polish Nobleman	350,000
van Dyck	Philip, Lord Wharton	250,000
Velásquez	Innocent X	360,000
Raphael	St. George and the Dragon	747,500
Rubens	Isabella Brandt	245,000
Hals	Man with a Red Sash	253,000
Rembrandt	Portrait of a Woman	287,500
Holbein	Duke Britanus	440,000
Dürer	Portrait of a Young Man	200,000
Memling	Virgin and Child with Two Angels	300,000
van der Weyden	Head of Woman with White Veil	250,000
Holbein	Edward VI as a Child	437,000
Vermeer	Girl with a Red Hat	290,000
Luini	Portrait of a Woman	290,000
Vermeer	The Lace Maker	400,000
Vermeer	Smiling Girl	350,000
Botticelli	Young Man in a Red Hat	280,000
van Dyck	Prince of Orange	55,000
	TOTAL	**$18,778,560**

XIV

Quality and its Importance

N THE SUMMER OF 1956 I VISITED THE KNOEDLER GALLERIES in New York and asked to look at Italian paintings. While it was expected that the paintings offered for sale would be of high quality, what actually was brought out was more than a surprise. At first the gallery representative brought out three or four fine paintings to which my reaction was the same: "Yes, that's a fine painting and no doubt authentic, but I just don't like it enough to buy it."

Then the attendants placed on the display easel one of the most strikingly beautiful paintings ever seen in a museum or anywhere else: a Magdalene, with brown hair tied in a charming bow, wearing a green tunic. The artist was Bernardino Luini, the Italian painter of the early sixteenth century. The expression, the pose, the rendering were near perfection. The painting stood on its own.

The price of the painting was reasonable, but reasonable from the point of view of a painting of this quality, not from the point of view of the author's painting budget.

The gallery representative could see the reaction to the Magdalene. He even offered to let the painting be "tried out" by hanging it in my apartment for a period of time.

This proposal was flatly rejected—but with regret. I knew instinctively that if the painting were ever hung in my home it would never leave, no matter what had to be done in order to raise the money to purchase it.

LUINI. *Magdalene.*
National Gallery, Washington, D.C.
(Kress Collection)

During the year our stocks at least didn't go down and we sold some property. One year later my wife and I were back at Knoedler's asking again to look at the beautiful Magdalene. What a feeling of dejection came over us when we were told that the painting had been sold, but that we would probably be seeing it soon —in the National Gallery in Washington.

It was discovered later that the Kress Foundation had purchased it, and that they were planning to give it to the National Gallery. Although we were disappointed we can say at least that that is where the painting belongs, for all the public to see. We will, however, always think when we see the beautiful Magdalene in the Museum, "Even though it isn't ours, our judgment of the *quality* of the painting is confirmed."

In our tour of dealers and art museums of Europe in the fall of 1959 we stopped off in Munich. In this city there is probably the largest dealer in Germany, Julius Boehler. We carried an introduction to Mr. Boehler from Dr. William E. Suida, then Curator of the Kress Foundation, and one of the world's leading art authorities.

Mr. Boehler showed us painting after painting in his large and impressive gallery. His stock was excellent and we were considering several paintings.

Then he brought out a less-than-life-size half-length portrait of a young Dutch girl painted by a Seventeenth Century Dutch artist. We were not sure who painted the portrait, and there is some disagreement among the art authorities. There is complete agreement, however, as to the quality of the painting. The quality is far too high for any except the very top artists of this period, and if it could be attributed with certainty to one of these it would rank among his finest works.

The price of the portrait was in the low five figures. It was not a low price for a portrait of a lady by an unknown Seventeenth Century Dutch artist, but the painting had to be judged in terms of quality alone. It had excellence. In terms of quality the price was fair if not low.

These two paintings have one striking thing in common: quality. One is early Sixteenth Century Italian. The other is Seventeenth Century Dutch.

Quality exists regardless of who did the painting, in what century he painted or in what country. The following paintings, each from a different School of art and a different country, illustrate the point.

The French Impressionist painting "The Canoeists at Lunch" in the Phillips Collection in Washington, D.C. can hold its own alongside not only other Impressionist paintings but alongside the works of any School of art. The variegated colors give the effect of living light. This work by Renoir will always rank at the top of the Impressionist School. It is a painting of quality.

From Nineteenth Century French painting we move back to Spain in the sixteenth century—to El Greco's magnificent portrayal of "The Burial of Count Orgaz" painted for the Church of Santo Tomé in Toledo. This painting combines

EL GRECO. *Burial of Count Orgaz.*
Church of Santo Tone, Toledo, Spain
Photograph courtesy of Anderson, Rome

portraiture with composition to create a feeling of supreme religious majesty. It is a masterpiece by anyone's standards, and another fine example of pure quality.

Our tour of Europe's museums and cathedrals during the fall of 1959 included a visit to Belgium. Headquarters were made at Brussels and from there day trips were taken to the museums in other Belgian cities. One Sunday morning an early train was taken to Bruges where, in brief succession, five museums were visited. After this tour was completed a train was boarded for Ghent and from the railroad station a trolley was taken to the Cathedral of St. Bavon. After looking at the paintings on the wall of the beautiful, but dimly lit, cathedral and its chapels, a doorway was observed which was blocked by a ticket collector. It was late in the day and the walk all around the city of Bruges and its galleries plus the train and trolley travel were not conducive to any great interest in seeing more works of art, most particularly if it was necessary to pay in order to see them.

Nevertheless, after a brief consultation, the fee was handed over and the little chapel was entered. On the wall hung a group of paintings so exquisite and so overpowering that for a time no comment could be made. The paintings comprised the altarpiece known as the "Adoration of the Lamb" painted in the year 1432 by Hubert and Jan van Eyck. Fortunately there was enough light so that the detail of the workmanship could be appreciated.

The main panel depicts a large group of people and angels worshiping the Lamb of God. Above the Lamb is an image of God the Father. The perfection of portraiture and the rendering of the fabric of the robe and jewels could hardly be improved upon by any School of painting in any era.

Although the altarpiece had been seen in reproduction many times, the truly breathtaking quality of the painting could not be realized until one stood there

RENOIR. *Canoeists at Lunch.*
Phillips Collection,
Washington, D.C.

HUBERT and JAN VAN EYCK.
*Ghent Altarpiece—Adoration
of the Lamb and God the Father.*
Cathedral of St. Bavon, Ghent

before the original. It was difficult to realize that it had been painted over 500 years ago.

The wings of the altarpiece open and close, and the guide showed the paintings on both sides. Several individual paintings are combined into this one altarpiece which illustrates so beautifully the adoration of the world for the Lord God.

The fact is difficult to comprehend that the canons of the Cathedral of St. Bavon once sold portions of the "Adoration," but through the fortunes of war the missing portions were returned to the Cathedral.

Miracles have been reported in connection with this altarpiece. It would seem that the perfection of workmanship is a miracle in itself.

From the year 1432 we move forward to the late years of the fifteenth century to Perugino's "Crucifixion" in the National Gallery in Washington. While the figures in this tryptich may be somewhat stylized as compared with the later

261

PERUGINO. *Crucifixion*. National Gallery, Washington, D.C. (Mellon Collection)

Raphael, the drawing and the application of the colors exhibit a technical excellence close to perfection.

Now let us find an example of quality in the Contemporary School. The portrait of Queen Elizabeth II was mentioned earlier but because of its excellence it should be mentioned again here as a prime example of quality today. It was painted by the Italian Pietro Annigoni.

Thus we can go through history and through the museums in search of quality, and when we find it it speaks for itself.

Quality is the essence of art value. For a painting to be worth anything it must have quality. The art industry is in a sense like any other industry. It is simply a different one. The dealers see paintings day in and day out. Paintings are their merchandise. Yet regardless of how many paintings a dealer sees it is unusual to meet one who is not thrilled when he looks at a masterpiece. His critical faculties are sharpened by long exposure to paintings, and over the years he has grown to recognize quality. Perhaps he does not say, "The psychic overtones are captivating," or, "The painting has almost perfect triangular symmetry."

It is far more likely that he will say, "That is a painting!" This is a simple expression of appreciation of quality. A fine painting speaks for itself. It radiates quality, and beauty is an integral part of quality. It exhibits a mastery that cannot fail to be recognized.

Yet the question sooner or later comes to mind: "How about putting a Raphael alongside a Modigliani; then what about quality?"

ANNIGONI. *Queen Elizabeth II.*
By courtesy of the artist
and the gracious permission
of Her Majesty

RAPHAEL. *Small Cowper Madonna.*
National Gallery, Washington, D.C.
(Widener Collection)

MODIGLIANI. *Mme. Amédée.*
National Gallery, Washington, D.C.
(Dale Collection)

The answer is that while quality most certainly is to a great extent *absolute,* still it must be judged in terms of each particular School of art. It should be measured against the standards of that School.

It is not likely that Modigliani had such intensive training as that received by Raphael under Perugino, his teacher, and under the influence of Leonardo da Vinci and Michelangelo. It is improbable that Modigliani could execute the composition, coloring and feeling of form, depth and space which flowed so naturally from Raphael's brush. Modigliani was trying to do something *different.* The quality of Modigliani should be judged by comparing him with early twentieth century painters, almost all of whom in the most prominent Schools emphasized various stages of Impressionism and later variations, including abstraction.

An individual brought up on the subdued colors and camera-like fidelity of the seventeenth century Dutch art—the art of Vermeer, Ter Borch, Rembrandt, and Hals—might be unable to judge whether a Modigliani, or a Klee, or a Pollock is good, bad, or indifferent.

Modigliani's works would appear to be primitive; Klee's works might look like the pictures painted by an adult copying a child's drawings; and Pollock's paintings might be a complete puzzle.

Yet when a photograph of an unrecorded Modigliani arrived from an Italian dealer a short time ago with an offer of the painting for sale, it did not take long to say, "This is a Modigliani and a good one. I wonder how much he wants for it?"

The quality was apparent, but the quality had to be determined by the standards of Modigliani's aims, background and times, in terms of his School of art; and this School of art has to be learned to be appreciated.

A successful collector of art must be a person who appreciates quality in art. He buys because the quality is there, and he arrives at his conclusion as to the quality through his native taste, through study of art and Schools of art, and through an intense enthusiasm for art and for collecting. He may be aided by connoisseurs and experts, and he should solicit such aid; but to be successful he must have the ability within himself to distinguish quality.

Edward G. Robinson sold his collection of French paintings, mainly Impressionists, for a price of $3,250,000. It is reported that he made $2,500,000 on the transaction. Mr. Robinson could hardly have done better no matter what combination of corporate securities he had bought. Yet successful collecting is not simply a matter of shrewd investment, or even primarily a matter of shrewd investment. It is obvious that Mr. Robinson collected the very best works of each artist that were available. He could recognize quality and he bought only quality.

It is true that van Gogh was emotionally upset. His training was not the most extensive. He often painted while inebriated, and it can hardly be said that he painted with painstaking care. In the end he was committed to a mental institution.

A painting was displayed by one of the smaller dealers in New York a short time ago as a possible van Gogh. The painting was rejected almost immediately with the comment, "No, it is too unsure. It is not done with a bold enough stroke. It doesn't hang together, and the colors are not positive enough."

The quality wasn't there. It was not a van Gogh.

A true collector treasures his finest paintings. He usually doesn't want to sell them even at a profit. He loves to look at them hanging on the wall and he never loses this satisfaction.

One of the very best signs of quality in a painting occurs when the painting gives the collector the impulse to wrap it up and take it to other collectors to see. There is always the thrill when one undoes the wrapping and says, "Take a look at that and tell me what you think of it."

A short time ago I bought a painting from a New York dealer, a painting not attributed to anyone. It was an allegorical scene of seven nymphs bathing, and an eagle flying overhead. Whether the painting was Italian or French was not certain, and it was suggested that it might even have been by a Dutch artist painting in Italy. The only thing certain was that it was done in the seventeenth century.

That evening my wife and I were having dinner with friends who were also collectors, and the new prize was brought along to the dinner. After dinner the four enthusiasts pored through reference books but could not determine either the allegorical subject or the artist. By 1:00 AM it was thought that the painting might be Italian, but although this was no certainty everyone at least agreed that the painting was excellent.

LOUIS BOULLOGNE. *Nymphs Bathing.*

The next day the painting was taken to an official of the Frick Art Museum and Art Reference Library. Dr. Becker, an official of the Museum, observed that the painting appeared to be outstanding; in fact he thought it advisable to take it to the Metropolitan Museum of Art. He suggested calling Dr. Eisner for an appointment.

Dr. Eisner looked at the painting the same afternoon but although he expressed admiration for it he could go no further than to venture the opinion that the painting was French. He suggested that it be shown to Dr. Walter Friedlaender of the Fine Arts Division of New York University, an expert on Seventeenth Century French painting.

At the Fine Arts Division identification was made. Dr. Friedlaender attributed the painting to Louis Boullogne who was court painter to Louis XIV.

The important point in this story is that everyone's reaction to the painting was the same, even though he did not know who did it. The quality stood out. The name of the artist who did a particular picture, although highly desirable to know at the time of purchase, sometimes can come later. To have an outstanding collection one does not always have to have every painting done by a big name. If the quality is there, the chances are that the work was done by an artist of importance.

Renoir painted no fewer than 6000 paintings. Certainly while he was painting some of them he must have had a headache or was getting a cold. It is very likely that how he felt affected the quality of the painting. As he grew older he gradually lost the ability to move his hands and fingers, so that the brush had to be strapped to his wrist. Under these conditions his paintings suffered. This unequal quality of work is certainly not confined to the work of any one artist. It is a concomitant of anybody's work, whether a singer, a writer or even a house painter.

We thus must judge quality against the School of art to which the painter belonged (and almost all belonged to some School) and against his other paintings.

To the Venetians of the sixteenth century accustomed to the monumental paintings of religious subjects and pageantry of Titian, Veronese and Tintoretto, very early Italian art must have seemed primitive indeed. These early artists had not mastered the technique of third dimension. Their emphasis was on pattern and line. Such was the art of Duccio and other Sienese masters of the fourteenth and early fifteenth centuries. It *was* primitive. Today these paintings are known as Sienese Primitives.

Do these painters have less value on today's art market than the later, better-developed Venetian masters? Not at all! No one can say that a museum does not prize a Duccio as much as a Titian, or that a Duccio is worth less than a Titian.

DUCCIO.
Calling of the Apostles Peter and Andrew.
National Gallery, Washington, D.C.
(Kress Collection)

Each artist must be judged in terms of his times, and his contemporaries—in terms of his group or School of art.

Similarly, what would the Venetians have thought of the paintings of Paul Gauguin? The Tahitian period of Gauguin does not recognize anything but the brightest, most strident colors; and although the Venetians can almost vie with Gauguin as to beautiful color arrangements, they would not have understood his lack of the third dimension. Gauguin stated that he painted flat because he saw things flat. Is Gauguin thus less desirable to own, and does Gauguin bring less than Titian? Definitely not!

If we understand that quality is the determinant in art, and that quality should be determined by reference to the School to which the artist belongs and by comparison with his other paintings, we can explain values and prices of paintings. We can hardly compare a Duccio with a Renoir, or a Giotto with a Braque.

Public taste, however, is changeable, and whereas in one period a particular School of art may be the thing wanted, 50 years later paintings by the artists of this School may be actually worthless. A painting for which the Nineteenth Century British artist Sir Lawrence Alma-Tadema refused 12,000g. ($66,000), a tremendous price to be offered for the work of any living artist, could not now possibly bring as much as $6000.

Just as the public does not want the works of Alma-Tadema, they do not want the work of his contemporary Edward Burne-Jones. This artist has fallen in favor equally far.

Value, then, is dependent upon quality of painting. There is an absolute quality of painting which leads one to say, "That painting is good. It has quality," whether by Giotto or Braque. But quality also implies comparison with the School (period and type of art) to which the painter belongs. Quality also implies a comparison with other works by the same artist.

Finally, quality is independent to a considerable extent of public taste which changes year by year among artists and among Schools of art. A whole School can and does decline because of a change in public taste. Values of the School, expressed in prices, decline, but quality within the School remains the same.

XV

What Makes an Artist Gilt Edge?

F THE CONNOTATION OF "GILT-EDGE" AS USED HERE IS THE SAME as the term applied to a security traded on the Stock Exchange, that is our purpose. Naturally the analogy cannot be perfect, but the general idea of the artist and the security is intended to be the same. A gilt-edge artist is one whose paintings command relatively high prices, whose firmness of price has been demonstrated over a period of years and whose prices are not likely to decline precipitately in any short period of time unless the economic system faces a catastrophe.

Under this definition few if any of the Contemporary painters can be considered gilt-edge. If Picasso is, and we could include him as a gilt-edge Modern, it is because his public acceptance and price have been demonstrated over a period of many years, and his gilt-edge paintings are not of recent origin but were produced long ago, criticized, and accepted and have over a long period commanded high prices. A good Picasso at the end of the year 1961 would command a price in six figures.

These are the gilt-edge artists whom we are going to analyze here. There are dozens of gilt-edge artists whom we could study, but we have chosen a workable number—six—and there is no question in anyone's mind that all six come under the definition "gilt-edge."

Rembrandt	El Greco	Gauguin
Vermeer	Renoir	Matisse

MOREELSE. *Portrait of a Gentleman.*
Parke-Bernet Galleries, Inc.

REMBRANDT. *Portrait of a Man.*
Corcoran Gallery, Washington, D.C.
(Clark Collection)

The first two are Seventeenth Century Dutch, the third Spanish, the fourth a leading French Impressionist, the fifth a leading Post-Impressionist and the last a French Modern.

Rembrandt began his career by painting in the traditional style of the Seventeenth Century Dutch School. The style was precise, photographic and subdued in color. This tight style is illustrated in the fine, typical portrait of a gentleman by Rembrandt's contemporary, Paul Moreelse (1571-1638). The portrait dated 1636 was sold by the Parke-Bernet Galleries on April 6, 1960.

To a considerable extent Rembrandt's "Portrait of a Man" painted in 1633 resembles the Moreelse in the painting technique and in the use of dark color.

We can compare two half length portraits of men to see Rembrandt's distinct departure from his Seventeenth Century Dutch School: the "Married Couple" in the Isabella Stewart Gardner Museum, and his self-portrait in the Metropolitan Museum in New York. The first is in the traditional tight, precise style, and the second is sketchy, employing heavy paint and using many colors, some bright, to achieve an impression of depth, psychological penetration, and grandeur.

The study of the evolution of Rembrandt's style is not simply one of going through his paintings chronologically to see how gradually the tight style gave way to the rough, heavy painting. He experimented even in his early years with the technique that was to develop into his mature style, and conversely in later years he occasionally reverted to the traditional style. He experimented in order to achieve the style that suited him, and it undoubtedly took years of experimentation for him to "find himself." It is certainly to be expected that those commissioning Rembrandt to paint their portraits described how they wanted their portraits to look, and some of them desired to have their portraits in the style of the era.

It was this final style of Rembrandt which made his lasting reputation. It represented a revolution in painting and at the same time it made Rembrandt's paintings instantly recognizable.

Jan Vermeer of Delft lived from 1632 to 1675. Jan van Goyen, his contemporary, lived from 1596 to 1656. Both painted landscapes, but unfortunately few of Vermeer's landscapes are known.

Jan van Goyen's "View of Overschie" in the National Gallery, London, is a typical and good painting of a river and a town beyond the river. The colors are subdued.

Vermeer's "View of Delft" in the Hague's Mauritshuis is a similar subject, but there is all the difference in the world between the two paintings, mainly because of the unique application of color by Vermeer which brings to mind the much later French Impressionist technique.

Vincent van Gogh, commenting on Vermeer's "Reader" in the Amsterdam Rijksmuseum said in a letter to a friend, "Do you know of a painter called Jan

REMBRANDT. *A Lady and Gentleman in Black.* (Detail) Isabella Gardner Museum

REMBRANDT. *Self-Portrait.* (Detail) National Gallery, Washington, D.C. (Mellon Collection)

van der Meer? He painted a very distinguished and beautiful Dutch woman in pregnancy. The scale of colors of this strange artist consists of blue, lemon-yellow, pearl grey, black and white. It is true in the few pictures he painted the whole range of his palette is to be found; but it is just as characteristic of him to place a lemon yellow, a dull blue and a light grey together as it is of Velásquez to harmonize black, white, grey and pink."

Van Gogh is describing Vermeer's unique style of painting. There was nothing like it in his Seventeenth Century Dutch School just as there was nothing comparable to Rembrandt's style.

Gabriel Metsu was a typical Seventeenth Century Dutch painter of interior scenes. He lived from 1629 to 1667. We can compare his "Woman Seated at a Table and a Man Tuning a Violin" in London's National Gallery, with Vermeer's "Soldier and a Laughing Girl" in the Frick Collection.

Vermeer's use of color combined with his intensely dramatic portrayal of bright light streaming into the room from the window makes his painting unique in the Seventeenth Century Dutch School.

Vermeer had another quality which has always been a puzzle to artists: the viewer seems to be looking through a heavy piece of glass or ice at the colors on the canvas. On occasion forms seem indistinct as though they were a fraction out of focus. The borders, as between the subject and the wall, are hazy. In the chapter on Fakes and Copies we will see how these unique qualities of painting stimulated the greatest art fraud of all time.

While it is a most difficult thing to trace the artistic origins of the work of any particular artist to see what influences were responsible for the development of his style, it is even more difficult to do it in a small space. We are dealing with

VAN GOYEN. *View of Overshie.*   VERMEER. *View of Delft.*
National Gallery, London   Mauritshuis, The Hague

VERMEER. *Soldier and a Laughing Girl.*
The Frick Collection

METSU. *Woman Seated at a Table.*
National Gallery, London

art from an investment point of view rather than art from the point of view of the historical determinants of the style of any particular Master.

We know, nevertheless, that from a traditional, accepted, non-radical style came Impressionism which was something new and which represented a revolt against the prevailing style of painting.

When we come to Renoir we can look for the background and antecedents to Watteau, Boucher, Fragonard, and Chardin. Renoir was also influenced by Diaz, Delacroix, Courbet, and Corot.

At the risk of oversimplification of what Renoir was as compared with the traditional and accepted School of his time, let us look at Chardin as compared with Renoir.

CHARDIN. *The Silver Goblet.* The Louvre, Paris

RENOIR. *Fruits of the Midi.*
Art Institute of Chicago (Ryerson Collection)

In the Louvre hangs "The Silver Goblet" by Chardin, a simple still life with three apples, painted in accordance with nature but with subdued colors.

Now let us look at a comparable painting by Renoir. "Fruits of the Midi" is also a rendition of fruits. It hangs in the Art Institute in Chicago. In the first place Renoir's colors are not only brighter than Chardin's, but brighter than the fruit actually is. In the second place, where Chardin was fairly true to nature, Renoir painted the fruits sketchily, without Chardin's delicate use of highlights; but Renoir's colors themselves are pleasing, and anything but dull.

Next let us compare a Courbet with Renoir. In the Glyptothek, Copenhagen is a picture by Courbet entitled "The Three Little English Girls." They are watching a performance from a seat in the audience. The drawing is fairly close to nature, and the identity of the girls might be recognized from the painting.

RENOIR. *Premiere Sortie.*   COURBET. *Three Little English Girls.*
Tate Gallery, London   Glyptothek, Copenhagen

In the Tate Gallery is a picture by Renoir with much the same subject matter and pose entitled "Premiere Sortie." If Courbet's "Three Little English Girls" were blurred considerably and dashes of color applied to create an impression of people in the background we would almost have Renoir's painting.

RENOIR. *Algerian Landscape.*
The Louvre, Paris

COURBET. *Le Remise des Chevreuils.*
The Louvre, Paris

Let us finally compare Courbet's "Le Remise des Chevreuils" in the Louvre with "Algerian Landscape" by Renoir, also in the Louvre.

Courbet's trees and animals are painted with considerable fidelity to nature with the color green predominating. Renoir uses alizarine crimson as a dominant color, but in addition seems to brush all of the rainbow onto the canvas. The bright colors themselves are pleasing, and while they are not applied with photographic fidelity the resulting impression is a beautiful synthesis of color and subject. His style is vastly different from that of the traditional artists of his time.

Next let us examine El Greco against the background of religious austerity and perfection of reproduction of forms and figures that characterized the "Great Spanish Period." In a typical Spanish picture of the era the colors are strong but true to nature. The use of light and shade is natural. The robes are carefully drawn. The faces are lifelike.

In the National Gallery in Washington is El Greco's "Laocoön" of the family struggling with the serpents. The colors are dramatic. The forms do not represent

EL GRECO. *Laocöon.*
National Gallery,
Washington, D.C.
(Kress Collection)

precision painting. They are a prime example of El Greco's famous elongations. The use of light is not subtle and natural. It is bright and seems to come from everywhere rather than from a single source.

The "El Greco characteristics of painting" convey the impression of intense struggle. The sky is stormy, and the light on the sketchy landscape eerie.

This painting is in sharp contrast to El Greco's masterpiece painted 20 years earlier—"The Burial of Count Orgaz"—a painting which, while characterized by bright colors and "El Greco forms," is more in the traditional high-fidelity, majestic, Spanish style.

It must be obvious that the later, elongated figure style of El Greco with its unusual color, all-pervasive light and liquid sketchiness is recognizable even by a person without much knowledge of the Schools and subtleties of art.

Our next artist to study is Paul Gauguin (1848-1903), the Post-Impressionist. Gauguin's characteristic period and style are represented by his paintings done in Tahiti (1891-1893 and 1895-1903). His painting "We Greet Thee, Mary" in the Metropolitan Museum of Art is typical of this Tahitian period with its blending of tropical colors and primitive two-dimensional rendering of form. The painting was done in 1891.

Earlier in his life he painted "Brittany Landscape." It is hardly possible to believe that the same artist painted the two pictures. The latter is done in traditional, orthodox style, with far more subdued colors. The perspective is normal and there is a general, mild tone of Impressionism.

PAUL GAUGUIN. *We Greet Thee, Mary.*
The Metropolitan Museum of Art, New York
(Bequest, Samuel A. Lewisohn, 1951)

PAUL GAUGUIN. *Brittany Landscape.*
National Gallery, Washington, D.C.
(Dale Collection)

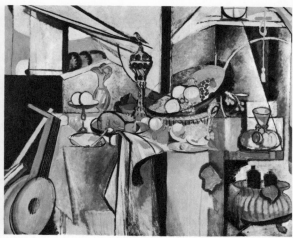

DE HEEM. *The Dessert*. The Louvre, Paris

MATISSE. *Variation on Still Life by de Heem*. Parke-Bernet Galleries, Inc.

It is out of such conservatism that Gauguin grew and against which he revolted, with the result that he developed his characteristic, primitive style.

Henri Matisse, sometimes called the father of Modern Art, was the leader of the Fauve (Wild Beast) School. Probably he, more than anyone else, is responsible for the many and varied Schools of art which sprang up in the early part of the present century and which led to the tremendous variety of non-pictorial paintings which exist today and which are being produced and displayed all over the Western world.

Two paintings mentioned earlier (see page 57) illustrate Matisse's objective: the first, a traditional Seventeenth Century Dutch still life by Jan Davidsz de Heem entitled "The Dessert," which hangs in the Louvre. One of Matisse's early occupations was to copy paintings in the Louvre and sell them to the French government for distribution to the French provincial museums. He copied this de Heem. Twenty years later he did a variant on this painting which represents his final style.

If one analyzes this variant certain things immediately stand out. The accuracy of drawing and of form are gone. The perspective is gone, and there appears to be no third dimension. Everything appears flat. The forms are made abstract, and one cannot easily determine where the table, for instance, begins and ends. Above all, the colors become strident, bright, unnatural and devoid of subtleties, shading, and the effect of light falling naturally on the subjects.

Matisse deliberately did these things to destroy photographic qualities and natural representations. He strove to make something that one liked to look at because of the employment of bright and contrasting colors, and forms that in themselves would please, regardless of their photographic accuracy or fidelity in representing nature. His paintings were not representations of nature, as the earlier

277

artists strove for; nor did he attempt to convey an emotion or thought or underlying message or mood as some of the later Schools have tried to do. He wanted to accomplish his object of painting pictures which would be enjoyed simply because of his use of color and pleasing forms. With Matisse the representational element of painting began to recede in earnest.

After first studying the Old Masters, Matisse absorbed Impressionism, then the Post-Impressionism of Cézanne, van Gogh, and Gauguin, including the Pointillists Seurat and Signac, and arrived at his own individual art. The representation of nature went far downhill with the Impressionists, further with the Post-Impressionists and much further with Matisse.

What, if anything, do all of these artists have in common that establishes a bond among them and places them in the "gilt-edge" category? In a general way we have examined Rembrandt, Vermeer, Renoir, El Greco, Gauguin, and Matisse by comparing them with their contemporaries and antecedents.

Each artist was an innovator. Each represented a departure from the traditional School of painting of his time. Each artist was either alone in his style or was a member of a relatively small group painting in a particular style; or each was the first, or a very early member, of that group, not a Johnny-come-lately.

Rembrandt was alone. Although others painted like him, they were his followers and students, and to a considerable extent they fell into the category of copyists. Just as the followers of Leonardo were so dominated by his personality and sheer ability as to have been able to develop little uniqueness on their own, so Rembrandt's followers—Bramer, Dou, Eeckhout, etc.—were to a considerable extent imitators, never achieving a great degree of individuality.

Vermeer was not only alone, but ahead of his time in the use of brilliant colors and light, in addition to being a skilled craftsman.

Renoir was also a unique painter and one of the very best of the relatively few, highly valued early Impressionists. The style of this group was a radical departure from the traditional Nineteenth Century French style of painting.

El Greco was alone in his style. No group or School formed around him except his own factory of assistants who executed orders for him.

No one painted like Gauguin in his Tahitian period. He is known as a Post-Impressionist, but this term is applied only for convenience. He does not belong to any School. We think of the names Gauguin and van Gogh together. Actually their painting techniques are far apart.

Finally, Matisse founded a School of essentially nonrepresentational art, one which made the pictorial representation of natural things secondary to the use of color and form so that the viewer would secure his satisfaction from these things alone. Whether the viewer likes or dislikes what he sees in Matisse is up to him, and he is privileged to like or dislike Matisse's art without studying the history of painting or the workings of Matisse's unconscious mind. Matisse was trying to achieve something. We know what he was trying to achieve, and that he was a serious, trained artist who could and did understand something of the techniques of painting. His style is unique because he deliberately chose to make it unique.

Another characteristic of all of these artists we have chosen for study is that they were either rejected or made the center of controversy in their early years. Rembrandt had difficulty in collecting his fee for his monumental "Night Watch" now in the Rijksmuseum in Amsterdam. Vermeer was completely overlooked after his death. In a survey of Dutch and Flemish masters of the seventeenth century, made in the general period of their work by Carel van Mander, Vermeer was not even mentioned despite the fact that the survey included some of the most minor artists. This oversight contributed materially to the oblivion into which Vermeer fell for centuries.

The entire School of Impressionism was scorned and derided when it first appeared, and Impressionist canvases could be bought for next to nothing. Renoir was no exception.

El Greco fell into almost complete oblivion after his death and remained in this state for about 300 years. Even his canvases in the basement of the Prado in Madrid were not recognized as being of any importance or even of being by El Greco until he was "re-discovered."

Gauguin found it difficult to locate a sponsor for a show of his paintings, not once but many times, even after his first visit to Tahiti during which stay he produced some of the canvases that are among those the most sought after today. At the time of his death a great many of his paintings were burned.

When Matisse contributed to the famous New York Show of 1913 he was so derided that he felt it necessary to write an open letter explaining that he was not an unsubstantial man.

There is one unfortunate characteristic which these gilt-edge artists have in common: only time proves their merit. They were not only rejected initially. They were vociferously denounced as are, to a considerable extent, innovators in all fields. Time alone secures their acceptance and establishes their value, and very often decades or centuries must pass before this acceptance becomes a reality.

A fifth quality the artists have in common is that they are often "re-discovered." A long time after their peak of painting or after their passing someone gets the idea that here is an overlooked artist of prime quality, and he attempts through scholarly research to indicate just why this was a great Master.

The final attribute that these six artists have in common is that they have inherently good quality. They all have a uniquely masterful painting style.

"Gilt-edge" is a term which is relative to time. It is not entirely absolute. "Gilt-edge" is a value and price term, and there is a time when artists are gilt-edge and a time when they are not. Rembrandt was not gilt-edge at the time of his death. He was in disrepute. Vermeer sank into oblivion shortly after his death, even though he was at one time President of the Delft Guild. Renoir received his gilt-edge recognition really only since World War II, and El Greco in the last 60 years. Gauguin and Matisse have taken on this attribute in perhaps the same period as Renoir, but we cannot go back to the 1920's and call Renoir, Gauguin, and Matisse gilt-edge masters. Whistler and Sargent were the gilt-edge Moderns of this period. To a considerable extent "gilt-edge" is a cyclical term and refers to the top of the value cycle in the history of sales of the artist's paintings in the art market. This subject of the value cycle will be taken up in the chapter on **Major Price Movements in Art.**

XVI

What Determines the Price of a Painting?

HO PAINTED IT" IS OBVIOUSLY THE MOST IMPORTANT THING ABOUT a painting in determining the price it will bring; but this is really only the starting point.

The question must immediately be asked as to how characteristic the painting is of the artist. A sale was held in one of the major world auction houses in the late 1950's which featured a portrait by Rembrandt. It had a good background of attribution but brought only a little over $10,000.

Why did a Rembrandt portrait bring so little? The answer is that it was not entirely characteristic of the artist. To a certain extent it looked like the work of Girard Dou, a follower of Rembrandt. Since there was even a small possibility that the painting might be by Dou instead of Rembrandt it could not command the price of an unquestioned Rembrandt.

The point illustrated here is that to bring a top price a painting must be thoroughly typical of the artist. The following is another example.

A New York dealer recently had a painting which was attributed to El Greco. It was a most unusual work with several hundred figures in it. It appeared to be signed in characteristic fashion. While El Greco is one of the artists in greatest demand at the present time the painting did not move for over a year. The reason is that it did not look completely characteristic of El Greco.

For a painting to bring a high price, even though the artist may be "gilt-edge," the painting must be typical, but it must also have been painted in a period of the artist's life which people have come to think of as characteristic of the artist.

Before Paul Gauguin went to Tahiti to paint he worked in Paris. The paintings of Gauguin that bring high prices are the Tahitian paintings with their bright, tropical colors, with particular emphasis on reds, scenes which usually include native girls. These Tahitian paintings have a distinctly flat appearance. The paintings of Gauguin's Tahitian period are so characteristic and so unique that they can hardly be mistaken for anyone else. His earlier French paintings are more conventional and like other paintings of the time.

Renoir lived from 1841 to 1919. Toward the end of his life he lost the use of his fingers and had to have the brush strapped to his wrist. The result is a very free style, one which is less precise and easier to imitate than his earlier style. This late style is less preferred than some of his earlier styles.

El Greco's painting falls into three fairly distinct periods and styles. He was born in Crete and painted there in the traditional Byzantine style. When he was about twenty-five years old he went to Venice and there fell under the influence of Veronese, Giorgione, Titian, and Tintoretto.

From Italy El Greco migrated to Toledo, Spain, and there developed his characteristic mannerist portrayal of elongated forms. This is the style which the buying public usually identifies with El Greco, not the Venetian style and certainly not the relatively unknown early Byzantine style. The price of El Greco's paintings reflects this identification and preference.

The value of a painting depends, therefore, not only on who painted it, but on how characteristic the particular painting is of the artist, and the period in the artist's career in which it was painted.

The next determinant of the value is subject: what is depicted. There are few Dutch landscapes more in demand at the present time than those by the Seventeenth Century Dutch artist Jakob Ruisdael. His paintings bring well into five figures.

Five years ago a magazine article appeared containing a description of a hypothetical Ruisdael and how what was in the picture determined its price. At about the same time a splendid Ruisdael was offered in New York—an unusually large painting of falling water with a hilly, wooded background. The price asked, and by a first-class gallery, was only $4500.

The type landscapes produced by Ruisdael which are the most in demand are not the waterfall scenes but the flat landscapes with great expanses of cloudy sky and perhaps a few little figures walking or riding along a winding, rutted dirt road. If there is a river or a windmill so much the better. Whether these paintings are any better inherently than the waterfall scenes is certainly debatable, but they are what the buying public wants and is willing to pay for.

In the paintings of some artists the technical differences which affect value are so numerous as to be bewildering. A Romney portrait, 26 by 30 inches, for instance, in which a man is wearing a black or plum colored coat, is one of the less valuable Romneys. If the dimensions are larger it is worth more. If, instead of a dark coat, the sitter is wearing a bright uniform, the value is higher; and if the subject is a lady the value is still higher, and possibly even higher if the subject is a child.

Gilbert Stuart, the painter of the famous George Washington portraits, may be our greatest American portraitist. His paintings of important personages done in America are very rare and very valuable, and his so-called Newport period paintings are highly sought after by at least one major museum.

Gilbert Stuart also painted, however, in England and in Ireland. The English and Irish period Stuarts are the Stuarts which are not so highly prized. If the portrait is half length of a man seated it is worth far less than a full length portrait. If the full length portrait is life size it is worth more than if it is full length but less than life size.

Almost every artist produced certain types of paintings whose contents or size makes them more or less valuable.

Inextricably interwoven with subject matter is quality. Obviously not all of the paintings by one artist are the same in quality. At the Lurcy sale in New York in 1957 the top price received for any painting was $200,000 for Renoir's beautiful garden scene entitled "La Serre." In the very same sale another Renoir entitled "Still Life: Fish" brought but $5500. The latter painting was exactly what the title said it was, and the catalogue description stated: "A dozen small fish . . . displayed strewn against a grayish-white background." The fish painting did not have the quality of the landscape.

The size of a painting is important in relation to value. A 30 by 36 inch painting, or thereabouts, is a very desirable size. It is impressively large, yet not too big to hang in a modern apartment or house. A Grand Canal scene by Canaletto of this size is the optimum.

Outsize paintings, as the over-large ones are called, are usually not in demand, since few people have the wall space to hang them. On the other hand, if the large painting is one of great quality by a much wanted Master, as, for instance, Rubens' "Adoration of the Magi" it is a museum piece. It brought the equivalent of $771,000 even though it could hardly get through the door of the auction room.

On the other hand one cannot turn down a Rembrandt landscape because it is too small. Many Rembrandt landscapes are small. That is one characteristic of them.

The condition of a painting is all-important. The better the condition the more valuable the painting. Whether or not the painting is restored extensively is a matter for experts to determine. What can be demanded is the privilege of seeing the painting under ultraviolet light. One New York gallery offered a painting to a museum in Baltimore a few years ago. The painting appeared to be in excellent condition until the ultraviolet light was turned on it in the darkened laboratory of the museum. At once the painting looked as though someone had filled it with buckshot from a shotgun blast. The restoration of the numerous tiny holes was done very skillfully, but the ultraviolet light showed up these restorations immediately. Obviously the painting was not in the condition it could have been in, and its value was far less than if these damages were absent.

Paintings by the early Italian Master Perugino are some of the most expensive works on the market. The values of Perugino approach those of Raphael. In New York a dealer has what appears to have been a Perugino "Madonna." If it were in good condition the price would be in the low six figures. In its present condition the painting is practically valueless and the dealer considers it a "throw-out."

An overcleaned, typical, signed Ruisdael recently sold on Third Avenue for somewhere in the neighborhood of $3500. It was worth no more simply because of its bad condition. Had it been in excellent condition the price might have been about $25,000.

The condition of a painting might roughly be classified into "Prime," "Good," "Damaged," and "Overcleaned." These are not official classifications used in the art industry, but they convey the idea. A prime painting does not have to look as though it was painted yesterday. In fact there is nothing the matter with a painting which has never been cleaned or relined with new canvas. Such a painting will have a dirty, yellowish, flat appearance, but it can easily be cleaned and relined by a good restorer. These never-cleaned paintings of the older Schools are rare, however, and even a yellowed painting may have been cleaned several times in its life, which life may be as long as 500 years or even longer. Old relining and minor damages do, however, help establish the age of an Old Master painting.

How the painting was cleaned, whether well or poorly, and how many times are the usual questions which must be asked of the dealer. Sometimes in well recorded paintings there is a history of the cleanings. Usually, however, one must arrive at his own conclusions from photographs, particularly x-ray pictures. Usually a dealer will not permit the prospective customer to clean the painting prior to its purchase to make an examination, although one London gallery cleaned a painting prior to its purchase so that I could make up my mind about it intelligently.

Theoretically, cleaning, when it is done properly, does not hurt a painting since all it does is remove the dirt and old varnish. In practice cleaning often takes off some of the paint too. The earlier the cleaning the greater the risk of damage to the paint itself, and for two reasons: earlier in the painting's life the paint was softer and came off more easily, and earlier restorers did not have the materials to clean without damage that are in existence today.

A major museum in Washington has a collection of Seventeenth Century Dutch paintings several of which are obviously damaged through overcleaning.

The next factor determining the price of a painting is its "pedigree" or degree of authenticity.

A well attributed Rembrandt entitled "Woman Plucking a Fowl" was sold in November, 1932, at the auction of the American Art Association-Anderson Galleries in New York. It measured 52 by 41½ inches—a fairly large painting. Its long pedigree is an example of an excellent attribution.

REMBRANDT. *Old Woman Plucking a Fowl.*
National Gallery, Washington, D.C.
(Gift, Dr. and Mrs. Walter Timme)

The painting is described in Smith's *Catalogue Raisonné of the Works of the Most Eminent Dutch Painters of the Seventeenth Century*. It is described in Dutuit, *The Complete Works of Rembrandt;* in Bode, *The Complete Works of Rembrandt;* in Hofstede the Groot in his *Catalogue Raisonné of Dutch Painters,* in W. R. Valentiner's *Rembrandt* and in Valentiner's *Rembrandt Paintings in America*.

This is an almost perfect authentication of a Rembrandt painting. Almost all of the great Rembrandt experts have certified it.

Clearly such a painting is in the category of a museum piece. It is now displayed in the National Gallery in Washington.

The great authorities on art are as well known in the art field as are the authorities in any other field—architecture, rocketry, and nucleonics, for instance, but we will reserve a discussion of the qualifications of an art expert to the chapter dealing exclusively with this subject.

In what collections was the painting included in the past? The Rembrandt "Woman Plucking a Fowl" was in the collection of Jan Six in Amsterdam. Jan Six was Rembrandt's patron. Although the painting may not actually have been purchased directly from Rembrandt, since the descendants of the original Jan Six purchased paintings too, we know that the Six family owned it in the year 1734 and sometime prior to that year. Since that time it has been in eight other well known collections.

Some prominent painting collections contained some doubtful items. Others were known for their consistent high quality as, for instance, the Jakob Goldschmidt Collection of Impressionists which included the "Seven Paintings for $2,186,000."

The advantage of owning a painting which has been in a prominent collection is that the collector in all probability studied the painting before he bought it and during his ownership of it. When the painting has appeared in several prominent collections it has the seal of approval of several collectors. More than one collector has had the opportunity to study the painting.

Another advantage of buying a painting that has been in collections is that the painting didn't just "come from nowhere." The "Woman Plucking a Fowl" didn't suddenly appear on the market. There are relatively very few years during which the whereabouts of this painting was unknown.

Many copies of Rembrandt exist—excellent copies—and many of the followers of Rembrandt painted like him. Carel van der Pluym is startlingly close to Rembrandt. Carel Fabritius and Gerard Dou (Rembrandt's pupils), van den Eeckhout, Govaert Flinck, Jakob deWet, and Aert de Gelder are all too close to Rembrandt for the purchaser's comfort.

In what important exhibitions was the painting shown? A museum often sets up a committee of experts to choose not only the paintings clearly the work of a particular artist, but excellent examples of his work, beautiful, authentic paintings which will benefit the exhibition in the eyes of the viewer, particularly the expert viewer. It is very embarrassing for a painting in an exhibition to be criticized by a visiting art expert or museum director. The selection committee or committees for the 1959 Venice Exhibition of Seventeenth Century Venetian Painters consisted of names as illustrious in the art field as a list of Nobel Prize Winners.

The Burlington Fine Arts Club was for years distinguished for its excellent exhibitions of paintings by Schools of art, as, for instance, the Umbrian Exhibition of 1910 which included such masterpieces as Raphael's "Small Cowper Madonna" now in the National Gallery in Washington, the "Madonna and Child" by Fiorenzo di Lorenzo, then owned by Sir George Salting, now in the National Gallery in London, and the Raphael "Predella Panels," one of which is in the Metropolitan Museum of Art and the other in the Isabella Stewart Gardner Museum in Boston. Similar distinguished exhibitions have been held in the Royal Academy and in the New Gallery in England.

If we again go back to the Rembrandt "Woman Plucking a Fowl," we find it was exhibited in the British Institution Exhibition, London, 1861, as number 17; in the Rembrandt Exhibition, Detroit Institute of Arts, May, 1930, as number 31; and in Florence, Italy in both 1737 and 1767.

Usually the people in a particular country know their art best. The display of a French painting in Paris speaks more for its authenticity and quality than its display in Spain, and an El Greco displayed in the Prado is thereby better authenticated than if shown in the Glyptotheque in Copenhagen.

Is there a signature? The Seventeenth Century Dutch artists frequently signed their paintings. The Italian artists of the same century and the following century rarely signed. Renoir signed the majority of his paintings, while Cézanne signed few of his. An authentic signature adds greatly to the value of a painting. A false signature detracts from a painting. Strangely enough, many real Rembrandts carry false signatures. Rembrandt did not sign all of his paintings, but to dispel any doubt, dealers over the centuries added what Rembrandt forgot.

Very fortunately most signature fakers are neither ingenious nor thoroughgoing. *Most* false signatures come off when the painting is cleaned, particularly if the signature has been added within the past 50 years so that the paint is still soft. Frequently these added signatures can be determined to be later additions as the new paint fills in the cracks when it should crack with the cracks. Ultra-violet rays will usually show the false signature as being different from the original paint.

Sometimes the signature is not characteristic of the artist whose facsimile signature can be studied in several of the dictionaries and directories of artists.

The difficulty of detecting fake signatures is the greatest in the case of Impressionists and French Moderns. The original paint is not old enough to provide a striking contrast to the added signature. Often the painting itself is not a faked imitation of the artist but the authentic work of another artist who painted in the same style. The "big name" is then faked on the painting of the lesser artist. The chapter on Fakes and Copies will go into detail on some very clever fakes that fooled even the top art experts.

The price history of a particular painting is important in determining whether its present asking price is fair. If the painting is a well known one and has been sold at public auction or sold privately but with a published price, this price offers some gauge of the market, and it represents what someone else thought of the painting and was willing to pay for it.

Often, however, the painting has no price history and may have been in the possession of the present owner and his family for years, perhaps even from the time the artist sold it originally. In such a case the price of a painting of similar size, subject matter and quality by the same artist may serve as some guide.

The Cézanne "Boy in a Red Vest" sold for $616,000. We can fortunately locate similar paintings by Cézanne on which it is possible to secure prices paid for them prior to this sale.

It was reported that in 1956 the David Rockefellers paid about $180,000 for a similar Cézanne, "Boy in a Red Vest."

In 1947 the Swiss munitions maker Emile Buehrle was reported to have paid $150,000 for a roughly comparable Cézanne. There is thus some price history.

Next, in determining the price of a painting, *who* offers the painting for sale is important. In the case of the $616,000 Cézanne the collection being sold was the Jakob Goldschmidt Collection, one known throughout the world for its excellence.

In the Spring of 1960 at the benefit sale in New York for the Museum of Modern Art a Georges Braque sold for $145,000, certainly a high price for this artist. The donor was Gov. Nelson Rockefeller. Quite aside from the fact that because the Governor and his family have traditionally had enough money to buy the best works of Braque or any other artist, there is a certain glamor to owning a painting from the Rockefeller family and from Gov. Nelson Rockefeller, a public figure.

One does not expect to make "discoveries" at major galleries such as Duveen, Knoedler, Wildenstein, and French and Company, but he does expect to get authentic paintings. The nature of these establishments is that they handle quality merchandise at a quality price, but at the same time, and because of this fact they are reliable. If they sold a fake or a copy as an original the sale could too easily make headlines and discredit the gallery perhaps permanently.

Besides these galleries there are some dozen other New York dealers of highest rank, many of them on East 57th Street.

The major auction galleries of the world are the next source of good paintings, and three stand out: Parke-Bernet in New York, and Sotheby's and Christie's in London, although there are other good auctions on the Continent.

Here, however, one must depend to a great extent on his own knowledge of values and on his evaluation of what is written in the descriptive material pertaining to each painting which is printed in the auction catalogue. All auction houses handle some paintings whose low price reflect their low quality, and only at a sale of a known high-grade collection can one be fairly certain of quality.

In London the auction houses appear to handle about everything anyone offers for sale. Parke-Bernet in New York is more selective. In 1960 a seemingly well recorded Goya from a prominent collection was annotated by the gallery to the effect that it was probably not by Goya. This is a good step toward opening the auction houses to worry-free patronage by inexpert buyers.

There are in every city small dealers who do not pretend to handle the quality paintings offered by the major dealers, and the next chapter will go more into detail on these dealers as well as the structure of the art market generally.

Where a painting is offered for sale and *when* it is offered are highly important factors in determining price. The art season is a winter season which starts in the fall and ends the following June. Most art buying is done in this season, and it is often done at night when the business of the potential buyers does not conflict with the sale. The Georges Lurcy sale was held in New York at 8:00 PM, November 7, 1957. The Arnold Kirkeby sale was held at 8:00 PM, November 19, 1958. The Goldschmidt sale was held in London in October, 1958. The season, the city, the gallery, and the time all help to determine the price a painting will bring.

Finally, *who* attends the sale is extremely important in determining the price the painting will bring. Of course *what* is offered determines to a great extent who attends as prospective buyers, but sales of quality paintings have been held which brought low prices because, for one reason or another, few buyers came. At the famous Lurcy sale in New York about 2000 people attended. In this group were Chester Dale and his wife, the great collectors of Impressionists and French Moderns, Mr. and Mrs. Billy Rose, James J. Rorimer of New York's Metropolitan

Museum of Art, the Henry Fords II and Mrs. Eleanor Roosevelt. A number of these notables came prepared to pay and pay high.

These, then, are the important factors determining the price of a particular painting:

1. Who painted it, and whether it is typical of the artist and painted in the most desired period of his career.

2. Quality in terms of the artist's other paintings.

3. Characteristics of the painting—subject and size.

4. Condition.

5. Pedigree—record of collections, exhibitions and other background.

6. Signature.

7. Who offers it for sale?

8. Where and when is it offered for sale?

9. Who attends the sale?

XVII

Where to Buy: The Structure of the Art Market

HE THREE MAIN ART SALES CENTERS OF THE WESTERN WORLD are London, New York, and Paris. For the season ended June, 1959, the major art auction house in New York as well as in the United States, the Parke-Bernet Galleries, sold over $10,000,000 worth of art objects. Their 1960 sales were $9,240,000.

For the 1959 season Sotheby's auction in London sold £5,756,742 ($16,-120,000) worth of art items, and the sales of the other major London auction, Christie's, were £2,783,490 ($7,800,000). The total of these two London houses was $24,000,000. In 1960 Sotheby's sales were $19,254,000 and Christie's $10,-360,000; the total of these two was approximately $30,000,000.

It is estimated that the third major center, Paris, sold $16,000,000 worth of art objects at auction.

In New York, in addition to the Parke-Bernet Galleries, the other auction houses are Savoy Art and Auction Galleries, Coleman's, Plaza, and Tobias Fischer, plus some lesser houses.

While the enumerated figures add up to nearly $55,000,000 in sales, the minor auctions and the auctions in other countries, including Charpentier in Paris, the Dorotheum in Vienna and Weinmueller's in Munich, add materially to this total.

If we add sales of major and minor galleries, private sales of art objects and other sales, which, while not primarily sales of art objects include some art objects, it is estimated that the annual volume of art objects sold in the Western world is about a quarter of a billion dollars. Paintings alone amount to roughly half this total.

The three or four major auction houses are more in the news than any of the other establishments in the art marketing business, primarily because the prices received by these organizations are published in the newspapers and make interesting reading. It was at such houses that the $771,000 Rubens "Adoration of the Magi," the $616,000 Cézanne "Boy in a Red Vest," and the $509,000 Hals portrait were sold.

An art auction is for three types of buyers: experts, buyers who bid only on the thoroughly authenticated paintings, and those who are willing to pay for an art object that may not be what it is labeled but which may be worth the purchase price for other reasons—because it is worth the price as a decoration or because the buyer loves it for itself and for other non-investment reasons.

The London art auctions which in the last two years have sold many paintings in six figures and collections in seven figures are burdened down with paintings which bear little relation to the names under which they are sold in the catalogue. In fact it has been a practice in London to indicate the degree of authenticity of a painting by the wording of its designation. If a painting appears to be authentic, a Rubens, for instance, it is designated "Sir Peter Paul Rubens." If it is less certain it is labeled "P. P. Rubens," and if it is very doubtful that it had anything to do with Rubens it is simply "Rubens."

When one reads over the typical catalogue of a London auction house for an unimportant sale (and such a catalogue is usually a thin one without illustrations) he may not be far wrong to estimate that about 20 per cent of the paintings, or fewer, are what they are labeled. If one compares the prices after the sale with the designations it will be immediately apparent that if a painting bearing the name of an illustrious artist brought a low price no one who was at the sale thought it was what it was designated, and conversely if the painting brought a high price it was probably authentic.

The art auctions are one of the main sources of great discoveries, and in a later chapter some startling discoveries at art auctions will be described. The fact stands out, however, that usually only experts or very knowledgeable collectors and dealers make discoveries.

Although the auction houses sell some of the finest and most unquestioned paintings in the world, as, for instance, the Goldschmidt Collection, even a good collector sometimes makes an honest mistake and has a copy of an authentic work in his collection or a school work or a mislabeled painting. The risk of buying at auction without definite knowledge of what is being purchased is a great one for the unaided investor.

The fact should be stressed, however, that great paintings are sold through auction houses, paintings with long histories, paintings authenticated by the most knowledgeable experts, paintings that have been in fine collections and have many times been displayed in important exhibitions or published in authoritative works. In fact the basis of price determination in this book is auction prices on authentic works, and it has been pointed out that as a general rule auction prices are below those of dealers.

While the major art auctions sell a number of art objects and are very much in the public eye, the organizations which stand at the top of the pyramid of the art marketing industry are the major galleries. Included in this group in New York are Knoedler and Company, Duveen Brothers, Newhouse, Paul Rosenberg, Rosenberg and Stiebel, Wildenstein, and French and Company. In London there are Leonard Koetser, Colnaghi and Company, J. Leger and Son, Marshall Spink, and William M. Sabin and Sons. In Amsterdam, there are Douwes Brothers and Peter de Boer; in Munich, Julius Boehler; in Florence, Mario Bellini; and in Paris, Durand-Ruel and Duveen.

While these are some of the largest dealers in the world, they by no means have a monopoly on the best pictures. There are many other dealers of first rank in every one of these cities and in other cities, including perhaps a dozen more quality galleries in New York.

It was the Knoedler Galleries in New York which arranged the sale of the Edward G. Robinson Collection of Impressionists and French Moderns for over $3,000,000 to Stavros Niarchos. It was also Knoedler who arranged for the sale of the Hermitage paintings from Russia to Andrew Mellon for nearly $7,000,000, including $1,166,000 for Raphael's "Alba Madonna" and $747,000 for Raphael's "St. George and the Dragon." Both of these paintings now hang in the National Gallery in Washington, D.C.

In some cases topflight European dealers are a little lower in price for top grade paintings than American dealers. The lesser European dealers are a little higher than the lesser American dealers, and very much higher in terms of their local currencies.

When a buyer is considering the purchase of a painting a guarantee should be requested as to the artist. The large dealers often give such a guarantee. The background and history of the painting should also be guaranteed, since it is not at all unusual for unscrupulous sellers to "trump up" backgrounds and collections in which the painting was included.

When there is no guarantee, and the authorship is questionable, a painting can still be excellent. A buyer who considers such a painting should have become somewhat of an expert with a sufficiently trained eye to make his own determination of its value. If, however, no guarantee is offered and the buyer is not sure of his ability to judge the painting it is best to obtain expert advice and assistance.

Still better is an agreement by the gallery to repurchase at any time the buyer does not want the painting. Such an agreement is rare but not impossible to secure. At least one New York gallery offers such an agreement. If all of the buyers who purchased paintings under this agreement requested the gallery to repurchase, the gallery would not become bankrupt. Its owner could retire on his profits. Such has been the rise in the painting market since the gallery first began offering this guarantee.

Under a guarantee from a good dealer the question of authenticity need not usually be proven. If the question is raised the gallery will usually repurchase. This is one of the great advantages of dealing with a good house. The repurchase agreement or guarantee of authorship should, however, be very carefully examined.

From the top of the art marketing pyramid we can draw the rest of the pyramid. The large and important buyers as a general rule buy from the large dealers as well as from the topflight collections being sold through auction. Very often the ultimate buyer uses a large dealer as agent and perhaps advisor as well when purchasing at auction. Rosenberg and Stiebel of New York was the buyer of the $200,000 Renoir at the Georges Lurcy sale, the highest priced painting sold. The real buyer was Henry Ford II.

At any major auction of an important collection of paintings the major galleries of the world are well represented. In the London auctions the names of the buyers are printed in the price lists published by the auction houses. Here the great gallery names like Wildenstein and Knoedler often appear. In fact one method of determining the authenticity of a painting sold at auction is to see who bought it. It is unlikely that Duveen Brothers will buy a copy, mistaking it for the real thing. If one has the patience to go through all of the auction catalogues of all of the major auctions for years back and at the same time is familiar with the painting stock of the major dealers some surprising things turn up. One auction painting sold in New York a few years ago for $1500. The painting appeared in the stock of one of the major New York dealers priced at $75,000, completely attributed after the dealer had purchased it.

The major galleries buy from the lesser dealers, and this fact further draws the art marketing pyramid. Almost all smaller dealers want to make a quick sale at a profit and are willing to take a smaller profit quickly rather than wait for a high price at some indefinite time in the future. The major gallery offers this possibility. The head of one of the largest New York galleries stated that over the past ten years he had purchased about $1,000,000 worth of art objects from a smaller dealer located in lower New York.

A typical transaction in which prices are known involved an object for which a smaller dealer paid $12,000. The item in this case was not sold to the larger gallery but was placed on consignment, and the asking price was $30,000.

Small dealers are always looking for the prime type of art object which the major galleries will want. Long experience tells a minor dealer when he runs across such an object. Usually such an item does not present problems of resale to a major gallery, and the sale can be negotiated quickly and at a profit. The large gallery has customers who will pay more for good quality paintings. Seldom can the small dealer command the same prices that the large dealer can for the same item.

Finally, whereas the sale of an art object at retail usually involves much looking by buyers, consideration, family conferences, some price haggling, and, perhaps, time payments, the wholesale transaction with the large gallery can be done quickly and with a minimum of fuss.

Some time ago a smaller New York gallery purchased a "Madonna and Child" by Giampietrino, a follower of Leonardo da Vinci. The painting was of quality and was shortly thereafter sold to a large uptown gallery. This gallery then offered the painting for sale at a price higher than could have been obtained by the small gallery, and eventually sold it.

A large gallery will often not handle a painting on which there is no background. It wants to be in a position to offer the background to the prospective buyer. Sometimes the gallery secures this pedigree with the painting it purchases for resale. Sometimes there is a great deal of time and money spent researching the painting. When this research is undertaken after the major gallery purchases the painting there is the risk to the gallery of finding out that the painting is not as good as originally thought.

This authentication is work, but when it is completed and the painting is finally established the gallery can offer a painting of authenticity to the buyer. For this work and this authenticity the buyer must of course pay, and this is one of the reasons the paintings sold by major galleries are not low in price.

The research undertaken by the large gallery in some cases discloses the fact that a painting purchased for relatively little money is in reality a lost masterpiece. Newhouse Galleries in New York, for instance, "discovered" a Ter Borch, one of the highest priced Seventeenth Century Dutch Masters.

This was also the case of the French and Company Davenport-Bromley Madonna by Leonardo da Vinci, and this story will be told in the chapter on "Discoveries."

In addition to the pedigree the major dealer will almost always produce attributions of the painting by well known art historians. Frequently their paintings are well recorded and sometimes illustrated in authoritative books. The dealer will show this documentation on request.

Any time a dealer has to make explanations it is time to be cautious. One of the explanations a dealer may give for a painting that does not look typical of the artist is that the painting is an early period work. Another favorite explanation is that the painting is a late work of the artist. One dealer had a beautiful Flemish Primitive which could not be identified. He told the prospective buyers that it was either a late van Eyck or an early Memling. The buyer could take his pick!

A major dealer is always ready to talk about the condition of the painting and will generally admit if it is not everything it should be. He may produce ultra-violet photographs which reveal overpainting and retouching of damaged places and he may produce x-ray pictures in order that the underpainting may be examined. The dealer Hirschl and Adler in New York owned an excellent Umbrian painting which was displayed with parts of the paint actually gone. This is the ultimate in honesty. The blank spots can easily and cheaply be blended in with the rest of the painting, but the dealer wanted the buyer to know exactly what he was getting.

The major galleries buy not only from major auctions and from lesser dealers but from private families, very often from the noble families of England who collected paintings over the centuries. The level of income tax in England is a factor in forcing the sale of the fine old mansions and castles at low prices and to a considerable extent the tax has the same effect on paintings, although the houses generally go first because of the large out-of-pocket expense required to operate them.

The beautiful Luini "Magdalene" sold by Knoedler a few years ago had been in the same English family for generations, and the story is the same with many other paintings which have come onto the market. Frequently the purchase of a fine painting from an old and noble family is a very delicate operation and involves more than going into the family home and asking, "How much will you take for that painting?" The job of go-between can often be a most valuable one which will mean the difference between securing the painting and not securing it. One of the greatest talents of the late Sir Joseph Duveen was his ability to approach diplomatically an unapproachable family and come out with a great painting at a price allowing resale at a profit.

A major gallery may have in its employ scouts who visit all kinds of sales looking for paintings or other art objects and who attempt to find paintings that private estates have for sale. In most of the large cities there are families who own paintings and who might under certain circumstances be induced to sell. Their primary reason for selling is often lack of funds. Frequently the collector himself has passed on and his widow may even have removed the paintings from her home and placed them out of the way in storage.

In some cases it is necessary to sell all of the items from an estate before settlement is made with the widow and other heirs.

The major galleries also sometimes use free-lance scouts. Recently a New York dealer sold me a splendid painting of the Umbrian School. Nothing of the background of the painting was known either to the dealer or to me, but the painting stood on its own. While I was drinking coffee in a small downtown lunchroom shortly after the purchase, a free-lance scout came in and sat down. I soon learned that it was he who had located and purchased the painting from a family on Long Island. He said, "I know it's a good painting, and I could have sold it to a large uptown gallery, but I like the dealer you bought it from, and I thought I'd let him have it."

From later research it was disclosed that the painting was a recorded master-piece displayed on several occasions including the famous 1910 Exhibition of Paintings of the Umbrian School at the Burlington Fine Arts Club in London.

Next let us look at the smaller dealers, those who do not confine their dealings to the prime Old Master paintings handled by the major galleries. In New York there are about 25 dealers in this category, although there are probably 1000 shops and dealers who at times handle paintings along with antiques and other objects. Some of these dealers are located on Madison Avenue, and these are the higher grade of the secondary dealers. It should be pointed out here that some of the top dealers in Contemporary paintings are located on Madison Avenue, and at least one prime dealer is located there. Many of the secondary dealers are located on Third and Second Avenues and on the cross streets from the thirties to the seventies.

While these dealers may handle a large quantity of second-rate Old Master paintings, a few copies or school pieces, as well as Schools of art and periods of paintings which are not in highest demand, occasionally excellent paintings appear in their shops. In one small shop on 62nd Street and Third Avenue in New York there has appeared an authentic, signed landscape by Jan van Huysum, a Botticini Madonna, an important recorded Magnasco and an excellent seascape by the Seventeenth Century Dutch artist Abraham van Beyeren.

The price level of the paintings in these secondary shops is about 50 per cent of the price a major dealer would get for the same works, and sometimes lower. Because of the lack of art scholarship of some of the secondary dealers and because they have neither time nor money to do much research these dealers sometimes offer the opportunity to the knowledgeable buyer to make "discoveries."

While there are perhaps 25 such minor dealers in New York handling Old Master paintings there are about 100 in London, 50 in Munich, 50 in Vienna, 50 in Rome, and over 100 in Madrid, to name only a few European cities with art dealers. American cities other than New York contain few dealers in these older paintings. The number of dealers in Contemporary paintings is, however, increasing, and all over the country.

In New York and a few other major art centers there are importers who deal in paintings on a large scale, some of them advertising several thousand paintings in stock at all times. They act almost solely as wholesalers and generally will not sell to the buying public, confining their sales to dealers in New York as well as dealers throughout the country. These importer-wholesalers do not specialize in top quality paintings and they usually do not sell to major galleries. Once in a while a fine painting comes through them, but this is the exception, not the rule.

The importer-wholesalers buy to a great extent in London, although they may go to Paris, Rome, and other cities where there is a plentiful supply of paintings. The secondary dealers patronize these importers, but frequently a secondary dealer will appear insulted if one asks him whether he buys from an importer. He considers the general quality of such wholesale imports as beneath him.

There is another group of importers separate from the importer-wholesalers of old paintings. These are the importer-agents for Contemporary artists. The demand and nature of the market for the works of Contemporary artists, primarily those located in Paris, has already been explained. It is sufficient here to point out that this type of importing is growing tremendously. The sole source for many of the Contemporary works is New York. If a dealer either in New York or in another city wants a painting by a particular Contemporary artist he must patronize the artist's agent in New York or else do without. Those artists in greatest demand are rapidly securing contracts from agents in New York for their entire output.

Finally in the art pyramid is the minor art auction, and it is one of the most fascinating parts of the entire art marketing structure. This is because of the possibility of making discoveries here.

In the United States when a collector or an estate desires to auction off art objects the first organization thought of is usually the Parke-Bernet Galleries in New York. For one reason or another, however, Parke-Bernet may not want a particular offering. There are only so many auction days in the art sales year, and Parke-Bernet may have enough good sales scheduled. The alternative may then be one of the other auctions.

On the other hand a collection or estate might well be offered to a smaller auction first. The owners or executors might feel that the smaller auction would produce just as good results. Sloane's auction in Washington has at times secured prices for paintings which would be hard to equal in a major auction.

Late in 1959 an auction house on 59th Street offered for sale a group of paintings many of which were miscatalogued. One painting was catalogued as having been done by the Italian landscapist Pannini. It was a Monsu Desiderio whose hitherto relatively unknown works have been rising rapidly in value. Another was labeled "Satyr in Landscape—Flemish." This was an understatement. It was by Jan Wildens, the excellent Seventeenth Century Flemish landscapist. A third painting was catalogued "Boucher." The painting was a beautiful Seventeenth Century Flemish work by Jakob Jordaens. The purchasers of these works not only bought fine paintings, but made discoveries, if they were knowledgeable as well.

A non-expert buyer can, however, very easily throw his money away trying to "discover" masterpieces in secondary auctions. In many of the Impressionist and Modern Sales by some of these minor auctions over 100 paintings will be sold in one night labeled "Renoir," "Cézanne," "Seurat," "Monet," and everyone else in the Impressionist, Post-Impressionist and Modern Schools, most of the paintings fully signed. Few will be more than optimistically attributed. The trick is to go into one of these "Impressionist" sales and manage to come out with one genuine Impressionist. It can be done, but it takes a knowledgeable buyer to do it.

The minor auctions are a great source of paintings for the smaller dealers, but they do not offer much of a supply for the large galleries, since the general run of paintings is not to be considered prime. These auction houses have little or no time to research 100 or 200 paintings in a lot, but a dealer may single out in the pre-auction display one or two paintings in Schools with which he is familiar and research these before he appears at the auction. By the time of the sale he has a definite idea of what he wants, some certainty as to the authenticity, and a definite price in mind which he can afford to pay in order to be able to resell at a profit.

Some out-of-town or even out-of-country buyers maintain agents in New York on a retainer basis or on a per-painting-purchased basis. When the agent locates something that might be of interest to one of these out-of-New York clients he calls the client, tells him what is up for sale, and secures a commitment from the client as to how high to bid. In the case of out-of-country buyers, and some of these are in Latin American countries, the agent sometimes takes a chance and buys without prior confirmation.

The art intelligentsia (the experts and knowledgeable amateurs) frequent major and minor auctions. Sometimes they discuss in advance what is up for sale and its degree of authenticity, provided of course this sharing of information will not result in competition among themselves.

Once in a while a masterpiece or near masterpiece goes through auction without background or authentication, but it is so obviously authentic that most of the dealers agree on what it is as well as its value. In such a case it is not uncommon for a group of dealers who have an interest in the purchase of such a painting to form a syndicate in order to avoid bidding against one another. One of their number will do the actual bidding. In this way competition is minimized as far as the dealers are concerned.

When the spokesman or bidder for the dealers' syndicate is high bidder and secures the painting another auction is held privately just for the participating dealers and the highest bidder gets the painting. The difference between the official auction price and this later private sale price is divided among the participating dealers. Obviously the practice is a monopolistic one, and the person selling through the auction suffers, but it is a practice prevalent in the art world.

In summary, it is wise for the collector to develop his taste, train his eye, and become a connoisseur before he tries to "discover" paintings.

Paintings can be purchased through a reputable dealer under his guarantee without risk, and prime paintings can also be purchased through auction, but here the trained eye or guidance of an expert will be necessary if paintings other than those with a well recorded background are to be purchased. Mistakes are, however, not serious if the price paid is not large. The important thing is to learn, and the best way to learn is to buy. When a person puts out his money for a painting he studies it so intensively that what he learns is sometimes worth the purchase price of the painting itself.

In the beginning, however, it is wise to be cautious and limit the amount spent to a certain maximum per painting, say $1000. If a collector loses a great deal of money on mistakes he is inclined to give up the whole thing in discouragement. This is to be avoided by testing connoisseurship slowly in small purchases until confidence is gained. *Where* you buy is important, but even more important is *what* you buy.

XVIII

The Art Experts

ELDOM CAN A BUYER GO TO THE ARTIST AND ASK, "DID YOU PAINT this picture?" Obviously if the artist is no longer living this is impossible. Relatively few pictures, furthermore, are sold by anyone who can state that he himself purchased them from the artist. An unbroken record of ownership from the artist down to the present is highly desirable but almost impossible to secure, even in the case of major museum works.

This is where the art experts come in. An art expert is a person who, because of education and training and because of particular knowledge of an artist or School of art, can state with authority that in his opinion a particular painting is by a particular artist.

This definition implies several things:

1. The expert must have education in the field of art or else his expertness is doubtful.

2. He must have experience in recognizing a particular artist or School of painting concerning which he professes to be an expert.

3. He confines his attributions to those artists and Schools with which he is thoroughly familiar.

It is most important to remember that these are the qualifications of an expert in the field of art in view of the "expert attributions" which appear from time to time.

The standards of an expert in any field are fairly well established. When, for example, a person appears before the Tax Court of the United States and claims to be an expert representing a company petitioning that Court for a tax refund, the attorney for the Commissioner of Internal Revenue is permitted to cross-examine him in order that the expert may establish before the Court his expert status. Usually an expert must have a Doctor's degree, and preferably from a prominent university. Next, he should have worked in the particular field in which he claims to have expert knowledge and he should have held some important positions in the field. If his expert knowledge is called upon in a specific situation it must be demonstrated that he is particularly qualified by possessing intimate knowledge in this specific situation. The qualifications for experts in the art field are to a considerable extent like those of any other expert, except that they are in the field of art.

In the early part of November, 1944, the Leon Schinasi Collection was offered for sale at the Parke-Bernet Galleries in New York. Included in the collection was the so-called "Madonna della Stella" painted by the Italian Master, Fra Filippo Lippi, who lived from 1406 to 1469. It was a painting on panel in tempera, measuring 32¾ by 24¾ inches, and brought $30,000.

A letter was cited in the description of the painting and was to be given to the purchaser. It was written by Bernard Berenson on July 26, 1929, and read in part, "You ask me to write down with my own hand the few lines I penned years ago about the Carl Hamilton Filippo Lippi that now belongs to you. I do so with pleasure:

"It is a painting of exquisite, tender feeling, fine composition, and very beautiful colour. Indeed I can recall no other picture by this most human of Florentine painters which is so glowing and radiant."

The painting also had authentications by Richard Offner, Lionello Venturi, Raimond van Marle, and W. R. Valentiner.

These expert authentications place the painting in the "above-suspicion" class.

Of all of the experts on Italian art, the one who has through the years been the most vocal and most in the public eye is Bernard Berenson. B. B. (as he is often called) was for years advisor to Sir Joseph Duveen on the purchase of paintings. He was also instrumental in locating fine works for Mrs. Jack Gardner whose "Fenway Court" in Boston is now one of America's important museums. The significant thing about his attribution of this Fra Filippo Lippi is that it *praises* the painting. B. B. was not always given to praise. In his *Italian Painters of the Renaissance,* Phaidon Press, Ltd., London, 1953, he states, page 133, "No wonder that we have given over Giulio Romano, Pierino del Vaga, Giovanni Franceschi Penni, Polidoro da Caravaggio, and their ignoble fellows to oblivion. It is all they deserve."

On page 164 of the same work he states, "If miserable decline was the lot of Ercole, who had come in contact with reality at second hand and with intellect at third hand, we may know what to expect from his pupil, Lorenzo Costa, whose contact with life and thought was only at third and fourth hand. He began with paintings, like the Bentivoglio portraits and the 'Triumphs' in San Giacomo in Bologna, which differ from Ercole's later works only in increased feebleness of touch and tameness of conception."

Finally, on page 203 he states, "The Mannerists, Tibaldi, Zuccaro, Fontana, thus quickly give place to the Eclectics, the Carracci, Guido, and Domenichino. Although counting many a painter of incontestable talent, and some few who, in more favouring circumstances, might have attained to greatness, yet taken as a school, the latter are as worthless as the former . . ."

Berenson had a knack of being able to damn the largest number of painters in the fewest possible words.

For this reason his glowing description of the Fra Filippo Lippi offered for sale could only have the effect of significantly increasing its value.

Offner has always been conservative in his assessment of paintings and has not been given to writing attributions for any and all paintings shown him, as have some experts.

Van Marle cites the painting in his scholarly work *Development of the Italian Schools*.

Finally, the painting was selected by W. R. Valentiner, Director of the Exhibition of Masterpieces of Art, New York World's Fair, 1939.

The important thing about attributions is "Who are the experts and what do they say about the painting?"

While the public has been made acquainted with the leading atomic scientists, since the atom has been so much in the public consciousness for the past decade, and in other fields the "greats" are known—architecture, commercial illustration, bridge building, etc.—expertness in the field of art seems to the public to be a kind of shadowy, little known talent possessed by relatively few people, mostly Italian, living somewhere or other in obscurity.

This is by no means the case, and in the sphere of art the experts are as well-known as in any other line. There is, moreover, a great amount of agreement in the art field as to the degree of competence of experts. The knowledge even goes so far as to classify the degree of expertness of a particular authority according to the period in his life. A great Dutch authority, for instance, is praised for his early attributions, but because of his failing eyesight his later attributions are not taken with the same degree of seriousness. As we will see, this failing on the part of this expert led to the greatest art swindle of all time.

In the field of Italian art, and the art of the Renaissance in particular, the following experts, specialists in their line as noted below, are considered to rank high among the great authorities of the century:

William E. Suida, late Curator of Research of the Kress Foundation, the largest collection of paintings in America.

Adolfo Venturi.

Bernard Berenson.

Roberto Longhi in early Renaissance art.

Antonio Morassi for Tiepolo, Magnasco, and Genoese art.

Herman Voss, late Renaissance and Baroque art.

Federico Zeri on Renaissance art.

Giuseppe Fiocco, Seventeenth and Eighteenth Century Venetian art.

Pietro Toesca on early Renaissance art.

Richard Offner on early Florentine art.

F. F. Mason Perkins on Sienese art.

Langton Douglas on early Sienese and Florentine art.

Hans and Erika Tietze, on Sixteenth Century Venetian art.

In particular Schools of art there are specialists, such as Enzo Carli, Director of the Galleries of Siena, Italy, on early Sienese art.

The Kunsthistorisches Institut in Florence, under the direction of Dr. Ulrich Middeldorf, is extremely knowledgeable in the attribution of Italian paintings in general. Dr. Middeldorf is also a leading authority on Renaissance sculpture.

Books have been written on certain artists, and these books and their authors are usually, though not always, authoritative.

Bertina Suida Manning is authoritative on the Genoese artist Luca Cambiaso as well as on Italian Renaissance and Baroque art, and Benno Geiger is authoritative on Alessandro Magnasco, whose works he catalogued.

The following are three examples of authoritative cataloguing of the works by particular artists:

Van Gogh by de la Faille.

Romney by Ward and Roberts.

Cézanne by Meier-Graefe as well as Lionello Venturi.

The Dutch painting "Woman Plucking a Fowl," attributed to Rembrandt and referred to in an earlier chapter, has an almost perfect authentication by a large group of the prominent Rembrandt experts. This painting is described in Smith's

Catalogue Raisonné of the Works of the Most Eminent Dutch Painters of the Seventeenth Century. It is described in Dutuit's *The Complete Works of Rembrandt,* in Bode's *The Complete Works of Rembrandt,* in Hofstede de Groot in his *Catalogue Raisonné of Dutch Painters,* in W. R. Valentiner's *Rembrandt,* and in Valentiner's *Rembrandt Paintings in America.* This work sold at auction in New York in 1932 now reposes in the National Gallery in Washington.

Some of the ranking authorities on Seventeenth Century Dutch art are:

W. R. Valentiner.
Hofstede de Groot who catalogued the works of the great Dutch artists of this period.
Abraham Bredius.
Gustav Glück, also an authority on Italian art.
Wilhelm von Bode.
Max Friedländer.
Jakob Rosenberg.
Leo van Puyvelde.
Ludwig Burchard.

These are not all of the authorities on Seventeenth Century Dutch art, but they are among the most prominent and have done a great deal of attributing over the past years.

The Netherlands Art Archives, and particularly Dr. S. J. Gudlaugssen of that organization, are present day authorities on this School of art, and Walter Bernt has written the exhaustive illustrated series of books on Dutch School of the Seventeenth Century, *Die Niederländischen Maler des 17. Jahrhunderts.* This set of books is a necessity for the collector of Seventeenth Century Dutch paintings.

In the field of German art and on the greatest German painter, Albrecht Dürer, in particular, Dr. Ernst Buchner, former Director of the Alte Pinakothek in Munich, Germany, is the best living authority.

Walter Friedländer is considered an important expert on Seventeenth Century French art.

Robert L. Manning of the Kress Foundation is a knowledgeable specialist on Baroque Italian Art and on the French artist Simon Vouet.

Today in America there are few authorities who authenticate paintings. Probably more authenticating is done by the Flemish art specialist Professor Erik Larsen of Georgetown University than by anyone else.

What is a good expert authentication of a painting?

In the first place, an illustration of the painting may appear in some authoritative book on the artist. A painting by an artist in the Leonardo School might appear in Suida's book, *Leonardo und Sein Kreis*. Such artists would be: Luini, Boltraffio, Solario, da Sesto, de Predis, Marco d'Oggionno, de Conti, Giampietrino and, of course, Leonardo. If the painting appears in this volume, it is recognized by the authority in the field and is well attributed. Berenson in his *Italian Pictures of the Renaissance-Venetian School* illustrates many pictures of this School and presents lists of authentic paintings. Inclusion in this book goes a long way to establishing the authorship of the paintings covered.

The Luini "Magdalene" offered for sale by Knoedler a few years ago appears as No. 160 in the book entitled *Bernardino Luini* by Angela Ottino Della Chiesa. This is a typical, excellent attribution. On the other hand, toward the end of 1960 another Luini was offered for sale at auction. Chiesa described the work as a "copy." Consultation of the book might well have deterred prospective buyers.

The recently sold $369,000 van Gogh is shown in *Van Gogh* by da la Faille.

One of the works on Italian art by an expert is Berenson's *Italian Painters of the Renaissance* cited above. A far more detailed work on Italian art is that of Adolfo Venturi, *Storia dell'Arte Italiana*. This is the bible of Italian art. If a painting is referred to in this work its authenticity is practically to be taken for granted.

In the same field of Italian art Raimond van Marle's *Italian Schools of Painting* is similarly authoritative, and there is finally Crowe and Cavalcaselle, *A History of Painting in Italy*.

These are recognized, excellent works on Italian art. But just as all experts are not of equal rank or ability, neither are all books in print. A recent book on a particular Dutch artist has been described by at least one art authority as, "Not worth the paper it is written on." Almost anyone can pick out an artist, read some books about him, reproduce paintings from museum photos and write a book. This procedure does not make the writer an expert—even on the one artist he writes about.

Max Friedländer's *Alt Niederlaendische Malerei* is the best and most competent over-all work in the field of early Flemish painting.

A group of works to which reference is continually made is the *Klassiker der Kunst* series, each book being written by a leading authority on the artist discussed. The series was published over a period of years by the Deutsche Verlags-Anstalt in Stuttgart and Berlin. They contain illustrations of the known paintings of many of the great Masters, including Raphael, Rembrandt, Titian, Dürer, Rubens, Velásquez, Michelangelo, Correggio, Donatello, van Dyck, Memling, Mantegna, Fra

Angelico, Holbein, Watteau, Murillo, Dou, Perugino, de Hooch, Leonardo, Giotto, Hals, and Signorelli. A few additional volumes are on less eminent artists. Although over a period of decades some attributions have changed in these illustrated works, as in the case of several Raphaels, still, this series has become authoritative and invaluable to the collector.

An attribution by a recognized expert (which is usually written on the back of a photograph of the painting) should accompany the painting if it is not a well-known, illustrated or recorded work. If an Italian Renaissance painting has certificates by Berenson, Suida, and Adolfo Venturi, it would probably be as close to being perfectly attributed as possible. In fact, any one of the three fairly well establishes the picture, but the more recognized authorities accept it the better.

There is probably not an expert alive, or who ever lived, who can honestly say that he did not make a mistake at some time. Shortly after World War II the great van Meegeren scandal broke in the newspapers. Van Meegeren was the famous forger of the Vermeers. At the time his painting entitled "Christ at Emmaus" appeared in 1937 it was proclaimed as Vermeer's masterpiece by Abraham Bredius and was purchased for the Boymans Museum in Rotterdam, Holland. The story will be gone into later, but it is sufficient here to point out that even the best of the experts make mistakes.

One would naturally believe that the paintings which hang in museums are all exactly and indisputably what the labels on them say they are. This is too often not the case, despite the most valiant efforts to find out who painted the pictures.

JOOS VAN CLEVE. *Woman with Rosary.*
Corcoran Gallery, Washington, D.C.
(W. A. Clark Collection)

GIORGIONE. *The Holy Family.*
National Gallery, Washington, D.C.
(Kress Collection)

In the W. A. Clark Collection in the Corcoran Gallery of Art in Washington there hangs a picture of a woman with a cap entitled "A Lady of the Pape Family" labeled Joos van Cleve, the Sixteenth Century Flemish artist.

This is what the experts have to say about this painting:

> Catalogue of Clark Collection to which the painting belongs—
> School of Holbein (German, first half of Sixteenth Century)
> Dr. W. R. Valentiner—Joos van Cleve (Flemish, 1520-1556)
> Jakob Rosenberg—Flemish, perhaps by Pieter Pourbus
> Julius S. Held—William Key (Flemish, 1515-1568)
> Dr. A. B. de Vries—suggests Martin van Heemskerck, or possibly Willem Key or a Dutch painter working in Antwerp."

The experts do not even agree as to the nationality of the painting—whether German, Flemish or Dutch, much less the specific artist. Yet it is certainly fine enough to be displayed in a museum.

The National Gallery in Washington has a painting from the Kress Collection entitled "The Holy Family" and labeled Giorgione. This is what the various experts have to say about it:

> Herbert F. Cook—Giorgione
> Lionel Cust—Giorgione
> Ludwig Justi—Giorgione
> Bernard Berenson at one time placed it "somewhere between Catena and the youthful Titian." However, in his *Italian Pictures of the Renaissance* he catalogued it under "Giorgione."
> Lionello Venturi—Catena
> G. Gronau—Master of the Allendale Nativity—later switched to Giorgione
> Sir Charles Holmes—Master of the Allendale Nativity
> Tancred Borenius—Master of the Allendale Nativity—later switched to Giorgione
> R. Longhi—Giorgione
> W. E. Suida—Giorgione
> G. M. Richter—Giorgione, with landscape by Sebastiano del Piombo
> Hans Tietze—Unknown pupil of Giovanni Bellini
> Adolfo Venturi—Interpreter of Giorgione, but not Giorgione
> Duncan Phillips—Assistant of Giorgione
> John Walker—Artist other than Giorgione
> Mario Modestini—Artist other than Giorgione

Regardless of authorship the painting is fine and of museum quality. If all of the experts agreed on who painted it, the value on the market would at least be doubled. Without this agreement, however, the painting still stands on its own as a fine example of Venetian art.

In another instance, the author has been told by two top art authorities that there are two Vermeers in one of our American museums which are questionable.

One of the most peculiar phenomena in our entire history of art experts is contained in one of the first really significant books to appear on the subject of the attribution of Italian art—*The Study and Criticism of Italian Art* by Berenson, published in London by George Bell and Sons in 1901. One of the main purposes of this book was to bring to the notice of the art world that a new Master had been identified and his name or title, created by Berenson, was Amico di Sandro; that is, "Friend of Sandro Botticelli." The artist, Berenson said, was close to Botticelli, but not quite so good as Botticelli, and he assigns painting after painting (some of which were formerly attributed to Botticelli) to this new artist.

Through the years of his art development Berenson apparently pondered the matter a good deal more, with the result that some time later he stated that after further study he had changed his mind and that there was *no* Amico di Sandro.

Mr. Berenson's aforementioned 1901 publication contains an illustration of a "Portrait of a Gentleman" which he has clearly labeled, "Copy After Giorgione." * This painting now hangs in the National Gallery where it is clearly labeled "Giorgione and Titian."

As a "Giorgione and Titian" a fair price for the painting would be upwards of $250,000. As a "Copy After Giorgione" which Berenson originally said it was, $2,500 would seem to be more of a fair price. If it were not a contemporary copy (a copy by an unknown artist done at the time Giorgione painted the original) but was a copy done say 100 years later, an equitable price would be perhaps only $250.

Such is the importance of experts, and one hopes when he submits a painting for attribution to the expert, that on that particular morning the expert got up on the right side of the bed!

---

* Although in the above mentioned 1901 publication he stated that the painting was definitely not even a copy by Titian, he apparently modified this opinion, as in his recent *Italian Pictures of the Renaissance,* published by Phaidon Press in London, 1957, the painting is catalogued as a "Titian."

XIX

Discoveries: Are They Possible?

N 1888 Christie's auction in London sold a painting from the William Rennie Collection labeled simply "Christ Healing the Blind" by Tintoretto. Neither the collection nor the painting was of particular significance since the sale was not mentioned in the *History of Christie's,* so thoroughly chronicled by H. C. Marillier in 1926. The fact that the painting was catalogued "Tintoretto" and not "Jacopo Robusti—Il Tintoretto," as was and is the custom for the authentic works, indicates the low esteem in which the particular painting was held by the gallery. The price confirmed this low opinion— 17½ guineas ($93.45). Yet the painting was large and could not escape notice— 46 by 57 inches. It consisted of a number of figures with an architectural background depicting the famous Biblical scene.

The same painting was offered for sale by the same auction house in May, 1958. The gallery apparently had the same opinion of its artistic merit in 1958 that it did in 1888—70 years earlier; only this time it was labeled "Veronese," not even "Paolo Veronese."

This time it brought not 17½ guineas but 36,000 guineas (approximately $105,000)—two thousand times the 1888 price. The successful bidder was the London dealer Geoffrey Agnew, and his unsuccessful competitors for the painting included among others the London dealer, Edward Speelman, and the American dealer, Julius Weitzner.

310

Just prior to the opening of the bidding on the painting Sir Alec Martin, Christie's expert, announced that in his opinion the painting was by El Greco. The rapidly mounting bids by leading dealers bore out Sir Alec's opinion.

When one sees the painting hanging on the wall of New York's Metropolitan Museum of Art he wonders how the quality and typical El Greco figures could have escaped anyone, particularly the characteristic elongated figure on the left side of the painting. The fine work is now in the collection of the Charles Wrightsmans, owners of the Vermeer "Blue Girl."

The quest for an Old Master painting is one of the most thrilling sports in the world, but without an intimate knowledge of a particular Old Master or School of Old Masters a person wastes his time and his money trying to make discoveries, and can easily fill his home with "school pieces" done in the shop of the Old Master by his students, as well as old copies.

In 1850 Christie's auctioned off a collection of paintings not considered to be of particular importance, owned by Francis Duroveray. In the sale was a small picture entitled "Apollo and Marsyas" which was listed in the sale catalogue as being by Mantegna, a renowned late Fifteenth Century Italian artist.

A Mr. Morris Moore instructed his agent, Mr. Emery, a London dealer, to buy the painting for him. Mr. Moore was certain the painting was a Raphael.

Mr. Emery purchased the picture for £70/7s. (about $350) for Mr. Moore's account.

PERUGINO. *Apollo and Marsyas.*
Formerly attributed to Raphael.
The Louvre, Paris

EL GRECO. *Christ Healing the Blind.*
Collection Charles B. Wrightsman.
Photograph by Taylor and Dull

Immediately Mr. Moore offered the painting for sale to London's National Gallery as a Raphael—at a "Raphael price." The Director of the National Gallery apparently did not share Mr. Moore's enthusiasm for the painting and so declined the offer.

In the meantime there was anything but agreement in London art circles as to who painted the picture. Some of the suggested artists were Timoteo Viti, Lorenzo Costa, and Francia.

Mr. Moore, the owner, was entirely unimpressed with these opinions and maintained that the painting could have been done by none other than Raphael. Mr. Moore took a trip to Venice where, in the Academia, he found a drawing of the same subject attributed to Montagna (not Mantegna, the artist Christie's catalogue attached to the painting). The drawing appeared to be a study for Mr. Moore's painting.

Mr. Moore was apparently a persuasive man, because he argued the officials of the Venice Academia into changing the attribution of their drawing to "Raphael."

Still few if any people other than Mr. Moore seemed to be convinced that the painting was by Raphael. For 35 years he tried to "prove" his painting. Finally, in 1885, when he was in his final illness, he offered the painting to the Louvre for what he considered to be a very fair price—£8000 (about $40,000) but with the stipulation that he would sell the painting only if it were clearly labeled on the frame "Raphael."

The Louvre met his terms!

Soon thereafter Mr. Moore passed on, happy in the thought that his attribution had been correct and that his efforts, which extended over almost a lifetime, were not in vain.

But this is not the end of the story. The painting is still in the Louvre. It is still considered by all the art world to be a fine work; but it is now recognized as a Perugino (the teacher of Raphael).

Which master is better? Which is rarer? Which master is worth more today— Raphael or Perugino? It is anyone's opinion. Mr. Moore's efforts were not unsuccessful. Through his purchase of the painting at Christie's he put it back into the limelight, thus saving it from possible oblivion. Incidentally, what appears to be the same painting can be traced back to Christie's sale of 1799 when it was sold for the equivalent of about $10. The painting would bring upwards of $100,000 today.

The eminent Bernard Berenson did at least as well as Mr. Moore, and his story can best be told by relating the painting to our visit to Berenson's beautiful

Villa I Tatti, just outside Florence, Italy in a small village called Settignano. It was the fall of 1959.

Count Giorgio Geddes, a friend of mine, offered to drive me and my wife out to the appointment at I Tatti. The offer was accepted as it was a 20 minute drive to the villa.

I Tatti was no disappointment with its beautifully landscaped grounds, and it was immediately obvious why Berenson wanted to live there.

It was discovered on arrival that unfortunately Mr. Berenson was not well and could not receive visitors, but his assistant, Signorina Gioffredi, offered to show the collection and library. Upon arrival our group had been ushered into the main drawing room to wait while the Signorina said good-bye to an American museum director and his wife who were paying a visit.

The drawing room was dominated by three magnificent panels depicting the Glorification of St. Francis. When Signorina Gioffredi returned and was asked about these panels she told a very interesting story:

Berenson discovered the panels in a junk shop in Florence around 1900. It was a basement shop where he had gone looking for kitchen chairs. He actually rescued the panels since they were scheduled to be cut up the next day. The gold background was considered to be suitable material on which to paint little imitations of Fra Angelico angels. He paid the shop its price—under $500—and carried home his treasure in his carriage. These "rescued" panels are part of an altarpiece by the important Sienese painter Sassetta, and are now considered to be this artist's masterpiece.

What the history of these panels was before finding their way into that basement junk shop no one knows, but in response to a question about their value in dollars Mr. Berenson was quoted as saying, "Five hundred thousand wouldn't buy them now."

In 1955 we made the acquaintance of the "Dean of Antique Dealers," Mr. Mitchell Samuels, late chairman of the board of French and Company in New York, and over the next few years many hours were spent discussing art with him and looking over the painting collection of his company. It was on one of the first visits to the inner vault and an impressive moment when he brought out a beautiful landscape by Rembrandt—one of the few genuine Rembrandts we had seen offered for sale. The price was about what would be expected—$150,000. The title of the painting was "The Villa of the Burgomaster Six."

In August, 1959, we visited the Prinsenhof in Delft, Holland where the Annual Art and Antique Fair was being held. After we had toured the fair we ate lunch in Delft and then took the train to Amsterdam with the object of visiting a number of dealers in that city. After we had knocked on several doors with no response we came to the conclusion that most of the dealers must be at the Delft Fair.

Then we met with success: Mr. Evert Douwes of Douwes Brothers, vice-president of the Antique Art Dealers' Association, was in his establishment and invited us in to talk and to have a cup of tea.

The conversation ran to discoveries, and Mr. Douwes gradually unfolded one of the most interesting stories of a discovery we had ever heard:

One Monday afternoon in the late 1920's, when he was returning from a sale in the English countryside, about 4:00 P.M., he went into Christie's to take a look at the pictures on display for the next Friday's sale. As he entered the room he saw the picture hanging next to the door was a figure subject by some Dutch master. The second was a landscape catalogued under the name "Rembrandt." This designation indicated that in Christie's opinion the painting might be a Rembrandt school piece.

Then, in Mr. Douwes own words, "I suddenly got a shock. I felt sure I was looking at a genuine landscape by Rembrandt.

"Without looking at another picture I left the auction rooms, drove to my office and phoned my partner in Amsterdam, asking him to send me over by that same night's boat one of my restorers, giving as a reason that there were so many sales to be viewed that week that I could not do them all by myself.

"Fetching him from the boat-train the next morning at 8:30, we drove straight to Christie's where, at this early hour, we had all the rooms to ourselves. According to our custom to view a sale for the first time separately, so as not to influence one another, I left him to his own devices and posted myself in front of some framed French mezzotints, where in the glass I could see the 'Rembrandt' and note our restorer's reactions.

"After having looked superficially at the first picture he stopped before 'the painting.' I saw him stiffen and look quickly to the left and to the right to see who was nearby. Then I saw him examine the painting closely and move on.

"I joined him after a while and casually asked, 'Well, did you find anything?'

"He could hardly conceal his excitement. 'Yes,' he answered, 'a Rembrandt.'

"I then said, 'Thank you, Jan. That is what I asked you to come over for: a confirmation of my first impression of yesterday.'

"At five o'clock the display rooms closed for the day, and just before that time I returned and asked an attendant to take down the painting for my closer inspection. I always gave them a half-crown for such service.

"I was satisfied that I had not been overenthusiastic and that the painting was in fact a Rembrandt. On Wednesday we went to the Wallace Collection in London to have a close look at their Rembrandt landscape. The plate glass prevented our comparing the brushwork but, at my request, they were kind enough to take the picture out of the frame and take it to a window where we could examine it at our ease. After closing time at Christie's we were again allowed to have another look at their picture.

"Then the real work started. On Thursday we went to the Arnold Witt Library (now the Courtauld Institute) and studied every one of their reproductions of Rembrandt landscapes and etchings, more especially the etchings, hoping to find that he had made an etching of the painting, thus attesting to its authenticity. I had no luck. I was very disappointed, forgetting at the moment in my excitement that an etching of the same subject would be a reverse impression of it.

"The truth came out later. Sure enough: there it was in the *Klassiker der Kunst,* 'Rembrandt,' volume of 1906 on Page 74.

"Next was the big day—the day of the auction. I was afraid to bid myself, so I got another dealer, a friend of mine, to bid for me. Since he was not a picture dealer there would be no indication that my firm was interested in acquiring the painting, and competition would not be stimulated.

"A very close friend of mine, a Dutch picture dealer in London, approached me the night before the sale and told me he intended to 'go for the picture' so we decided to do so in joint account.

"I got the painting—for about $6000.

"As soon as I had my hands on it I took it to Holland and to the eminent authority on Dutch art in the Hague: Abraham Bredius. Bredius looked at the painting, then turned to his valet who was holding it up for him and said, 'Take a good look at this painting. It is one of the few genuine Rembrandts that have come to light in the last ten years.'

"From there I went to the other Dutch art authority, Hofstede de Groot. After studying the painting over the weekend he too pronounced it genuine.

"Now that," Mr. Douwes concluded, "is the history of the Rembrandt landscape that presently belongs to French and Company in New York—the painting that Mr. Mitchell Samuels showed you."

On December 2, 1944 the Parke-Bernet Galleries in New York sold a painting of a Madonna and Child, 24¼ by 16½ labeled "Milanese Master of the Circle of Leonardo da Vinci." The painting brought $3500.

On November of the following year the same painting was offered again by the same gallery. This time it realized only $1500. Whether or not it was bid in by the owner, apparently no one was willing to offer over $1500 for it.

Then the painting went under the scrutiny of the experts, and the leading authority in the United States on Renaissance Italian art, Dr. William E. Suida, pronounced it to be by Leonardo da Vinci himself, together with his pupil Marco d'Oggiono, and was in fact the lost "Virgin of the Violets" from the well-known Davenport-Bromley Collection. The painting found its way into the Jacob Heiman Collection in Los Angeles. Mr. Heiman, who wanted to retire, sold this painting along with some others from his collection to a leading New York dealer. This dealer priced the painting at $75,000. In 1960 it was sold to a European buyer.

There is another interesting story of a discovery from French and Company, one told us by Mitchell Samuels shortly before his passing. We took the story down word for word, and we reproduce it here exactly as he told it to us:

"In the very early 1920's our Gallery was at 6 East 56th Street, and we had a large warehouse at 5 to 9 East 59th Street. Our warehouse skirted the Sherry-Netherland Hotel, and we also had a part of the building that faced Fifth Avenue.

"One day as I was coming from the warehouse to our Gallery, I passed an alley near O'Reilly's Auction House. In the alley I saw an ash can with what appeared to be a drawing sticking out. I glanced at it and asked the O'Reilly janitor what the drawing was doing there. The janitor said that the auctioneer had told him to burn the drawing since he couldn't get a bid of even a dollar for it. The janitor threw it into the ash can.

"I happened to have $2 in my pocket, and I offered it to the janitor for the drawing; but he replied that $.25 would be fairer—enough to buy a 'skittle of beer.'

"I left him the $2 under protest, and I looked over the drawing as I walked along 59th Street. I saw immediately that it was of fine quality. As it was a little out of skew in the frame I shook it to get it straight, and lo and behold it was signed 'Winslow Homer.'

"I took it to one of my friends at Knoedler's who was a specialist on Homer, but before I had an opportunity to tell him anything about the drawing, he offered me $2500 for it.

"A few weeks later one of my very good clients called me up to remind me that I hadn't been in touch with him recently. He said that in the meantime he had bought some fine things. I asked him what he had bought and he said, 'One of the finest things I have bought is a Winslow Homer drawing.'

"I went over to his home. Yes, it was the same drawing. He had bought it the day after I had sold it. He paid $6500.

"This rescued drawing was later exhibited in the Metropolitan Museum of Art in the Winslow Homer Exhibition."

In the year 1925 the Detroit Institute of Arts purchased a panel painting of St. Jerome attributed to the Flemish Primitive Petrus Christus for $18,000. The painting never secured the enthusiastic acclaim of the art world. Certain sections of it were weak.

In 1956 a complete restoration of the painting was undertaken by William Suhr. Gradually the real picture emerged. The weak areas had been overpainted. The painting was, Mr. Edgar P. Richardson, Director of the Detroit Institute, announced, not by Christus but by Jan van Eyck, one of the top Flemish Primitives from whose brush fewer than 40 paintings are known to exist.

Before the cleaning the authorship of van Eyck was suspected, but the weak areas were not of the quality of van Eyck's painting. The painting was, furthermore, dated 1442, and van Eyck died in 1441. The conclusion therefore seemed logical that the part that appeared to be by van Eyck might have in fact been done by him, but the rest, the weaker portions, might have been done by Petrus Christus (a pupil of van Eyck) after van Eyck died.

The date too was overpainted. It was a forgery and came off in the cleaning.

LEONARDO & D'OGGIONO.
La Virgen de la Violete de Davenport-Bromley

JAN VAN EYCK. *St. Jerome in His Study.*
Detroit Institute of Arts

The Detroit Institute, in response to a question as to how much the painting was worth, pointed out that two years previously the Frick Collection had purchased a painting by van Eyck in combination with Petrus Christus for $750,000, and that their newly discovered van Eyck was worth at least this much.

In May, 1930 New York's Metropolitan Museum of Art sold a group of paintings selected from the Havemeyer Collection. Included in this group was one painting listed as "Portrait of a Grey Bearded Old Man in Doge's Dress" by the "School of Titian." It had been acquired 50 years previously from the Duchess of Berry, daughter-in-law of Charles X of France.

This painting was purchased at the sale for $400 by Dr. W. R. Valentiner, at that time Director of the Detroit Institute of Arts.

William Suhr, restorer for the Detroit Institute, saw that the picture was greatly overpainted and started to remove the outer layer of overpaint on the forehead and right eye of the figure. Under this paint on the eye Mr. Suhr found another eye in a slightly different position and done by another artist.

The portrait emerged as a genuine Tintoretto. The present Director of the Detroit Institute of Arts, Edgar P. Richardson, states that the painting is "Definitely a work by Tintoretto and represents the first doge painted officially by Tintoretto, after he succeeded Titian as court painter to the republic."

At the time of the discovery the painting was valued at $150,000.

TINTORETTO. *The Doge Girolamo Priuli.*
Detroit Institute of Arts

TINTORETTO. *The Doge Girolamo Priuli* (detail).
Detroit Institute of Arts

Mr. Robert Manning of the Kress Foundation once told us, "You can find a good painting anywhere, even in the gutter." Apparently you can find a good painting in anything from a museum sale to a junk shop and even a trash can.

In the late 1950's the Metropolitan Museum of Art had another sale of paintings that it did not wish to keep. We looked at the exhibition prior to the sale in the Parke-Bernet Galleries in New York. One painting caught my eye. It was a Madonna and Child labeled "School of Cima," late Fifteenth Century Italian Master. The painting was fascinating not because of its beauty but because of its downright ugliness and its poor condition. The impression was so adverse that I called my wife over to give the painting special attention. I turned to her, and in words entirely foreign to the field of fine arts, remarked, "Isn't this a dog!"

She agreed, and we left the display rooms with the firm resolution not to attend the sale.

Mr. Leon Medina, the New York dealer, attended the sale, however. For some reason he often bids on paintings without first examining them prior to the sale. Perhaps he feels that the law of averages will not let him down in the long run. Yet, with his admittedly poor eyesight it is difficult to foretell just how this theory will work out.

Mr. Medina was at the sale and he bought the painting for $500. At the time he made the purchase a fair appraisal would have been that he had overpaid by about $350; but he felt he had something fine and he turned it over for cleaning to Bartolo Bracaglia, one of New York's top restorers. Mr. Bracaglia took a look at the painting and asked, "How much did you pay for this?"

"Five hundred dollars," answered Mr. Medina.

"I'm afraid you have thrown your money away," remarked Mr. Bracaglia, "but if you want me to clean it I'll do what you say. It's your money."

Mr. Medina returned to his shop and waited for the cleaning to take place. A few days later his phone rang, and Bracaglia's excited voice on the other end of the line said, "Please come down to the studio and take a look at your painting."

Mr. Medina lost no time in making his way to the studio on Washington Square where a great many of the paintings belonging to the Kress Foundation were being restored, along with Mr. Medina's Madonna.

The painting by Cima that emerged was nothing short of beautiful and in excellent condition. I can well recall the shock of seeing it after restoration. It was shortly thereafter sold by Mr. Medina for $4000, and at that price it was a bargain.

How do these paintings become hidden beneath inferior painting? One explanation is that a restorer long ago undertook to "correct the deficiencies" in painting skill of the Master and became overenthusiastic in regard to his own skill.

The following story seems improbable, but it is true and illustrates the point well:

A prominent American artist whose works sell in four figures painted a portrait of an admiral's wife. The painting was given to her after three poses and she took it home very much pleased with it because it had been given to her as a gesture of friendship. She hung it on the wall proudly. Comments from members of the family, including the admiral were, however, a bit disappointing. One particular comment was, "I don't like that arm. It is unfinished."

After a year had passed the wife, who was also an artist, finished all her own uncompleted paintings and found she had run out of canvases. She then noticed the painting on the wall that looked so "unfinished." She started "improving" it herself.

Very soon the entire canvas was covered with new paint. She couldn't improve the arm without retouching adjacent areas, and one brush stroke led to another until gradually the picture lost all resemblance to its original self. Since she did not know that overpainting could be cleaned off she finally threw the painting out in disgust.

Will the painting one day turn up, and if so will anyone think to have it cleaned or x-rayed? Probably not.

It is interesting to speculate on how many overpainted masterpieces there are in existence now. It is entirely probable that there are many unrecognizable "improved paintings"—some by great artists—waiting to be rediscovered under layers of overzealous "touching up."

It is reported that under a painting by Vermeer in the National Gallery in Washington there is another entire painting also by Vermeer. In this case the Master apparently didn't like his own painting and tried to do a better job and still not waste his materials. This is one painting which will probably never be "rediscovered."

Dr. William E. Suida played the key role in the discovery of a now well-known museum masterpiece. He first saw the painting a number of years ago in Vienna. It was the custom in those days for picture peddlers to carry paintings from dealer to dealer. These peddlers were called runners for lack of a better term, but it described their activity well, since they were constantly running here and there with paintings.

One of these runners had with him a large panel painting. At night he would check the panel in the cloakroom of a restaurant or hotel for "safekeeping" and then return for it the next day to take it to another possible customer. Since for a long time the runner had been unable to sell the panel and had no idea who painted it he took it to Dr. Suida and asked him about it.

It is quite a tribute to Dr. Suida's unselfish nature that at this point instead of purchasing it for himself at the very low asking price he said, "The painting is by Piero della Francesca and I would like very much to publish it."

To make a long story short, he never heard from the runner again, and could not locate him to discuss the possibility of publishing the painting. Not too many months later, however, the painting appeared again. It had been purchased by the Frick Collection at a price well into six figures. It is considered one of their most valuable and highly treasured works. Those who know this story shudder to think of such a magnificent work of art having been carried daily through the streets and checked night after night in a cloakroom.

These are a very few stories of the discoveries of masterpieces that have taken place over the years. Discoveries take place every year, many discoveries; but dealers

PIERO DELLA FRANCESCA. *St. John the Evangelist.*
The Frick Collection

who make discoveries are not inclined to publicize them. A sales argument is not very persuasive that runs, "I found this painting in an old attic. I paid $50 for it. You can have it for only $10,000."

On the other hand there are many false and deliberately engineered "discoveries" that are designed to trap the inexpert, gullible buyer. Very often the "art authorities" who attest to the authenticity of these paintings are questionable in the extreme; and these are often the "authorities" who charge the most for their attributions.

In summary, however, the real discoveries far outweigh the trumped-up ones, and it is only too bad that as the art market booms on, as art consciousness penetrates the public mind, and as the supply of available paintings is progressively depleted, fewer and fewer discoveries remain to be made.

XX

The Author Discovers

N THE FALL OF 1959 MY WIFE AND I VISITED VERY NEARLY EVERY art dealer of prominence in London. There is always the hope (but not too much expectation) of making a discovery. The object was to see what paintings were for sale on the European art market, and their prices, and to add one or two prime Dutch examples to our ever-growing collection. After a few days in London it became evident that the British dealers possess an art scholarship which is remarkably high, to say the least—without making any comparisons—and are extremely hospitable and gracious.

The gratifying thing about the hunt for paintings in London is that the store owner, although often wearing a stiff collar and striped pants, offers to show every single painting in the shop and is generally more than willing to get paintings down from the top shelves or to receive them as you pass them down to him from the top rung of the ladder.

After looking over about two hundred paintings in this way, in one of the Old Bond Street shops, we came to an unframed painting lying in the corner on the floor. It was covered with discolored varnish and just plain dirt so that it was difficult to see the colors. The subject appeared to be a pastoral scene and the quality seemed excellent. There was a possible signature which might or might not turn out to be authentic. A price of $170 was agreed to, subject to cleaning, which the dealer said he would have done by his own restorer.

In a few days I returned to the Bond Street shop to look at the cleaned painting.

The proprietor gave his reaction to it first: "When I came to work this morning," he said, "I asked where we got the new painting. I didn't recognize it after it had been cleaned."

It was apparent why. Under the grime was possibly one of the finest Seventeenth Century Dutch landscapes by Nicholas Berchem. There were his typical, fluidly painted cows, sheep, shepherds and shepherdesses, with a background of rocky hills and an expanse of blue sky. The signature was clear and genuine. It immediately came to mind that the dealer would probably not want to go through with the sale once he had seen the quality of the painting; but if he had such feelings he did not show them. He was true to his word and produced a bill of sale as "by Nicholas Berchem" and seemed genuinely pleased with our discovery.

In the attribution of paintings, however, one must go to great lengths to make doubly sure that the paintings are authentic. In the case of the Nicholas Berchem a photograph was immediately dispatched to the Netherlands Royal Art Archives. The reply came back, "A characteristic work by the hand of Nicholas Berchem."

Then, to determine the value of the painting it was necessary to check the market, which revealed that Berchem works were selling in a range from medium low to middle four figures. (A Berchem, "The Return from the Hunt," brought 1300 guineas at auction in April, 1960, at Christie's.) An authority of note, on the other hand, felt that the pastoral would bring more than $3500 at retail.

The painting, however, was not for sale. As soon as the uniquely fine quality was uncovered, it was destined for the museum collection which we are assembling for an Eastern college. The painting is now hanging where student artists can study it and where visitors can enjoy it for generations to come. Thus, we have a happy ending to this London shopping expedition.

In the late 1950's a large and prominent gallery moved to smaller quarters on Madison Avenue in New York and was forced to reduce stock. Some of the paintings were sold at reduced prices or through less prominent dealers; and through a dealer who handled a large number of these paintings I purchased one of a pair of Seventeenth Century Dutch portraits. The portrait was of an aristocratic young woman in the typical period costume of black dress and white ruff. Since the portrait of her husband was not as attractive, it was not purchased. These works were attributed to Jan Verspronck, one of the circle of Frans Hals, but a fine painter in his own right.

Somehow the name Verspronck never quite fit the portrait, but the tag bearing the name Verspronck from the major gallery was left on the painting until proof could be obtained as to who was really the artist. Known for certain, however,

NICHOLAS BERCHEM. *Pastoral Landscape.*
Courtesy City College of New York

THOMAS DE KEYSER. *Portrait of a Lady.*

was that the painting had beautiful quality, was large and imposing, was in good condition, was unquestionably Seventeenth Century Dutch, and cost only $300.

Shortly after it was purchased a prominent dealer came down from New York to visit us and brought with him photos of the paintings he had for sale. While he was in the house he saw the new acquisition and suggested the name of Nicholas Elias. At the time his scholarship seemed surprising, since Elias is a lesser known artist, and rarely have any of his paintings been seen in any museum in the United States or for sale by any dealer; but the matter was dropped there.

Some months later, during a visit to The Hague in Holland to work on the authorship of several paintings, our marveling at the dealer's scholarship ceased, for there in the archives were the portraits of the Dutch girl and her husband—attributed to Nicholas Elias.

The story can be pieced together like this: the dealer knew he could buy the painting from the major gallery reasonably because it was not by Jan Verspronck, the big name carried on the label. He secured photos of the paintings and rushed them to the Netherlands Royal Art Archives for attribution. The Archives mentioned the minor master Nicholas Elias, whereupon the dealer lost interest in their purchase.

The story just begins here, however. The expert in the Netherlands Art Archives who was examining the photo of the portrait in our presence thought it looked particularly good and said so. He had then located the photograph in the file with the attribution to Nicholas Elias but was not satisfied with this attribution and decided to consult a colleague in the Archives. They agreed on another attribution—to the very prominent Seventeenth Century Dutch artist, Thomas de Keyser.

After some discussion, they thought it advisable to seek the opinion of the Director of the Archives. His opinion was quick and sure—Thomas de Keyser. The mystery was solved and, upon further research, the only question was "Why hadn't it been seen before? It is so obvious!"

The Lady, now correctly attributed to Thomas de Keyser, is valued in the high four figures and hangs over the fireplace in our home in a position of honor. It is understood that the companion piece was sent to a dealer in Chicago, but its whereabouts is unknown.

The advice of Mitchell Samuels, late Chairman of the Board of French and Company, should not be forgotten: *"Buy a quality painting, not a name."* This could well be the collector's motto.

The summer season is slow in the art business. The major art auctions are suspended during the summer months. The major dealers go to Europe to buy for the winter season, and the small auctions are patronized by fewer and fewer people until they also often shut up shop. One always hopes a good collection will be offered for sale through a small auction in the summer and that the sale will be held on a weekday at noon. The summer season, plus a weekday, plus noon means that the major dealers who are in Europe cannot attend. The dealers who are left may not want to close up shop to attend. Men buyers are usually at work, and women have their household chores to occupy them. One wonders why auctions are held at such times, but they sometimes are, and it was at one of these auctions in New York that I purchased a beautiful painting.

The painting was discolored when it was first spotted on the wall of the Savoy Art and Auction Galleries, but the quality was not hidden. On the back of the panel was printed "Van Deelen and de Wet" and the picture portrayed the "Liberation of St. Peter." Although the name on the back did not authenticate the painting, the painting, nevertheless, appeared excellent and of the period.

It was then noted that the picture boasted an authentic Dutch frame and such frames are becoming very rare. If the painting did not clean up well at least the frame could be used.

I decided to come back to bid and hurried about my business the day of the auction in order to be there when the painting came up for sale. The bidding started at the surprisingly low figure of $25, and the raises were apathetic. The auctioneer's hammer banged down on my bid of $55.

A quick cleaning by the restorer revealed a beautifully detailed, absolutely authentic painting by the two collaborators, Dirk van Deelen and Jacob de Wet, the former an important painter of church interiors and the latter of the circle of Rembrandt. The cleaning also revealed the date 1635 and the signatures of both artists on the bases of two of the church columns. Several months later the director of one university art gallery on seeing the painting asked if it could be presented to his institution. This was a very flattering request for a painting which cost only $55.

Every collector tends to think that he knows more of the authorship of paintings than a dealer does, so that when he goes out looking, although he may not admit it, he speculates at least a little on the possibility that this may be the day he discovers in the back of a shop, under a stack of old, worthless canvases, a painting which is priced at $25 and turns out to be a genuine Rembrandt or a Cézanne.

It was in this spirit of adventure that my wife and I entered a shop in George-town, Washington, a few years ago and a small, beautifully painted portrait of a man, which appeared to be Seventeenth Century Dutch, immediately caught our eye. The quality was unmistakably fine, but just who the artist might have been was not apparent. The surface had yellowed, but under the discolored varnish could be seen traces of a signature. Permission was asked of the dealer to take the painting into the daylight for further examination. After moving it about in order to let the sunshine fall on it in just the right way and several minutes of inspection through the magnifying glass (which I carry for just such occasions), it was decided that there was a signature—"Werff."

That started research which led quickly to the conclusion that in all probability this was a signed Adrian van der Werff (1659-1722), court painter to the Elector Palatine Johann Wilhelm. The outstanding characteristic of van der Werff is that he painted with consummate perfection and secured a likeness rivaled only by photography. The dealer was paid the $90 he asked and the painting was taken to the restorer to be cleaned.

Alas, although the dirt came off with the cleaning, so did the "Werff" signature. This meant only one thing—that the signature was a fake—for, if it were signed by the artist, it would not have come off more easily than the rest of the paint.

The painting was re-examined carefully before being put back in the frame. It was of even higher quality than had been thought at first. Then something exciting was noticed. A small patch of canvas to the right of the figure appeared slightly different in color from the rest of the background. As there was little to

DIRK VAN DEELEN and JACOB WILLEMZ DE WET. *The Liberation of St. Peter.*   VAILLANT. *Portrait of a Man.*

lose since the "Werff" signature had come off, the restorer was requested to clean the discolored place and clean hard.

It required the strongest chemicals and vigorous elbow grease, but gradually the real signature became visible, carefully covered up many, many years ago— "W. Vaillant."

The explanation of this faking is that in his lifetime probably no painter was more highly praised than Adrian van der Werff. The Elector Palatine so admired his enamel-like finish and technical perfection of drawing that he contracted for all the paintings produced by this Master in nine months out of every year. There was great competition among the public to buy the artist's works in the three "free" months in the year. At the end of the seventeenth century no artist received higher prices for his paintings. When the King of Poland was in Rotterdam in 1710 even he could not find one painting by van der Werff to purchase.

The style of Wallerant Vaillant is very close to that of Adrian van der Werff, and Vaillant painted just a little earlier. He was born in 1623 and died in 1677.

This is a typical example of "faking"—to take an artist who himself is good and close in style to the one aspired to, blot out his signature and falsify one.

How long ago this falsification was done one can only guess. While at the end of the seventeenth century van der Werff was in huge demand, public taste changed, and it is not absolutely certain that today Vaillant is ranked below van der Werff. Since most of Vaillant's paintings now hang in the palaces of Europe, and few hang in the United States or are on the market here, it is a minor treasure worth several thousand dollars. Thus a genuine, fine painting of quality, not by van der Werff but by Vaillant, was added to our collection.

328

One of the Third Avenue dealers in New York once had a corner of his shop reserved for what he called "the Junk Pile." For the most part it *was* a junk pile containing paintings severely damaged, overcleaned, of poor quality to begin with, or simply nondescript nineteenth century canvases.

One day in the early years of my collecting, I visited this shop. The dealer announced that he had a "School of Luini" painting, but that it was much damaged. Since Luini or "School of Luini" is almost impossible to find, this announcement aroused interest and considerable skepticism.

The painting he brought out was in poor condition indeed. To begin with, it was frameless. Originally it had been on canvas, but in order to preserve the canvas which had deteriorated it had been cemented onto new plywood. The re-mounting job was not bad, but the painting was. The subject was a Madonna and Child, but the Child was poorly modeled. The leg was not a good physical like-ness, and the foot contained four instead of five toes. The only colors visible in the entire painting were shades of dull, dirty, brownish yellow. I still don't know why I bought it. Certainly it was nowhere close to Luini, but the $50 was paid and the painting taken home.

When the "masterpiece" was cleaned by the restorer it was transformed. After the poor overpainting was removed the four toes became five, the colors were revealed—blues and reds became apparent—and the flesh tones became natural.

GUGLIELMO CACCIA. *Madonna and Child* (before overpainting was removed)

GUGLIELMO CACCIA. *Madonna and Child* (after overpainting was removed)

When Dr. W. E. Suida saw the painting it took little time for him to render his verdict: "The painting is by Guglielmo Caccia, known as Il Moncalvo, Middle Sixteenth Century painter, and this is one of the best examples of his work."

In New York City several years ago one of the Old Master dealers passed on. It is a question what to do with the stock of such a dealer, often amounting to hundreds and sometimes thousands of paintings. In this case the dealer's widow chose to sell the entire stock to another dealer, a friend, for a flat cash sum.

The purchasing dealer was in a good mood when I walked into his shop. He had the purchased stock in his cellar and he allowed me to inspect it. After a morning in the cellar I selected one small painting, a sketch of shepherds, horses and sheep. Although the painting was sketchy, it had a definite strength, and I bought it for $50.

As my wife and I were having dinner that evening with good friends, Robert and Bertina Manning, who are experts on Italian art and are enthusiastic about new painting discoveries, the recent acquisition was taken along to show them. Robert Manning unwrapped the painting and sat on the sofa in the lobby looking at it for a few minutes. When he handed it back he said, "Castiglione," and Bertina Manning agreed. Visiting the Manning's home later that evening we viewed their several Castigliones. The similarity was unmistakable. Castiglione,

CASTIGLIONE. *Biblical Scene.*

CASTIGLIONE. *The Prodigal Son.* Photograph by Brenwasser

an important Middle Seventeenth Century Genoese painter who could paint figures, sheep and accessories masterfully, is one of the painters of the Italian Baroque who is rapidly growing in popularity.

The newly acquired Castiglione was not a large one nor an important one, but a good little sketch thoroughly characteristic of the Master. Better still, a new artist had been added to the collection. Another artist had been learned by the purchase of one of his works. At the time of this purchase we knew little of Castiglione. Now he has become a favorite and his works are sought.

One week in New York late in 1960 we made the rounds of several dealer friends to see what was new. One, who on occasion buys some very fine things and then sells them to other dealers, displayed a charming Isabey from a prominent collection. This was tempting until he brought out another painting and said he didn't know who painted it, but thought that it might have something to do with Fragonard. It was a sketch in oil on paper over canvas. The price was $60.

It took about one minute to determine that the painting was by Castiglione. It was happily purchased. The sketch is quite typical of Castiglione, larger than the first one acquired and in perfect condition. After cleaning, the coloring appeared stronger and the masterful brush work in this sketch endeared the works of Castiglione even more completely to us both. The subject is "The Prodigal Son" and it has a value of about $2500.

This painting might have been overlooked had there not been previous schooling in Castiglione by the Mannings, and to them full credit and thanks are given.

Toward the end of the 1950's, one of the European countries purchased a magnificent town house for the residence of its Ambassador and his family. The house is located a few blocks away from my home on a quiet street in Washington. One of the city's large banks had arranged the sale and was also planning to sell the contents of the house for the owner. The bank went to much trouble to inventory every item, identify it, and secure an appraisal of it.

At a dinner party the wife of the Ambassador, on learning of my interest in paintings, very graciously invited me to see the paintings and furnishings for sale in the mansion. A meeting was arranged with her and an official of the bank a few days after the dinner party.

After an hour in the house it became evident that no paintings were of particular interest—several even being copies or school pieces. As no opinion was asked, no comment was made, especially since the valuation sheets contained appraisals running, in the case of some paintings, well into four and even five figures. The furnishings, however, were exquisite and I had no desire to undermine the ability of the bank to get a high price for the contents of the house.

Still, there was a feeling of embarrassment, as both the Ambassador's wife and the Vice President of the bank gave their time for me to look over the paintings and I had no interest in any of them. Frantically I looked around for something to buy—a set of books or a snuffbox or a tapestry—and my eye settled on a stone statue on a marble pedestal standing near the main staircase. All that could be guessed was that the head was ancient Roman or Greek or maybe a late copy of this style. The nose and chin had been broken off and had been carefully replaced with new stone.

The bank representative, after consulting his valuation sheets, came up with the pronouncement of the appraisers: "Statue on Pedestal—As Is—Appraised price—$50." "I'll take it." It was not much of a purchase, but at least the kindness of the Ambassador's wife and the bank official was not completely in vain.

"What exactly are you going to do with that?" asked my wife, since she was not consulted about the purchase.

"I don't just know, but it looks like something genuine and fine."

"What makes you feel that it is genuine and fine?"

"I'm not sure, but it just seems good to me and I think I'll give it to City College in New York. The Chairman of the Art Department, Professor d'Andrea, is an expert on sculpture and he'll be able to identify it for me. You'll see."

"Yes," she said, "that's exactly what I'm afraid of. He is very likely to tell you that a firm near Pittsburgh fifty years ago used to turn out these things at the rate of thirty a week and sell them for $5 apiece."

"If he says that, I won't give it to the College. I'll take it back to Washington and we can use it for a door stop."

"Not in my home," she said, and that for the time being closed the subject.

The statue looked heavy—very heavy—and it seemed extravagant to hire professional movers to take a $50 statue to New York when it was doubtful whether it was worth anything.

The only solution was to load it into the car and drive it to New York when we had to go on other business. Finally the bank ordered that the purchase be taken out of the house and we drove the car around to pick it up.

Never before had I tried to move such a heavy art object. It could be lifted only about one inch from the floor and this could be accomplished only because it had projections from the marble base in the right place for lifting. But even when it was lifted by the projections it could not be moved sideways even an inch.

The solution was to drag it over the marble floor—and in so doing put a score along the floor. There were visions of the foreign country calling off the whole purchase of the house, and the bank's suing me in consequence.

At last the statue was pulled to the car, but it was a complete impossibility to get it into the trunk. It was impossible to lift it that high, and even if it could be lifted the operation would so dent the trunk ridge as to cost more in repairs to the car than the statue was worth. The best thing that could be done was to lift half of the statue, lean the head against the inside of the car, lift the base and slide the whole thing inside. By this time I fervently wished that neither the statue nor the house had ever been seen. We scheduled an immediate trip to New York, hoping to be able to deliver the statue to the Head of the Art Department of City College when he was not in his office, so that he would not be in a position to reject it before our return to Washington.

On the way to New York my wife had time to renew the doubts about the wisdom of the course being followed. Suppose the statue was a fake or one of numerous copies? Only discredit could result from bringing such a thing to City College.

Her logic prevailed, and before delivering it we visited a dealer in lower New York, one specializing in sculpture. We left the car in a dark corner of a public garage, with the statue in it, hoping in a way that someone would steal it in our absence and thus solve the whole problem.

When the dealer heard the word "statue," however, he was out of his shop in a hurry and into the garage. He took just one short look into the dim back seat of the car and asked, "Would you care to tell me what price you paid for that?"

"Fifty dollars," I replied.

"Would you take $200 for it?"

The answer was out very nearly before the offer was made. In fact, $25 would have bought it.

The "Statue on Pedestal—As Is—Appraised Price $50" turned out to be a prime example of authentic Second Century A. D. Roman sculpture. Needless to say the dealer's retail price was not $200.

This chapter is the story of what one collector has discovered—for little money. I have made more significant discoveries, but generally for very much more money. I have other paintings which were thoroughly authenticated and whose value was known by the dealer when he sold them. I had to pay the market price for them. But this chapter shows what has been done and indicates what may still be done in the future in the way of discovering fine works for little money.

Several points should be made about these stories of treasure hunting.

In the first place, I had some idea about what I was buying. I knew the schools of art fairly well from constant study.

In the second place, I bought on the basis of quality alone. The paintings looked excellent to me, not like copies or school paintings. The only exception to this principle of buying was the Il Moncalvo Madonna, and the success in this purchase can be attributed only to plain beginner's luck.

What was the outcome from an investment point of view? If all of the art objects discussed in this chapter are grouped it is fairly certain that after identification they have a fair appraised value at retail of at least ten times what was paid for them, and they will be worth more as time goes on. The artist of every painting was identified with certainty. This determination helps the value enormously.

Against the selling price should of course be charged the time to locate the paintings, the travel expense to New York and elsewhere, the cost of a good art reference library, and the mistakes—the purchase price of those paintings which did not turn out to be what I hoped they would.

Most of these discoveries will never leave the collection during our lifetime. They are loved. We are always pleased to look at them when we pass where they hang on the wall.

XXI

Fakes and Copies—and a Discovery

Y SEEING HOW FAKES ARE PERPETRATED ALMOST EVERY DAY AND have been perpetrated all through history one can gain knowledge as to how to avoid being taken in by this ever-recurring swindle.

In 1955 German Chancellor Konrad Adenauer attended a gala event, significant in the history and heritage of Germany and in the art world: the rededication of the restored murals in Lübeck's St. Mary's Church. That the event was of national importance was signified by the fact that 2,000,000 anniversary postage stamps were printed for the occasion.

Then two individuals were arrested: Lothar Malskat and Dietrich Fey—for faking the murals. Malskat told the complete story. The faking of the Lübeck murals was only a far greater and more difficult assignment for Malskat than his faking had been up to that point in his artistic career. In Malskat's words, "I was allowed to stop fabricating French Impressionists. Fey had a better job for me: I had to go back to the Middle Ages."

This was what Malskat had to do in order to fabricate the Biblical scenes in the Lübeck Church. But when "that crook Fey took all the credit and most of the money" Malskat decided to reveal the hoax.

The job to be undertaken was one of cleaning the old murals and restoring them. Malskat soon found out that there was little to restore, and that pieces of the murals crumbled in his hands. So he filled in the blank places with his own creations, and these blank places were practically all that remained of the original murals. He painted pictures of historical personages with likenesses of his school-mates and local laborers. The likeness of the Holy Virgin was based on photographs of former German movie queen Hansi Knoteck.

A visiting art scholar admired a figure of one of the prophets. The prophet was in reality Malskat's father, a second-hand clothing dealer in Koenigsberg. The Gothic king, on the other hand, was actually the Russian Gregory Rasputin.

A girl student based her doctoral dissertation on the murals. She wrote, "The splendid figure of Mary bears the brush marks of Gothic genius."

When the forgery was revealed to her, the student angrily pointed out that the murals were still remarkably similar to the Gothic murals in Lübeck's Holy Ghost Hospital.

Malskat's reply was, "I also painted those."

The story did not end with the conviction of Malskat and Fey. The Lübeck Church Superintendent asked to be retired. The Art Director of Lübeck moved to the East German Zone and his assistant was abruptly pensioned off.

A fantastic forgery took place in the late 1920's, extending into the year 1930. It involved the name of one of the greatest French painters of all time—Millet.

For 10 years Jean Charles Millet, grandson of the famous painter, and Paul Cazot had been producing and selling fake art, mainly faked Millets. One paint-ing had been sold for $60,000 in England.

Usually the young Millet sold the forged paintings for about $4000 and signed his grandfather's name to them. There was a written guarantee which accom-panied each painting signed by Charles Millet, the son of the painter. Charles Millet's signature was forged. Cazot was the one who actually did the faking of the paintings.

The job of faking was helped considerably by the fact that the canvas and wood frames were actually from genuine old paintings of the period in which the famous Millet painted.

In June, 1930, the young Millet was jailed for a year, but on a charge of circulating worthless checks, not on a charge of forging the paintings.

Shortly after the young Millet's arrest, an artist by the name of Charles Chaplin stated in an article in the magazine "Mercure de France," "Millet's work can easily be copied." He went on to support his position by stating that he had painted a picture of a herd of pigs on a rugged mountainside. The picture was purchased by Madame Halévy, wife of the French composer, for $120. On the death of Madame Halévy a dealer purchased the picture for $16. He effaced Chaplin's name and forged the signature of Millet. He then sold the picture as a Millet to an American for $2000.

Some of the most effective faking occurs when genuine paintings of other artists are decorated with fake signatures of greater masters of the same period and sold as being by the more eminent artist.

Probably the most faked artist who ever lived was Corot. H. C. Marillier, the chronicler of Christie's auction house stated, "America . . . was flooded to suffocation by Corots of doubtful ancestry. The legend goes that at one time they were being imported at the rate of four thousand a year. Corot may have reduced his system to a formula, and been able to paint endless still pools with pale verdure in his studio, but he could scarcely have manufactured them in anything like such quantities as this."

The statement has been made that in his life Corot painted 2000 pictures, 5000 of which are in America.

At the time of his death in 1923 the French Doctor Jousseaume had in his possession 2414 spurious Corots: paintings, drawings and detrempes, which he had bought as being authentic over the years from obscure dealers at low prices.

At a recent sale in New York a Corot and a Paul Truillebert were sold. It is interesting to compare the two paintings. Truillebert was a follower of Corot and so close to the Master that it is said a genuine Truillebert is rapidly becoming a collector's item. Many if not most Truilleberts have had the artist's signature replaced by that of Corot, and the paintings were sold under the name of the greater artist.

In this type of fake there is little work for the forger to do. The age of the painting does not have to be "created" since both artists painted in approximately the same period.

Emile Bernard, the French Modern, worked with Paul Gauguin in Brittany. In the Paris World's Fair of 1937 one of Bernard's paintings was displayed as a

COROT. *Ville d'Avray.*
National Gallery, Washington, D.C.
(Gift, Count Cecil Pecci-Blunt)

Gauguin but was quickly withdrawn when Bernard himself appeared and stated that he had painted the picture.

In the same way Pierre Grimm discovered one of his paintings which bore the signature "Bonnard," the French Modern. The "Bonnard" had an accompanying certificate of authenticity. Similarly Michel Kikoine is passed off as Soutine.

But let us go back to the Millet case. Five years after the discovery of Millet's forgery factory he was again in the news. The case had still not been concluded. Millet's defense now was that the dealers who had purchased his forgeries knew that the paintings were forgeries, so that they were the malefactors, not he.

These defenses, however, did not prevail, and Millet and his accomplice Cazot were jailed for six months and fined 500 francs apiece (the franc being worth 6.64¢). The dealer who brought the suit was awarded 120,000 francs to be paid by Millet, Cazot and Cazot's former wife, also an accomplice.

All this took place in February, 1935. In December, 1935, Millet was again in the news. He was sentenced to jail for swindling art collectors. He received an additional sentence of 15 years for stealing a painting entrusted to him for cleaning.

One wonders how far he could have gone had he not been caught. Among other things he stocked the Barbizon Museum in the town which gave its name to the prominent School of French painters—with "masterpieces by Millet."

The Millet forgeries were nothing as compared with the forgeries that were shortly to rock the art world to its foundations. After the complete record of the van Meegeren forgeries is studied one wonders whether there is one genuine painting in the world. The author talked with many dealers and art experts in the United States and in Europe about these forgeries, particularly to those in Holland.

Henri (Han) van Meegeren sold eight pictures purportedly by Vermeer and de Hooch for a grand total of $2,289,000. His forgeries might still be unrevealed were it not for the fact that he was hauled into court on a charge of selling national treasures, namely great Dutch Old Master paintings, outside the country, and particularly to an enemy country—Germany. For his last forgery, "Christ and the Adultress" German Field Marshal Hermann Goering paid $495,000. Van Meegeren's major works are listed on the following page.

"Christ at Emmaus" was purchased in 1937 and had hung for seven years in Rotterdam's Boymans Museum at the time of van Meegeren's confession in 1945.

The ironical part of the position taken by van Meegeren in his trial was that he was a good Dutchman, not a traitor to his country who would sell national treasures to the Germans. To prove his loyalty it was necessary for him to prove himself a forger. This he did by painting still another "Vermeer," "The Young

Christ at Emmaus (as by Vermeer) ....$	174,000
The Card Players (as by de Hooch)	117,000
A Drinking Party (as by de Hooch)	87,000
Christ's Head (as by Vermeer)	165,000
The Last Supper (as by Vermeer)	480,000
Isaac Blessing Jacob (as by Vermeer)	381,000
Washing of Christ's Feet (as by Vermeer)........	390,000
Christ and the Adultress (as by Vermeer)	495,000
Total	$2,289,000

Christ Teaching in the Temple." He did this work before judicial witnesses in a period of two months between August and October, 1945. In the end he was convicted of forgery.

In 1932 van Meegeren was a moderately successful artist, but one who felt he had received more than his share of criticism in the art world. He thus set out to prove not only to the art world but to the world in general his worth as a painter. This he proposed to do by painting a picture so much in the manner of Vermeer that the whole world would be fooled.

Now van Meegeren could have made a copy of a known Vermeer, and possibly in the style of Vermeer. Copies are easy forms of fakes. They require no originality whatever. They are not created—not the idea, not the composition, not the drawing. Copies usually lack the natural spontaneity of the artist's own painting.

One of the first things which is done when a "discovery" appears is to search for all photographs of paintings by the artist to find an identical painting, or two paintings by the artist which the forger could have combined in his forgery into one—the head from one painting, the body from another, or one figure from one painting by the artist and the second figure from another of his paintings. When an identical painting by the artist is found (without variations) this often ends the search, and the "discovery" is sent back to where it came from.

The existence of the exact painting elsewhere does not invariably throw out the painting as being a copy, however. Van Dyck, for example, often did the same painting twice or even a greater number of times. Gilbert Stuart did possibly 70 originals of George Washington. These duplications by the Master are called replicas, not copies. Copies are done by someone else.

Sometimes the similar paintings are school or workshop pieces, done in the shops operated by the Master. Usually a school piece is worth far less than the work of the Master. A Rubens workshop piece is worth less than one-tenth of the price of a painting by Rubens himself, unless it can be shown that the "hand of the Master" is in the painting—that his own brush painted it at least in part.

In the case of El Greco, replicas and workshop pieces are extremely common, and the replicas and even the pieces done by the workshop sell for prices in line with those originals by the Master.

Vermeer, however, as far as we know, did no replicas. If van Meegeren had produced a copy of a known Vermeer it would probably have been rejected immediately. He furthermore did not want to produce a copy. He wanted to create something that was his own, but something that was good enough to pass as the work of Holland's rarest and highest priced Master.

In 1932 he started to purchase materials for the "Vermeer." For four years he conducted experiments in painting "Vermeers." By 1936, four years later, his method was perfected, and in a period of six months of actual painting and processing he turned out his first "Vermeer"—"Christ at Emmaus." This painting he took to Paris and turned over to a lawyer to sell for him. The lawyer sold it to a prominent Amsterdam dealer, but before the sale the authentication of one of the leading authorities on Dutch art was secured, although at the time the great authority was aging. Here are the exact words of this authority describing the new "Vermeer":

> "It is a wonderful moment in the life of a lover of art when he finds himself suddenly confronted with a hitherto unknown painting by a great master, untouched, on the original canvas, and without any restoration, just as it left the painter's studio! And what a picture! Neither the beautiful signature 'I. V. Meer' (I.V.M. in monogram) nor the *pointillé* on the bread which Christ is blessing is necessary to convince us that we have here a—I am inclined to say—*the* masterpiece of Johannes Vermeer of Delft, and, moreover, one of his largest works (1.29 m. by 1.17 m.), quite different from all his other paintings and yet every inch a Vermeer.
>
> "In no other picture by the great Master of Delft do we find such sentiment, such a profound understanding of the Bible story—a sentiment so nobly human expressed through the medium of the highest art."

The Amsterdam dealer then sold the painting to the Boymans Museum in Rotterdam where it hung for seven years.

A news account of the time states, "But only a reproduction in full colours permits the formation of an adequate idea of the almost unearthly loveliness of this magnificent painting. It is difficult to know what to admire more—the majestic simplicity of the composition, or the drama the artist has instilled into this moment of dawning recognition by the disciples and the maidservant of the Saviour risen from the dead. Dr. Hannema, the Director of the Boymans Museum, has sent us a very interesting account of the history of the picture. 'A Dutch girl living in Het Westland,' he writes, '—the region behind the town of Delft—married, in 1885, a Frenchman. The family of the girl had always been in possession of the Disciples at Emmaus, and gave it to her as a wedding present. The young couple took the picture to Paris. As they did not know anything about the quality and value of pictures and the house was small and the canvas large (50¾ x 46 in.), they put it away in a cupboard, where it was found by a Dutch lawyer after their death, in 1937.' "

The story was certainly well prepared and well accepted. When one reviews the pictures in the catalogue of the paintings in the New York World's Fair of 1939 he is inclined to smile when he sees this van Meegeren reproduced in an advertisement of the Amsterdam dealer who proudly proclaimed that it was he who had sold this masterpiece to the Boymans Museum.

Van Meegeren's task of faking was not an easy one. The x-ray probes beneath the surface, and van Meegeren had to use an old canvas. Had he not removed all of the original Seventeenth Century Dutch painting from the canvas the x-ray would have revealed it.

The pigments used by Vermeer were hand ground and of uneven size and shape. Modern pigments are machine-prepared and are far more uniform. Van Meegeren had to hand grind his pigments out of the materials Vermeer used, or the spectroscope would have identified some of them as being other than those used originally by Vermeer.

Van Meegeren then had to "age" his paint so there would be no trace of oil in it. It would then be impervious to alcohol which will remove new paint but not the fully dried Seventeenth Century paint.

He bought brushes of badger hair. These were what Vermeer used. He even filled his studio with Seventeenth Century antiques, not in order to paint them, but to put him in the artistic element in which Vermeer worked and to put him in the frame of mind of Vermeer himself.

One can go through all of these motions and still not come up with a "Vermeer." Van Meegeren had studied Vermeer for years in conjunction with his art education in Delft, where Vermeer had lived and worked. He studied not only Vermeer's technique of painting but his subject matter as well. It occurred to van Meegeren that he would have to create a new and undiscovered period of Vermeer, a middle period between his early religious period, represented by his painting of Christ in Scotland, and his late, non-religious scene period. This "middle period of Vermeer" was to be a religious period and of a style which, although related to the early and late periods, was still to be distinct. If the style was not exactly like either the early or the late period, van Meegeren felt he would have a chance to get away with his forgery since exact comparisons with Vermeer's paintings of the same period as the forgery would be impossible. Every artist paints in a particular way at a particular time in his painting life. It is this characteristic that allows unsigned paintings to be identified.

In Vermeer's case the job of faking was far greater than in the case of the usual artist. Vermeer's paintings have a unique characteristic. The borders, as, for instance, between the sleeve of a garment and the background, are peculiarly blurred, and the entire painting often seems "out of focus," as though one were looking at the painting through a sheet of ice.

To duplicate this effect van Meegeren baked his pictures in an oven. Perhaps Vermeer did the same, but we will probably never know. Baking, however, entails the risk of bubbling the paint if sufficient heat is applied to harden the paint so that ordinary solvents, including alcohol, will not remove it. The solvent test is one of the first to be applied to suspected paintings.

Van Meegeren conducted experiment after experiment. Finally he hit upon the right combination. Before he dipped his brush into the paint he first dipped it into a combination of phenol and formaldehyde. These chemicals permitted

VAN MEERGEREN. *The Washing of the Feet* (after Vermeer).   VERMEER. *Christ in the House of Mary and Martha.* National Gallery of Scotland, Edinburgh

drying in the oven to the point at which the pigment would pass as old paint of the seventeenth century.

When the painting was removed from the oven it was still not ready to be "rediscovered." There was no crackle. To supply these cracks of age van Meegeren designed a roller two feet thick, and carefully and slowly rolled the painting around it. The paint, being almost rock-hard, cracked in the characteristic pattern of the old seventeenth century pictures.

This was still not enough, however, and van Meegeren set out to make the cracks more prominent by filling them with India ink, a medium which left particles so small as to be difficult of detection under the magnification that would certainly be used to prove or disprove the picture later on.

There was one final process used by van Meegeren to create an impression of age: he pried off small pieces of the paint and deliberately damaged the canvas underneath.

After the completion of the painting there were various transactions, including the "discovery" and authentication which led up to its sale to the Boymans Museum for $174,000 of which van Meegeren kept $120,000.

This was the beginning of a series of "Vermeers" and "de Hooches." In the spring of 1940 van Meegeren bought a painting by the seventeenth century artist Hondius representing a hunting scene with two horses and riders, their dogs, and the birds they had killed. The Hondius which a later x-ray revealed was then painted over with a "Vermeer." This Hondius was purchased from Evert Douwes of Amsterdam who did not know the part the painting was to play in the great forgery scandal. Mr. Douwes pointed out that at such time as the van Meegeren overpaint is removed there will be a discovery of a real Hondius.

This "Vermeer" of the Last Supper, together with a head of Christ, van Meegeren sold for the huge total of $645,000. Yet he didn't even bother to remove the Hondius picture underneath. The dealer who had handled his first painting, "Christ at Emmaus" also handled "The Last Supper," "Christ's Head," "Isaac Blessing Jacob," and a "de Hooch."

In many respects it was unfortunate that the Rotterdam industrialist and collector, D. G. van Beuningen, purchased a "de Hooch" as well as two other paintings, as we shall see.

It was the eighth and final picture that was to be van Meegeren's undoing, "The Adultress," which was sold to Gen. Goering for $495,000. In 1945 "The Adultress" was found in Goering's collection at Berchtesgaden by Allied investigators, together with a bill of sale. From this bill of sale the painting was traced back to van Meegeren.

At this point van Meegeren had to prove he was not a traitor to his country, and under the eyes of the police and court he painted the final van Meegeren-Vermeer of "The Young Christ."

The trial was a quick one, and van Meegeren was sentenced to one year in jail. His sentence never began. The reason is not known. Perhaps the admiration for van Meegeren's feat overshadowed his crime. The suits of the injured buyers of his paintings were entirely separate from this trial. Perhaps the feeling in Holland was one of concealed, but genuine, pleasure that van Meegeren had hoaxed Gen. Goering—not only hoaxed him but in effect traded one fake Vermeer for 200 authentic Dutch paintings that Goering had removed from Holland. This repatriation was a real service to Holland.

In any event van Meegeren died before he had served any time on his sentence.

How was van Meegeren able to get away with his forgeries? In the first place. he was a trained, practiced, and competent artist, and he was all these things in a country whose heritage is art. He was not considered a great artist, but he did distinguish himself through capturing prizes for his paintings. He was driven by what he considered inadequate recognition by the art critics to hoax these critics and to prove to the world that he could paint like Vermeer, enough like Vermeer to fool the experts who placed Vermeer at the top of their list and van Meegeren somewhere down toward the lower end. He did this. He took almost five years to produce "Christ at Emmaus," but his constant application achieved his goal.

Scientific tests could have been used to disprove van Meegeren's paintings. In later paintings, those he made after "Emmaus," the x-ray spotted the old painting beneath the van Meegeren. The spectroscope did in fact prove that the color blue used in one of his paintings was not in existence in the time of Vermeer. This error on the part of van Meegeren was not an oversight. The chemist from whom he ordered the type of blue Vermeer used was out of the pigment and used his own discretion in filling the order with the blue that was later detected.

Even in his first "Vermeer" of "Emmaus" some white from the original painting that van Meegeren tried to remove still remained. This small patch of paint could have been detected by the x-ray. In fact the ultraviolet ray might have picked it up.

"Christ at Emmaus" does not resemble any other real Vermeer, but then there are only about 35 known and accepted Vermeers. Van Meegeren invented a period of Vermeer from which there are no known paintings. This invention of a period helped him to get by with his forgery. When one compares the head of Christ in "Emmaus" with some of the heads painted by van Meegeren under his own name the relationship is obvious. But no one was looking for van Meegeren's paintings to compare with the new "Vermeer." One of van Meegeren's paintings hangs in a back hallway in a hotel in The Hague. It is competent, but a person would hardly want to buy it as a work of art, but rather as a novelty since it was by van Meegeren, the great forger. Perhaps in order to win the approbation of the art critics van Meegeren should have spent as much time on his own paintings as he did on the "Vermeer."

The story does not end here, however. In order to consider all the evidence in the forgery trial, an International Committee was set up, headed by Dr. P. B. M. Coremans, Director of the Central Laboratory of the Belgian Museum. This was a committee of art experts who were assigned the job of advising the court whether, in their expert opinion, the paintings were forgeries. The committee advised that they were forgeries.

Years after the trial Mr. D. G. van Beuningen, the Rotterdam industrialist and art collector, brought suit against Dr. Coremans over the authenticity of "The Last Supper" which was sold to Mr. van Beuningen as a Vermeer. It was Mr. van Beuningen's contention that the "Last Supper" for which $480,000 was paid was a real Vermeer, whereas the others, with the possible exception of the first one, "Christ at Emmaus," may have been fakes.

The government provided Dr. Coremans with an attorney, but he had to employ his own attorney in addition, and had to go to immense trouble to accumulate scientific evidence that "The Last Supper" was a van Meegeren forgery.

In building up his defense, Dr. Coremans visited Nice, where van Meegeren had painted "Emmaus." Here he found another "Vermeer." This was also a "Last Supper"—painted over a picture of two children in a goat cart by the Seventeenth Century Dutch artist Govaert Flinck.

It is obvious why the experts are reluctant to question paintings even when they know they are fakes. They do not want to be criticized or sued. I have seen Mr. van Beuningen's paintings only in photographs. Maybe they are the finest Vermeers ever turned out by the Master himself, despite much evidence to the contrary.

In September, 1950, the van Meegeren forgery of "Christ as a Young Man" was auctioned off for $800. In the same month in Amsterdam two van Meegerens were offered for sale. When the first was put up for sale C. J. Snoeijerbosch, an artist from Maersfoort, Holland, stood up and claimed that he, not van Meegeren, had painted the picture. The painting was passed by the auctioneer. Then the

VAN DYCK. *Portrait of Cornelius Vander Geest*
(after the faked portion was removed).
National Gallery, London

second van Meegeren was put up for sale. Mr. Snoeijerbosch stood up again and objected. This time he was disregarded, and the painting was sold—for the equivalent of $15!

Fakes are not always easy to spot. An important van Dyck portrait of Cornelis van der Geest that has been in the National Gallery in London for well over a century was demonstrated to be in part a forgery by means of x-rays. Only the head was painted by van Dyck. The body was added in the eighteenth century by carefully joining onto the original wood panel on which the painting was done another panel on which the bust was added. The forger placed the brand of the Antwerp Guild on the back of the added panel, smoothed both panels to a continuous surface so that one could not easily see where van Dyck's panel ended and the forger's began, and put heavily darkened varnish over the picture to disguise his addition. Because of the larger size the painting would bring a higher price.

In 1955 the prominent London dealer Leonard Koetser announced that the "Virgin and Child" by Francia in the National Gallery in London was a forgery, and that he owned the original, which was for sale for $50,000.

Sir Philip Hendy, a British Museum Director, and other authorities agreed. Sir Philip stated that as a masterpiece the National Gallery picture was worth $28,000, but that as a forgery its value was problematical.

The greatest field of all for the art forger is Impressionists and Moderns. There are thousands of spurious paintings of these Schools in America alone. In some of the smaller auctions there are hundreds of paintings offered for sale in just one session. Often few if any are authentic. Yet they bear the signatures of Renoir, Picasso and about anyone else who ever painted an Impressionist or

GREGORY STAPKO. *Copy of "The Loge" by Mary Cassatt.*

MARY CASSATT. *The Loge.* National Gallery, Washington, D.C. (Dale Collection, Loan)

FLAVIA HALLORAN. *Girl, in the manner of Renoir.*

RENOIR. *Girl Wiping Her Feet.* Magnin Collection, San Francisco

Modern picture. The author was once introduced to a gentleman who had the distinction of being one of the artists who so successfully added the false signatures to some of these spurious paintings.

Many of the buyers actually think they are getting a Cézanne or a van Gogh for $200. When I glanced at one of the several purchases of two couples who were busily loading their treasures into their car at the end of one of these auctions, I remarked, but with some reservation, that the painting might be by Chagall.

"Might be?" retorted the wife of one of the buyers. "It *is* a Chagall!" In further defense she went on, "You don't always have to pay thousands of dollars for a Chagall. Besides, this auction has the highest reputation."

As I departed I heard one of the purchasers say to the other, "Hey, Dave, this signature looks kind of funny."

In October, 1946, the French police arrested Jacques Mairesse in connection with an art falsification ring which produced Utrillos, Picassos, Renoirs, Rodins, and others of the Modern and Impressionist Schools who were starting to boom in the art market.

It is interesting to note what Juliette Claude Latour, the artist who produced the forgeries, had to say. She stated, "Modernist art is the easiest thing in the world to copy and to falsify."

She admired classical art only, but she said that it would be impossible for her to imitate Leonardo da Vinci or Velásquez.

"But I can copy any modern painter," she told investigators. "My Utrillos are better painted than the Master's."

Utrillo is said to have studied long before he pronounced one of Mlle. Latour's copies, signed with his name, spurious.

It takes more time and more talent to produce "Old Masters," but my wife and I got the shock of our lives in Florence, Italy, when we were walking from the bridge over the River Arno to the Pitti Palace. Along the route there was a rather run-down shop filled with what appeared to be antique paintings. Since the personnel of the shop were all in the back room, the paintings were examined in some detail. The canvases were not only old but they were patched in several places. While a number of the paintings appeared to be strangely vague under dark varnish, some of them appeared to be painted with zest and well executed.

Then one of the shop personnel came out to greet us. He assured us that every painting in his shop was a fake. When we persisted in questioning about a particular painting that had an antique look to it, since we feel we know something about Renaissance Italian art (and this was the type art the shop contained), the attendant became even more positive. *All* the paintings, he said, without exception, were fakes. The shop attendant said he knew because he painted some of them himself.

The question is, who bought these paintings and what were they sold as.

In Madrid there was another shock in store. One day my wife was apparently suffering from an attack of "painting nerves." This illness is caused by looking at too many paintings in too condensed a period of time; so I visited the Prado alone, and after a few hours there took a cab to the Rastro, Madrid's "Flea Market." There some of the most beautiful "Flemish Primitives" were discovered. They were obviously newly painted, but they had the look of the Old Masters. The sight was so impressive that I went back to the hotel to get my wife out of bed and dressed, regardless of how she felt, so that she could see these masterpieces. She was not too enthusiastic about the trip until she took one look at the "Flemish Primitives." After a few minutes of looking, the thought apparently came into both of our minds: what if these paintings were cleverly cracked to simulate age, and what if the cracks were filled with India ink and the entire paintings covered with a dark varnish? Would they defy immediate detection? That was enough art for one day!

The forgery of antiquities is one of the oldest occupations in the world, and the longer ago the forgery was done the more authentic it looks, unless, of course, the pigment used was poor, in which case the telltale color gives away the forgery.

In 1496, when Michelangelo was 21 years old, he imitated an ancient sleeping marble cupid. This he buried in the ground. Later it was dug up. An art dealer paid 30 ducats for it and sold it to Cardinal Riario, a collector, for 200 ducats. This incident proved to Michelangelo's satisfaction that he was as good as the ancients, just as van Meegeren's forgeries established his worth in his own eyes.

Denis Rouart tells the interesting story of the young Renoir. At this particular time in Renoir's life he was unknown and unaccepted as a painter. Fortunately for Renoir, the well-accepted Barbizon painter Diaz saw the young man's work and liked it. Diaz took it upon himself to market Renoir's paintings, passing them off as having been painted by Rousseau, a contemporary painter. Nowadays, the fakers would like to pass off Rousseaus as having been done by Renoir.

There is an interesting story of a fake, or of a discovery, or both, depending upon how one wants to look at it:

In Rome in 1959 we visited the small art shops on the Via del Babuino at the bottom of the Spanish Stairs. While walking through one shop looking at the various paintings hanging on the wall my wife handed me a note. It read, "Hercules Seghers."

It was immediately apparent what she meant. She thought she had discovered a landscape by the eminent Seventeenth Century Dutch artist Seghers. His landscapes are somewhat similar in size and manner of painting to those of Rembrandt, and they are worth about as much—$150,000.

I spotted the painting and a short look convinced me that this was an apparently good attribution. The painting was relatively small of a conflagration in a city, and the fire seemed almost real. Since the proprietor knew no English and I knew no Italian the negotiations contained a certain element of interest.

In the end the painting was purchased for $185; but this was not all. Its export had to be approved by the Fine Arts Commission. It took three days to secure this permission, but finally the package was officially sealed with the lead stamp of the Commission so it could be taken out of the country.

The next stop was Madrid, and here the treasure was opened. Reference books were secured and the Prado was visited to compare the painting with those hanging in the Museum; but the more comparisons were made, the more convincing became the thought that the painting was not by Seghers, but possibly by Rembrandt. Landscapes by Seghers and Rembrandt are often confused.

Plans to leave Madrid and return to the United States would have to wait. Instead a trip to Amsterdam was scheduled where both Rembrandt and Seghers could be studied in the Rijksmuseum, and in the Mauritshuis and Netherlands Royal Art Archives in The Hague. The collection of drawings in Rembrandt's house was studied for a clue to the scene painted, and the neighborhood was explored to find out if there was a church tower nearby like the one in the conflagration scene.

The studies seemed to confirm the possibility of Rembrandt as the artist and so London was revisited to study the Rembrandts in the National Gallery and in

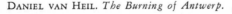

DANIEL VAN HEIL. *The Burning of Antwerp.*

the Wallace Collection, as well as photographs in the Witt Library of the Courtauld Institute. A photograph was made of the painting, including large sectional blow-ups for better detailed study and comparison.

On returning to the United States, since the matter was still not concluded, two things were done:

1. The painting was cleaned. This was done to test the paint. It did not appear to need cleaning; but when the painting came back from the restorer there was a disappointing shock. It did need cleaning! Off came the characteristics of Rembrandt. The scene was still one of a conflagration, in perfect condition, but obviously not by Rembrandt—or Seghers either. Someone had carefully put on Rembrandt's telltale characteristics of painting.

2. Photos of the painting were sent to the Netherlands Royal Art Archives and to Evert Douwes, the Amsterdam dealer.

Back came the attributions from Holland. Both the Archives and Mr. Douwes stated essentially the same thing: "A scene of the burning of Antwerp by Daniel van Heil." The Art Archives added that in all probability the painting was signed. So it was: DVH for Daniel van Heil, and the signature had been hidden by the "Rembrandt overpainting."

How was it possible to think that the painting might have been by Hercules Seghers or Rembrandt? In looking over the latest catalogue of the paintings offered for sale by the large Amsterdam dealer Peter de Boer, it was noted with interest that one of the paintings was a Daniel van Heil. This sentence was contained in a description of the picture:

> "It is difficult to explain the resemblance of some parts of this painting with the works of Hercules Seghers."

No $150,000 Rembrandt or Seghers was purchased in Rome for $185, but a fine, authentic Daniel van Heil—a good, rare Seventeenth Century Flemish painting worth about $2500. It was both a fake and a discovery, but even more important it taught the lesson again that when one buys a quality painting for little money, he does not usually go wrong—and the knowledge he gains can be secured in no way as thoroughly and as lastingly as when he buys a painting and does the research himself.

XXII

The Buyers in the Market

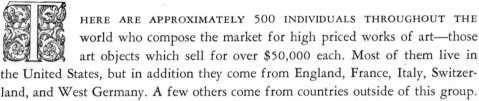HERE ARE APPROXIMATELY 500 INDIVIDUALS THROUGHOUT THE
world who compose the market for high priced works of art—those
art objects which sell for over $50,000 each. Most of them live in
the United States, but in addition they come from England, France, Italy, Switzerland, and West Germany. A few others come from countries outside of this group.

These buyers purchase anywhere. They keep in touch with major dealers and
major auctions in all countries waiting for a fine piece of art to appear, and they
will buy in any market, either directly or through an agent.

The $616,000 Cézanne "Boy in a Red Vest" from the Goldschmidt Collection
was purchased by Paul Mellon of the Pittsburgh banking family. It is believed
that out of the seven Goldschmidt paintings sold for a total of $2,186,000 Mr.
Mellon bought three. This is the magnitude of purchase of one of the top collectors.

In the Lurcy sale in 1957 the top priced painting, Renoir's "La Serre," went
to Henry Ford II for $200,000. This painting represents the quality of the col-
lection of this family.

Gov. Nelson Rockefeller donated, for the benefit of the Museum of Modern
Art, a Braque that brought at auction $145,000. In the same sale William A. M.
Burden, the American Ambassador to Belgium, donated a painting which brought
$200,000—a Cézanne still life.

When it became necessary for Edward G. Robinson to dispose of the fine collection of Impressionists and French Moderns that he had so painstakingly built up over the years, it was tanker king Stavros Niarchos who purchased it for over $3,000,000.

At least three American private collections are in the "Great" category by any standards: the Robert Lehman Collection which is heavily on the side of the Old Masters, some of them among the masterpieces of the world, the Chester Dale Collection, primarily of Impressionists and French Moderns, and the Duncan Phillips Collection, in many ways comparable to the Dale Collection.

The most active private collector in the world today is probably Walter P. Chrysler, Jr. His entire collection is reported to number over a thousand, and the dollars invested in it in the millions. Unlike most collectors Mr. Chrysler does not stick to a few Schools of art, such as Impressionists and French Moderns. While he has these, and some of the best that could be purchased, he has an entire collection of Seventeenth Century Dutch paintings and one of French Barbizons. In fact when he was buying Barbizons a few years ago abroad, the size of his purchases alone had an effect on the market. Mr. Chrysler can be credited with more than driving the Barbizon market up, if he did. He anticipated a reversal of the trend to an up-market, and he anticipated it by several years.

Most collectors do not sell in any organized way. Mr. Chrysler is the exception to the rule. Over the years since the end of World War II he has put on rather elaborate sales, in addition to selling a few pictures in a general painting sale. To some extent he may be getting rid of items he no longer has a preference for; yet some of the things he has sold are of top quality, and the quality was reflected in the price the paintings brought.

While the purchases and sales of these important individual art buyers are spectacular, the art market could not exist on them. In fact it is not designed for this type buyer. Both dealers and auctions make their livings on a vastly larger group of buyers with far less money to spend on a particular painting.

In an effort to find out some of the characteristics of this wider market for paintings, a questionnaire was sent out to a large sample of dealers. The questionnaire was sent out in the fall of 1960 and reached dealers all over the United States. The sample was large in that it reached those dealers responsible for the majority of painting sales in the country, since the coverage of New York City was extensive. During the same period individual interviews were conducted with dealers along the East Coast, and primarily in New York City. During the fall of 1959 personal visits were made to about 700 dealers throughout Europe, and the information secured from these dealers supplies background material for the American survey.

While the dealers who were surveyed throughout the United States were not classified in advance as to what kind of paintings they handled or what Schools they dealt in, the returns left no doubt as to the major type of art handled. About 50 per cent of the dealers stated that they sold only Contemporary paintings, while 34 per cent more stated that they sold Contemporaries along with other Schools. French Modern paintings were handled by 30 per cent of the dealers, almost always along with other Schools, and 20 per cent sold Old Masters, almost always in conjunction with other Schools.

The next question required an answer as to the type of buyer, both from an income point of view and the point of view of the purpose of the buyer in purchasing.

Less than 15 per cent of the purchasers were reported to be (1) Wealthy people buying for decorating their homes and (2) Wealthy collectors; but if to these wealthy collectors there is added (3) High salaried people, these three groups represent 65 per cent of the buyers.

One of the significant findings is that if we add (1) Medium salaried people and (2) Low salaried people, these two groups together amount to 35 per cent of all customers. Many of the dealers stated that their customers were all in the low salaried group.

In order to get an approximation of the size of the operation of each dealer it was requested that each one state, if he wished, the number of paintings he sold per year. Most of the dealers fell into the Under-50-Paintings-Per-Year category. Half as many dealers sold over 200 paintings per year each.

One of the larger dealers had some surprising things to say about his market. He stated, "An amazing number of younger people buy paintings of the better type and pay out of low salary or allowance." At the same time he stated that most of his sales, about 80 per cent, fell into the $100 to $500 category. He added, "There is a whole new class of collectors buying for prestige purposes and for profit, using paintings as a form of currency."

Well over half the dealers surveyed stated that their market was in the under-$500 class. Only 10 per cent of the dealers were in the over-$1000 class exclusively, and there is probably a good deal of "Prestige Bias" on the part of the dealers answering this question in this way.

The most unexpected information came from the dealers in connection with the trend of art prices in the year 1960 as compared with 1959. The main purpose of this question was to check the price charts prepared for this book from a survey of auction prices and from a sampling of dealer prices in the Schools of art surveyed.

Between January and December, 1960, the trend of many commodity prices in the United States was down—new cars, used cars, lumber and wood products, machinery and motive products, household appliances, industrial raw materials, metals, and all commodities other than farm and food. The most significant index which showed a rise in this period was the Consumer Price Index.

The history of the stock market in the year 1960 was one of up one step and down two. The *New York Times* Combined Average of 50 Stocks dropped from a high of 420 on January 4, 1960 to the low 300's late in 1960.

In light of this history of declining prices let us review the things the art dealers had to report in October, 1960:

Very nearly all of the dealers surveyed throughout the country stated that their 1960 prices were the same or higher than their 1959 prices. Only 4 per cent stated that their prices were lower. Thirty-six per cent stated that their prices were definitely higher and the rest said that they were the same. At almost exactly the same time that this survey was made the *New York Times* Stock Price Index touched 315 (Oct. 25, 1960) and dropped to that level from 420 in January.

In response to the query as to whether the art business of each dealer was better in 1960 as against 1959 or worse, 69 per cent of the dealers stated that it was better, 26 per cent stated that it was worse, and the rest stated that it was unchanged.

In October, 1960, a businessman visited one of the large New York dealers. and inquired about the prices of several of the paintings offered for sale. He apparently had definite feelings about the prices quoted, because he remarked, "I guess you don't much want to sell these paintings, do you?"

The head of the gallery replied, "No, not much. You see, they appreciate in value every month. We have enough cash income, and how are we going to replace this quality painting?"

Throughout the year 1960 business in the United States generally declined, but the painting business did not. Yet the number of dealers who reported poorer business in 1960 than in 1959 was proportionately greater than those who reported lower prices. The drag down of business was apparently being felt in a pressure on painting sales, even though slight, and a continuation of the downtrend in business would eventually get around to affecting painting prices, for under the pressure of declining sales, prices must give way. But there is a lag in this downtrend in the art industry and it has a profit cycle which varies in length and amplitude from the general business cycle.

At the same time that the dealers of the country were surveyed, a survey by questionnaire was made of the museums in order to find out what they were purchasing and what they intended to purchase in the future: whether Old Masters, Modern French Art, Contemporaries or what. The survey was sent to the leading museums throughout the country and to a number of smaller museums, including college and university museums. The sample was a very large one, and the returns were very nearly 100 per cent.

The replies from 54 museums were studied in detail because they presented significant facts. These museums replied to the question, "What were the last three paintings you purchased, and when did you purchase them?"

These 54 museums reported purchases of 133 paintings. Of this total, over half (70) were purchases of the works of Contemporary artists, and out of this total purchase of Contemporaries by far the largest sub-group is American paintings. Twelve of the museums stated that they concentrated on the purchase of American art of all periods, not just Contemporary American art.

Of the 133 purchases listed, 61 were made in the year 1960 and 27 in 1959, a total of well over half of the purchases having been made within the past two years.

There are a relatively few great masters included in the group of purchases. One museum purchased a Nattier and a Hubert Robert. A second purchased a Carel Fabritius. Both of these museums were organized within the past five years and are reaching hard to achieve the status of fine collections of art.

An art museum in the middle West purchased a painting by the Expressionist Kandinsky and also had the foresight to purchase a Georges de la Tour in 1956, long before the notable purchase of the famous de la Tour by the Metropolitan.

Included in the group of significant purchases are Sully, Lawrence, Robert Henri, Monet, Homer, Terbruggen, Pissarro, Cranach and Benjamin West.

The Wadsworth Atheneum in Hartford, Conn. has long been admired for its excellent collection of paintings. Over the years the policy of purchase seemed to be to buy fine, beautiful paintings of Schools of art not in great demand at the time and to set off this collection by a relatively few prime masterpieces, such as Rembrandt, El Greco, and Zurbaran.

A statement of the Director of the Atheneum, C. C. Cunningham, affirms this opinion. He says, "I don't think I or any museum director or curator can know nowadays what our next purchase is going to be. There are naturally certain areas in which we are interested and in certain artists. If one waits for the right desiderata to come along, one often misses first rate things which one doesn't happen to be looking for at the moment. The Sebastiano del Piombo and the Bassano are a case in point and they help considerably our representation of Venetian painting."

This statement is not only a declaration of policy of one museum, but it reflects the intelligent attitude of all buyers in today's art market. What was available ten years ago may well not be available today, and one may wait for the rest of his life to buy a Perugino and in that time pass up a fine Gilbert Stuart and a Winslow Homer. In another ten years no Stuarts or Homers may be available either!

In the same vein, Willis F. Woods, Director of the Norton Gallery in West Palm Beach, Fla., says, "Our present aims include acquisitions of American paintings of the present and past decade, and Chinese paintings and calligraphy of Ming and earlier dynasties. However, we have an opportunistic point of view."

Mrs. Mary O. Steele, Assistant Director of the Santa Barbara (Cal.) Museum of Art, states, "We are being given a magnificent collection of 40 to 50 American paintings—1750 to 1950—and it is likely we will confine purchases to paintings which will fill in any gaps in this collection—unless, of course, something outstanding which we could not afford to do without but could afford to buy, comes along."

There is a striking amount of agreement among museum directors as to the quality of paintings sought.

David G. Carter, Director of the Rhode Island School of Design, states, "Our interest is first in quality and then in a particular school."

Otto Karl Bach, Director of the Denver Art Museum, says, similarly, "We are interested in high quality paintings of all areas and periods."

Charles H. Sawyer, Director of the University of Michigan Museum of Art, says, "I would say that like most college museums we aim to collect pictures of quality rather than names. There is first the fact that we cannot afford to compete with the larger museums for name pictures and a second factor that the study and reinforcement of an attribution is one of the attractions for a university museum with graduate students in the History of Art. I do not wish to say that we collect chiefly anonymous pictures, but we are not seriously concerned if the attribution is changed after purchase provided the picture maintains its identity as a significant work of art and as a useful teaching instrument."

Finally, Laurence Sickman, Director of the William Rockhill Nelson Gallery of Art in Kansas City, Mo., says, "We perforce operate on a more or less opportunistic basis. We are interested primarily in quality and find it extremely difficult to attempt a planned program of acquisition in the painting field. . . . We purchase for quality rather than attempting to build up a complete historical sequence even though the examples may be inferior."

In the survey of the museums of the country the question of attribution of paintings and their discovery was injected, just to see if anything of interest would be reported. Considerable interest was reported, and these are the most notable reports:

John Richard Craft, Director of the Columbia Museum of Art, Columbia, S. C., tells a not-uncommon story of a change in attribution. He says, "As has been the case with any museum director of experience, I have had many occasions *to participate in* what might be called 'discoveries' or changes in attribution. Most recent was a beautiful neatly signed 'Corot,' which turned into a beautiful neatly signed Paul Desire Trouillebert (French, 1829-1900). This was a landscape, 'Paysage près de Rouen.' "

Peter Guille, Director of the Sterling and Francine Clark Art Institute of Williamstown, Mass. says, "As to reattributing any of our paintings, this we have done in a minor way with two, one, Dirk Bouts to Studio of Dirk Bouts, another, Botticelli to Studio of Botticelli."

Along the same line, David G. Carter, Director of the Rhode Island School of Design, reports, "I have had the pleasure of reattributing certain pictures, the most important is a 'Crucifixion' which I give to Alejo Fernandez, formerly given to Isenbrandt."

Finally, Willis F. Woods, Director of the Norton Gallery and School of Art, reports a Luca Giordano reattributed to Valerio Castello, a Marten van Heemskerck reattributed to Giovanni Bezzi, and a Master of 1518 reattributed to Jan Mandyn.

Mr. Woods sums up not only his own experience in reattribution but the experience of many museum directors when he says, "I regret that the effect of several of our efforts at reattribution has been demotion rather than upgrading."

One report of a museum director is a borderline case, in which it is not clear whether the reattribution was good or bad. Philip C. Beam, Director of the Bowdoin College Museum of Fine Arts, says, "The way in which we have 'discovered' works of art also needs some qualification. I made an important reattribution soon after I arrived at Bowdoin and discovered that a number of paintings attributed to old masters were in point of fact excellent copies by John Smibert who painted them when he visited Italy."

Smibert (1688-1751) was one of our earliest American painters, and the first English painter to arrive in America. His paintings are not only much sought after but will be much more sought after as the years go by.

A number of quite important reattributions, or discoveries, were, however, reported.

Denys P. Myers, Assistant Director of the Baltimore Museum of Art, says, "As for 'discoveries' the enclosed current issue of our News contains an article on a small Guardi which has been reattributed to Guardi. It was formerly given to Crespi, a rather more minor master."

Mrs. Loren Eiseley, Assistant Director of the Pennsylvania Academy of Fine Arts, tells this interesting story. She says, "In common with other museums we have occasionally changed the attribution of some painting from a 'great' name to that of 'unknown artist.' We have had the other kind of experience also, that of being able to substitute a correct attribution for a wrong one. Within my recent memory was the case of a portrait of Henry D. Gilpin, 6th president of the Academy, and a prominent Philadelphian. For many years the portrait was attributed to Samuel B. Waugh, a not very distinguished painter. In 1956 it was discovered, largely through the observation and study of our conservator, that the portrait of Mr. Gilpin was not by Samuel B. Waugh, but was an excellent example of the work of Henry Inman (1802-1846). Since we have many other examples of the work of Henry Inman, the only explanation for the mistake not having been rectified long before it was, must be laid to the fact that the portrait in question had hung in a certain room for a long time, along with portraits of other Academy presidents, and no one had paid any particular attention to the attribution.

"We were able, happily, further to substantiate the fact that the painter was Inman (although the work speaks eloquently for itself) on studying the Board minutes for 1876. It appears that the Academy originally owned a Samuel Waugh portrait of Mr. Gilpin, but that an exchange for the one by Henry Inman was later made. The cataloguing of the era was at fault, so that records were not changed properly."

Mr. C. C. Cunningham of the Wadsworth Atheneum tells his interesting story of a discovery. He says, "When I was in the Museum of Fine Arts, Boston, Mr. Plaut and I may have perhaps discovered the Gentile Bellini 'Portrait of a Doge' in that collection. You will find an account of this in their Bulletin, copies of which are in the Library of the National Gallery and the Library of Congress."

Miss Mildred Goosman, Registrar of the Joslyn Art Museum of Omaha, tells a short story of a notable discovery. She states, "Several years ago we purchased two paintings from a man who had bought them in a second hand store for the frames. These have been attributed to Joseph Vernet."

Emily Hartwell Tupper, Registrar of the Seattle Art Museum, sums up the whole attribution situation on works of art in these words: "We are continually attempting to alter and refine our attributions and dates. . . . In Museum connoisseurship one is often on very uncertain ground so changes are continually being made."

This statement summarizes the great difficulty in purchasing art, particularly the art of the older Schools and that later painting which is subject to forgery. It is one of the main reasons for the existence of Art Historians and Experts and it represents one of the greatest hazards in buying paintings. It is the reason for all the emphasis in this book on: Who says Rembrandt painted it, what dealer sold it to you, and does he guarantee it?

Although no question was asked in the survey of art museums as to how much is spent by the museums on paintings, no fewer than 18 museums volunteered the information that they buy few or no paintings because their budgets are either too small or actually nonexistent.

This is a strange situation at a time when all over the world there is a contest going on to buy paintings, the demand coming from both private buyers and museums. For the past five years the European dealers have conducted what amounts to a raid on the American supply of paintings, so that these will no longer be available in this country. They will be gone forever; and while our tax laws encourage the purchase of art by wealthy people in high income tax brackets to give to museums, encourage the long-time owners of collections to present them to museums and educational institutions, and encourage discoveries of works of art, just like our uranium buying program encouraged the discovery of this element, still other countries place direct restrictions on the flow of paintings out of their lands. It is wondered also how many of the members of the Boards of Trustees of American Museums know of the values of paintings, how many have realized the extent of the appreciation of works of art since the war, and how many have restricted the budgets of museum directors while the trustees themselves have had adverse experience in their personal stock portfolios.

In the fall of 1960 a questionnaire was sent out to a sample of the larger corporations of the country to find out just which corporations owned painting collections, what the collections included, why they were purchased, what use had been made of them, whether the purchase program was still going on, and whether any of the paintings had been sold or would be sold. It was hoped to determine whether paintings were purchased because they were considered a good investment, for advertising purposes, for prestige, or decoration.

Out of the total number of questionnaires sent out over half of the answers (and the answers were nearly always supplied in response to the questionnaire) indicated that the corporation did have a painting collection or at least a few quality paintings. Of course it must be pointed out that only the larger American corporations were surveyed, and it was known in advance that certain corporations did have collections.

One of the leaders of the group of corporate collectors is Hallmark Cards, Incorporated. This company has conducted five competitions for artists from 1949 to the present. The first three competitions were centered around a Christmas theme, as might be expected from a manufacturer of greeting cards, but the last two competitions stressed neither Christmas nor cards.

For the first Hallmark Card Award over 10,000 artists competed. The contest was administered by the Wildenstein Galleries, and the contestants came from every state of the United States, from Alaska, Hawaii, the Virgin Islands, and France.

In 1952 a second contest was held, this time for watercolors, and the area from which artists submitted entries was broadened to include all of the countries of North, Central and South America, and Western Europe.

The third contest held in 1955 was an invitational contest in which the works of 50 artists were purchased outright from which the judges chose 10 prize winners.

The fourth contest held in 1957 was also an invitational contest at which 50 artists were invited to submit paintings. This contest differed from the previous one in that in this no theme was specified.

This 1957 contest was far more than the ordinary art contest which produces possibly one excellent work, 20 per cent good works and the remaining 80 per cent productions of little value. It included such artists as Hopper, Sheeler, Piper, Vlaminck, Buffet, Wyeth, Hurd, Eugene Berman, and Paul Sample. It was a contest of men, not of boys.

The fifth contest, that of 1960, assembled the works of 57 "painters of promise," which is presumed to mean that they have not yet "arrived."

Since the awards were started the works of 357 artists from 27 nations were represented, and there have been 85 exhibitions in 36 different museums throughout the country. Approximately $250,000 in commissions and prizes were paid out by the company.

Hallmark Cards is also a sponsor of the Scholastic Magazine Art award competition for high school students and through this participation has acquired 125 student paintings which are available for display in museums, schools, and other institutions. The company also awards three art scholarships annually to high school students to study for one year in an art school or university.

The company makes a sharp distinction between these art-sponsoring activities and its purchase of art material for its cards.

Mr. T. D. Jones, Director of the Department of Arts and Sciences of International Business Machines Corporation, made the following statement:

"The IBM Department of Arts and Sciences was organized as the Fine Arts Department in 1939 as an educational and goodwill activity of the Company. The acquisition of paintings from all the countries in which IBM was represented was the first project of the Department. Thus, local art juries in each of 79 countries chose two paintings by living artists of their country for inclusion in the collection. Subsequently, contemporary paintings from each of the 48 states and U. S. possessions, selected by local art juries, were assembled in two collections. These International and United States Collections were exhibited at the World's Fairs held in New York and San Francisco in 1939 and 1940.

"The IBM Department of Arts and Sciences has for some time placed emphasis upon the acquisition of scientific exhibits. Significant are a collection of working models of Leonardo da Vinci's inventions.

"Specific touring exhibits are loaned, without charge, upon written request, to museums, educational institutions, civic groups, and other non-commercial organizations. Exhibits also are made available to banks, department stores, and other business concerns. During 1959 more than two and a half million people in 237 cities and towns throughout the United States viewed the IBM exhibits."

Mr. Jones stated that, "The objective of the Department has been to broaden the scope and extend the educational value of IBM arts and sciences activities as an important part of the company's public relations program."

International Business Machines has gathered together a first rate collection of paintings which includes works by such artists as Washington Allston, Bellows, Benson, Bierstadt, Mary Cassatt, Constable, Copley, Corot, Eakens, Glackens, Hartley, Hassam, Homer, Hopper, Inness, John, Millet, Moses, Orozco, Charles Willson Peale, Prendergast, Remington, Reynolds, Romney, Sargent, Gilbert Stuart, Utrillo, Vlaminck, Waugh, Benjamin West, Dufy, Marin, Whistler, and Wyeth. This is not a second rate collection in any sense of the word and must be classed near the top in quality among collections of American corporations.

Clairol, Inc. is an example of a smaller company which makes use of art in its corporate activities. It has an annual National Fine Arts Competition for beauticians sponsored by the Clairol Art Foundation. The winning paintings look surprisingly good.

The company stated, in addition, "Our company owns several paintings which were purchased principally for decorative purposes and because the executives of the company enjoy good paintings. I don't believe they were purchased out of any feelings about prestige, investment, or profit."

Abbott Laboratories has a somewhat different purpose in their art purchases. Mr. Charles A. Walz, the company's Art Director, stated, "The paintings were purchased for reproduction in Abbott Laboratories advertising to physicians around the world. This is the basic purpose for which all of our art is commissioned or purchased. Abbott Laboratories has been commissioning and purchasing fine art for use in its advertising since 1938." The artists in the collection include Paul Sample, Aaron Bohrod, Fernand Leger, Thomas Hart Benton, Utrillo, Laurencin, Rouault, Charles Burchfield, Grant Wood, John Steuart Curry, Milton Avery, Jimmy Ernst, Raoul Dufy, Salvador Dali, Braque, Shahn, and Afro.

Bradley L. Wilson, Art Director of General Electric Company, stated that the policy of the company is to "commission twelve paintings each year for our calendar. This has been continued since 1926. Almost 400 paintings are on loan now from coast to coast and in Canada."

The Ford Motor Company has purchased American paintings which are lent for exhibition purposes throughout the country. It is known as the Ford Times Collection of American Art. It contains the unbelievable number of 7250 paintings. There have been over 650 showings of these paintings which have been collected over a period of 12 years from commissions for Ford publications.

Standard Oil Company of New Jersey commissioned a number of artists to depict the role of petroleum in the war years 1940-1945. The group of artists who did the paintings includes Thomas Benton, and while the paintings have a commercial theme they are art nevertheless and the subject matter does not hide their fine quality.

The John Hancock Mutual Life Insurance Company has a group of about 100 paintings, mainly of great Americans or typical American scenes, by such eminent Contemporaries as Andrew Wyeth and Peter Helck.

The Du Pont Company has in its Hotel du Pont in Wilmington an excellent group of paintings, most of them naturalistic American, although the Italian landscapist Zuccarelli is included. Both N. C. Wyeth and Andrew Wyeth are included.

Manufacturers Trust Company in New York has in addition to such first rank Contemporary artists as Lyonel Feininger, Jimmy Ernst, John Marin and Ben Shahn, Old Master paintings by C. W. E. Dietrich and Pannini. All of their paintings are set off beautifully by their furniture in their executive offices which can be described by no other adjective than "superb." Ray Lockwood, executive vice president, proudly pointed out one huge desk that the bank had to work on for some time before the purchase could be consummated. It seemed that bidding against the bank was a European king, and only the pressure of his other duties allowed the bank to make the purchase in the absence of the king from his country.

Corporate ownership of what can be considered genuine art collections is something relatively recent in the United States, but such ownership represents a definite corporate movement and interest. The H. J. Heinz Company of Pittsburgh typifies the new companies entering the field of art collection. Mr. C. G. Koepke, Assistant to the Chairman, said, "Our corporate art collection is still in its infancy. We really only started acquiring art in the summer of 1958. Both Mr. and Mrs. Heinz are great art enthusiasts and they have personally selected every painting or sculpture we have purchased so far. Many of them were purchased abroad." The Heinz collection includes Boudin, Rouault, Braque, Stuart Davis, Soulages, Venard, and John Kane. The start of this collection is very auspicious.

Perhaps the attitude of the company just coming into the field of art purchase and art collection is best epitomized by Mr. Albert Arenberg of Luminator Harrison of Chicago. Mr. Arenberg wrote:

"We have several office locations and a number of branch warehouse locations. The branch warehouses have counters at which industrial and dealer customers come to pick up merchandise which our subsidiary, Harrison Wholesale Company, stocks.

"When the Woman's Board at the Art Institute in Chicago opened an Art Rental Gallery we rented about twenty pictures from them and they agreed to move them from one branch to another, at intervals of several months. Later on, we purchased the group of pictures and circulated them ourselves. Subsequently, we've bought an occasional picture—over the last few years.

"The purchases were largely those of Chicago artists . . . we thought they'd make our premises more interesting to people who came to them. We felt they'd also develop a greater interest in cultural activities on the part of our employees . . . many of them are painting themselves and have reacted favorably to the management's display of interest in art.

"Incidentally, we've assisted employees financially in taking various study courses, attending opera and orchestral concerts.

"We've had occasions when customers have inquired about purchasing our pictures—and we have referred them to the Art Rental Gallery at the Art Institute.

"We expect to continue to buy paintings of younger artists."

This company apparently thought the paintings would do two things: make the premises more attractive to the customers and to the staff of the company. It went into its art program conservatively—by renting first, and buying only when the program appeared to be a success. Both customers and personnel apparently liked the program since there were customer inquiries about selling the paintings and employee interest in art was stimulated by the knowledge that the management also liked art. The management followed up this interest by assisting the employees in their art pursuits, and finally decided to purchase more paintings.

These, then, would seem to be the main reasons for the existence of corporate collections:

1. Direct advertising where the painting is reproduced along with the advertising copy
2. General public and community relations
3. Decoration
4. Employee and customer relations

There is little or no attempt on the part of American corporations to invest in art simply because it is a good monetary investment, and although a number of corporations have indicated in the survey that they had sold paintings or would under certain circumstances sell them, their primary objective seems to be to keep and to build up the collection.

XXIII

Major Price Movements in Art

N COMPARING THE PRICE OF PAINTINGS OF A PARTICULAR ARTIST or School of painting over a period of years so as to get a price trend, the following difficulties and objections are always present:

1. The paintings are not comparable, even though by the same artist
    A. They are not all of equal quality.
    B. One may be beyond question the work of a particular artist, and the other may be questionable.
    C. One painting may be in an excellent state of preservation, and the other damaged and possibly overpainted.
2. One painting may be unknown and the other from prominent collections. A history of previous ownership carries a degree of authenticity as well as prestige.
3. The subject may be just different enough to make the paintings fall into different price categories.
4. The paintings may be from different periods in the painting life of the artist and thus of different value.
5. The size of two paintings by the same artist is rarely close enough to make them exactly comparable.

These objections do not exist where the *same* painting has been sold at public auction more than once and thus where we have two recorded prices.

On January 8, 1926 the sale of the paintings from the famous Billings estate took place at the American Art Association in New York.

On November 23, 1934 the same gallery sold the Eli B. Springs Collection. In this collection there were at least 11 paintings formerly in the Billings Collection. All paintings were examined from photographic reproductions to make sure they were the same.

These were the prices of the 11 paintings sold twice at auction, the first time in the pre-depression year of 1926 and the second time in 1934, the year of maximum depression unemployment:

Artist	Painting	1926 Price	1934 Price	Per Cent Decline
Maris	Under the Willows	$ 8,500	$ 1,400	84%
Diaz	La Mare aux Chenes	2,400	1,200	50
Ziem	Venice	6,400	2,100	67
Cazin	La Route	9,500	2,600	73
Dupré	Landscape with Fishermen	17,500	2,900	83
Troyon	La Charette de Foin	16,500	2,200	87
Rousseau	Bosquet d'Arbres	25,000	5,000	80
Daubigny	La Saulaie	12,500	2,100	83
Corot	Mantes	11,500	3,300	71
Corot	La Charette de Grès	27,000	11,100	59
Corot	Ville d'Avray	21,500	10,500	51

The effect of the Depression on prices can be judged, first by noting the decline of all of the paintings taken together. The decline in prices was 74 per cent with the 1934 prices 26 per cent of those received in 1926.

The comparison would show the effect on painting prices of the Depression were it not for the fact that all of these artists were in a downtrend at the time. Taste had changed, and other artists and Schools were preferred. The artists in this group were "the ones to own" in the 1910's and '20's, but they became passé in the '30's.

Corot did not go down with the permanence that the other artists did. Corot's decline was 60 per cent, while the other artists declined 80 per cent. Conversely Corot declined to 40 per cent of his pre-Depression level and the other artists to 20 per cent of that level.

We can learn more of the effect of the Depression by studying other paintings which were sold prior to the Depression and then during the Depression.

In the same Billings Sale of 1926 Corot's "Cavalier in the Country" was sold for $30,000. In December, 1934 the same gallery, American Art Association, sold the same painting for $13,000. The decline was 57 per cent, and the decline approximates that of the other three Corots sold in the Billings and Springs Sales.

ART PRICES FOR SAME PAINTINGS
BILLINGS SALE, 1926 – E. SPRINGS SALE, 1934

PRICES IN PERCENTAGE

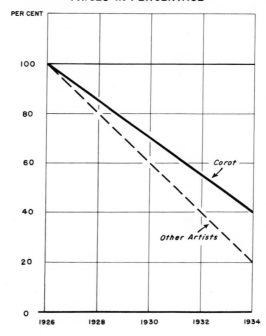

In 1928 the Daubigny (Barbizon School) "Evening, Ducks and Cattle" was sold for $2750. The same painting was sold in the early Depression (November, 1931) for $1400. The decline in price was 49 per cent in three years.

Still another example of the effect of the Depression on the prices of paintings is the double sale of a Childe Hassam (American Impressionist) in February, 1928, and again in March, 1933. The painting was entitled "Listening to the Orchard Oriole." The two prices were $2300 and $400. The decline was 83 per cent.

In this case Hassam cannot be considered an Impressionist from a price point of view. His change in classification from American School to Impressionist came later, and this change greatly affected the price of his paintings. Here in these two sales he was regarded as another American painter, although a good one, who somewhat went out of style. Had Hassam been considered an Impressionist the price decline would almost certainly have been less steep.

In January, 1925, a painting by the American landscapist George Inness sold for $1650. The title of the painting was "Rome, the Appian Way." The same painting sold in November, 1934, for $1050. The price decline was 36 per cent, and this is probably a good example of the effect of the Depression, since most of the artists used as examples up to this point were falling out of public favor at the time and were in long-term price downtrends which would have been present regardless of any Depression.

Later we will return to the effect of the Depression on the price of paintings. There are, however, a number of paintings sold twice through auction which demonstrate the postwar trend of art prices, particularly in the decade of the '50's, and we will look at these next.

The American artist George Bellows is the first illustration. His "Newsboy" was sold January 10, 1952 for $1000. Four years later "Newsboy" was sold for $2000, an increase of 100 per cent.

In 1954 two fine Canaletto Venetian scenes were sold in London by Sotheby's. In 1958 they were sold again by the same gallery.

	Price in 1954	*Price in 1958*
View of the Church of the Redentore	£6,800	£7,500
St. Giorgio Maggiore	5,500	7,500

Another Canaletto was sold at the Parke-Bernet Galleries in New York, once in 1942, and again in 1955. The title was "Grand Canal—Venice," and the two prices were $4200 and $6750.

"The Family" by Chagall was sold three times at the following prices:

October 22, 1952	$1,550
April 18, 1953	2,000
November 12, 1953	2,200

Now let us note the prices of two modern Italian paintings by Giorgio de Chirico:

"La Rivage de la Thessalie"

Jan. 17, 1945	$1,500
Jan. 25, 1956	1,950

"Castor and Pollux"

Dec. 13, 1950	$550
Jan. 6, 1954	800

The next price we compare is that of the Spanish Contemporary Salvador Dali. His painting which was sold twice is entitled "Labyrinth."

May 23, 1951	$600
Jan. 25, 1956	900

The price increase was 50 per cent in five years.

Not all paintings showed a price rise in the '50's, even though the School to which a particular painting belonged was a rising one. Take, for instance, the Impressionist Edgar Degas whose "Three Dancers" was sold in New York in 1953 for $29,000 and again in London in 1958 for £11,000 ($30,800), practically the same price.

Although the French Modern André Derain has certainly been on the rise, and his "Jeune Homme au Chapeau Feutre" was auctioned for $600 in 1946 and again for $1800 in March, 1956, the painting sold for a third time in November, 1956, and brought only $1400.

Derain demonstrates the rise in painting prices beginning in the 1950's when his "Portrait of a Woman" brought $750 in 1948 and $800 in 1952.

Finally, let us examine the prices of paintings sold twice through auction to see the effect of the Postwar painting trend when these paintings all belong to Schools of art in the ascendance:

Artist	Painting	First Sale Date	Second Sale Date	First Price	Second Price
Manet	Les Petits Cavaliers	1949	1954	$ 4,250	$ 5,250
Modigliani	Madame Hebuterne	1956	1958	10,500	11,500
Renoir	Portrait of a Lady	1950	1952	2,000	2,300
van Gogh	Paysanne Ratissant	1955	1959	5,500	9,000

These artists fall into the general over-all categories of Impressionists and Moderns. All show increases in price between the two dates.

Even in the 1950's the Schools of art which were out of public favor did not show the increase in price that paintings in general did, as evidenced by the following sales:

Artist	Painting	First Sale Date	Second Sale Date	First Price	Second Price
Diaz	L'Amour	1944	1950	$1,200	$ 650
Diaz	The Goddess of Love	1949	1953	400	300
Diaz	Venus et l'Amour	1945	1951	650	400
Gainsborough	Philip Dupont, Esq.	1935	1950	6,000	1,100
Hoppner	Eliz., Duchess of Devonshire	1947	1958	1,900	1,600

The two Schools represented here, French Barbizon and British Eighteenth Century Portraitists, were Schools which were declining in popularity and price, and this decline was not reversed by the boom of the 1950's, at least in the case of these paintings.

Finally, let us note the results of selling paintings twice on dates close together:

Artist	Painting	First Sale Date	Second Sale Date	First Price	Second Price
Kisling	Young Provincial Girl	Jan. '44	Jan. '45	$ 500	$ 550
Kokoschka	The Hunters	Jan. '50	Apr. '50	1,100	725
Rubens	Head of One of Three Kings	Mar.'28	Apr. '29	4,500	4,000
Russell	The Princess	Dec.'56	Oct. '57	600	500
Utrillo	Aubervilliers	July '57	July '58	£9,200	£7,000
Utrillo	Vue d'un Chateau	Jan. '58	Jan. '59	$4,100	$4,250
Vuillard	Woman with Blue Apron	Mar.'49	Mar.'50	1,000	625

The motives behind these close-together double sales are not known. What is known is that quick profits on the resale of paintings are not usual, and this fact was mentioned earlier in this book. Sometimes losses resulted, even in the 1950's, and even in the most popular Schools and artists.

A prime example of the unlikelihood of quick profits on quick purchase and resale occurred in the case of the Picasso "Mother and Child" reportedly bought in 1957 for $185,000 and sold in 1958 for $152,000 with a resulting loss of $33,000. Vlaminck's "Le Potager" also mentioned in an earlier chapter was sold in 1957 for $17,000 and resold in 1959 for $15,000, a loss of $2000 plus commission to the auction house.

Let us now see if we can measure the price movement of the entire art market over the period from 1925 to 1960. Since 1925 is used as the starting date, the effect of the Depression of 1920 and 1921 is not recorded. In 1925 the country was moving upward in the business cycle toward the boom, so that the full effect of the Great Depression and recovery on art prices can be recorded.

The job of preparing an index of price movement in art is similar to that of preparing a price index in commodities or stocks. The task is one of picking out the artists whose prices represent an adequate sample of all art prices, and recording price changes as accurately as possible.

The problem of establishing a price index in the art market is, however, far harder than that of establishing an index of commodity or stock prices, for these reasons:

1. There are many more artists whose works appear on the market than listed stocks or traded commodities. In the Seventeenth Century Dutch School alone there are 2000 artists, and in the Seventeenth Century Flemish School possibly as many as 2500 artists—4500 artists for just these two Schools, without taking into con-

sideration the remaining artists of the world in every period throughout art history.

2. Whereas one share of Shell Oil Common is just like another share for purposes of price comparison, and one pound of electrolytic copper is just like another, no two paintings by the same artist are exactly comparable or exactly matched in price.

3. Because any one artist has produced only a limited number of paintings, and only a relatively small percentage of these is on the market at any one time, the market is imperfect, and a market price is a somewhat intangible thing.

With these limitations as to the value of any Art Price Index clearly in mind, let us first take *all* the Schools of art we have reviewed and make a price index out of them.

This is very inclusive as an index of the International Art Market, but it does not represent the vast majority of paintings sold. This vast majority of paintings consists of those works which are national or local in market and which bring up to perhaps $500 or $1000. In this great numerical group are the following paintings:

1. Local traditional nineteenth and twentieth century paintings whose market is largely in the country of origin.
2. School works of the great artists in any period and School, and paintings turned out by followers of these great artists. They are frequently mislabeled "Leonardo," "Titian," "Raphael," etc.
3. Paintings of artists whose style is similar to that of major artists or copyists of major artists. These paintings are frequently "assisted" by false signatures.

The Art Price Index does not necessarily include this group of works although it *may* reflect its movement. The index represents International Art, that art which is sold in many countries and which has something of an established market price in many parts of the world. A Corot, for example, is marketable in its native France, but it is just as easily marketable in London or New York. Probably Canaletto sells better in London than in his native Italy.

First, then, we will list all of the Schools of art we have reviewed to date in order to make an over-all price index which we can later modify in order to make it more representative of the art market.

Italian Schools

Primitives, such as Duccio and Cimabue
Painting to the year 1450, represented by Fra Angelico

Late Fifteenth and Early Sixteenth Century, represented by Bellini
Great Venetians—Titian, Tintoretto and Veronese
Baroque—including the Carracci
Eighteenth Century, including Tiepolo, Pittoni and the Canal Painters

Dutch Schools

Seventeenth Century Major Artists, including Hals, Ruisdael and van Goyen
Seventeenth Century Minor Artists, represented by Nicholas Berchem
Nineteenth Century, represented by Josef Israels

Flemish Schools

Seventeenth Century Portraitists, represented by van Dyck
Seventeenth Century Landscapists and Genre Painters, represented by Teniers

British Schools

Eighteenth Century, including Gainsborough and Romney
Nineteenth Century, including Cox, Birket Foster, Pettie and Alma-Tadema

French and Other Moderns

Impressionists, including Renoir, Monet and Manet
Post-Impressionists, including Cézanne, van Gogh and Gauguin
Important Moderns, including Matisse, Picasso, Braque and Léger
Eight Moderns, including Derain, Dufy and Modigliani
Ten Moderns, including Chirico, Kisling, Miro and Laurencin
Barbizons, including Daubigny and Corot
Expressionists, including Kirchner and Kokoschka

American Schools

Moderns—Prendergast, Glackens, etc.
Nineteenth Century, represented by Sargent
Old Masters—Gilbert Stuart

If we average these 23 Schools and Sub-Schools of art with 1925 as the base year which we will make equal to 100 per cent, we have a *starting point* for an Index of Price Movement of the Art Market. This is the average taken at five year intervals:

Over-all Art Market Price Index

1925	100%	1945	189%
1930	139	1950	344
1935	121	1955	609
1940	170	1960	1274

This index must now be refined. There are six Schools within the Italian category. While Italian art is the most important single School from the point of view of museum collections, it is doubtful whether from the point of view of the International Art Market it is six times as important as, for instance, the Impressionists. It should not be given six "votes" in the average and the Impressionists only one "vote" even though Italian art has six subdivisions.

There are few authentic prime grade Italian Primitive paintings on the market, and few of the painters who produced up to about the year 1450, like Giotto and Fra Angelico. The main Canal Painters, Canaletto and Guardi, and Bellotto can be eliminated from the index, although it is possible to trace the prices of these artists through the years very well.

In the Dutch School, Berchem has been eliminated as representing the Small Dutch Masters. His prices are not representative of the School because of Berchem's steep rise in esteem since the war.

Israels has been eliminated together with the Nineteenth Century Dutch School. This School has almost ceased to exist as an important and preferred School internationally, and it is so large that Israels alone may not be a good sample. By way of apology to this School of art it can be said that it is possible for this School to decline in price very little without hitting zero, and at some time in the future it will almost unquestionably rise again.

In the revised index, the Flemish Portraitists have been represented by both van Dyck and Rubens, not just by van Dyck. This change has been made for two reasons: Rubens alone is an important element in world art, and, although the price curve of Rubens is not like that of van Dyck, these artists together are a significant part of the art market, past and present, and they represent two of the four really important Seventeenth Century Flemish painters.

The third Seventeenth Century Flemish master is a relatively minor one pricewise—David Teniers. He has been selected to represent the lesser, but extremely numerous, Flemish genre painters, and landscapists.

Dutch and Flemish art of the seventeenth century are very similar and closely allied. We now have three divisions of this art in the index to go along with three Italian divisions, with the result that Dutch and Flemish art on the one hand

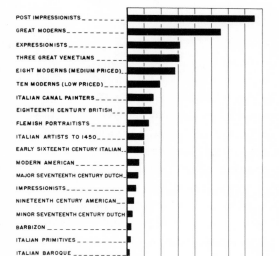

PERCENTAGE INCREASE IN ART PRICES
BY SCHOOLS OF ART
1960 VERSUS 1955

POST IMPRESSIONISTS
GREAT MODERNS
EXPRESSIONISTS
THREE GREAT VENETIANS
EIGHT MODERNS (MEDIUM PRICED)
TEN MODERNS (LOW PRICED)
ITALIAN CANAL PAINTERS
EIGHTEENTH CENTURY BRITISH
FLEMISH PORTRAITISTS
ITALIAN ARTISTS TO 1450
EARLY SIXTEENTH CENTURY ITALIAN
MODERN AMERICAN
MAJOR SEVENTEENTH CENTURY DUTCH
IMPRESSIONISTS
NINETEENTH CENTURY AMERICAN
MINOR SEVENTEENTH CENTURY DUTCH
BARBIZON
ITALIAN PRIMITIVES
ITALIAN BAROQUE
NINETEENTH CENTURY DUTCH
AMERICAN OLD MASTERS
NINETEENTH CENTURY BRITISH

0   200   400   600   800

SCHOOLS OF ART   1955 PRICE   PER CENT

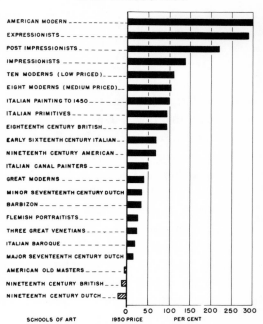

PERCENTAGE INCREASE IN ART PRICES
BY SCHOOLS OF ART
1955 VERSUS 1950

AMERICAN MODERN
EXPRESSIONISTS
POST IMPRESSIONISTS
IMPRESSIONISTS
TEN MODERNS (LOW PRICED)
EIGHT MODERNS (MEDIUM PRICED)
ITALIAN PAINTING TO 1450
ITALIAN PRIMITIVES
EIGHTEENTH CENTURY BRITISH
EARLY SIXTEENTH CENTURY ITALIAN
NINETEENTH CENTURY AMERICAN
ITALIAN CANAL PAINTERS
GREAT MODERNS
MINOR SEVENTEENTH CENTURY DUTCH
BARBIZON
FLEMISH PORTRAITISTS
THREE GREAT VENETIANS
ITALIAN BAROQUE
MAJOR SEVENTEENTH CENTURY DUTCH
AMERICAN OLD MASTERS
NINETEENTH CENTURY BRITISH
NINETEENTH CENTURY DUTCH

0   50   100   150   200   250   300

SCHOOLS OF ART   1950 PRICE   PER CENT

and Italian art on the other are now given equal weight in the index.

Eighteenth Century British art is left in the index, but Nineteenth Century British art has been eliminated since it has for some time declined in price to a very low point and does not carry great international weight.

The Moderns may perhaps be overemphasized in the index, with the division of this School into three parts by price class of artists; but Modern Art is now extremely important in total dollars of painting sales, as indicated by the increased number of "All Modern" sales in London and New York in the 1950's. The least expensive division of the Moderns has consequently been eliminated, but the Expressionists have been retained in the index.

Finally, American art has been included with three divisions—Modern, Nineteenth Century and Old Masters, the last category being mainly portraitists. While the price of American art is low as compared with international art prices generally, and American art is in light demand outside America, this overemphasis on American art has been permitted because this is an American book, and American art is plentiful on the American market.

This, then, is the revised Art Price Index:

Revised Art Market Price Index

1925	100%	1940	81%
1929	165	1945	102
1930	100	1950	150
1933	50	1955	290
1935	71	1960	981

The Index rises to a peak of 981 per cent as against 1274 per cent in the All-Inclusive Index. This lowering has been caused by the removal from the index of Italian Primitives, Italian Painting to 1450, and the one artist Nicholas Berchem. The removal of these groups is not meant to imply lack of importance but merely that they do not form a significant proportion of the paintings offered for sale.

From 1925 which is equal to 100 per cent, prices rose 65 per cent to 1929 and then dropped to a low point of 50 per cent at the bottom of the Depression. The pre-Depression boom prices were not again approximated until the 1950's.

A most important factor bearing on this price index is the changing attitude of the public toward paintings. While the Depression certainly limited the ability of prospective buyers to acquire paintings, other equally important factors were at work influencing the art market. The Depression philosophy which to an extent included feelings of antagonism against the wealthy and paintings, which were some of the attributes of wealth, plus the trend toward functionalism, or simplicity, in decor had a deadening effect on art sales for a long time.

In order to overcome the influence of these long term or trend factors influencing the art market we will have to find a measure of the influence of pure business conditions on art prices. We will have to note price rises and falls over intervals shorter than the five year intervals we have used up to this time, because these five year periods allow the long run trend factors to come into play to influence prices.

To determine this short run effect of business conditions generally on prices in the art market, we have closely examined the price curves of every artist we have surveyed to find particular years, fairly close together, in which a price trend is clearly indicated. It does us little good in determining the effect of the Business Cycle to note that in 1925 the average price of a Hals was 100 per cent and in 1941, 125 per cent. What happened in between, say from 1929 to 1932, and from 1932 to 1935? What we want to know is what happened to prices going into the Depression and what coming out, and what happened going into World War II and what coming out of the war.

These are the prices of particular artists going into the Depression:

DEPRESSION PRICE BEHAVIOR OF ART
(1925 = 100%)

Artist	Year	%1925 Price	Year	%1925 Price	Price Decline in Percentage Points
Dutch School					
Hals	1928	100%	1935	40%	60%
S. Ruisdael	1929	120	1932	16	104
van Goyen	1930	130	1934	30	100
Berchem	1929	700	1932	300	400
Israels	1929	100	1932	20	80
British School					
Cox	1929	100	1932	14	86
Birket Foster	1930	350	1933	300	50
Turner	1930	160	1932	25	135
Romney	1929	100	1932	33	67
Hoppner	1930	250	1934	45	205
Gainsborough landscapes	1930	100	1934	50	50
Gainsborough portraits	1929	100	1930	90	10
			1935	70	30
French School					
Corot	1928	100	1930	45	55
			1931	20	80
			1933	10	90
Diaz	1929	60	1932	48	12
			1934	20	40
Italian School					
Bellini	1930	100	1933	45	55
Guardi	1929	200	1930	100	100
American School					
Inness	1929	200	1933	66	134
French School					
Matisse	1929	100	1934	50	50
Monet	1930	200	1933	150	50
Gauguin	1930	100	1936	50	50
Cézanne	1930	100	1932	20	80

Where the 1925 average art price was 100 per cent, the 1929 average was 165 per cent, and the Depression average about 58 per cent. The index had dropped 107 points.

The basis of the selection of the artists included in the above table was the availability of a price in the Depression so the effect of the Depression could be determined. It should be mentioned again that unlike the stock market the paintings of one particular artist are not sold regularly. In some cases two or three or more years may go by and not one of the artist's pictures will appear on the art market. To construct the above table every artist surveyed in this book was studied to see which ones had prices recorded just before the Depression and then in the Depression.

The pre-Depression price index number is often not 100 per cent. We have considered the year 1925 as 100 per cent in all cases, but many artists rose higher than that figure in the boom months before the collapse, and at least one artist declined.

The average decline in price between the prosperity peak and the Depression was 62 per cent. A painting bought for $10,000 before the Depression was worth on the average $3800 in the Depression.

While this sample which we have used is very small, it is fairly safe to conclude that few artists went down to the worthless point in the Depression as did some stocks.

Decline in Art Prices in the Depression
(in per cent)

Hals 60%	Gainsborough portraits 10%
S. Ruisdael 87	Corot 90
van Goyen 77	Diaz 58
Berchem 57	Bellini 55
Israels 80	Guardi 80
Cox 86	Inness 67
Birket Foster 14	Matisse 50
Turner 84	Monet 25
Romney 67	Gauguin 50
Hoppner 82	Cézanne 80
Gainsborough landscapes ..50	Average Decline 62

The next determination to make is the effect on art prices of the economic recovery from the Depression low of 1932-1934.

We have sampled this effect in the same way, by finding artists whose prices are well recorded in the Depression and then recorded again later on in the 1930's or even the early 1940's.

RECOVERY PRICE BEHAVIOR OF ART
(1925 = 100%)

Artist	Year	%1925 Price	Year	%1925 Price	Price Recovery in Percentage Points
Dutch School					
S. Ruisdael	1932	16%	1941	30%	14%
Berchem	1936	300	1937	700	400
			1939	1000	700
Israels	1932	20	1935	30	10
Flemish School					
Rubens	1931	50	1935	75	25
			1939	120	70
			1940	150	100
Spanish School					
Murillo	1934	10	1939	20	10
British School					
Cox	1932	14	1937	30	16
Turner	1932	25	1941	35	10
Romney	1932	33	1941	33	0
Gainsborough landscapes	1934	50	1937	300	250
Gainsborough portraits	1935	70	1941	70	0
French School					
Corot	1933	10	1937	17	7
			1941	20	10
Daubigny	1931	16	1935	42	26
Bouguereau	1932	20	1936	50	30
Italian School					
Canaletto	1932	8	1937	20	12
Guardi	1932	40	1939	100	60
American School					
Stuart	1932	45	1939	165	120
Whistler	1932	16	1940	268	252
Sargent	1932	14	1935	115	101
Hassam	1932	20	1935	100	80
Impressionists					
Monet	1933	150	1935	150	0
			1940	150	0
Degas	1934	25	1941	80	55
Gauguin	1936	50	1940	200	150
Cézanne	1932	20	1939	80	60
Average		*44%*		*125%*	*81%*

All artists show a price recovery with the exception of the British portraitists Romney and Gainsborough, who were temporarily out of style. There was also a lack of interest in Monet paintings. Unfortunately the artists in this table are not all the same as those in the earlier table of prices going into the Depression, so that the percentages in the two tables are not strictly comparable.

Art Price Recovery from the Depression
(in per cent)

S. Ruisdael	47%	Bouguereau	60%
Berchem	70	Canaletto	60
Israels	33	Guardi	60
Rubens	67	Stuart	73
Murillo	50	Whistler	94
Cox	53	Sargent	88
Turner	29	Hassam	80
Romney	0	Monet	0
Gainsborough landscapes	83	Degas	69
Gainsborough portraits	0	Gauguin	75
Corot	50	Cézanne	75
Daubigny	62	*Average Recovery*	56

The price decline into the Depression for our sample was 62 per cent. The recovery was not based on exactly the same sample, so that a strict percentage comparison is not possible.

To illustrate one difficulty, if a $10,000 painting declined to $2000 there would be an 80 per cent decline; but if the same painting then recovered to $10,000 again the increase would be 400 per cent, although it had retrieved in dollars just what it lost.

To minimize this difficulty, the recovery in dollars was divided by the figure to which it recovered (in the illustration, by $10,000); and the result is 80 per cent recovery—not strictly correct mathematically, but a good approximation for our purposes.

The recovery of prices in the sample which we used was 56 per cent—not too far under the loss of 62 per cent into the Depression.

If, on the other hand, a person bought all of his paintings in the Depression and resold them at the end of the decade of the 1930's, his return on his money would have been 253 per cent, and in addition he would have had his initial capital returned to him.

The war is the next important event to examine in connection with the price of art. In order to determine the war's effect we have compared as many pairs of prices as we can on the same artist, the first just before the war, the second near the war's end—1945.

WARTIME PRICE BEHAVIOR OF ART
(1925 = 100%)

Artist	Year	%1925 Price	Year	%1925 Price	Price Increase in Percentage Points
Dutch School					
Hals	1941	40%	1945	70%	30%
Berchem	1939	1000	1943	500	−500
Israels	1940	28	1943	48	20
			1946	65	37
Spanish School					
Sorolla	1939	100	1943	1050	950
English School					
Hoppner	1941	100	1944	33	−67
French School					
Corot	1941	20	1945	30	10
American School					
Whistler	1940	268	1945	100	−168
Hassam	1941	100	1946	60	−40
Modern School					
Picasso	1940	100	1945	220	120
Braque	1941	100	1945	550	450
Vuillard	1940	100	1945	220	120
Chirico	1940	100	1944	320	220
Kisling	1939	100	1944	300	200
Impressionists					
Monet	1940	150	1944	350	200
Degas	1941	80	1944	150	70
Cassatt	1939	70	1946	120	50
	Average	97%		188%	91%

In the war art prices as a general rule went up. Only four prices in the sample went down. One was Hoppner, the Eighteenth Century British Portraitist, who was in a downtrend and going out of style temporarily. Two others were Whistler and Hassam in the American School, who had risen so greatly in the recovery phase of the business cycle from the early 1930's to 1940.

In this period the Impressionists and Moderns began to become popular. Monet rose 133 per cent, Degas 88 per cent and Cassatt 71 per cent. The five Moderns in the sample rose 222 per cent during the war. There was, however, a temporary situation in England early in the war when it was not clear whether

POSTWAR PRICE BEHAVIOR OF ART
(1925 = 100%)

Artist	Year	%1925 Price	Year	%1925 Price	Price Increase in Percentage Points
Dutch School					
Berchem	1945	600%	1953	1600%	1000%
Israels	1946	65	1952	40	−25
British School					
Cox	1945	160	1953	100	−60
Hoppner	1944	33	1953	15	−18
French School					
Corot	1945	30	1946	35	5
Bouguereau	1945	20	1950	40	20
American School					
Stuart	1946	100	1952	100	0
Whistler	1945	100	1948	100	0
Inness	1945	100	1946	133	33
			1952	166	66
Hassam	1946	60	1948	40	−20
Moderns					
Matisse	1945	400	1950	700	300
Picasso	1944	220	1950	220	0
Braque	1945	550	1946	900	350
Segonzac	1946	200	1952	250	50
Gris	1945	100	1946	260	160
Marin	1944	100	1950	200	100
Miro	1946	100	1950	250	150
Expressionists					
Kirchner	1946	100	1949	100	0
Impressionists					
Renoir	1944	2100	1948	2100	0
Monet	1944	350	1948	350	0
Degas	1944	150	1948	153	3
	Average	*155%*		*210%*	*55%*

paintings would have any value whatever. Prices dropped so far as to be unbelievable. For this reason and because of the bombing of the British art auctions and an inability of the auction houses to publish adequate catalogues with illustrations during the war, the war years contained in this study are dependent on the experience in the American auctions.

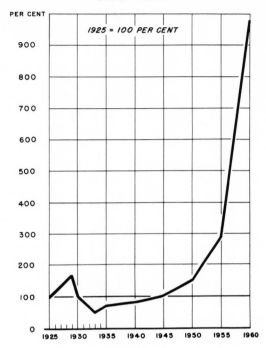

ART PRICES IN PERCENTAGE
1925 - 1960

PER CENT

1925 = 100 PER CENT

900

800

700

600

500

400

300

200

100

0

1925 1930 1935 1940 1945 1950 1955 1960

Let us look at prices in the immediate postwar period, between the war's end in 1945 and the year 1950. A new era in art and art prices was being ushered in in this five-year postwar period.

There were four declines in the postwar period: Israels, Cox, Hoppner, and Hassam. Israels and Cox were in a period of long term decline—both nineteenth century artists. Hoppner was going out of fashion, while Hassam was declining along with the American School in general and had not yet been "identified" with the Impressionists.

Two other artists in the American School show no price increases because of the long term down trend in this School—Gilbert Stuart and Whistler.

The ironical thing about the modern artist Picasso, the Impressionists Renoir, Monet, and Degas, and the Expressionist Kirchner is that they all fail to show price increases in this period. It was not until the 1950's that they were to be in the forefront of the painting boom.

The rest of the artists show substantial price increases in the immediate post-war period.

Let us now follow the price index from the year 1950 down to the end of the decade in order to determine which Schools are rising the fastest as compared with other Schools.

383

Prices by Schools of Art 1955 as Compared with 1950
Per Cent of Rise (or Fall)
(1950 = 100%)

American Modern	300%	Italian Canal Painters	50%
Expressionists	290	Great Moderns	40
Post-Impressionists	220	Minor 17th Century Dutch	35
Impressionists	138	Barbizon	32
Ten Moderns (Low Price)	110	Flemish Portraitists	26
Eight Moderns (Medium Price)	103	Great Venetians	23
Italian Painting to 1450	100	Italian Baroque	19
Italian Primitives	94	Major 17th Century Dutch	15
Eighteenth Century British	94	American Old Masters	−5
Early Sixteenth Century Italian	67	Nineteenth Century British	−12
Nineteenth Century American	63	Nineteenth Century Dutch	−20

In this period the Modern Schools and the Impressionists clearly head the list in price increase, while the Nineteenth Century British and Dutch Schools are at the bottom of the list and show actual price declines.

Let us now look at another list of Schools of art in descending order from those with the greatest price increases between the years 1955 and 1960 down to those with the least rise.

Prices by Schools of Art 1960 as Compared with 1955
Per Cent of Rise (or Fall)
(1955 = 100%)

Post-Impressionists	754%	Modern American	73%
Great Moderns	557	Major 17th Century Dutch	68
Expressionists	307	Impressionists	52
Great Venetians	306	Nineteenth Century American	38
Eight Moderns (Medium Price)	282	Minor Seventeenth Century Dutch	30
Ten Moderns (Low Price)	195	Barbizon	24
Italian Canal Painters	161	Italian Primitives	21
Eighteenth Century British	148	Italian Baroque	16
Flemish Portraitists	127	Nineteenth Century Dutch	0
Italian Artists to 1450	100	American Old Masters	−5
Early Sixteenth Century Italian	100	Nineteenth Century British	−18

Several things are apparent from this table. In the first place the price increases for the five year period from 1955 to 1960 are vastly greater than those from 1950 to 1955. The Post-Impressionists Cézanne, van Gogh, and Gauguin increased 754 per cent compared with 220 per cent for the previous period.

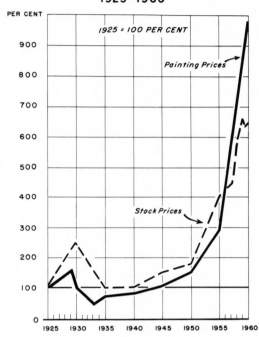

ART PRICES VERSUS STOCK MARKET
PRICE HISTORY IN PERCENTAGE
1925-1960

Again in this table the Impressionists and Moderns show the greatest price increases, although the Venetians, Veronese, Titian, and Tintoretto, show a great increase as do the Canal Painters, Canaletto and Guardi.

As in the previous table Nineteenth Century British and Dutch, as well as American Old Masters, are at the bottom of the list.

A highly interesting comparison can be made between the Revised Art Price Index and Stock Prices for the years studied: 1925 to 1960. In the first place the drop off of painting prices in the Depression was not nearly so severe as the drop in stock prices. The recovery from 1940 to 1950 is roughly parallel. Stocks then forged ahead of painting prices for the next five years. Then despite the bull market in stocks after the 1957 recession, painting prices forged far ahead of the stock market to the year 1960, and despite the setback in the stock market in that year, painting prices still rose.

XXIV

Building a Collection Today

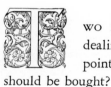WO KEY QUESTIONS WHICH SHOULD BE DISCUSSED BY ANYONE dealing with the investment value of art are: From an investment point of view should paintings be bought now and if so, what should be bought?

The 1950's saw a boom in art such as has possibly never appeared before in history. As we turn into the 1960's the boom does not show any signs of turning into a decline.

Prices of art have been rising at a phenomenal rate. They obviously cannot continue up forever, any more than the stock market or wholesale prices can; but at the turn of the decade into the 1960's there was a definite upward trend in the art market, while at the same time many Schools of art were not overpriced.

First, let us consider the Schools of art which do *not* appear to offer the best outlook or prospect for a collector. These are eight:

1. Flemish Primitives

This School is almost completely unobtainable at the present time. Occasionally a little fragment or pencil drawing by Jan van Eyck or Rogier van der Weyden appears on the market and brings a tremendous price in relation to the intrinsic merit of the object as a work of art. When a larger work appears it is often not typical, or everyone does not agree as to its authenticity, or it is in poor condition.

With the exception of some of the lesser masters in this School, there are so few items offered for sale as to make the Flemish Primitive market almost nonexistent.

2. *Italian Schools Earlier than Baroque*

This is the art of Italy prior to the year 1550. While occasionally a typical, fine Veronese, Titian, or Tintoretto appears on the market, this is the earliest Italian School which can be secured at all—Sixteenth Century Venetian. A Leonardo, a Raphael, a Giotto are to all intents and purposes not on the market. When a second line artist appears, such as Fiorenzo di Lorenzo or Antoniazzo Romano, the price is well into five figures and sometimes higher. The smallest names in the School are generally not wanted and are not the best from the point of view of building a collection or making a sound investment.

3. *German Sixteenth Century Art*

The art of Dürer and Holbein is rarely on the market, but when it does appear the price is well into six figures. From these leaders, and perhaps Grünewald, there is a big step down to the lesser Sixteenth Century German artists such as Strigel, Cranach, and Baldung-Grien. Yet even these Sixteenth Century German artists are not in great enough supply to form a large market, and they bring prices in five figures.

4. *The Important Classical Spanish Artists*

There are very few Spanish artists in this category. The greatest are Velásquez and El Greco, and both are extremely rare. In the past 35 years hardly one excellent Velásquez has appeared on the auction market. Ribera and Murillo have come onto the market occasionally, but extremely few Zurbarans and Goyas. Although there are certainly Spanish artists other than these, they are not nearly as well accepted on the international art market.

5. *French Artists of the Eighteenth and Seventeenth Centuries*

In this group are Chardin, Boucher, Fragonard, Poussin, and Lorrain. Too few of these masters appear on the market to be of any significance or to provide much availability, and the lesser French artists of these centuries are less valuable, or unidentified, or both. The prices of the major works that do appear are very high, as for example, the Georges de la Tour recently purchased by the Metropolitan Museum of Art in New York for a sum in the high six figures.

6. *Chief Impressionists and Post-Impressionists*

Although there does not seem to be any price weakening in this group, which includes Renoir, Monet, Manet, Sisley, Pissarro, Degas, Seurat, Signac, Cézanne, van Gogh, and Gauguin, the prices are very high, and often a painting will sell in six figures. How far this group can rise in price is problematical.

7. *The Great Moderns*

In this group are included Matisse, Picasso, Braque, and Léger. They have risen far and are often in six figures. Whether they can continue to rise, and if so how far, is not known; but the purchase of just one painting in this group involves a very sizable investment for anyone, no matter how wealthy he may be.

8. *Nineteenth Century British*

This is a School which is at low ebb. It has shown little sign of recovering in price. Perhaps this low ebb is an indication that it will go up simply because it is at so low a point, but it is very much in the position of the railroads and the oil companies. Probably they will rise sometime; but while we are waiting around for this movement to start, other things are going up rapidly.

There remain then the Schools which it is felt are good from the collector-investor's point of view. These are eight in number:

1. Baroque and Eighteenth Century Italian
2. Seventeenth Century Dutch
3. Modern
4. Expressionists
5. Lesser Impressionists and other Major French of the Period
6. American
7. Eighteenth Century British Artists
8. Contemporary

There is some significance to the order, but not a great deal. The Baroque and Eighteenth Century Italian Schools have been unspectacular in their rise, but certain, although they have not experienced the great rise of the Moderns, Expressionists, Lesser Impressionists and other Major French. These three groups (categories 3, 4 and 5) are likely to rise faster for a time than the first two, but their certainty of rise is less than in the Italian and Dutch Schools. American and Eighteenth Century British have a great deal to rise, and the rise is not yet well started. There is more doubt about their uptrend than in the earlier categories. Contemporary art is going up, but it is primarily the leaders in the group who are rising, not all Contemporary artists simply because they are Contemporaries.

While in general it is not a good policy to buy the lesser artists and the followers in any School, the height of the market in the Impressionists makes the purchase of the major artists very difficult; and those who want the Impressionists have been buying the lesser names and driving this market up.

Probably the School to buy from the point of view of the one most in vogue is the Expressionists. This is a very particular style of art, however, and the School has been placed fourth rather than first as it contains more of the element of fad than the other Schools.

The American School is a large School, and available, and to date the prices within this School have not risen so high as to make the paintings beyond the reach of all but the most wealthy. The quality of the paintings is, in general, good; they are pleasing; and as time goes by they should have more of an established place in art.

The Eighteenth Century British School of Gainsborough, Romney, and Reynolds has long been in the doldrums. After the war Gainsborough landscapes started to become popular and rise in price until they went almost out of sight. Then, in the latter part of the 1950's, Gainsborough portraits started up and are now within sight of the landscapes. The other artists are, however, still available and at reasonable prices in relation to Gainsborough, but their trend is up. Our early American portraitists are very similar to the British of the period and can logically fit into such a collection.

We finally arrive at Contemporary Art. These are the artists of today. There is at present the greatest welter of producing artists in centuries, and a choice among them becomes difficult. While the leaders of the group have risen in price by leaps and bounds, including the American, Jackson Pollock, and the Frenchman, Nicholas de Staël, it is not clear just which of the others will finally be recognized over a period of time, and which will fall by the wayside as being of only passing moment. It is not simply a matter of studying price trends. Some very peculiar artists have shown a sharply rising price trend, and we do not have a history behind these artists to judge either their lasting quality or the firmness of their acceptance by the art world. We can only use our best judgment as to the quality rather than base our judgment on short run price trend.

One of the least satisfactory ways to collect is to buy just one painting at a substantial price and expect that that is a good investment. It is like risking everything on just one stock; and few responsible financial men would advocate such a program. What is necessary is to select paintings by several artists within the School or Schools of one's choice.

We have thus chosen ten to fifteen paintings in each School of art as a possible collection. Such a program hedges against the decline in price of any one artist, but it does more than that: it builds something that provides joy to the owner and which should provide considerably more intrinsic pleasure than do the pictures on the stock certificates.

The formation of a collection does still another thing for the buyer: it forces him to know something about the School of art he has chosen to collect. He has twelve or fifteen paintings. They form an important part of his home and his life, much more than does one painting. There are more paintings and there is a larger investment. Such a group of paintings is very persuasive as an educator; and without education in the particular field of art interest, a person might as well not collect. Authentic paintings by big names are often offered at what appear to be bargain prices. Everyone agrees on the authorship; but the paintings are not typical of the master and thus do not have the value, either aesthetically or monetarily, of the master's other works. Only a knowledgeable buyer could have told this. Technically the painting was by the master, but it was not a sound purchase. Only long and patient study will educate a buyer enough so that he may be able to detect such distinctions in quality.

An art purchaser must learn the School of art he collects and the particular artists he has chosen to collect. This is why suggestions are made for *collections within the same School of art*. A person can certainly mix Schools of art if he wishes and choose a Renoir, a Romney, and a Ruisdael for his home; but it is unlikely that he can hold down his job and at the same time be even a semi-expert on a combination of Impressionist painting, Eighteenth Century British and Seventeenth Century Dutch art.

The following tentative collections of selected artists' works in each School have been put together on the basis of (1) what is available, (2) what artists have a consistent standard of good quality, (3) what artists appear to be rising in price or at least not declining, and (4) what will make a balanced collection and be pleasing in one's home.

Rough estimates of prices have been used. Sometimes these are auction prices of paintings which have been examined from photographs. Sometimes they are dealer prices in established markets; and sometimes they are the prices of actual paintings which have been located off the beaten path. At any rate, they represent the maximum prices which I myself would be willing to pay for each artist listed from my knowledge of current prices and of particular paintings which are, or were, recently on the market.

SEVENTEENTH CENTURY DUTCH AND FLEMISH

First List

Rembrandt	$150,000
Hals	50,000
Ter Borch	50,000
van der Heyden	10,000
Rubens	30,000
van Dyck	25,000
A. Cuyp	15,000
Steen	15,000
Jacob Ruisdael	35,000
Salomon Ruisdael	25,000
van Goyen	35,000
van Huysum	25,000
	$465,000

Second List

Franz Post	$ 3,000
van Ostade	2,000
van Goyen	8,000
van der Neer	5,000
Jan Brueghel	5,000
Avercamp	10,000
van Huysum	7,500
David Teniers	5,000
van Dyck	10,000
Master of Winter Landscape	7,500
Berchem	5,000
de Momper	3,000
	$71,000

Third List

Maes	$ 2,500
S. Ruisdael	5,000
de Keyser	2,500
J. G. Cuyp	1,000
Savary	2,000
Siberechts	3,500
van Beyeren	3,000
Jan Both	3,000
Jan D. de Heem	2,500
Brouwer	2,500
Berck-Heyde	3,000
van Kessel	2,500
	$33,000

Fourth List

de Wet	$ 800
Beeldemaker	500
van Lint (Hendrick)	800
Bramer	300
Martin van Heemskerck	300
Peter Neefs	500
Verkolje	600
Caspar Netscher	800
Alex Adriaenssen	500
Peter de Bloot	300
Adam Willaerts	500
Bart. Breenbergh	300
	$6,200

Obviously omitted from the first list is Jan Vermeer. His paintings are priceless and probably unobtainable. In nearly the same category is Peter de Hooch. It is extremely difficult to get good, authentic, typical works by him, and for topnotch de Hooch paintings $250,000 is not an unreasonable price.

The $150,000 for the Rembrandt would require some careful searching. While $50,000 would buy a small Rembrandt, about the size of a sheet of paper, and a really important Rembrandt would cost $500,000 up, the sum of $150,000 should buy a good, fairly large Rembrandt, remembering that time is required to locate it; and while there are many atypical Rembrandts and "maybe-Rembrandts" on the market from time to time, and with seemingly good attributions, these are not the ones a collector should buy.

While a good interior scene by Ter Borch might cost $150,000, some effort applied to looking around might result in securing one for $50,000, or at least a good portrait of a man or woman.

The Rubens and van Dyck paintings will both have to be portraits, although they can well be excellent ones, since Biblical and mythological scenes cost much more. A $50,000 Hals would be a small one.

Three top landscapes are included—by Jacob Ruisdael, Salomon Ruisdael, and Jan van Goyen—and at the prices listed in the first and highest priced group these scenes should be excellent ones.

The final picture on the first list is a good flower painting by the leading Dutch flower painter Jan van Huysum.

The first list is not only a list of masters who are rising in value, but it represents the best Seventeenth Century Dutch art as well as a beautiful and balanced collection.

The second list includes landscapes by Franz Post, Jan van Goyen, Aert van der Neer, Jan Brueghel the Elder, Hendrick Avercamp, the Master of the Winter Landscape, Nicholas Berchem, and Joost de Momper, a flower piece by van Huysum, an interior scene by David Teniers the Younger, one by Adrian van Ostade, and a portrait by van Dyck.

The collection should give the pleasing impression of the first one, but is less expensive and at the same time will include masters whose works are increasing in popularity.

The third list includes an important portrait or portrait group by Nicholas Maes, landscapes by Salomon Ruisdael, J. G. Cuyp, Savary, Siberechts, van Beyeren and Both, a good portrait by de Keyser, an interior or yard scene by Adrian Brouwer, a flower piece by Jan van Kessel, and a city or canal scene by Berck-Heyde, who is very much like van der Heyden but less expensive. All of the artists included on this list are popular and are growing in value.

The fourth list is the so-called low-priced list. It does not contain artists who are growing in value at the rate of the artists on the first three lists, but there is a good chance that they too will appreciate. All are excellent artists, and their prices can hardly go down under present conditions. The important thing is that for the listed prices, good paintings by these artists can usually be secured, and paintings which are by no means inferior to some of those on the other three lists, except that they are not in such great demand.

Moderns

Salvador Dali	$10,000
Utrillo	15,000
Raoul Dufy	12,000
Chirico	2,500
Rivera (Cubist period)	7,500
Raffaelli	2,500
Sorolla	5,000
Chagall	10,000
Derain	9,000
Kisling	3,000
Laurencin	5,000
Lurcat	2,000
Valtat	5,000
	$88,500

It is recognized that the leading Moderns have not been mentioned here: Matisse, Picasso, Léger, and Braque. The possibility of including one or more of these leaders should not be ruled out, particularly if one knows his paintings well and is able to shop around; but the prices of the Big Four are very high at the present time.

This sampling gathers together, in a small collection, works which when chosen carefully should be some of the most significant and beautiful of the Moderns, as well as works by Modern painters who are rising in popularity.

Expressionists

Marin (watercolor)	$ 2,500
Matta	1,500
Nolde	5,000
Jawlensky	2,500
Kandinsky	3,000
Kirchner	3,000
Mendersohn-Becker	2,500
Kokoschka	7,500
Meidner	1,500
Schmidt-Rottluff	3,000
Munch	10,000
Schiele	2,500
Klimt	1,200
	$45,700

The leading Expressionists have been included on this list, even Munch, despite his recent rise to great heights. The Abstract Expressionist Matta has been included as he has been increasing rapidly in popularity. At least one artist is included at a low figure—Klimt—although his output has been drawings, rather than paintings. The particular Klimt oil painting was seen in a small shop recently and is both recorded and illustrated as one of the most important early Klimts.

Impressionists

Renoir	$15,000
Monet	15,000
Friess	2,500
Guillaumin	5,000
van Rysselbergh	2,500
Corinth	3,000
Cassatt	20,000
van Gogh	12,000
Ceria	3,000
Carrand	2,500
Maufra	5,000
Loiseau	2,500
	$88,000

This collection has deliberately been put together on a most conservative basis. The total cost is less than one large Renoir would bring; yet it includes some of the most important members of the Impressionist School. The Renoir will have to be small, but it need not be of quality lower than that of large Renoirs.

The same price might buy a fine Monet if some shopping is done. The Cassatt can be a very important, large one; the van Gogh will probably be of the Nuenen period. The rest of the group are less known but excellent artists and the paintings at the prices listed can be significant ones. Some of the leaders of the School, at least in their production of paintings, have been deliberately omitted from the list because of their tremendous prices.

For comparison purposes an Impressionist-Modern list has been drawn up. Whereas the above list includes a van Gogh of the Nuenen period, which is not the preferred period, the second list contains an important, typical van Gogh. Possibly the price of $12,000 for the van Gogh on the above list could secure a good single figure from the typical van Gogh period.

This list has been prepared for illustrative purposes only, and there is no recommendation implied that these artists should be bought at the present time, although it is certainly possible that they will continue to rise in value. It is an illustration of what it would cost to get together a collection of some fine works by these artists—works of importance.

First Rank Impressionist-Modern

Braque	$ 30,000
Picasso	30,000
Léger	30,000
Matisse	50,000
van Gogh	150,000
Gauguin (Tahiti)	250,000
Cézanne	150,000
Manet	75,000
Renoir	75,000
Degas	35,000
Toulouse-Lautrec	90,000
Monet	30,000
	$995,000

American

Sargent	$ 5,000
Hassam	7,500
Luks	7,500
Sloan	5,000
Duveneck	5,000
Shinn	2,500
Bellows	5,000
Homer	20,000
Remington	5,000
Twachtman	1,500
Russell	3,500
Waugh	3,500
Robert Henri	5,000
Eakens	15,000
Inness	1,500
	$92,500

In many ways this is a well balanced collection of American art. In this area there are many possible combinations and price choices. Eakens and Homer are high priced, and the prices quoted here would require shopping around. A good, relatively small outdoor scene by Homer might cost $35,000, and a really important sea scene as much as $150,000. Eakens could run well over $15,000.

The Eight vary in price from as much as $35,000 for Prendergast to under $1,000 for Davies.

The above collection is, however, balanced and does include many of the important artists in the American School with the exception of the earlier portraitists who are classed with the British portraitists because of certain similarities of style and artistic background.

Eighteenth Century British Artists and American Portraitists

Gainsborough	$15,000
Romney	7,500
Raeburn	5,000
Hoppner	3,500
Reynolds	5,000
Bonington	3,500
Turner	5,000
Lawrence	4,000
Gilbert Stuart	5,000
Charles Willson Peale	5,000
Thomas Sully	3,000
Benjamin West	3,000
John Singleton Copley	5,000
	$69,500

The list includes all of the most important artists in the British and American portrait group of the period plus the British landscapists Turner and Bonington. While $3,500 should buy a fairly good Bonington, a Turner Impressionist-style seascape would run to far more money; but $5,000 should purchase a good water-color or small oil.

The price of Gainsborough varies sharply. A portrait of a woman might cost in six figures, and a really important group portrait or a group in a landscape might approach $500,000. On the other hand, a good half-length portrait of a man might be purchased for under $15,000.

A well-known portrait of a lady by Romney might cost $75,000, but a dark-coated, half-length portrait of a man might be purchased for $10,000 or less.

In buying paintings in this School of art it must be remembered that color is all-important. The present market places great emphasis on color, as it does in other Schools of art as well, but particularly in this School; and the brighter the colors generally the higher the price. This is one of the main reasons for the low prices of Gilbert Stuart. Probably taste will shortly change and Gilbert Stuart will rise in price, but at the present time his prices could hardly be lower in relation to the quality of his painting.

This list, which for lack of space can include but a fraction of the important Contemporaries, leans very heavily in the direction of the American Scene artists. There is little element of fad in this School, and as time passes and the scene changes the group will increase in popularity, if it follows the pattern of the

Matured Contemporary

Walter Sickert	Thomas H. Benton
Robert Brackman	John Steuart Curry
Leon Kroll	Reginald Marsh
Yasuo Kuniyoshi	Peter Hurd
Andrew Wyeth	Eugene Speicher
Grant Wood	Pietro Annigoni

Contemporary Abstract Artists

Lionel Feininger	Severini
Bernard Buffet	Guttuso

Schools of other countries. Age alone will add value to the outstanding American Scene painters. It will be noted that the dividing line between Contemporary American and Historical American painters is not a sharp one.

Our sample includes Andrew Wyeth, a beautiful landscapist and an expensive one. It does not include the spectacular Jackson Pollock (the "drip artist") or Nicholas de Stael, both of whom have skyrocketed in popularity. Because of their tremendous price rise they have not been selected here, whereas they obviously should have been included on any list prepared a few years ago.

Pietro Annigoni has been included because of the monumental quality of his paintings and his acceptance by museums while his prices remain relatively low.

The Abstract Artists included are considered to be among those who have the most substance and have been proven over a number of years.

All of the artists are in the four figure range, but the range is wide from the low end to $10,000 or over in some cases. Because of this wide range, plus the fact that prices in this group are changing rapidly, individual prices have been omitted.

A highly interesting collection of the most contemporary Contemporaries is being drawn together by the Chase Manhattan Bank. A budget of $500,000 has been established for the purchase of paintings and sculpture, and between February, 1960, and the end of the year, 81 paintings and 10 pieces of sculpture were purchased, and the purchase program is continuing. The important thing about the choices of artists made is the nature of the purchasers. It consists of an Art Committee composed of David Rockefeller, chairman (President of the Chase Manhattan Bank and a major collector), Mr. Alfred H. Barr, Jr., and Miss

Dorothy Miller of the Museum of Modern Art, Mr. Robert B. Hale of the Metropolitan Museum of Art, Mr. James J. Sweeney, formerly of the Guggenheim Museum, Mr. Perry Rathbone of the Museum of Fine Arts, Boston, and Mr. Gordon Bunshaft of Skidmore, Owings and Merrill, architects for Chase Manhattan's new building. It is possible that this combined talent will not only pick works of art which are attractive but will have foresight in selecting artists whose work will have more than passing significance.

MAJOR ART WORKS PURCHASED FOR THE CHASE MANHATTAN BANK'S NEW BUILDING
BY THE ART COMMITTEE

Artist	Title	Medium	Size
Afro	Estate in Palude (1957)	Oil on canvas	45 x 64
Josef Albers	In Late Red (Homage to the Square) (1959)	Oil on masonite	40 x 40
Milton Avery	Sandbar (1959)	Oil on canvas	34 x 60
Milton Avery	Conversation (1956)	Oil on canvas	40 x 50
Leonard Baskin	Porcupine (1951)	Woodcut	21 x 27½
Renato Birolli	Landscape (1956)	Crayon Drawing	19¾ x 15¼
Elmer Bischoff	Cityscape with Orange Light (1959)	Oil on canvas	47½ x 59¾
Elmer Bischoff	Landscape (1959)	Oil on canvas	68 x 68
James Brooks	Loring (1957)	Oil on canvas	78 x 66
James Brooks	Embo (1960)	Oil on canvas	48 x 44
James Brooks	Gananogue (1960)	Oil on canvas	48 x 54
Charles Burchfield	July Wind Rustling (1948)	Water color	40 x 30
Charles Burchfield	Pink Locusts and Windy Moon (1959)	Water color	33 x 40
Charles Burchfield	Street Light Shining Thru Rain and Fog (1917)	Water color	25½ x 16
Charles Burchfield	Sunflowers (1917)	Water color	22 x 18
Kenneth Callahan	Cascade Mountain Drawing, Series II (1954)	Ink on paper	26 x 40
Kenneth Callahan	Cascade Mountain Drawing, Series III (1955)	Ink on paper	25 x 38
Nicolino Calyo	American Landscape with Indians (1853)	Oil on canvas	32 x 43½
Thomas W. Chambers	Hudson River Landscape (circa 1840)	Oil on canvas	22 x 30

Artist	Title	Medium	Size
Carroll Cloar	Corner at Marked Tree (1960)	Tempera	28 x 40
George Cope	Wild Duck, Hanging on a Green Barn Door (1910)	Oil on canvas	22 x 16
Edward Corbett	Mt. Holyoke #2 1960 (1960)	Oil on canvas	68 x 50
Leonardo Cremonini	The Bull Tamers (1951)	Oil on canvas	39½ x 55
Nanno de Groot	Landscape #1 (1959)	Oil on canvas on board	23 x 18
Nanno de Groot	Landscape #5 (1959)	Oil on canvas on board	27 x 26
Luis Feito	Sun Spot (1959)	Oil on canvas	28½ x 36
Fritz Glarner	Relational Painting, Tondo No. 45 (1956)	Oil on masonite	25" in dia.
Fritz Glarner	Relational Painting, Tondo No. 46 (1956-57)	Oil on masonite	45½" in dia.
Fritz Glarner	Relational Painting, No. 79 (1956)	Oil on canvas	52½ x 44
Leon Golub	Head XXI (1959)	Oil on canvas	42 x 66
Robert Goodnough	The Survivors (1959)	Oil on canvas	45 x 45
R. LaBarre Goodwin	Theodore Roosevelt's Cabin Door (1905)	Oil on canvas	69 x 34
Jose Guerrero	Fire and Apparitions (1957)	Oil on canvas	80 x 100
Jose Guerrero	Blues Converging (1960)	Oil on canvas	57 x 51
Jose Guerrero	Black Penetration (1960)	Oil on canvas	51 x 62
Edward Lamson Henry	Station on Morris and Essex Railroad (circa 1864)	Oil on canvas	15 x 24
Genichiro Inokuma	Kabuki II (1958)	Oil on canvas	79 x 72
Gyorgy Kepes	Garden of Light (1959)	Oil on canvas	60 x 60
Karl Knaths	Pine and Dune (1959)	Oil on canvas	36 x 42
Gerd Leufert	Composition V B-14 (1959)	Oil on canvas	34 x 36
Conrad Marca-Relli	Untitled (1959)	Collage (oil and canvas on canvas)	43 x 39
Conrad Marca-Relli	27 October 1959 (1959)	Collage (oil and canvas on canvas)	6' x 7'
Norma Morgan	David in the Wilderness (1956)	Engraving	18 x 35¼
Kyle Morris	Evening Image (1958)	Oil on canvas	60 x 72
Walter Murch	Carburetor (1957)	Oil on canvas	32½ x 27½
Sam J. Ntiro	Chagga Home (1958)	Oil on hardboard	46¾ x 34½

Artist	Title	Medium	Size
Sam J. Ntiro	Carrying Poles (1956)	Oil on canvas	20 x 16
Sam J. Ntiro	Clearing Building Site (1957)	Oil on canvas	20 x 16
Sam J. Ntiro	Maize Harvest (1960)	Oil on canvas	20 x 16
Kenzo Okada	Ise (Temple in Japan) (1959)	Oil on canvas	72 x 84
Gabor Peterdi	The Big Tree II (1957)	Etching	20 x 23
Gabor Peterdi	Burning Rocks (1959)	Etching	33 x 23
Gabor Peterdi	Wings of the Ocean (1958)	Etching	32 x 23
J. F. Peto	Forgotten Friends: Candlestick and Books on Table (circa 1890)	Oil on canvas	$15\frac{7}{8}$ x $10\frac{1}{2}$
Larry Rivers	Me III (1959)	Oil on canvas	58 x 52
Kay Sage	Signal to Signal (1954-55)	Oil on canvas	57 x 45
Charles Shaw	Cap Martin (1960)	Oil on board	10 x 14
Charles Shaw	Road to Tomorrow (1959)	Oil on canvas	30 x 40
Pierre Soulages	23 March 1960 (1960)	Oil on canvas	$57\frac{1}{4}$ x $57\frac{1}{4}$
Malcolm Spooner	Untitled (1960)	Oil on canvas	29 x 40
Hedda Sterne	Queens No. 1 (1958)	Oil on canvas	72 x 42
N. H. Stubbing	Greek Vigil (1959)	Oil on canvas	52 x 39
Kumi Sugai	Kiri (1959)	Oil on canvas	77 x 38
Alfred Sully	Bison Bull (circa 1850)	Oil on canvas	15 x 20
Carol Summers	The Dark Vision of Xerxes (1958)	Color woodcut	$38\frac{3}{4}$ x $26\frac{3}{4}$
Carol Summers	Monte Amiata (1960)	Woodcut	47 x $38\frac{1}{4}$
Carol Summers	Hudson River Sunset (1959)	Color woodcut	39 x 38
Esteban Vicente	No. 4—1958 (1958)	Oil on canvas	48 x 60
Bryan Wilson	Birds in Grass	Oil on canvas	74 x 76
Jack Youngerman	Black-Red (1959)	Oil on canvas	70 x 100

Purchased Dec. 6, 1960

Artist	Title	Medium	Size
Ernesto Barreda	Sol (1960)	Oil on canvas	32 x 32
Ernesto Barreda	Cal 1 (1960)	Oil on canvas	32 x 32
Robert Crippa	Figure 1960 (1960)	Collage of cork	78 x $78\frac{1}{2}$
Alfred Jensen	The Work (1960)	Oil on canvas	72 x 46
David Lund	The Wall (1960)	Oil on canvas	$47\frac{1}{4}$ x $59\frac{1}{2}$
Conrad Marca-Relli	Runway #5 (1959)	Collage (oil and canvas on canvas)	67 x 56
Georges Mathieu	Park Avenue (1957)	Oil on canvas	6' x 6'
Joan Mitchell	Slate (1959)	Oil on canvas	$77\frac{1}{4}$ x $74\frac{3}{4}$
Frank Roth	Avril (1960)	Oil on canvas	67 x $62\frac{1}{4}$
Kumi Sugai	Fubuki (1959)	Oil on canvas	64 x 51

BAROQUE AND EIGHTEENTH CENTURY ITALIAN

First List		*Second List*	
Pittoni	$ 7,500	Maratta	$ 2,000
Guercino	10,000	Bacciccio	2,500
Domenichino	10,000	Baschenis	2,500
Reni	7,500	Zais	3,500
Strozzi	10,000	Battoni	3,500
Piazzetta	10,000	Marieschi	2,500
Annibale Carracci	10,000	Solimena	2,500
Castiglione	7,500	Pannini	6,000
Magnasco	8,000	Monsu Desiderio	4,000
Rosa	7,500	Giordano	5,000
Ricci	10,000	Crespi	7,000
		Corrado Giaquinto	7,000
	$98,000		**$48,000**

The Canal painters are not on either list—Guardi, Canaletto, or Bellotto. These are extremely high in price and might even equal the entire cost of the second list—for just one painting by one of the three. Similarly the landscapist Zuccarelli has been omitted because he is rare and very high priced.

The first list has on it the excellent landscapist Castiglione and a landscape by Salvator Rosa. The Second List has on it the architectural painters Monsu Desiderio, Pannini, and Marieschi, and these landscapes give balance to each collection.

We have prepared one final list as a summary and a challenge. It contains the names of the greats of all time, those artists who have been tested through the centuries and accepted as the best. Some of the recent painters and some of the Contemporaries may gain places on this list of immortals, but only the test of time and the elimination of fad can place them there. It is an impossible list from the point of view of actually being able to accumulate such a collection at the present time. The prices are realistic if the paintings ever become available, however. A few people such as Paul Getty, the Rockefellers, Paul Mellon, and Robert Lehman could afford to put this proportion of their assets into a collection of paintings, and some of them have made a good start on such a list; but who now, in a lifetime, could ever find even a substantial number of these masters' excellent, typical, important works?

van der Weyden	$1,500,000
van Eyck	1,500,000
Master of Flemalle	1,500,000

Memling	1,000,000
Vermeer	1,500,000
Rembrandt	500,000
Rubens	500,000
Dürer	750,000
Holbein	500,000
Velásquez	750,000
Giorgione	1,000,000
Piero della Francesca	1,000,000
Leonardo da Vinci	2,000,000
Perugino	750,000
Raphael	1,000,000
Fra Angelico	1,000,000
Botticelli	750,000
Giotto	500,000
Titian	500,000
	$18,500,000

XXV

A Look to the Future

N THE RECESSION OF 1957 WE WERE LITERALLY DELUGED WITH Wall Street brokers up here to buy paintings from us." This story was told by an official of one of the largest galleries in the world. The stock market was in a decline, and business in general was at least ill. The motive was what to do with funds rather than any more artistic motive.

The brokers were right, and their analyses led them in the right direction. In a recession paintings tend to hold up better than either the stock market or prices of commodities, although in a real depression there is no justification for assuming that art prices will not decline significantly.

In 1957 the trek of the brokers uptown would have been appropriate for the additional reason that the art market was embarking on one of the greatest periods of uptrend in its entire history.

Paintings are a good investment and they will remain so until there are definite signs of a serious depression. They are a good investment as compared with other investments, including real estate and the stock market.

Strangely enough, however, the important collectors of paintings usually do not sell. They look upon their paintings as their treasures and a major love of their lives to which of course a price tag can be attached but which usually need not be turned into cash during their lifetimes. It is enough to know that the value is there and that it can be passed on to heirs or public institutions as their contributions to the culture of society.

This same philosophy holds true for the tremendously numerous smaller collectors with very few exceptions. There are few investors interested in a profit to be realized in dollars. A few investors have apparently bought for resale. One of these in the postwar period got together a medium grade collection of Impressionists and sold it in the late 1950's in seven figures and at a tremendous profit.

For the reason that most collectors buy paintings to keep, the question of where to sell has been left to the last chapter. There is to date no sales channel designed for those who have paintings to sell with the exception of the art auction.

For a moment let us postpone discussing the art auction as a means of disposing of paintings and turn to dealers. Since dealers are the day-to-day trade channels through which paintings are sold, it would seem logical for a collector who wants to sell paintings to sell to the dealer.

In order to sell to a dealer at anything like the value of the painting, the painting must be sold to a large dealer, and in order to realize any price, the painting must be an authentic, quality painting. It must be to all intents and purposes above reproach and in addition, it must be by a master of considerable standing since this is the type painting the major galleries handle.

It is useless to go into a major New York gallery and say, "Here is a fine Venetian portrait that I own. I think there is a good chance of its being a Tintoretto. I don't have its background, but it certainly is a good period painting."

There is an American agent for a well-known Italian collection. Over the years some of the better paintings from the collection have been sold, but there are still some good paintings left to be sold, along with some school pieces and some questionable ones. A major gallery was approached by the American agent who had photos of every painting and detailed descriptions. The agent got nowhere in the sale of the collection or any part of it. The head of the gallery told me, in connection with the collection, "Yes, I had known of the availability of this collection for some time, but the paintings are not prime."

The agent then approached another New York gallery and was asked to wait in the outer office downstairs while the photos of the paintings were taken upstairs to one of the gallery officials. The photos were shortly returned with the curt statement that the gallery was not interested.

A gentleman from the South, an industrialist and politician, put in excess of $150,000 into a collection of paintings. He took photos of the paintings into a major gallery in New York and offered the collection for sale. His fate was the same—not interested!

The next logical step would seem to be to take the painting to a minor dealer. Here the price is often so far under what the owner thinks is fair or even paid for the painting, that the experience is both discouraging and humiliating.

Frequently a dealer will suggest that the painting be left on consignment. From the point of view of the seller this procedure theoretically gives him a chance to get a large part of the full retail price, as the dealer will frequently ask a commission of 20 per cent.

The results are often, however, not entirely as anticipated. The dealer does not have his own funds tied up in the painting. If he sells the consigned painting he pockets 20 per cent of the selling price; but if he sells his own painting he pockets 100 per cent, and has this money with which to stock another painting. The seller consequently finds that his consigned painting is relegated to the back of the shop where it may very well be covered with dust because of infrequent showings to prospective customers.

A friend of the author who lives on Long Island has a collection of paintings worth upwards of $1,000,000. One evening the author asked idly where a particular painting in the friend's collection came from. It was a good painting, but not a great work of art. The reply was somewhat unexpected. The collector said, "In order to get that painting I had to trade in exactly 14 paintings plus cash. I wanted the painting and the dealer had me."

It was difficult to conceive of any 14 paintings from the particular collection being required as trade-in on the particular painting in question.

Twice the author went back to the dealer from whom he purchased particular paintings because they were not what he wanted. In one case the dealer wouldn't take back the painting even in trade. In the other case I bought the painting to give to my wife for a birthday present. She didn't like the painting, and it was immediately returned to the dealer, who said, "Don't worry. Just hang it on the wall where it was before and I'll resell it for you."

"How long was it hanging on the wall before I came along?" I asked.

"Three years," was the quick reply.

On the other hand, I decided to sell a painting that didn't seem to fit into my collection. It wasn't an important painting, and so it was consigned to a Third Avenue dealer with instructions to get whatever he could for it.

Shortly after consigning it, the painting was sold. The net to me after the commission to the dealer was exactly five times the painting's cost.

In the fall of 1960 a Canaletto was offered for sale privately by the agent for an estate. The price at which it was offered to a museum official was $5000.

It took little review of the price charts used in this book to determine that the offering price was under the market. The painting was shortly thereafter offered to a New York dealer, and it is understood a transaction quickly took place—at a sum vastly in excess of the $5000. This was a prime painting from a prominent family, owned by that family for generations, and the canvas was signed on the back. This was a painting which should have been offered to a large New York dealer for sale, and was so offered.

We come now to the auction market. Probably the best place to offer an Impressionist painting or a Modern painting is the auction, and it is likely that the auction will secure a higher price in many cases than can a dealer, even a large New York dealer. Conversely, the buyer of Impressionist and Modern paintings might well look first at the large New York dealers before he looks at the auctions. If, then, the seller of a Renoir has a choice to make between selling at the auction or selling to a dealer, the prima facie choice might well be the auction, since if the retail price of the auction house is higher than that of the dealer, the net to the seller would be still less if he sells to the dealer, because the dealer has to make a mark-up which will likely be in excess of the auction house's selling commission.

If a person is seeking a Rembrandt, a Velásquez or a Fra Angelico, the place to go is to the best dealers. These items do not frequently appear on the auction market. It might be necessary to wait a long time to buy such a painting at auction. If, however, he has some flexibility as to what he purchases he should watch the auctions. He can buy at auction for anywhere between 10 and 75 per cent of the retail price.

While the smaller American auctions frequently have fine paintings, and the smaller auctions offer the knowledgeable collector the opportunity to make discoveries, the great bulk of the better works of art go through the Parke-Bernet Galleries, and there is a serious attempt made to identify the paintings, as well as other works of art correctly. Because a painting dealer handles only paintings, he should be in a better position to identify them correctly than is the auction house which deals in all manner of art objects and furniture. Some dealers will guarantee both authorship and background, whereas the auction house does not offer such a guarantee. On the other hand, if a serious question is raised about any art object with the large auction house the house will often take back the object and refund the price.

Where a well-known painting is offered with a known background of ownership and authenticity there is no difference between the dealer and the auction house as to reliability or warranty. In unquestioned works of art a warranty means little because it is not likely to be invoked. The Parke-Bernet Galleries recently sold a Della Robbia plaque, an obvious masterpiece and an object of great beauty. The price realized was $40,000, and it is understood that it was bought by the Metropolitan Museum of Art. While the price was justified by the high quality it is doubtful whether any dealer would have been able to secure a higher price.

There are two other advantages of selling through auction. The first is that a transaction will take place and the object converted into cash, and that this transaction will take place quickly. If the quality is reasonable an entire collection of paintings or other objects of art can be sold through auction, whereas any one dealer may take only a few of those offered.

Finally, if the price reached by the bidding is not high enough, in the opinion of the seller, he can bid in his item himself, but of course pay something to the auction house for handling the offering.

The entire discussion on how to sell paintings leads one fairly directly to one conclusion: it is the best policy in collecting, from an investment point of view (as well as from any other point of view) to buy fine, unquestionably authentic works of art by accepted masters whose works will speak in the art market for themselves, telling of a masterful brush, excellent quality, and prime condition.

The immediately obvious way to select Schools of painting and particular artists to purchase is to review price trends as reflected by preferences by reviewing the various appropriate chapters in this book, at least using these as a take-off point.

If we compare prices by Schools of art in the year 1960 with those in the year 1955 we see that the School showing the greatest rise is the School of the Post-Impressionists—Cézanne, van Gogh and Gauguin. These artists were at a level of 754 per cent of their 1955 price level in the year 1960. The School of next greatest price rise was the School of the Great Moderns—Matisse, Picasso, Léger and Braque. These rose to 557 per cent of the 1955 level. Third were the Expressionists who rose to 307 per cent.

This table predicted exactly what took place during the winter season of 1960, although it was prepared months before the season opened.

But if one is giving investment advice his first concern is that the person does not lose money, and his second is that he stands a good chance of making money. This is a distinctly conservative approach. It is the type of advice which might be offered by the Financial Vice President of a corporation to the Board of Directors for the employment of funds for a period of years in a theoretical situation in which the only feasible investment was paintings. If the wrong advice was given the corporation might lose money and all chances of the Financial Vice President's ever succeeding to the Presidency might be over. In such a theoretical situation conservatism is the better part of valor. These would be possible recommendations, not *all* the best recommendations, and certainly not recommendations for a quick speculative gain, but conservative recommendations for the purchase of fine paintings:

Italian School
    Canaletto
    Guardi
    Sebastiano Ricci
    Pittoni
Dutch School
    van Goyen
    Jacob Ruisdael
    Salomon Ruisdael
    Hobbema
Impressionists and French Moderns
    Renoir
    Utrillo
British School
    Gainsborough landscapes
    Gainsborough portraits

The reasons for these selections, and the order of the selections from first down to last are these:

1. The artist must have painted enough pictures to provide a present ample supply on the market so that something approaching a market price exists.

2. The paintings by the particular artist should not be too diverse as to value depending on size, subject, dress of those in the portraits, variance in style of the artist over his life span, etc.

3. The presumption should be that the painting offered is authentic. A genuine Rembrandt is a rare object on the art market, but there are many doubtful Rembrandts offered. There are fewer doubtful van Goyens.

4. There should have been a rise in prices of the particular artist to the present time, but not a frightening rise, a rise so fast and to such a height that a debacle is suggested at some time in the future. For this reason the Expressionists are not emphasized here.

5. The size of the investment in each painting should not be too high, and at the same time not too low. A Gauguin is a fine painting to have and at the present time a good investment, but it is risky to invest over $100,000 in one painting.

On the other hand, there are some good $500 paintings on the market, but it takes many of these to equal let us say the $20,000 that one might consider as an investment in paintings in general.

6. The paintings while being good investments should be paintings of beauty and quality, regardless of what the market is doing. It is likely that paintings lacking in quality and beauty will not long hold their value, because they lack the substance of great art.

7. The size of the painting must be optimum, that is, it must fit into an apartment or a modern home which does not have huge wall spaces on which to hang enormous altarpieces.

With this underlying philosophy, namely that it is better to buy conservatively and to buy works of Masters long accepted, at least from an investment point of view, let us try to forecast the future art market and the direction of future preferences for art.

There is no question but that for the past several years there has been a decided preference for non-realistic painting, and by non-realistic is meant the Schools of art beginning with the Impressionists and going through the Post-Impressionists, the French Modern, the Central European Expressionists, the Abstract Expressionists, and Abstract Surrealists.

While there exists a great demand for Abstract painting and there is little question that this type painting is in vogue in the year 1961, this School may already be over the top in public preference. The great difficulty with it is that it does not demand the techniques on which painting excellence through the centuries has been built—drawing, third dimension, composition, a feeling of space, and a general craftsmanship. There is certainly a place for Abstract Art but the criteria for judging its excellence or lack of excellence are too obscure.

While there are a few good abstract painters, painstaking workers who at the same time get a spark of brilliance into their productions, painters carefully trained in the techniques of painting, unfortunately for the School there are too many hangers-on, too many painters who do not know the techniques of painting but who have latched onto a School which does not require excellence of drawing, effective use of color, or third dimension.

On the part of the public there is still the inevitable comment, "I don't understand it, but then I don't have a profound education in art." It is possible that one day this great uninformed public will learn the criteria by which to judge art, including Abstract Art, and will reject the School.

In addition there is a great deal of topnotch critical opinion against a large segment of Abstract Art, some of it coming from the most influential newspapers in the country and in the world. This critical opinion tends to mold public opinion.

For these reasons it is possible that the Rorschach-type of Abstract Art is already on the downgrade. At any rate the prices of the leaders of the School price-wise are at such a high level that a red flag should be raised, or at least a yellow caution flag.

One step away from Abstract Expressionism is Central European Expressionism. While it is felt that this art is on safer ground than Abstract Expressionism, it too is characterized by a vagueness in drawing, color application, and third dimension. The time may soon arrive when the idea conveyed may not be enough for the collecting public and they may demand craftsmanship too.

In the end the investor-collector always arrives back at the same question in his selection of works of art: Is the *quality* there?

Index